METS

BY THE

NUMBERS

METS
BY THE
NUMBERS

*A Complete Team History
of the Amazin' Mets by Uniform Number*

JON SPRINGER WITH MATTHEW SILVERMAN

Foreword by Howie Rose

SPORTS
PUBLISHING

Sports Publishing books may be purchased in bulk at special discounts
for sales promotion, corporate gifts, fund-raising, or educational purposes.
Special editions can also be created to specifications. For details, contact the
Special Sales Department, Sports Publishing, 307 West 36th Street, 11th Floor,
New York, NY 10018 or sportspubbooks@skyhorsepublishing.com.

Sports Publishing® is a registered trademark of Skyhorse Publishing, Inc.®,
a Delaware corporation.

Visit our website at www.sportspubbooks.com.

10 9 8 7 6 5 4 3 2 1

Library of Congress Cataloging-in-Publication Data is available on file.

Cover design by Tom Lau
Cover photo credit AP Images

Print ISBN: 978-1-61321-869-3
Ebook ISBN: 978-1-61321-886-0

Printed in the United States of America

To Ivan, in memory of his Aunt Jen

CONTENTS

FOREWORD

Willie Mays was one of the greatest baseball players of all time; perhaps the best of all those living today.

Kelvin Torve, as I recall, is a very nice person.

These two gentlemen should never be confused as baseball players, but in the early 1990s they were, and it makes for the delicious type of anecdote that fills this entertaining book.

Mays, of course, played most of two seasons with the Mets in 1972 and 1973. Following his retirement, the Mets did not issue his famous number 24 to any other player, although the number was never officially retired. Then, in 1990, Torve, a career minor leaguer, spent some time with the Mets. For no apparent reason, when he took the field for his first game as a Met, he did so wearing number 24.

This, of course, was surprising, and all these years later, Jay Horwitz, the team's vice president of media relations, recalls the incident and shakes his head while chuckling, wondering why Torve was given Willie's number. What he really gets a kick out of is why people care, but they do; and that's the reason you're reading this book.

Torve's heist of the famous number was a short-lived issue. He wore number 39 from his second game on, through parts of the 1990 and 1991 seasons, but it's a fun piece of Mets trivia. The far more deserving Rickey Henderson wore the number during his time with the Mets and donned it again as a coach. Torve is now free to wear it in whatever line of work he pursues today.

I've always enjoyed keeping track of uniform numbers. They define players in a variety of ways, so much so that players' nicknames are occasionally a reflection of the numbers they wear. Some members of the 1986 Mets referred to manager Davey Johnson not as "Skip," or "Davey," but as simply "Number 5."

On a couple of occasions when I worked on the air with Tom Seaver, I called him "41." I did so to pay tribute to a man who actually took part in a no-hitter for the New York Mets, but little did Tom know I wasn't referring to him. That's how we come to Gordon Richardson.

Richardson had been a part of the St. Louis Cardinals world championship team in 1964, but by the next spring he was a Met. In March 1965, at Al Lang Field in St. Petersburg, Richardson, wearing number 41, combined with Gary Kroll to no-hit the Pittsburgh Pirates. I don't remember what number Kroll wore, and if I did, I wouldn't tell you. You'll just have to read the whole book. But I can tell you that Richardson was the last Met to wear number 41 before Seaver began his Hall of Fame career in 1967.

You're not the only one who cares about uniform numbers. They mean a lot to the guys who wear them, too. That's why, when the great Warren Spahn joined the Mets in 1965, Ed Kranepool gave up the number 21, presenting it to Spahn, and took number 7, the number he would wear throughout the rest of his Mets career. To this day, no matter who wears 7 for the Mets, I always think of Kranepool.

Ron Swoboda will always be remembered as number 4, but he wore 14 as a rookie in 1965. The next year, longtime Cardinals third baseman Ken Boyer joined the Mets, and Swoboda surrendered 14. Following the trade of Boyer to the Chicago White Sox during the 1967 season, number 14 became available for its original owner, Gil Hodges.

Hodges wore the number the night the Mets played their first game in the National League, on April 11, 1962, and reclaimed it when he was named manager for the 1968 season. Less than three years after leading the Mets to the 1969 world championship, Hodges passed away, and his number was retired.

Only four Mets, plus Jackie Robinson, have had their numbers retired by the Mets, but in my opinion there should be more. I've long felt that Keith Hernandez's number 17 should be on the outfield wall because he was clearly the soul of the team that provided the best series of seasons the franchise has enjoyed. One could also make the case for Dwight Gooden's 16, and Darryl Strawberry's 18, although their personal problems have precluded that honor to this point. I would argue that Jerry Koosman, the winningest left-handed pitcher in Mets history, is worthy of his number 36 being considered for retirement as well.

That's one of the fun things about tracking uniform numbers. They provide great fodder for debate, as well as trivia. Which brings us back to Willie Mays. I have never felt that the Mets should retire his number. He was a great player—as a Giant—but some Met, at least in my opinion, probably should have worn 24 long before Kelvin Torve. That number is still essentially preserved in Mets mothballs, but if someday the Mets decide to honor Willie for his contributions to baseball in New York as a Giant as well as a Met by permanently retiring it, I say go for it.

If that day ever comes, Jim Beauchamp should be part of the ceremonies. Someone had to give 24 to Willie when he became a Met. You probably remember that Beauchamp took number 5 after Mays came aboard. If you didn't, that's all right. That's what this book is all about. Have fun.

—**Howie Rose**
June 2007

INTRODUCTION TO THE SECOND EDITION

*When he last managed to articulate his message, I embraced him. He
had come out of the steamy depths to tell me ever-so-bravely that he,
too, was a Daffodil-11.*
"My brother," I said.

—Kurt Vonnegut, *Slapstick*

Since the research underpinning this book was first published on the Internet seventeen years ago—and particularly, since the first edition of this
book hit the streets in 2008—the world has been witness to a small revolution in which I'm proud to have played a small part.

Once a neglected and under-researched statistic, the uniform number
today has emerged from a phenomenon residing only in the mind of the
fan to a commodity widely discussed and available everywhere. Since '08,
reference sites like baseball-reference.com have added uniform numbers
to their data sets. News of player uniform changes race through the fan base
at the speed of Twitter—a medium that today includes accounts dedicated
entirely to uni-number changes with thousands of followers. Once upon a
time, the mbtn.net website was one of the only places in the world to find this
stuff, and though it remains the definitive and most precise record out there,
it's not alone anymore. Mets by the Numbers gave birth to a tiny cottage
industry: Thanks in part to Skyhorse/Sports Publishing and my busy col-
laborator Matthew Silverman, fans of the Cubs, Yankees and Red Sox have
all seen books published on their club's uniform number histories, modeled
after this one.

Why? Because it's the way the mind of the fan works. So many of us deeply
associate the players and the uniform number they wear, if only unconscious-
ly. Uni numbers help us remember PIN codes and locker combinations. They
inspire us to buy jerseys. And if you listen to them, they will tell you a story.

Here's how: Since a uniform number can be worn by only one player at
any one point of time, a number defines that player's unique moment in
team history in a way that's more precise than almost any other statistic.
Isolate the number, and you have a broader history—what Vonnegut called
an "artificial extended family"—linking one player's moment to the next's.
Yesterday's Jon Matlack is today's Steven Matz, and tomorrow never knows.

Reverse-engineer a progression of uniform numbers and a history of transactions and the front-office philosophies behind them are laid bare. Find the point where a player changes numbers and there's a story there to tell.

Instances of teams wearing numbers date to the nineteenth century. The Cleveland Indians formally introduced the practice in 1916, and the St. Louis Cardinals followed a few years later, but it didn't really take off until the 1929 Yankees assigned their players numbers that corresponded to their position in the batting order, which is how Babe Ruth became 3 and Lou Gehrig 4, and so on. By 1932, all major league teams were doing it.

Yet in a sport obsessed with statistics, uniform numbers are a kind of final frontier. The data contained in this book is proudly unofficial, gathered the only way it could have been—over a lifetime of fandom and refined with the help of scorecards, archival newspaper accounts, transaction records, photos, and video—and presented in a way that's both authoritative and fun.

Since the first edition hit shelves in 2008, some 300 new players have put on a Mets uniform for the first time, while the organization endured a punishing financial crisis, subsequent tear-down, and an inspiring rebuild that brought them to the World Series for the first time in fifteen years: Those stories and more have been woven into the narrative. This book sheds new light on forgotten numerical history (the five Mets who wore No. 41 *before* Tom Seaver); digs a little deeper into the familiar lore (revealing something about Kelvin Torve *other than* the fact he once wore No. 24); and reveals more facts and figures about the team its players including a history of its ever changing uniforms. I hope I've provided both a useful reference book, and a fun read. There is no quiz at the end. As Casey said, you could look it up.

Jon Springer
February, 2016

* * *

How to Read This Book
This book was assembled during the 2015–16 offseason, so statistics are as current as publishing allows. To data set includes only those numbers assigned to players on the active roster in-season, whether they played or not, as

well as primary coaches and managers as listed on an official scorecard. That means: Rube Walker, yes; Batboy Jim, no. Garth Brooks, no; Mac Suzuki, yes.

The lists of statistical leaders and a progression of numbers that accompany each chapter are based on the performances of players only on the dates that they wore or have worn that number (in Chapter 7, for example, Ed Kranepool's numbers don't jibe with his career Met stats because the three seasons he spent wearing No. 21 are counted separately and listed in that chapter). In a few cases where precise dates have proven unknowable (George Theodore's switch from 18 to 9, for example), we made our best estimate based on the data we gathered and don't figure to be off by much. Player names are in **bold** in a chapter if they actually wore the number, and years given refer only to the seasons he wore those digits.

"Number of times issued" means the number of times a number was issued to a new or returning player nonconsecutively. For example, Greg McMichael in Chapter 36 counts for one player but two issues since No. 36 was reissued between the time he left the team and when he returned.

Career statistical leaders are based on a minimum of plate appearances or innings pitched, relative to the larger set (roughly 100 for both, with some exceptions).

Dates that accompany each player in the progression refer to the years (partial or full) that the player performed for the Mets. Dates in parenthesis indicate the starting or ending date for players *only in those cases where there were multiple issues of the same jersey in the same year.* For an even more detailed look at precise dates (as well as a continually updated progression), consult mbtn.net. Corrections and comments, plus any book-related inquiries, may also be directed to the site.

Finally, we have included an all-time alphabetical roster for quick reference.

More than 1,000 players, and another 100-plus coaches and managers, have worn the Mets uniform since 1962. This is the story of all of them, told in a totally new way.

The Mets line up numerically along the lines at Citi Field during the 2015 World Series.

#1: LEADING OFF: MOOKIE WILSON

"Number 1 is my number because . . . that's the number they gave me in spring training."

Turned out to be a pretty apt decision, at least when it came to **Mookie Wilson** (1980–89), who would become the epitome of No. 1, arguably the most beloved Met of all time, and, appropriately, the leadoff hitter in a discussion of numerical Mets history.

Selected by the Mets in the second round of the 1977 amateur draft out of the University of South Carolina, Wilson arrived in September of 1980 displaying all the characteristics fans expect in a No. 1: aggression at the plate, speed and daring on the base paths, range in center field, and an enthusiasm worthy of his number.

Years of cheerful service through the lean early '80s were rewarded when Wilson found himself at the plate for the most important turn at bat in Met history. His 10th inning, Game 6 confrontation with Bob Stanley of the Red Sox in the 1986 World Series would produce the most important wild pitch in team history (Brad Clontz's in 1999 rates second) and, of course, a slow ground ball destined to roll past Bill Buckner and into baseball's collective consciousness forever.

After the arrival of Lenny Dykstra, and a concurrent shoulder injury in 1985, Wilson would increasingly be platooned in left field and center field, and with judicious use his on-base percentage improved during the second five years of his ten-year stay at Shea. He was traded in the bloody summer of 1989, by then having set all-time Met records in stolen bases

Dan Carubia

Mookie Willison in March of 1988, year No. 1 for the Mets in Port St. Lucie.

(281) and triples (62), although each of those marks would fall to another great leadoff hitter, Jose Reyes.

Wilson remains a revered Met who reappeared in the No. 1 jersey in coaching roles (1997–2002 and 2011).

Ever since Earle Combs of the Yankees donned No. 1 in 1929, helping usher in the practice of uniform numbers throughout baseball, No. 1 has traditionally been associated with scrappy, speedy, leadoff hitters.

Richie Ashburn led off the very first Mets game in 1962. He flew out to center, though later in the game he singled and scored the first run in Mets history. A future Hall of Famer, Ashburn certainly possessed No. 1–like qualities, although many, particularly his speed and once-pristine fielding, had eroded by the time he'd reached the Mets. Nevertheless, the thirty-five-year-old Ashburn was probably the Mets' best overall player in their inaugural season, with a .424 on-base percentage—he was 27 plate appearances shy of qualifying but would have been the NL's leader that year—and a .306 batting average. His retirement following the '62 season left the Mets in want of a dependable leadoff hitter and center fielder for years to come.

Lance Johnson joined the Mets in 1996 as a veteran free agent signee from the Chicago White Sox, and before anyone knew it he set team records that year for hits (227), runs (117), and triples (21) in a season—the hits and triples records still stand. Johnson had trouble repeating that performance in 1997 and feuded with manager Bobby Valentine before being sent back to Chicago (this time, to the Cubs) in the first trade of Steve Phillips's reign as general manager.

Johnson, who was known as "One-Dog" to teammates in reference to his uniform number, suited up in No. 51 for the Mets just once—on September 1, 1996—while the Mets inducted Mookie Wilson into the club's Hall of Fame. "We had to do what we could to make his day perfect," Johnson told the *New York Times* afterward.

They haven't all been perfect days. **Luis Castillo** (2007–10) was a Met for four years—only Mookie logged more games in the No. 1 jersey—but as far as Met fans are concerned only one game mattered. That of course was June 12, 2009, in Yankee Stadium, when Castillo backpedaled for what should have been a game-ending popup by Alex Rodriguez in shallow right field, only to have the ball clank off his glove for a stunning, two-run, game-ending error. Dos manos, Luis.

Castillo wasn't as terrible as that most nights. He'd tortured the Mets as a member of the rival Marlins early in his career, never lost his ability to reach base, and did what he could for the doomed 2007 Mets upon being acquired in a stretch run trade. But his subsequent four-year contract from the Mets was about three years longer than necessary. Predictably, the chubby, slap-hitting Castillo was in rapid decline by year three and never played professionally again after the Mets released him with a year still to go on his deal.

There have been other disappointments in the No. 1 jersey. **Tony Fernandez** (1993) should have worked out but didn't: the four-time All-Star shortstop was acquired in an off-season trade with the Padres, but got off to a brutal start with the '93 Mets, hitting .225 and looking like he'd rather be waiting for a bus than playing baseball. Exasperated, the Mets unloaded him in mid-June to Toronto, where he'd starred his first eight seasons in the majors. He promptly hit .306 for the Blue Jays, including 18 triples in 94 games, and won a World Series ring.

Fernandez's arrival prompted **Vince Coleman** (1991–92) to change his number from 1 to 11, but he was a loser in any disguise. Signed to a rich free-agent deal just as Darryl Strawberry departed to the Dodgers, "Vincent Van Go" showed only traces of the speed that made him a three-time 100-base stealer with St. Louis. He brought precious little else to the Mets lineup while battling hamstring injuries, beat reporters, and team authorities. He is remembered best for throwing an M-100 firecracker from a car outside Dodger Stadium in 1993, injuring three bystanders, including a two-year-old girl.

The budget-minded Mets gambled that **Chris Young** (2014) could be a bargain comeback candidate but the veteran outfielder got hurt in his very first game, then whiffed his way to a midseason release. His comeback came instead with the Yankees. Young inherited the No. 1 jersey from electrifying utilityman **Jordany Valdespin** (2012–13), who had a flair for the dramatic (his five pinch-hit home runs in 2012 is a single-season team record; and six overall is tied for second all-time) along with the kind of insufferable ego that made him unpopular with teammates and opponents alike. Hard to say which shot was harder: John Buck's pie-the-face following a Valdespin walkoff grand slam, or the Justin Verlander fastball to the walnuts Valdespin absorbed without the good sense to have worn a cup that day.

Over the eighteen years between Ashburn and Wilson, No. 1 went to twelve men. **Cliff Cook** and his replacement, **Duke Carmel**, in 1963 combined to hit .229 in reserve outfield duty. Low-average slugging third baseman **Charley Smith** (1964–65) followed and led the '64 Mets in home runs with 20—he's the only No. 1 ever to pull off that feat. **Eddie Bressoud** (1966) was a stopgap shortstop peddled to St. Louis following the 1966 season for **Jerry Buchek** (1967–68), a part-time infielder with a knack for power—his 14 home runs as a second baseman in 1967 was the highest until Jeff Kent came around in 1993. Minor league vets **Kevin Collins** and **Bobby Pfeil** split reserve duties and the No. 1 jersey with the 1969 Mets.

The 1970s brought more brief visitors: part-timers **Lute Barnes** (1972–73), **Gene Clines** (disappointing compensation in exchange for Duffy Dyer in 1975), **Leo Foster** (1976), **Sergio Ferrer** (1978–79), and, making a pre-managerial appearance, **Bobby Valentine** (1977–78).

Following Wilson's decade of service, the No. 1 jersey went to reserve outfielders **Lou Thornton** and **Chuck Carr** in 1990; to reserve infielder **Kevin Baez** in 1993; and was split between prospects **Fernando Viña** and **Ricky Otero** in 1994.

Who was the Opening Day second baseman for the NL East Champion 2006 Mets? Give yourself a hand if you recall **Anderson Hernandez**.

Before there was Mookie, there was Bobby Valentine for a 1977 Mets team that was far from No. 1.

JacobKanarek/FromWorsttoFirst

Hernandez (2005–06), like his predecessor **Esix Snead** (2004) wasn't long for the Mets. The 2015 champs had negligible contributions from two wearers of the No. 1 jersey—scrappy rookie outfielder **Darrell Ceciliani**, followed by **Eric Young** in a limited return engagement.

Number 1

Number of times issued: 32 (28 players, 1 coach)

Longest tenured: Mookie Wilson (10 seasons, 1,116 games)

Best single seasons: Lance Johnson, 1996 (.333/.362/.479, 21 triples, 50 stolen bases); Wilson, 1982 (.279/.314/.369, 55 RBIs, 58 stolen bases); Richie Ashburn, 1962 (.306/.424/.393); Luis Castillo, 2009 (.302/.387/.346, 77 runs scored, 20 stolen bases)

Career statistical leaders: Home runs (Wilson 60); RBI (Wilson 342); batting average (Johnson .326)

Lineup by the Numbers

Mookie Wilson matched his uniform number to his slot in the starting lineup in 681 regular-season games during his career with the Mets, the most times a uni number has aligned with a batting order slot in Met history.

Following is a list of Met players whose jersey number aligned with their slot in the batting order most often (through 2015). Note that in more than 1,300 career games, Bud Harrelson never once batted third (nor has Curtis Granderson through his first 312 games as a Met). In 2015, Kirk Nieuwenhuis snapped a fifty-three-year streak, becoming the first and only No. 9 slotted into the 9th spot in a batting order.

1. Mookie Wilson   681 games
2. Justin Turner   95 games
3. Richie Hebner   11 games
4. Rusty Staub   250 games
5. David Wright   245 games
6. Mike Marshall   37 games
7. Hubie Brooks   115 games
8. Chris Cannizzaro   58 games
9. Kirk Nieuwenhuis   1 game

#2: MARVELOUS MARV AND THE TERRIBLE TWOS

A catcher who couldn't throw, a manager in disguise, a reviled acquisition, and a man whose initials were M.E.T., but whose play was B.A.D. Mets who have worn No. 2 are remembered for reasons they might not have wanted.

Take **Marvin Eugene Throneberry** (please!), the very first Met player to suit up in No. 2, acquired with the best of intentions but destined to become a lasting symbol of the futility of the dreadful-but-endearing '62 Mets.

Throneberry, who arrived in a trade with Baltimore in May 1962, was the kind of player the young Mets were willing to take a chance on: he'd shown good power in the minor leagues, hitting 40 home runs in consecutive seasons with the Yankees' Denver farm team. Although he'd since bounced to the Kansas City A's and Baltimore Orioles organizations, the Mets brass felt Throneberry could thrive if given the everyday opportunity—and the need was urgent with Gil Hodges' knees already giving way. The Mets willingly parted with the first player they'd selected in the expansion draft, Hobie Landrith, to acquire him.

"Marvelous Marv" would hit .238 with 16 home runs for the '62 Mets, but where he really excelled was in the field of pitiable comic relief. He committed a league-leading 17 errors at first base, and twice was called out for missing a base on what otherwise would be triples. Legend has it Casey Stengel charged out of the dugout to protest the injustice on one, only to be interrupted by third-base coach Cookie Lavagetto. "Forget it, Case," Lavagetto said. "He didn't touch first either."

But Throneberry's earnest struggles struck a chord with Mets fans anxious to cheer for anything, and he became something of a fan favorite as a result.

Throneberry was considerably less popular with the front office following a contract squabble prior to the 1963 season, and was farmed out by May, never to return to the big leagues. His legend lived long after his career, thanks in part to a magnificent portrayal of himself in Miller Lite beer ads.

Dark glasses, a black hat, and a fake mustache weren't part of the official uniform, but when manager **Bobby Valentine** (1996–2002) donned them during a 1999 game, he wasn't supposed to be there anyway. His reappearance in the Shea dugout in disguise following an ejection came during the course of a remarkable week in which the manager must have felt he had nothing to lose: three members of his hand-picked coaching staff had just been fired, eliciting Valentine's offer of his own head on the chopping block: If the Mets didn't improve over their next 55 games, he dared, fire me. They would go 40–15 over that stretch.

No man since Casey Stengel embodied the role of Mets manager quite like Valentine, who in six-plus years proved one of the most charismatic and divisive personalities in Mets history. While his tenure was marked with feuds with players (Todd Hundley, Pete Harnisch, Bobby Bonilla), the media (Murray Chass, Marty Noble), and general manager Steve Phillips, Valentine was rarely outmanaged by the other guy and was always fascinating to think along with. Astutely dubbed "The New Perfesser" by the *Village Voice*, Valentine won 536 games as a Mets manager, second only to Davey Johnson's 595.

Dan Carubia

The throwing woes of Mike Piazza were child's play next to Mackey Sasser.

Mackey Sasser hit well enough to be a capable backup for catcher Gary Carter, but a mystifying throwing ailment prevented him from being Carter's successor. An adequate receiver with an otherwise strong throwing arm, Sasser suffered from an inability to return the ball to his pitcher in one try: delays while he repeatedly pumped his arm before throwing frustrated Sasser and his team-mates alike, but opponents took little pity, swiping bases on him with impunity.

The condition seemed to worsen after the Mets let Carter go, leading to the Mets use of seven different catchers in 1990—six of whom couldn't hit—and Sasser's eventual conversion to a utility player. The free-swinging lefty compiled a .283 career average as a Met with good doubles power. He hit .307 over 100 games in 1990.

That the Nolan Ryan-for-**Jim Fregosi** swap was the worst deal in Mets history is barely debatable—the question remains where it ranks among bad trades in baseball history.

Yet when the swindle was orchestrated in December of 1971, the Mets were confident they got the better of it. After all, Fregosi (1972–73) was a six-time All-Star shortstop with the Angels and was viewed as the long-awaited answer to the Mets third-base whirligig, which was already becoming famous. They had Wayne Garrett around but didn't trust him, Tim Foli wasn't yet ready, and **Bob Aspromonte** (1971), the starter for most of the 1971 season and Fregosi's predecessor in the No. 2 jersey, had been released. Above all, the Mets believed they were contenders and could afford to go for it with a veteran, even if it meant the sacrifice of a few young prospects.

But they hadn't done their homework. An injured foot requiring surgery in 1971 had convinced the Angels that their twenty-nine-year-old star player was rapidly approaching the breakdown stage. If Ryan's frequent injuries and famous wildness—a fact driven home by dreadful performances late in 1971—warranted a trade, Fregosi was probably the wrong target and came very expensively, given the Angels' lack of leverage. And then there was the fact that Fregosi had never played an inning of third base in his 1,392-game major league career.

Sure enough, Fregosi never regained his form. Injuries limited him to 101 games in 1972, when he batted just .232 with five home runs, the worst numbers of his career. By 1973 he'd fallen out of favor with fans and management and was dealt to the Rangers in mid-season. The bounty? Undisclosed cash payment.

The Terrible Twos also included outfielder **George Altman** (1964), the prize in the Roger Craig trade who saw his career take a sudden turn for the worse with the Mets. Shortstop **Jose Oquendo** (1983–84) provided dazzling fielding but a weak bat as a teenager for Bambi's Bandits in 1983; he'd develop into an excellent utility player and later a regular second baseman with the Cardinals. **Chuck Hiller** (1965–67) served as the poor-fielding, left-handed-hitting piece of a second-base platoon in the mid-1960s and hung around the organization for decades afterward as a coach and organizational instructor.

Fiery ex-Phillie **Larry Bowa** (1985) played the last games of his career during the Mets' 1985 stretch drive and continues to hold down the shortstop position on the "They were Mets?" all-time squad. **Roy Staiger** (1976–77) was a well-regarded prospect but showed little beyond a strong glove at third base. **Kevin Elster** (1986) made his debut on the last day of August in 1986—just in time to become an instant World Champion. He wore numbers other than 2 for the balance of his Mets career. **Jimmy Piersall** was assigned No. 2 when he joined the Mets in 1963, but he switched to 34 after two days. Ex-Yankee infielder **Phil Linz** (1967–68) spent the final two years of his career as a Mets backup.

Justin Turner in 2010 became the first player to wear No. 2 since reserve outfielder **Damon Buford**, who'd arrived in the Bobby Bonilla trade fifteen years earlier. The jersey between their tenures belonged to Valentine (who had previously worn 2 as a coach in 1985), then to coaches Gary Pettis and Sandy Alomar. A squat, redheaded infielder, Turner (2010–13), made good contact even when not smashing pies into his teammates' faces. After the Mets let him go (there were whispers his conditioning wasn't great, although that much appeared self-evident), a determined Turner unexpectedly became the best hitter on a stacked Dodger club.

It's widely hoped that **Dilson Hererra**'s best days are still to come but as of the writing of this book it's not certain when, where or in what number they'll be. The Columbia-born infielder arrived from the Pirates organization in the Marlon Byrd trade and made brief appearances in the No. 2 jersey in 2014 and 2015. But when the '15 Mets traded for **Juan Uribe** during Herrera's time in the minors, No. 2 went directly to Uribe. (Herrera resurfaced in September wearing 16.)

Uribe, for his part, fit right in. A barrel-chested, crusty, cigar-chewing veteran of two World Series champions, Uribe overnight turned the Mets reserve corps from a weakness to a strength and kicked off their transition from a mere contender to a team with designs to win. He returned from a late-season injury in time to play in his third World Series. His only Mets postseason at-bat resulted in a run-scoring single to spark a four-run rally in Game 3.

Brock Pemberton, a switch-hitting first baseman with a name fit for a quarterback, got a brief audition as a twenty-year-old in 1974, and an even shorter one as a twenty-one-year-old in 1975. **Phil Mankowski** (1980) was acquired from Detroit as another potential solution to the Mets third-base issue but made two errors in the first inning of his very first start there.

Bill Almon (1987), a former #1 overall pick by the San Diego Padres out of Brown University, twice had brief stints as a Mets utilityman, donning

25 (1980) and 2 (1987). **Tom Grieve** (1978) passed through New York on his way to the Texas Rangers' front office. A day after part-time outfielder **Wayne Housie** (1993) was traded away, No. 2 went to newly arriving infielder **Doug Saunders** for his only big-league appearances. For more on that story, see sidebar below.

Number 2

Number of times issued: 26 (22 players, 1 manager, 3 coaches)

Longest tenured: Bobby Valentine (manager; 7 seasons, 1,003 games), Mackey Sasser (5 seasons, 420 games)

Best single seasons: Mackey Sasser, 1990 (.307.344/.426); Juan Uribe, 2015 (6 HR, 9 doubles, .430 slugging in 44 games)

Career statistical leaders: Home runs (Marv Throneberry 16), RBI (Sasser 133), batting average (Sasser .283)

METS UNIFORM HISTORY: A STITCH IN TIME

It was still only June, but the 1993 Mets were already 22 ½ games out of first place and fading fast when they finally bit the bullet and put Howard Johnson retroactively onto the disabled list. The last surviving hitter from the club's late '80s glory years, Johnson had been unable to shake a viral infection that made him weak, dizzy, slumping and unable to participate for several days. The shorthanded club recalled infielder Doug Saunders from Class AAA Norfolk for the first time, but getting Saunders into a uniform was another struggle entirely.

Russ Gompers, left, and Eric Krause put name and number to back on all the Mets uniforms at Stitches in Whitestone.

"It was a Saturday," recalls Russ Gompers, owner a Whitestone embroidery shop known as Stitches. "I was food shopping with my wife and kids. When I got home that night I had a phone message from my friend Steve Cohen who at the time had a sporting goods business in Astoria. 'Russ. It's Steve. We've got an emergency. Call me at this number.'"

Gompers did as he was told, not knowing the number he called belonged to the equipment office at Shea Stadium. A panicked Charlie Samuels answered, desperately seeking someone who could stitch a Doug Saunders jersey in time for Sunday's home game. The Mets regular stitcher had gone AWOL, and mutual friend Cohen had recommended Gompers.

"You take care of me on this," Samuels said that night, "and I'll give you all my work!"

Within the hour the club had sent over a fresh Mets jersey, letters and numbers to Gompers's shop in nearby Whitestone, and Gompers got to work. So that he would arrange the letters in the proper style, they also sent over a jersey of recently demoted outfielder Ryan Thompson to use as a model since it had the same number of letters as "Saunders."

Twenty-three years later, Gompers, an affable former trucker and unabashed fan of the orange-and-blue, proudly remains the official uniform stitcher of the Mets. (Interestingly, he recalls that the jersey he prepared for Saunders that night was a No. 12, and not No. 2, though on matters like these he gladly defers to his nephew, Eric Krause, who runs the shop with him).

In addition to affixing names and numbers on team jerseys, Stitches over the course of the baseball season performs any number of uniform related tasks for the Mets and often, visiting clubs and umpire staffs, including custom embroidery on shoes and chest protectors, plus various repairs. He designed and made several of the team's patches out of his small factory, which includes a number of embroidery machines, a room where three or more seamstresses work at sewing machines, and piles of assorted parts—spare numbers, reels of thread, boxes of gear for clients.

The Mets are only a small part of Stitches' overall business but at the same time it is high-profile, fun, and frequently hectic: Lest Yoenis Cespedes play barechested in his debut, Gompers has learned not to plan vacations at the trade deadline. He cops to have occasionally influenced the issuing of numbers, like when the trade bringing the Mets Mel Rojas in 1997 resulted in an accidental assigning of two 51s (acquiree Rojas and overlooked coach Mookie Wilson). Gompers saw the easy solution—with Lance Johnson going away in the same trade, he simply stitched Mookie a new 1, and all was right in the world again.

#3: REAL NEW YORKERS

It took **Curtis Granderson** less than two years to obliterate the all-time mark for home runs by a Met No. 3, and that includes his less-than-impressive debut season in the jersey in 2014. If that's an indictment of the 21 other men to labor in No. 3, so be it.

Like Carlos Beltran, George Foster, and Vince Coleman, Granderson was a newly acquired star outfielder who struggled in his first season in orange and blue. Arriving from the Yankees as Sandy Alderson's highest-profile free agent signing to date, Granderson said all the right things—real New Yorkers *are* in fact Met fans—but he appeared miscast as a middle-of-the-order slugger and struggled to bat .227 with 20 home runs.

Curtis Granderson found his old power stroke in the leadoff spot in 2015 with 26 homers while also leading the team in steals.

Granderson's 2015 season—26 home runs, 76 RBIs, 91 walks, and 98 runs scored, nearly all from the leadoff slot in the batting order—made him arguably the best everyday player on the World Series-bound Mets. Moreover he is a solid citizen and club ambassador who's easy to root for. Let's face it: If all he'd done was create the 'We Follow Lucas Duda' Instagram account, Granderson might also have been the most valuable Met.

Over a thirteen-year playing career with the Mets, **Bud Harrelson** never wore a uniform number other than 3 and never played an inning at any position but shortstop.

A Mets constant who distinguished himself with feistiness and hustle, Harrelson (1965–77) earned two world championship rings (one as a coach), two All-Star Game appearances, and a Gold Glove. He then had a second, shorter and far more difficult career as a Mets manager.

Harrelson was a star in the field but not in the highlight reels. Steady but rarely breathtakingly so, he positioned himself superbly, caught whatever was hit near him, and threw accurately and on time. At the plate he consistently provided meager but reliable production, supplementing a near complete lack of power (7 career home runs) with general heads-up play, and the ability to reach base via the bunt and the base on balls.

Part of Casey Stengel's "Youth of America," Harrelson signed with the Mets out of San Francisco State University shortly after he turned nineteen years old in 1963. So impressed was Stengel with the young infielder at spring camp in 1964 that the manager lobbied, albeit unsuccessfully, to take him north. It wouldn't be until 1967 that Harrelson established himself as the Mets' everyday shortstop.

In the championship season of 1969, Harrelson was one of only four regular starters under manager Gil Hodges' platoon system—Cleon Jones in left, Tommie Agee in center field, and Jerry Grote behind the plate were the others—embodying the baseball truism about strong defense up the middle winning championships. Many fans recall Harrelson best for his dusty brawl with Pete Rose during the 1973 National League Championship Series: Harrelson, although giving away size to Rose, acquitted himself well as the Mets, who kayoed the heavyweight Big Red Machine.

Ironically, Harrelson's career as a manager was a case of decent statistics obscuring a shaky day-to-day performance. Given the unenviable task of succeeding Davey Johnson, Harrelson struggled to hold together fragments of a crumbling dynasty and lasted less than two seasons despite an overall winning mark. Although strongly influenced by Gil Hodges, Harrelson appeared to lack his managerial idol's presence and confidence.

Harrelson was on the coaching lines (wearing No. 23) while a successor in the No. 3 jersey, **Rafael Santana,** replicated Harrelson's role as the no-hit, good-glove shortstop on a Mets championship team. Santana (1984–87) lasted four years as a Met, three as a starter. Reliable defensively, Santana was a poor hitter, providing little of the extras in terms of speed or on-base skills that Harrelson could.

By the time **Carl Everett** (1995–97) had begun to realize his tremendous potential, he was already on his way out. A first-round draft pick of the Yankees out of Hillsborough High in Tampa, Dwight Gooden's alma mater, Everett had all the tools but had already worn through two organizations when he arrived in an astutely orchestrated trade with Florida following the 1994 season. Everett really began to blossom in 1997, providing explosive power, clutch hits, and ability in any outfield position, becoming one of the most promising young players on the suddenly contending Mets. Then Shea Stadium day-care staff alerted authorities of their concerns the Everett family may have been abusing their children.

The incident—which for a time cost the Everetts custody of their two kids—didn't sit well with the family-friendly image the Mets were promoting. Everett was unloaded cheaply, to Houston for doomed reliever John Hudek, following the 1997 season. Everett would go on to greater accomplishments on the field with the Astros and Red Sox and even grander displays of temper and curious behavior.

Vance Wilson (1998–2004) one day will tell his grandkids that he backed up the two greatest catchers of his era—Mike Piazza with the Mets and Ivan Rodriguez with the Tigers. They totaled twenty-six All-Star appearances and seventeen Silver Sluggers between them. Not bad for Wilson, a 44th-round draft pick who didn't arrive in the majors to stay until age twenty-nine.

Richie Hebner arrived reluctantly on the eve of the 1979 season and overnight became the third baseman he no longer was and the cleanup hitter he was never suited to be. His offseason job as a gravedigger, however, was a perfect match for the comatose '79 Mets.

A hardscrabble New Englander who might have also made a career as a

Dan Carubia

Carl Everett was a key part of the 1997 Mets turnaround, but he left under a cloud.

hockey player, Hebner was a mainstay of the terrific Pirates teams of the early 1970s but had already been transitioned to a first baseman by Philadelphia when the Mets acquired him (for pitcher Nino Espinosa in a deal that certainly didn't go New York's way). Hebner knocked in four runs in his Met debut but things went downhill from there. A target of fan abuse and a symbol of a futile franchise, he was unloaded shortly after his only season in New York.

Left-handed-hitting French Canadian slugger **Tim Harkness** replaced Marv Throneberry at first base for the Mets in 1963. While his overall numbers were unimpressive (10/41/.221), Harkness is remembered for hitting two extra-inning walk-off home runs that season, including a 14th-inning grand slam to stun the Cubs. His trade to Cincinnati in 1964 for Bobby Klaus stunned teammates and Harkness alike, resulting in Harkness refusing to report to the Reds' farm team in San Diego until the Mets reluctantly provided him a $2,000 bonus.

Gus Bell was the 1962 Opening Day right fielder but lasted just five weeks in a Met uniform before being sent to Milwaukee as the player to be named in the previous winter's trade for Frank Thomas. Bell (1962) was

Lou Longobardi

If there are giveaway days in Mets hell, you might be handed Richie Hebner's No. 3 on jersey day. It would, of course, be a doubleheader. Against the Phillies.

one of the better power hitters in the National League in the 1950s, but he was all but washed up by the time the Mets selected him in the expansion draft. In 101 at-bats for the Mets, Bell hit .149. Another expansion draftee, **Ed Bouchee,** suited up in No. 3 after Bell disappeared in '62. Bouchee (1962) was a burly power-hitting first baseman with bad hands, suiting him perfectly to be a backup to Throneberry.

Billy Cowan (1965) was acquired from the Cubs to be the everyday center fielder in 1965. Despite a good glove, Cowan was an abysmal free-swinger (.179 batting average, .205 on-base percentage, 5 five walks, and 45 strikeouts in 162 plate appearances). He was traded in August. Reserve infielder **Mike Cubbage** wore No. 3 in 1981 but No. 4 when he took over briefly as Mets manager in relief of Harrelson a decade later. **Miguel Cairo** had a good reputation as a reserve when he arrived in 2005 but spent entirely too much time making starts for injured teammates.

Veteran reserve **Damion Easley** (2007–08) was a terrific pinch hitter who spent the last two seasons of an 18-year career with the Mets. That each of those years ended in the agony of just missing the playoffs was doubly sad for Easley, who retired with the dubious distinction as having played the most games in the majors without appearing in a postseason series: 1,706.

Easley's role as the veteran reserve infielder went to **Alex Cora** in 2009, but as with most Mets backups in Citi Field's first season, Cora spent way too much time filling in for injured starters. Eventually, injuries to both thumbs ended his year. He returned in 2010 wearing No. 13, without much luck. **Josh Satin** (2011–2012) would also spend time in both No. 3 and No. 13 during his Mets bench career.

Other No. 3s were short-lasting infield reserves **Sergio Ferrer** (1978), **Mario Ramirez** (1980), **Junior Noboa** (1992), **Darrin Jackson** (1993), **Luis Rivera** (1994), **Luis Hernandez** (2010) and **Omar Quintanilla** (2013). Not a Babe Ruth among 'em.

Number 3

Number of times issued: 27 (23 players, 2 coaches, 1 manager, 1 DNP)

Longest tenured: Bud Harrelson (13 seasons, 1,322 games)

Best single seasons: Granderson, 2015 (.259/.364/.457, 26 HR, 91 walks, 98 runs); Harrelson, 1970 (.243/ .351/.309, 95 walks, 23 stolen bases, 8 triples)

Career statistical leaders: Home runs (Curtis Granderson 46); RBI (Harrelson 242); batting average (Damian Easley .273)

Step Right up and Teach the Mets: From Batter's Box to Coach's Box

Promoting from within was a few years in coming for the Mets. The early coaching staff mostly played when John McGraw ruled the Polo Grounds. Casey Stengel, who'd been 33 when he'd starred for McGraw's Giants in the 1923 World Series, kept the Mets beat writers in stitches at his old stomping grounds. Crabby coach Rogers Hornsby scared the pants off the greenhorns, while pitching coach Red Ruffing could regale the beleaguered staff with tales of playing with Babe Ruth. It was all good stuff, but it didn't translate into wins.

The first Mets to join the coaching ranks were Hall of Fame players at the end of the line. Yogi Berra and Warren Spahn served as part-time players and full-time coaches in 1965. Berra, just fired by the Yankees despite winning a pennant as a rookie manager, caught just five games; Spahn flew the coop after three months, 12 losses, and untold headaches working with the hopeless pitching staff. He opted to pitch a few final games in San Francisco and did not coach in the majors again until 1972. Rusty Staub was a player-coach in 1982, but his role soon changed to unofficial advisor and official pinch hitter.

Gil Hodges was the first former Met to manage in the majors. He first managed expansion Washington in 1963 and then took over the Mets in 1968. (Both the Senators and Mets traded players to acquire him as manager.) Hodges was also the first former Met to manage a world champion. Eight former Mets have followed him as manager at Shea, with varying degrees of success. Six of them, like Hodges, were infielders. Unlike Hodges, though, five apprenticed as coaches for the club.

Player	Position	Number	Coach	Number	Manager	Number
Yogi Berra	C	8	1965–71	8	1972–75	8
Warren Spahn	P	21	1965	21		
Gil Hodges	1B	14			1968–71	14
Joe Pignatano	C	5	1968–81	52		
Roy McMillan	SS	11	1973–75	51	1975	51
Willie Mays	OF	24	1974–79	24		
Joe Torre	1B	9			1977–81	9
Bud Harrelson	SS	3	1982, 1985–90	53, 23, 3	1990–91	3
Rusty Staub	OF	4, 10	1982	10		
Bobby Valentine	2B		1983–85	53, 22, 28, 2	1996–2002	2
Mike Cubbage	3B	3	1990–96	4	1991	4
Chuck Hiller	2B	2	1990	22		
John Stephenson	C	49, 19, 12	1992–93	51, 32		
Dallas Green	P	27			1993–96	46

Bob Apodaca	P	34	1996–99	34		
Mookie Wilson	OF	1	1997–2002, 2011	51, 1		
Randy Niemann	P	46, 40	1997–99, 2001–02, 2009–10	45, 48, 52, 55		
Al Jackson	P	15, 38	1999–2000	54		
John Stearns	C	16, 12	2000–01	12		
Sandy Alomar Sr.	SS	5	2005–07	2		
Willie Randolph	2B	12			2005–07	12
Rickey Henderson	OF	24	2007	24		
Howard Johnson	3B	20, 44	2007–10	52, 20		
Tim Teufel	2B	11	2012–15	18		

Note: Position refers to primary position as a Met. **Bold** indicates manager (including interim managers). Coach and manager only include years in those capacities as Mets.

#4: TRADE BAIT

Shed no tears for **Wilmer Flores**. If he has a teary goodbye that sticks, it will be just another instance in a recurring theme for guys who have put on the No. 4 jersey over the years: Join the team, inspire a postseason run, and get out of here.

Naturally, it's happened four times.

Rusty Staub (1972–74) was one of the most complete ballplayers of his time; packaging power, on-base ability, clutch hitting, and terrific defense in right field (he led the National League in assists in 1974 and '75).

Acquired from Montreal just prior to the 1972 season for Ken Singleton, Tim Foli, and Mike Jorgensen, the left-handed-hitting Staub was leading the Mets in home runs and RBI before a fractured hand requiring surgery interrupted his season and derailed any hopes for the once-promising Mets. Staub returned in 1973 to set a then-team record with 36 doubles and provide 3 home runs as the Mets upset the favored Cincinnati Reds in the playoffs. In the 1973 World Series, Rusty led all hitters with a .423 batting average despite playing with a shoulder damaged so badly in a collision with the right-field wall at Shea that he was forced to throw underhand.

As he had been in prior stops in Houston and Montreal, Staub was a great fan favorite, which made his trade to Detroit for Mickey Lolich following the 1975 season all the more infuriating. Approaching 10-and-5 rights (ten years of major league service, five with one club) giving him the power to veto a trade, a front office skittish about the newly won gains of the players association figured to act while they still controlled their hitting star's destiny. The Mets would right that mistake six years later, however, and Rusty would write an exciting final chapter to his career . . . as we'll see in Chapter 10.

Robin Ventura is always going to evoke mixed feelings. Signed as a free agent in 1999, Ventura (1999–2001) was a legitimate MVP candidate

Dan Carubia

Robin Ventura was as good as any No. 4 the Mets have seen—and there have been some exceptional players to don the number.

(he finished sixth in the voting, just ahead of teammates Mike Piazza and Edgardo Alfonzo) and a team leader who introduced "Mojo Risin'" to the Met vocabulary. He capped his first year as a Met with the unforgettable "grand slam single" that dramatically ended Game 5 of the '99 NLCS. But the goodwill generated by that first season would be severely tested by the two injury-plagued and disappointing campaigns to follow. His stock had dropped so low by the end of 2001 (21/61/.237) that the Mets felt comfortable trading him to the Yankees, leaving conflicted Mets fans the choice of either cheering for his continued mediocrity or rooting against the comeback they all believed he had in him. Predictably, his results as a Yankee were a mix of good and terrible.

In Michael Lewis's bestseller *Moneyball*, Billy Beane, the Oakland general manager, described former farmhand roommate **Lenny Dykstra** as "perfectly designed emotionally to play the game of baseball." Don't linger too long on what that says about ballplayers.

Hyperactive, foul-mouthed and pint-sized, Dykstra (1985–89) wore No. 4 but played like a No. 1 (and probably thought he was a No. 44). He hit .278 with 104 doubles and 116 stolen bases as a Met and shined in the 1986 postseason: his home run off Dave Smith in the bottom of the ninth inning won Game 3 of the NLCS against Houston, and his leadoff triple off Bob Knepper sparked the 9th-inning rally that tied that series' epic and decisive Game 6. Dykstra's leadoff home run in Game 3 of the World Series at Fenway Park was the first step in the Mets' climb out of a deep hole against Boston.

In June of 1989, Dykstra, his giant wad of chewing tobacco, and Roger McDowell were dispatched to Philadelphia for Juan Samuel in a deal that to this day draws wails of regret from Mets fans. He'd go on to lead the Phillies into the 1993 World Series, finishing second in the National League MVP voting to Barry Bonds that year.

He wasn't much of an outfielder any other day, but his diving catch of Brooks Robinson's liner in Game 4 of the 1969 World Series helped make **Ron Swoboda** an all-time Mets hero.

"Rocky" socked 19 homers as a twenty-one-year-old rookie in 1965 (wearing No. 14, which he set aside for Ken Boyer in 1966). Though he never developed into a true slugger, Swoboda (1966–70) had a flair for the unexpected: it was his pair of two-run homers that defeated the Cardinals despite Steve Carlton striking out 19 Mets in September 1969. His 8th-inning double brought in the go-ahead run in Game 5 of the World Series to set the stage for Kooz, Cleon, and the rampage at Shea that followed. And along with teammate Tom Seaver, Swoboda became something of a spokes-man for the champion Mets and what they represented in those turbulent times. Swoboda left unhappy after a 1971 trade to Montreal (Don Hahn came in exchange). He eventually returned to New York, first as a Yankee, then as a sportscaster of some renown.

Swoboda was batting in the 1979 Old-timers Day game at Shea Stadium when the tape covering the nameplate on his No. 4 jersey peeled away revealing . . . BOISCLAIR. One of those bit players whom Met fans tend to remember vividly, **Bruce Boisclair** (1976–79) was a gangly outfielder with a wide left-handed stance who enjoyed some success as a part-timer and pinch hitter (.293, 21 doubles, 4 HR, 44 RBIs in 307 ABs in 1977).

As for Flores, he packed a career's worth of memories into his first full season with the Mets in 2015. A fine minor-league hitter in search of a field-ing position, the not-yet twenty-four-year-old Venezuelan was as surprised as the rest of us to find himself installed as

There's no doubt about chief spokesman for No. 4: Ron Swoboda.

the starting shortstop; but he was the last of us to know he'd apparently been traded to Milwaukee in a deadline deal for former Met Carlos Gomez. Tipped by the reaction of fans at Citi Field during a game July 29, a stunned Flores openly wept on the field, an event serving as booster engine for a #MetsTwitter rocket that had spread word in the first place.

The story took another dramatic turn when it was revealed after the game that the deal was off—the Mets apparently didn't like the medical report on Gomez—providing an extraordinary reprieve for the emotional Flores. He received standing ovations for the rest of the year: none more raucous than after ending a Mets–Nationals game two nights later with a 12th-inning walk-off home run, unforgettably gripping the Mets logo on his chest as teammates mobbed him at home plate.

Flores played shortstop throughout the 2016 postseason after Ruben Tejada was hurt, yet questions remain as to the role of Flores on the field. He needn't worry about his role in Mets history, or in the hearts of fans.

Former Brooklyn hero **Duke Snider** hit 14 homers in a nostalgia tour as a Met in 1963. As strange as it must have been for old Dodgers fans to see the Duke calling the Polo Grounds home, it was even stranger watching him don a Giants uniform in 1964.

Original Mets second baseman **Charlie Neal** might be considered the franchise's first-ever big-money goof. The inviting left-field deck of the Polo Grounds—not to mention his Dodger bloodlines—persuaded the Mets to trade Lee Walls and $75,000 of George Weiss's "mad money" to Los Angeles for the pull-hitting infielder following the expansion draft. But Neal aged quickly (the early Mets had a way of doing that to people) and shuffled off quietly in 1963.

Utility man **Bob Bailor** (1981–83) was the key player sent to the Dodgers in 1983 (along with reliever Carlos Diaz) in exchange for a portly minor-league southpaw named Sid Fernandez. That remains one of the shrewdest deals the Mets have ever made.

Number 4 is either inspired or insipid. And we've completed the inspired part . . .

Weeks after the Lenny Dykstra trade in September 1989, career minor-leaguer **Lou Thornton** was patrolling the Shea outfield in Dykstra's old No. 4. (Thornton would return in 1990 wearing the No. 1 jersey of another displaced fan favorite, Mookie Wilson.) **Wayne Graham** (1964) was best known for managing Rice University's baseball team wearing 37 in honor of his manager, Casey Stengel. **Jose Moreno** (1980) came over in the deal with Richie Hebner and was about as memorable. Long Islander **John Valentin** played the final games of his career with the 2002 Mets. **Chris Woodward** (2005–06) backed up Jose Reyes when Reyes needed little backup.

Ben Johnson hit .185 in 2007 and cost the Mets Heath Bell, who might have come in handy in the late innings of that September's collapsible lead. With Johnson gone, **Anderson Hernandez** switched from No. 1 to No. 4 upon the '07 trade deadline acquisition of Luis Castillo: He logged but a single at-bat in the jersey, and flew out to left. Rotund catcher **Robinson Cancel** made his Mets debut in No. 4 in 2008; he'd be back for longer bench stays in 40 and 29. **Argenis Reyes** took No. 4 following Cancel and briefly teamed with Jose on an All-Reyes middle infield. **Wilson Valdez** hung around for parts of 2009 before inexplicably developing into a useful spare part for the Phillies. Once upon a time **Angel Berroa** was the AL Rookie of the Year; little evidence of that 2003 accomplishment remained as he finished his big-league career with the Mets in 2009.

Thirty-eight-year-old backstop **Henry Blanco** teamed with thirty-four-year-old Rod Barajas in 2010 to forge a rather uninspiring catching combination. Young catcher **Mike Nickeas** took No. 4 in 2012 after newly signed Ronny Cedeno took the No. 13 Nickeas wore in his first visits.

The 2011 Mets clumsily moved on from the Luis Castillo Era by gambling on Rule 5 pick **Brad Emaus** as their Opening Day second baseman. He was no Famous Emaus, though, and was gone after two-and-half weeks. Speaking of recent Opening Day gambles, there's **Collin Cowgill**, whose Mets career peaked on his first day. The starter in center field and leadoff hitter to open 2013, Cowgill's grand slam punctuated an 11–2 laugher over the Padres. Within weeks he'd played his way out of the lineup and into a trade: No more Cowgill.

Number 4

Number of times issued: 28 (24 players, 3 coaches)

Longest tenured: Ron Swoboda (5 seasons, 602 games), Lenny Dykstra (5 seasons, 544 games)

Best single season: Robin Ventura, 1999 (.301/.379/.529, 32 HR, 120 RBIs)

Career statistical leaders: Home runs (Ventura 77, Swoboda 50); RBI (Ventura 265, Swoboda 254); batting average (Dykstra .278, Staub .273)

Now Playing at the Drive-In: RBI by the Numbers

Former No. 4 Rusty Staub enjoyed a fifteen-year reign as the Mets' all-time single-season RBI leader, although his one-time record of 105 RBIs, set in 1975 (while wearing No. 10) and tied by Gary Carter in 1985, has been bested sixteen times since then.

Despite the help of 265 RBIs from Robin Ventura and 254 from Ron Swoboda, No. 4 collectively ranks no better than ninth on the Mets' all-time list of runs batted in by uniform number. (Rusty's No. 10 was weighed down by too many Reys—Ordoñez and Sanchez—to make anyone's list.) No. 5 has taken a commanding lead in the category with the 2,000-RBI plateau approaching, thanks largely to David Wright. Recent pushes from sluggers Carlos Delgado and Lucas Duda has shot No. 21 into second place with 1,657 RBIs through 2015, followed closely by No. 15.

Following are the top 10 uniform numbers by RBI through 2015:

No.	RBI	Notes
5	1,938	David Wright (956) accounts for nearly half; John Olerud (291) and Steve Henderson (227) contribute nicely.
21	1,300	Cleon Jones (511), Carlos Delgado (339), and Lucas Duda (318) are the top three.
15	1,633	Carlos Beltran delivered 599 of them, followed by George Foster (361) and Jerry Grote (357).
7	1,523	Steady Eddie with 555; Jose-Jose-Jose-Jose with 423.
9	1,379	Five triple-digit RBI men, led by Todd Hundley (388) and Gregg Jefferies (205).
20	1,378	Order the ribeyes for Howard Johnson's (625), make Mark Johnson (23) pay.
12	1,369	John Stearns (292) and Jeff Kent (252) lead.
18	1,336	Former Mets career RBI king Darryl Strawberry carries the load with 733.
4	1,331	Robin Ventura leads (265), with Ron Swoboda (254) a close second and Trusty Rusty (192) a distant third.
17	1,089	Keith Hernandez loves his rib-eye steaks, he ate 468 as a Met. All other 17s can eat burgers at Keith's Grill at Citi. No discount.

#5: MR. WRIGHT

Thank you, David Wright. Thanks for being the most accomplished all-around offensive player the Mets ever developed. Thanks for saying all the right things when they stick a mic in your face. Thanks for twice signing contracts to extend your stay with the Mets. Thanks for your determination to fight back from those dreadful injuries. Thanks for the funny way you stick your tongue out when you throw, and for so fastidiously adjusting your sweatbands, batting gloves and uni-top as you dig in to the plate. Thanks for showing your socks on day games and pulling those cuffs down at night. Thanks for the eye black. Thanks for being the lead subject in a discussion of Met No. 5s that we'll barely need to update when our kids' kids are Met fans.

Dan Carubia

Captain David Wright leads by example, and that example has him at the top of most Mets franchise records.

Selected by the Mets out a Virginia high school as a between-round "sandwich pick"—compensation for having lost Mike Hampton to free agency the previous winter—Wright was the 38th overall selection in the 2001 amateur draft and forced his way to the majors a little more than three years later. Had Wright been given a choice of uniform number, he may have taken No. 8 in honor of his boyhood idol, Cal Ripken of the Orioles.

But the Mets had another Hall of Fame infielder in mind when they issued Wright No. 5. "I always liked [No.] 5 for a third baseman," Charlie Samuels, the Mets equipment manager, told Marty Noble of MLB.com in 2005. "And George Brett wore it. But I wouldn't have given [Wright] a single digit if I didn't think he'd be a special player."

Where talented players tend to have positive character attributes assigned to them regardless of their actual character, Wright over the years has proven to be the genuine article; the organization man who's too good to be fake. When fans wailed in 2005 that Willie Randolph had the temerity to bat him seventh in the lineup, Wright diffused any controversy by humbly explaining it offered him opportunities to learn. He paid respect to veterans, granted interviews, made promotional appearances, signed autographs for kids, maintained a Manhattan apartment, started a charity foundation, and did every promo and PSA imaginable.

As of this writing, Captain America has captured most of Ed Kranepool's longevity records and owns career Met marks for most runs, hits, singles, doubles, RBIs, strikeouts, walks, total, bases, sacrifice flies, and times hit-by-pitch. He's a modest Wright-like season (17 home runs and 44 RBIs) from becoming the first Met to reach 1,000 ribbies. Among Mets with 1,000 at-bats, Wright ranks second in batting average (.298), seventh in slugging average (.492), and fourth in on-base percentage (.377). He won Gold Glove and Silver Slugger awards in both 2007 and 2008 and has made seven All-Star teams.

He's the only remaining Met to have played for Art Howe, Willie Randolph, or played a home game at Shea Stadium, contributing to two division winners while enduring more bad seasons than he deserved. It says here he'll be the last man ever to wear No. 5.

Until Wright came along, No. 5 was best exemplified by **John Olerud.** Perhaps the best pure hitter the Mets ever employed came to New York in brilliant bit of thievery. Misinterpreting the first baseman's legendary patience at the plate as a lack of aggression, the Blue Jays took pedestrian starter Robert Person off the Mets' hands and paid $5 million of Olerud's $6.5 million 1997 salary. Olerud hammered home the folly of this deal by having the best three-year stretch of his career with the Mets, amassing 63 home runs, 291 RBIs, and a .315/.425/.501 line: His season *and* career batting and on-base percentages through 2015 remain the highest in Mets history among players with 1,000 at-bats, and his slugging ranks fourth all-time.

In 1998, Olerud shattered Cleon Jones's twenty-nine-year-old club record for batting average in a season, and Johnny O.'s .354 mark is still unmatched.

Olerud also came through when it counted. He hit .438 in the Mets' 1999 Division Series win over Arizona, including a home run in the crucial Game 1 victory over Randy Johnson, and .296 in the following NLCS against Atlanta with two home runs. Sadly, it would be his Mets swan song, as he packed his sweet swing and departed for Seattle as a free agent following the season.

Olerud complemented his uniform by wearing a flapless batting helmet in the field. This was not a fashion statement but rather a precaution—and a message to his mother he'd be careful out there—after having suffered a brain aneurysm while in college.

Style, however, was the specialty of Olerud's successor in the No. 5 jersey, the flamboyant free-swinging Japanese outfielder **Tsuyoshi Shinjo.** Shinjo (2001, 2003) wore gigantic orange sweatbands and seemingly couldn't help but add flair to his motions: he hopped before catching every fly ball, and his home runs were frequently accented with a casually arrogant flip of the bat (especially arrogant given that he homered once every 50 or so at-bats, but as Jose Batista and Yoenis Cespedes go, Shinjo was a pioneer).

Although imported primarily to be a reserve, injuries and ineffectiveness among regular starters provided Shinjo more playing time than the brass might have imagined in 2001. He responded by being perhaps the team's most exciting player that year, getting 10 home runs, 23 doubles, and 56 RBIs in 400 at-bats. The Mets traded him to San Francisco following the '01 season, but they missed Shinjo's contributions in 2002 enough to re-sign him in 2003, dressing him again in the No. 5 jersey. However, the 2003 go-round was considerably less effective (1 HR, .193 batting average in 114 at-bats) and injury-riddled. Shinjo returned to Japan, where he revived his career as the Jim Palmer of the East: a noted men's underwear model.

Casey Stengel famously explained that without a catcher, a team would have a lot of passed balls. And with that, the Mets chose lefty-swinging catcher **Hobie Landrith** with their very first pick in the 1961 expansion draft. A thirty-one-year-old veteran of four organizations, Landrith (1962) in fact allowed three passed balls in a Mets career that lasted less than a month before he was shipped to Baltimore for Marv Throneberry. His 45 at-bat Mets average of .289 wasn't passed by any 5 with more than 5 ABs until Olerud came along.

But Landrith's legacy was the passed ball and that jersey saw plenty of those on the backs of a handful of reserve catchers. Colorful **Joe Pignatano** was by far the most colorful of the bunch: Brooklyn born and a Brooklyn

Dodger, he famously hit into a triple play in the last game of the 1962 season and then retired to a long career as Mets bullpen coach, cultivating the first tomato crop in Shea's right-field pen. **Norm Sherry,** like his former team, was born in New York and moved to Los Angeles, was acquired following the 1962 season and destined for pinch-hitting duties in 1963, his final season. California kid **Chris Cannizzaro** switched from No. 8 in 1965 for the Mets to make room for another veteran New York catcher playing out the last days of his career: Yogi Berra.

Glide into 5 with Ed Charles, 1969 Met and franchise poet laureate.

Ed Charles, who arrived early in 1967 and lasted through 1969, became the first wearer of the No. 5 jersey to make it more than one season for the Mets. The veteran third baseman, known as the "Glider" for his running style, served as a platoon third baseman—and unofficial poet laureate. He led the 1968 Mets with 15 home runs and led the dancing line on the mound seconds after the 1969 World Series ended.

Charles's retirement weeks later, however, triggered one of the most foolish trades in team history when the Mets packaged young outfielder Amos Otis and pitcher Bob D. Johnson to Kansas City for **Joe Foy**.

The trade was a masterpiece of poor timing and wasted resources. Before the 1969 season the Mets had been so high on Otis they wouldn't part with him even though there were indications they might have pried Joe Torre loose from Atlanta if they had. Instead they tried making Otis a third baseman, and when that experiment failed (.158 in 93 at-bats as an outfield reserve and pinch hitter), he stayed in Gil Hodges's doghouse. With his value to the Mets clearly down they shopped him and, in the last deal made before the death of GM Johnny Murphy, brought back Foy. While talented, he came with questions about his attitude and associates. Foy subsequently flopped as a Met: .236, 6 HR, 22 SB in 35 attempts, rumors of involvement with drugs, and Otis's former spot in the Hodges doghouse. Foy was let go in the Rule 5 draft the following winter. Otis, naturally, went on to five All-Star appearances and a solid seventeen-year major league career at his natural position: center field.

Steve Henderson did the best he could to relieve the emptiness Mets fans felt from the Tom Seaver trade in which he was acquired, but Hendu could only do so much. Called to the majors for the first time following the trade, Henderson (1977–80) immediately took over left field, hit .295 with 12 home runs and a team-leading 65 RBIs in just 99 games, narrowly losing the Rookie of the Year vote to Andre Dawson of Montreal. But "Stevie Wonder" never much improved on his rookie season over the ensuing three years. His career highlight as a Met

See Hendu run! Steve Henderson comes in to score as John Stearns (12) welcomes him home.

Jacob Kanarek/From Worst to First

was a game-winning, three-run homer to cap a 7–6 comeback win over San Francisco, briefly convincing fans that the "magic" was indeed back in 1980. He was traded following that season for a second helping of Dave Kingman.

Davey Johnson mixed old-school fundamentals with a pioneering approach to analytics en route to becoming the Mets' winningest manager (595–417), its best percentage winner (.588), and their all-time leader in games managed. Johnson, who served from 1984 to 1990, believed his job was to position the team to score more runs than the other guys and didn't care much for policing the clubhouse, chatting with reporters, or babying pitcher's arms. His clubs fired off five consecutive 90-win seasons.

Sandy Alomar Sr. spent only two months of his fifteen-year career with the Mets in 1967 but during that period conceived his son Roberto, who'd play for the Mets 35 years later. Both Alomars, by the way, would be traded to the White Sox in August (thirty-six years apart), and the Mets would be better off without both: the father batted .000, and the son seemed to exude about that much enthusiasm. Senior came back to the Mets as part of Willie Randolph's coaching staff in 2006 and would be joined by another son, Sandy Jr., in 2007. **Mike Howard** (1981–83) was the opening-day right fielder for the 1983 Mets, but his future evaporated with the call-up of twenty-one-year-old man child Darryl Strawberry later that spring.

Pinch-hitting specialist **Jim Beauchamp** (1972–73) suited up in No. 5 when the Mets traded for Willie Mays, who took the No. 24 off of Beauchamp's back. Fleet outfielder and Notre Dame Alumnus **Shaun Fitzmaurice** had a 9-game Met and big-league career in September of 1966. That was a lot more action than **Jerry Moses** saw in 1975—the veteran catcher was on the active roster but never appeared in a game as a Met.

Jim Gosger wore three numbers as a Met—5 was the last, in 1974. Curly-haired backup catcher **Charlie O'Brien** was also a three-number man, wearing 5 in 1991 between stints in 33 and 22. Then there was utilityman **Jeff McKnight** for whom 5 was the second of the team-record five jersey numbers he'd appear in.

Promising catching prospect **Brook Fordyce** lasted only a few weeks in 1995. He was succeeded later that year by **Chris Jones**, a right-handed hitting reserve outfielder who hit .362 as a pinch hitter with three home runs through '96. Former Dartmouth lefty QB **Mark Johnson** (2000, 2002), traded years in the No. 5 jersey with Shinjo, but had his best Mets year wearing No. 20 in 2001.

Francisco Estrada appeared in only two games for the 1971 Mets but holds the record for games caught in the Mexican League during his 26-year career there. Free-swinging lefty power hitter **Jeromy Burnitz** (1993–94) wore No. 5 in his first go-round with Mets. Utility infielder **Mike Phillips** (1975–77) was acquired as insurance for the injured Bud Harrelson and had his moments for the Mets, including hitting for cycle at Wrigley Field in June of 1976. Phillips and Olerud (1997) are the only Mets to wear the same number to hit to the cycle. And Phillips is the only Met to strike out his first time up and still go cycling the same day. Call it the K-cycle.

Number 5

Number of times issued: 27 (23 players, 1 manager, 1 DNP)

Longest tenured: David Wright (12 seasons, 1,546 games), manager Davey Johnson (7 seasons, 1,102 games), Steve Henderson (4 seasons, 497 games)

Best single season: John Olerud, 1998 (.354/.447/.551, 22 HR, 93 RBIs); David Wright, 2008 (.302/.390/.534, 33 HR, 124 RBIs); David Wright, 2007 (.325/.416/.546, 30 HR, 107 RBIs, 34 SB)

Career statistical leaders: Home runs (Wright 235, Olerud 63); RBI (Wright 956, Olerud 291); batting average (Olerud .315, Wright .298)

Just Your Average Mets: Batting Average by the Numbers

It took the Mets fifty years and one controversial finish to finally get themselves a batting champion.

On the season's final day in 2011, Jose Reyes led off the bottom of the first inning with a bunt along the third base line off the Reds' Edinson Volquez at Citi Field. Reaching first with an easy infield single, Reyes—at his request—was removed for pinch-runner Justin Turner and retired to the clubhouse with a season-ending .337 batting average to edge Milwaukee's Ryan Braun, who went hitless to finish at .332. It was the impending free agent's final game as a Met.

Reyes's hit-and-sit act triggered more than a little controversy, particularly among the Play the Game the Right Way Police, who were quick to point out it had come on the seventieth anniversary of Ted Williams's decision to play both ends of a season-ending twinbill with a .400 batting average in the balance (Williams went 6-for-8 to finish at .406. He may also have walked uphill to and from Fenway Park in the snow). Reyes for his part had no apologies. "I don't care what people say," he told reporters afterward. What the critics overlooked were dozens of instances of similar shenanigans to preserve and affect numbers throughout baseball history. Manager Joe Torre sat Lee Mazzilli on the final day of the 1977 season so as to protect Maz's .250 batting average. Two-fifty! Ballplayers are sensitive about numbers and you're holding the evidence.

Former No. 5 John Olerud owns marks for both the highest single-season batting average in Met history (.353 in 1998, finished second in the National League that year to Larry Walker of Colorado) and the highest career hitting percentage for players with 1,000 or more a-bats (at .315, Olerud as of 2015 was the only career hitter north of .300). David Wright is just south at .298, but it's enough to push No. 5 past all others through 2015 in composite batting average for unis accumulating more than 4,000 at-bats. That cutoff disqualifies 31's team-best .286, nearly all the result of Mike Piazza's .296 career average—and that number won't be getting any more ABs. Here are the top five qualifiers through 2015:

No.	AB	Hits	Avg.	Note
5	13,582	3,783	.279	Olerud and Wright FTW.
13	5,329	1,464	.275	Edgardo Alfonzo (.292 career average) accounts for roughly half of 13's all-time hits.
7	14,076	3,806	.270	Jose Reyes was a .292 career hitter; Ed Kranepool hit .266 as a 7.
18	2,692	728	.263	No. 18's average exactly Darryl Strawberry's career average.
17	10,174	2,661	.262	It's Keith Hernandez (.297 career) and Felix Millan (.274 wearing 17). Pitcher Bret Saberhagen (.151) hit twice as high as first third baseman, Don Zimmer (.077).

#6: THE SIX-PACK

A reserve first baseman by the name of **Jim Marshall** was the first player to wear No. 6 in Mets history. On May 7, 1962, the Mets traded Marshall to the Pittsburgh Pirates for Vinegar Bend Mizell, a veteran lefty who unbeknownst to the Mets had won the last game of his major league career a few weeks earlier—against the Mets.

On the same day they traded away Marshall, the Mets flipped Don Zimmer to the Cincinnati Reds for **Cliff Cook,** a beefy country slugger whose résumé included a Most Valuable Player award from the American Association the year before. Cook arrived, was given the No. 6 jersey most recently belonging to Marshall, and was installed as the regular third baseman until bad hands cost him his starting job and a bad back ended his season. By July, Cook had surrendered the No. 6 jersey to **Rick Herrscher**, a middling utility infielder whose entire major league career would begin and end as a 1962 Met.

One year into their history and the Mets had issued No. 6 three different times to three different players. And to this day, it's their most frequently issued uniform number.

No. 6 would be issued to multiple players again in 1964; 1966; 1967; 1990; 1997; 1998; 2004; 2008; 2009; 2012; and 2013. In 1990 three men again wore the No. 6 jersey; in 2004 and 2008 four different guys wore the number.

Altogether, forty-two players and one coach have worn No. 6 heading into 2016, well ahead of the next most popular number in Met history—29, issued thirty-seven times. The Six Pack includes two Ricks, a Ricky and a Rich; two Carloses; two Marshalls; two Jims; and three Mikes. There's Omar and Phillips and Weis(s). There's a Johnson and a Nixon.

Wedged between Wright and Reyes; the weird neighbor of Olerud and Kranepool, 6 is the official address of the Met scrub. Even the most accomplished No. 6 in team history had a scrubby quality to him.

Wally Backman (1981–88) was an undersized, hardheaded infielder who, were it not for exceptional grit—and a champion in manager Davey Johnson—might well have suffered the same fleeting fate of every other man to wear the No. 6 jersey.

After hitting .548 as a seventeen-year-old high school shortstop in Beaverton, Oregon, the Mets selected Backman in the first round of the 1977 amateur draft (Mookie Wilson went in the second round). Listed at 5-foot-9 and 160 pounds, Backman relied on hustle, a good batting eye, and nominal switch-hitting skills (a natural lefty hitter, he consistently struggled from the right side) to reach the majors by 1980, but physical calamities and his own fiery temper kept him from staying there.

Backman debuted in September of 1980 (wearing No. 28), hitting .323 as a replacement for the injured Doug Flynn at second base, but he railed at being stuck behind veteran Frank Taveras at shortstop in 1981. Backman briefly staged a retirement when sent to the minors that season and was not invited back when play resumed following the strike. In 1982, Backman split time with Bob Bailor at second base but was lost for the season after breaking his collarbone in a bicycle accident. In 1983, frustrated at backing up the smoother-fielding yet weaker-hitting Brian Giles, Backman was yo-yo'ed between New York and the Tidewater farm club three times in the season's first two months and publicly campaigned for a trade.

Yet Backman's May 1983 demotion turned out to be the break his career needed, pairing him up at Tidewater with Davey Johnson, a believer in offense who would become the Mets manager in 1984. "The Mets sent down Backman and Ron Gardenhire and kept Brian Giles and Jose Oquendo," Johnson recalled in the *New York Times,* "and I thought they improved my ball club and hurt theirs."

With Johnson installed at Shea Stadium in '84, Backman followed, and rewarded his manager's faith with the best stretch of his career during the

Mets' best era. Paired with fellow speedster Lenny Dykstra atop the Mets lineup, Back-stra (as the press dubbed the diminutive duo) terrorized opposing pitchers while setting up the big guns that followed. Although often platooned—Backman was a .164 hitter as a Met from the right side as opposed to .306 from the left—he always seemed to find his way into a key spot in a tight game. Backman was traded to Minnesota following the 1989 season and left behind a .283 career batting average and a .353 on-base percentage over nine years with the Mets.

No doubt inspired by Johnson, Backman embarked on an eventful postcareer managing journey that most recently led to the Mets' Class AAA team in Las Vegas, where he presides over the 51s, conspicuous as ever in No. 6.

Until Backman came along, and pretty much since he left, No. 6 has been a hot potato. After three 6s in '62, reserve middle infielder **Larry Burright** (1963) wore it for two weeks. **Bobby Klaus** held it for two years, the number's first extended stay. Taking over at second base while Ron Hunt nursed various injuries, Klaus clubbed a 10th inning walkoff home run, delivering the Mets' first win of 1965. Klaus, who hit 12 homers that year despite batting just .191, was sent to Philadelphia in the Dick Stuart trade after the '65 season and never resurfaced in the majors.

Jim Hickman, whose customary No. 9 had been swiped by manager Wes Westrum, hit the last two of his 60 career home runs as a Met wearing No. 6 in '66. Earlier that year No. 6 was briefly on the back of **Lou Klimchock**, whose entire Mets career encompassed five hitless pinch-hitting appearances (with three strikeouts). Not to be out-Klimchocked, **Bart Shirley** was hitless in all 12 of his plate appearances with the 1967 Mets.

The highest batting average ever achieved by a Met No. 6 belongs to **Bob Johnson**—the infielder of 1967, and not the 1969 pitcher of the same name. Scooped up on waivers from the Orioles in May of '67, he proceeded to hit .348 over 246 plate appearances while filling in at all four infield positions. He was deftly flipped to Cincinnati after the season for Art Shamsky.

Al Weis gave the Mets four seasons of suboptimal regular-season play, and a single resplendent World Series. Weis, who came over from the White Sox in the Tommie Agee trade, was a skinny reserve middle infielder who rarely showed any power, or much else. In his best season, 1969, his OPS+ was 53, which was 47 percent below comparable player ranks.

Weis nevertheless hit the game-tying home run in the seventh inning of the Mets' decisive Game 5 of the 1969 World Series, and was 5-for-11 with a homer, three RBIs and four walks in the series—that's .455/.563/.727/1.290

Al Weis confers with manager Gil Hodges before a game in 1969.

in slash numbers. Weis received the Babe Ruth Award, a World Series MVP given each winter by the New York baseball writers chapter that is separate from the traditional Series MVP presented after the final game; Donn Clendennon took the better-known Series MVP prize in '69.

Weis achieved a .191 batting average, a .252 on-base percentage, and hit 4 home runs over four seasons in the shackles of No. 6. But he'll always have Game 5.

September call-ups **Greg Harts** and **Rich Puig** occupied No. 6 in 1974 and 1975 respectively, amassing 12 turns at-bat and 1 hit (Hart's) between them. Outfielder **Mike Vail** took 6 in 1976 and 1977 following an eye-opening '75 debut wearing No. 31. Vail never followed through on his early promise—they actually envisioned him as a potential replacement for the foolishly traded Rusty Staub.

Veteran outfielder **Jose Cardenal** (1979–80) boasted one of the best afros in team history but otherwise was an inconsequential member of inconsequential Mets clubs. He put on the number on August 4, 1979, and his sentence ended exactly one year later. He left on his own recognizance to Kansas City, where he ended his career in the World Series. Cardenal was the last man to wear No. 6 before Backman's triumphant run.

Mike Marshall (again, not the pitcher) was notable for being the guy the Mets got for Juan Samuel in a trade, which was good, and the guy who replaced Keith Hernandez at first base, which was, obviously, very bad. The Mets were better off with Dave Magadan at first base in 1990 and recycled Marshall's number to **Alex Treviño**, making his second appearance with the Mets, then to **Darren Reed**, who switched to No. 6 upon the acquisition of Tommy Herr, who preferred Reed's No. 28.

Outfielder **Darryl Boston** (1991–92) began his Mets career wearing No. 7 but switched to wearing No. 6 when Hubie Brooks was reacquired in 1991. **Joe Orsulak** was a throwback player—at times, looking as though he were thrown back to the 19th century. Manning a corner outfield slot for three years on a semi-regular basis, Orsulak was a Jersey product who played with a reckless style and maximum effort, compiling 17 home runs wearing No. 6—at the time, an all-time club record. If Al Leiter was the Mets' Bruce Springsteen, Orsulak was its Southside Johnny.

No. 6 was the first jersey the Mets issued in 1996 to one-time All-Star infielder **Carlos Baerga**, who did more damage—to the Mets, not necessarily the opposition—wearing No. 8. **Manny Alexander**, who replaced Cal Ripken at shortstop in Baltimore but was stuck behind Rey Ordoñez in New York, wore 6 until he was flipped to the Cubs in Steve Phillips's inaugural trade in 1997. The Mets later that year issued No. 6 to **Carlos Mendoza**, a speedy outfielder selected in Tampa Bay's expansion draft the following winter. Worry not, for the Mets countered by acquiring speedy outfielder **Rich Becker** (1998) only to see him flame out spectacularly with 42 whiffs in 100 at-bats. No. 6 would subsequently go that year to weathered veteran **Tony Phillips**, a solid hitter, at least before he was thirty-nine years old and a Met.

Melvin Mora, a Venezuelan soccer player who arrived with the Mets by way of Houston and Taiwan, was a revelation in 1999 spring training and arrived later that year to spark the Mets. He scored the run that forced a one-game playoff with Cincinnati, and his throw from left field to nail Jay Bell at home plate in the 8th inning of the decisive Game 4 of the Division Series against Arizona proved one of the most pivotal defensive plays in Mets history. The Mets never seemed to know what to do with Mora (1999–2000), whose ability at so many positions undermined his efforts to establish himself at one. Shortstop, however, was not one of them, and when Rey Ordoñez was injured in 2000, the Mets sacrificed Mora to Baltimore for the surer hands of Mike Bordick in a trade they'd live to regret. After the Mets'

World Series loss to the Yankees, Bordick went back to Baltimore as a free agent to play next to Mora, an All-Star third baseman.

Spunky outfielder **Timo Perez** (2000–03) appeared nearly as suddenly as Mora, and like Mora, he'd play an important role in a Met playoff drive, providing a spark as an injury replacement for fast-fading outfielder Derek Bell. However, Perez's legacy is tainted by the inexcusable base-running mistake in the pivotal Game 1 of the World Series, failing to run hard on a two-out double off the top of the wall by Todd Zeile and getting thrown out at home in a play that excruciatingly shifted the momentum of the entire event. In games that mattered far less, Perez had some success as an outfield reserve, but he was often injured and was finally swapped to the White Sox just prior to the 2004 season.

It was following Perez' departure that the No. 6 legend really took off. Four different men wore it both in 2004—**Ricky Gutierrez, Gerald Williams, Tom Wilson, Jeff Keppinger**—and again in 2008—**Gustavo Molina, Nick Evans, Abraham Nuñez, Trot Nixon**. Keppinger, who hit .284 making his big-league debut with the Mets in '04, would be traded for a subsequent No. 6, **Ruben Gotay** (2007), who also hit well (.295) in a brief stay in New York. Evans, a right-handed first-baseman-outfielder who always appeared as though his contact lenses were bothering him, spent four years bobbing between the Mets and AAA, with his appearances frequently interrupting other 6s who came and went: Nuñez, Nixon and **Ramon Martinez** (2009) among them.

No. 6 was the first of three Mets unis worn by reserve shortstop **Omar Quintanilla** (2012); the number went later that year to disappointing catcher **Kelly Shoppach.**

Marlon Byrd (2013) was a bargain pick-up who in two-thirds of a season in New York managed to hit more home runs than any other man to have ever worn the No. 6 jersey (21) before being flipped to Pittsburgh at the trade deadline for promising infielder Dilson Hererra. Byrd's number then went to skinny reserve outfielder **Matt den Dekker**, who hung around for parts of the 2013 and 2014 seasons before he was turned into lefty reliever Jerry Blevins. Assistant hitting coach **Pat Roessler** occupied No. 6 for the 2015 season, unfortunately blocking it from guys who might have been more appropriate occupants. Give it up, Pat. The scrubs need it back.

Number 6

Number of times issued: 46 (42 players, one coach)

Longest tenured: Wally Backman (9 seasons, 765 games)

Best single season: Backman, 1986 (.320/.376/.385, 18 doubles, 13 stolen bases); Marlon Byrd, 2013 (.285/.330/.530, 21 HR, 26 2B, 71 RBIs)

Career statistical leaders: Home runs (Marlon Byrd 21, Timo Perez 18, Joe Orsulak 17); RBI (Backman 156; Perez 114, Orsulak 114); batting average (Bob W. Johnson .348, Ruben Gotay .295, Jeff Keppinger .284).

The Joy of Six: Most Popular Numbers

Just ask Darren Reed or Lou Klimchock—unpopular players are often the cause of popular numbers. Following is a list of the jersey numbers most frequently issued to players in Mets' history through 2007. For a list of the least issued numbers, see Chapter 30.

No.	No. of Players to Wear It	Notes
6	42	Issued a team-record four times in 2004 and 2008.
29	36	Ike Davis and Steve Trachsel at the top.
19	35	Most games as a 19: Roger Cedeno.
34	35	Noah Syndergaard might already be the best of them—although another hard-throwing Texan, Nolan Ryan, wore it for a couple of weeks as a teenager in '66.
38	35	12 players in nine years between Roger Craig (1963) and Buzz Capra (1971).
43	35	Issued twice in '66, '97, '98, '02, '06, and '15.
35	34	Longest tenure: Dillon Gee (6 seasons); best wearer: Rick Reed.
26	32	One All-Star selection: Dave Kingman.
11	31	30 position players; 1 pitcher (Cory Lidle).
17	30	Unissued since 2010 after making Keith Hernandez watch its abuse from the booth.
33	30	17 pitchers; 13 position players.
1	29	Everyone wants to be No. 1; most should think twice.

#7: STEADY EDDIE

When **Ed Kranepool** hung up his No. 7 jersey for the last time, the event drew little notice (to be fair, a lot of things that happened in Flushing in 1979 were like that). There was no tearful retirement press conference, just a quiet refusal by the Mets to offer a 1980 contract—a sentiment subsequently echoed by the twenty-five other clubs declining to select Kranepool in the free-agent draft that fall. "There was talk of giving him a day at Shea Stadium last season," a Met publicist told the *New York Times* the following spring, "but nothing ever came of it."

He was only thirty-four years old.

It was hardly the usual farewell to a player who, at the time, held virtually every meaningful offensive record in the history in the franchise, including games, hits, doubles, RBIs, and home runs. He was also a local product, the team's first high-profile amateur signee, the only player to spend every year of the franchise as an active player, and the senior player on the team for thirteen years running. He was the kind of all-time hero only the Mets could produce.

Kranepool signed with the Mets for a reported $85,000 bonus shortly after graduating from James Monroe High in the Bronx in June of 1962. The talent-starved team gave the seventeen-year-old opportunities almost immediately, as Kranepool split brief visits to the minors between stretches on the Mets bench, before assuming a starting role at first base in 1965.

Smart-aleck Mets fans of the era once flashed a placard asking whether Ed Kranepool was over the hill. Who knew? Kranepool's career as an everyday player might have peaked as a twenty year old in 1965, when he played a career-high 153 games and was named an All-Star for the only time. Kranepool had fair power, but he was slow afoot, nobody's idea of

Jacob Kanarek/From Worst to First

The solid swing of Ed Kranepool was a Mets constant in the 1960s and 1970s, and it took time and Captain America to knock him from atop the team record books.

a defensive wizard, and occasionally appeared disinterested and surly.

The Mets for their part seemed to be forever looking to replace him. He'd be displaced as the Mets first baseman in 1969, waived and sent to the minor leagues in 1970, only to rebound with his best overall season in 1971 (14/58/.280/.340/.447 in 421 at-bats). From there he became a part-time outfielder/first baseman and effective pinch hitter for the balance of his career, a role for which he finally won the admiration of fans. Kranepool hit .396 as a pinch hitter between 1974 and 1978, including .486 in 1974.

While Darryl Strawberry, and later, David Wright, eventually toppled most of Kranepool's power and production records, his longevity itself still remains a Mets standard. Even discounting the 208 games Steady Eddie played at the beginning of his Mets' career wearing No. 21—no, he wasn't born wearing 7—his 1,645 games in No. 7 through 2015 still held a 99-game edge on Wright. And Wright still needs nearly two full seasons to catch Steady Eddie for all-time games played.

The Mets finally got around to inducting Kranepool into their Hall of Fame in 1990. By then, his uniform number had been redistributed to **Hubie Brooks** (1981–84, 1991). Brooks, a line-drive hitter with a reputation for clutch hitting, arrived along with the wave of promising early '80s Mets and looked, like Kranepool, like he'd be a longtime occupant of the jersey. But Brooks was sacrificed in the Gary Carter trade so that his comrades would taste a world championship. By the time the Mets reacquired Brooks in 1991, that juggernaut was already in decline (as was Brooks).

Future National League MVP **Kevin Mitchell** was only a rookie in 1986 when he played five positions during the year and then capped the season by coolly lining a two-out single to keep the Mets' slim hopes alive in the epic World Series Game 6. It was Mitchell who crossed the plate with the tying run on Bob Stanley's wild pitch that Mookie Wilson so deftly jackknifed away from. Amid rumblings that he was a bad influence, Mitchell was dispatched after the season in the Kevin McReynolds trade.

A rare product of the Mets farm system who was even better than the wildest hype, shortstop **Jose Reyes** (2003–11) was probably the most exciting position player the team ever produced.

Arriving as a nineteen-year-old in 2003, Reyes fought injuries and a botched conversion to second base in 2004, and struggled to reach base often enough to be effective in 2005 before a breakout 2006 (30 doubles, 17 triples, 19 home runs, a .300 batting average, and a .354 on-base percentage). Reyes set a previously unimaginable mark of 77 walks in 2007 and along the way mercifully wiped Roger Cedeño's name from the Mets record books with 78 stolen bases.

Reyes at his best played with a joie de vivre that was palpable: It inspired fans to sing. There was no thrill like the moment Reyes lined a ball to gap, turned first with no intentions to stop at second, and arrived at third base with a head-first slide wearing a dirt-covered jersey and a magnetic smile as bright as the stadium lights. By the time he was done in New York—the threadbare Mets offer of zero years and zero dollars no match for Miami's 6-year, $106 million free-agent pitch—Reyes had represented the Mets in the All-Star Game four times and obliterated all-time team records for stolen bases (370) and triples (99) while becoming the only Met to ever win a league batting title (.337 in 2011) or stolen base crown (three times running).

Few jobs in baseball are lonelier than Mike Piazza's understudy, but catcher **Todd Pratt** (1998–2001) sure made the most of limited stage appearances. His heart-stopping home run off the edge of Steve Finley's glove in deepest center field in the 10th inning in Game 4 to clinch the 1999 Division Series ranks among the most dramatic and unexpected thrills in team history. In July 2001 the Mets shipped Pratt off to the Phillies for **Gary Bennett** (2001) in a straight-up uni/catcher's gear swap. Bennett had just one plate appearance as a Met, and he doubled.

Juan Samuel (1989) arrived for Lenny Dykstra and Roger McDowell in a trade signaling the impending crumble of the Mets' would-be 1980s dynasty. It was a bad fit all around. Comfortable playing second base and wearing No. 8, the Mets played Samuel in center field and dressed him in No. 7 (Gary Carter still had 8 then). An all-or-nothing kind of hitter, Samuel gave the Mets almost nothing (.228/.299/.300 in 86 games). He was shuffled to Los Angeles following the season for Mike Marshall in a spiral of decreasing returns.

The first Met to wear No. 7 was **Elio Chacon** (1962), the Venezuelan shortstop destined to live forever as a key figure in the (probably apocryphal) "Yo La Tengo" story. At the risk of telling it again: Chacon and center fielder Richie Ashburn agreed that the English-challenged Chacon would back off on a popup if he heard Ashburn call, "Yo la tengo" ("I've got it"). Popup to short center, Ashburn calls the Spanish phrase, Chacon backs off . . . and left fielder Frank Thomas, oblivious to the arrangement and foreign tongues, flattens Ashburn as the ball hits the ground.

Telling it over and over seems to have obscured the untold story of why the Mets held Chacon in such poor regard. Whatever Chacon did to get on the bad side of Casey Stengel is a pity, because, without overselling his modest credentials, Chacon was the kind of player the early Mets didn't see nearly enough of. A speedy shortstop selected from Cincinnati in the expansion draft, Chacon hit just .236 with little power, but drew 76 walks in just 449 plate appearances in '62—fifth in the National League that year—and the most walks by a Mets shortstop until Bud Harrelson in 1970.

His defense was much derided—the "Yo La Tengo" story probably contributed to that perception—but the stats show he played every bit as well as the average shortstop in 1962. And despite staying in the Mets farm system for years, Chacon never appeared with the big club again, tagged by Stengel among those players who "failed here before" and not welcomed back.

Following Chacon in the No. 7 jersey were brief visitors **Chico Fernandez** (1963) and **Amado Samuel** (1964). Though we found no evidence Amado Samuel and Juan Samuel were related, both were middle infielders hailing from San Pedro de Macoris in the Dominican Republic, the cradle of more than fifty major league players. Fernandez clubbed 20 home runs for the Tigers in 1962 but was suddenly washed up upon his arrival in New York.

John Christensen (1985) wasn't destined to last with the Mets. He was assigned a pitcher's number (35) upon his promotion as a rookie in 1984 and assumed an outfielder's number only after Joe Sambito arrived in 1985. Christensen possessed decent right-handed power and a pretty good eye but didn't make enough contact—either with the ball or the starting lineup. The Mets met his desire for a new start by including him in the Bobby Ojeda deal following the '85 season. The Red Sox would later include Christensen in their trade for Dave Henderson, assuring Christensen would play a small role in assembling both sides of the 1986 World Series combatants.

The Mets reissued No. 7 following Reyes's departure. Bench coach **Bob Geren** (2012–14) got it but put No. 7 aside in 2015 when young catcher **Travis d'Arnaud** requested it as an alternative to the No. 15 he was issued as a rookie. His batting eye and throwing arm could be better, as could his health, but d'Arnaud made up for starting just 64 times at age twenty-six by catching every inning of the 2015 postseason and clubbing three home runs.

Other Magnificent Sevens included fringe players **Clint Hurdle** (1987), **Chuck Carr** (1990), **Daryl Boston** (1990), **D.J. Dozier** (1992), **Jeff McKnight** (1993), **Charlie Greene** (1996), and **Jason Phillips** (2002). All but Dozier, a two-sport player who also lined up in the Minnesota Vikings backfield, and Greene spent at least some of their Mets careers in a number other than 7.

Number 7

Number of times issued: 21 (19 players, 2 coaches)

Longest tenured: Ed Kranepool (15 seasons, 1,645 games)

Best single season: Jose Reyes, 2006 (.300/.354/.487, 19 HR, 17 triples, 64 stolen bases); Reyes, 2008 (.297/.358/.475, 16 HR, 19 triples, 56 stolen bases); Hubie Brooks, 1984 (.283/.341/.417, 16 HR, 73 RBIs, 6 SB, 24-game hitting streak)

Career statistical leaders: Home runs (Kranepool 106); RBI (Kranepool 555); batting average (Reyes .292, Kevin Mitchell .277).

Seven-Eleven: Numbers Most Frequently Appearing

The Mets have played 8,608 regular-season games in their history. If you went to any of them, ever, there's about a 50/50 chance you'd have seen a No. 11 or a No. 7 on the field. And while longtime occupants like Ed Kranepool and Jose Reyes boost the No. 7 appearances, No. 11 overcomes it by way of sheer volume: Only three seasons in Mets history have come without a No. 11, despite only a few of them—a Wayne Garrett here, a Ruben Tejada there—to last very long. In fact, it's been Tejada—Reyes's successor at shortstop—who has pushed No. 11 past No. 7 for most games all time in recent years, while 7 spent three years not accumulating games on the back of coach Bob Geren. And if David Wright spent more time on the field and less on the disabled list, third-place No. 5 might have caught up too.

Following is a list of the most frequent appearances in a game by uniform number through 2015, and the percentage of all Met games in which that number appeared.

No.	Games	Percentage of Games Appearing	Notes
11	4,442	51.6%	There's been nearly as many games with a No. 11 playing than Met games ending in a loss (4,480, or 52%).
7	4,273	49.6%	Ed Kranepool suited up in No. 7 a staggering 1,645 times.
5	4,208	48.9%	Wright (1,546 games through 2015) may one day lead No. 5 to the top, but it'll likely end there.
15	4,181	48.6%	Grote to the max: 1,235 games squatting.
12	4,080	47.4%	John Stearns played a team-high 718 games in 12 to edge out Ken Boswell (670).
21	3,935	45.7%	Cleon Jones with about twice as many games as the next guy, Lucas Duda.
3	3,874	45.0%	Bud Harrelson's 1,332 games lead the way.
4	3,757	43.6%	Ron Swoboda paces the pack with 602 games.
6	3,681	42.8%	Most popular number not most popular with managers.
9	3,674	42.7%	Todd Hundley played 719 games, including 150 behind the plate in 1996.

#8: KID

Getting **Gary Carter** into a Mets uniform was a strenuous exercise in give-and-take.

To receive the catcher who would change a promising 1984 Mets team into a true contender in 1985 and beyond, the Mets had to surrender four players to the Expos: infielder Hubie Brooks, just then coming into his own; catcher Mike Fitzgerald; and prospects Herm Winningham, an outfielder, and Floyd Youmans, a pitcher. Parting with Brooks left the Mets an infielder short, so just prior to making the Carter deal, general manager Frank Cashen made a separate trade, sending pitcher Walt Terrell to Detroit for young third baseman Howard Johnson.

Once the Mets and Expos agreed to the terms of the trade for Carter, they had to seek the perennial All-Star's approval. As a player dealt in the midst of a multiyear contract, Carter had the right to demand a trade: he'd waive that right in exchange for the Mets extending his no-trade clause through the expiration of the contract in 1989. But where Carter was concerned, one point was nonnegotiable.

"One thing I have to have," he told Cashen, "is No. 8."

No. 8 was Carter's lucky number. It represented both his birthday (April 8) and wedding day (February 8). "I'll never wear anything else," he said. For the Mets, he represented No. 8 with class, charisma, and passion through the life of his contract, and he was vital in achieving the objective the Mets had in mind when they acquired him.

Carter's line single started the two-out, 10th-inning Game 6 World Series rally in 1986, and earlier in that contest, he provided the 8th-inning sacrifice fly that allowed the game to go into extra innings. He drove in 9 runs in the '86 World Series, including the tying run in the 6th inning of Game 7, and hit 3 home runs.

Carter was celebrated, and sometimes criticized, for his enthusiasm and willingness to accommodate, earning him the nicknames "Kid" for the joy he took on the field and "Camera Carter" among detractors for his seeming love of attention. He was the ideal pitchman for Ivory Soap. Kid announced his arrival in New York by hitting a 10th-inning, walk-off home run off Neil Allen of the Cardinals on opening day in 1985, en route to a 32/100/.281 season, probably his best as a Met.

Creaky knees eventually sapped Carter's effectiveness and he left at the end of his contract, following a .189 campaign in 1989. He'd return to the organization as a minor league manager and earn Hall of Fame recognition in 2003. The Mets have not issued No. 8 since he entered Cooperstown.

More than half of the Mets players to wear No. 8 have been catchers. You can thank **Yogi Berra**, acquired by the Mets as a player-coach. Berra kept the former designation for all nine of his plate appearances as a Mets player, but he would also occupy No. 8 as a coach until 1971 and as a manager from 1972–75.

Named to the manager's position while the Mets were still reeling from the death of Gil Hodges, Berra would never be confused with his predecessor as a leader of men (his teams went 292–296 over three-plus seasons) or strategist (starting Tom Seaver on short rest in Game 6 of 1973 World Series), but he nonetheless took a flawed squad to Game 7 of the World

Yogi Berra led the 1973 Mets to the World Series four years after Gil Hodges took the team there for the first time.

Series in 1973, proving "It ain't over till it's over."

Yogi also said, "If you can't imitate him, don't copy him." But from the beginning, Mets catchers—and those who doled out the numbers—have gravitated toward 8. It began with **Chris Cannizzaro** (1962–64), who was stuck behind Tim McCarver in the Cardinals organization when the Mets selected him in the 1961 expansion draft. Cannizzaro was a fine defender, but the Mets never liked his bat enough to make him anything more than a backup. He hit .311 in limited duty with the Mets in 1964; when used in 54 more games the next year he batted .183. Cannizzaro did not play much in the majors until another expansion draft opened up yet more new markets for mediocre backstops: In 1969 he became the first catcher in San Diego Padres history.

Berra put on No. 8 in 1965 and no other Met wore it until **Dan Norman** uneasily—and ungracefully—slid it on in 1979, four years after Yogi had been fired as manager. The number made up for lost time in 1982. Switch-hitting backup catcher **Rick Sweet,** whose surname described his afro and accompanying mustache, spent the early part of '82 season in No. 8 before being sold to Seattle. In late June the Mets turned the jersey over to journeyman infielder **Phil Mankowski** (who'd appeared in 1980 wearing No. 2). Finally in September, the Mets recalled Class AA catcher **Ronn Reynolds** (1982–83), a tough, defensive-minded catcher who remained a Mets backup in No. 8 until the early part of the 1983 season (and returned in 1985 wearing No. 9, thanks to Carter).

John Gibbons, whose shot at succeeding Mike Fitzgerald as starting catcher ended when Carter was acquired, was the No. 8 whose name might have been the title of this chapter in an alternate universe. Gibbons was the third of three first-round selections by the Mets in the 1980 amateur draft (24th pick overall). The Mets famously selected Darryl Strawberry with the first overall pick and later got Billy Beane picking 23rd. Gibbons's breakout season at Class AA Jackson in 1983 (he batted .298/.375/.515 with 18 home runs at age twenty-one) allowed him to surpass Ronn Reynolds among the Mets up-and-coming catchers. Writing in *Newsday* in 1984, Marty Noble dreamily described Gibbons as "a rookie catcher with ability and eyes bluer than Paul Newman's."

Injuries eventually arrested Gibbons's progress: A broken jaw in 1984 cost him his first opportunity and he wouldn't get a second—other than a brief backup role wearing No. 35 in 1986. Also in the official records is a September callup in 1985 when he was issued No. 43 but did not appear in a game. Gibbons later become a hot managerial prospect with the Mets organization, which led to two stints as manager of the Toronto Blue Jays.

Reserve outfielder **Dave Gallagher** (1992–93) was the first Met to be issued No. 8 following Carter's 1989 departure, and he had some success pinch-hitting for the dreadful Met teams of 1992 and 1993. In 2001 **Desi Relaford** was terrific in a utility role (8/36/.302), and was sent to San Francisco with outfielder Tsuyoshi Shinjo in the deal for pitcher Shawn Estes. Relaford's perfect inning of mop-up relief pitching on May 17, 2001, leaves him the lowest-numbered Met to ever toe the rubber. For the record, third-base coach

Dan Carubia

Carlos Bearga left his old uniform number in Cleveland, not to mention all his old batting numbers.

Matt Galante (2002) was the last Mets employee to wear the number.

Like a lot of veteran American League infielders en route to the Mets (Fernandez, Alomar, Sanchez, et al.), **Carlos Baerga** (1997–98) suffered an accelerated career decline at Shea. His acquisition for Jeff Kent was a pretty bad deal for the Mets (Baerga, who'd worn No. 9 as a four-time All-Star in Cleveland, spent most of his first two months as a Met in 1996 playing first base, wearing No. 6, and being hurt.) Baerga hit better at second base in No. 8 (.273/.307.379), but 18 homers in two years as a Mets regular was about what he'd averaged each year in Cleveland from 1991–95. And to think it seemed like the Mets were getting the better second baseman . . .

Number 8

Number of times issued: 14 (11 players, 4 coaches, 1 manager)

Longest tenured: Gary Carter (5 seasons, 600 games)

Best single season: Carter, 1985 (.281/.365/.488, 32 HR, 100 RBIs); Carter, 1986 (.255/.337/.439, 24 HR, 105 RBIs, 3rd in NL MVP vote)

Career statistical leaders: Home runs (Carter 89, Carlos Baerga 16); RBI (Carter 349, Baerga 89); batting average (Desi Relaford .302, Baerga .273)

Out of Circulation: A Modest Proposal

The Mets have never said publicly whether it was a simple mistake or a clandestine experiment that resulted in issuing No. 24 to journeyman Kelvin Torve in 1990.

Inadvertently or not, by doing so they'd broken a promise made by deceased owner Joan Payson that the team would leave No. 24 unoccupied as a tribute to Payson's favorite player, Willie Mays. When writers and fans—often better stewards of Mets history than the club itself—revolted, Torve was soon dressed in the less controversial No. 39.

The Torve Affair highlighted the oddity of numbers that have not been officially retired by the club but have been taken out of circulation, on a temporary or semi-permanent basis. Mays's 24, Gary Carter's 8, and Keith Hernandez's 17 are a few such examples of uniform limbo affecting the Mets.

While several players wore No. 8 in the years following Carter's departure, the uniform appeared to get scarce around the time "Kid" was receiving consideration for the Hall of Fame and has been conspicuously unissued since his induction at Cooperstown in 2003. Some observers pegged this as a signal that the Mets would "officially" retire No. 8 in honor of Carter (as the Expos did), but as of this writing, no such plans have been made.

The Mets were exceedingly charitable when reissuing No. 17, to the point where its appearance on the backs of un-Mex-like (if sadly, Met-like) jobbers like David Newhan, Dae Sung Koo, and Jose Lima was getting the attention of Hernandez himself, pontificating from the broadcast booth (not to mention fans, whose tendency to profess outrage blossomed along with social media). This appears to have resulted in a greater sensitivity on the part of the Mets: No player has worn 17 since Fernando Tatis walked off in 2010.

As for 24, it remains in limbo, save for the Met tenure of Rickey Henderson, who insisted on wearing 24 when he joined the Mets but first sought and received an OK from Mays. (Henderson reappeared in 24 as a Met coach in 2007.)

The Mets, we'd argue, would do well to "retire" 24 in honor of Payson, without whose generosity the club might never have existed, while simultaneously commemorating the player with which she's most closely associated. Becoming the first club to honor a woman with a retired number would also be a high-profile, progressive move for an organization interested in positioning itself behind diversity and inclusion in thought if not always in deed.

If they're worried Mays isn't sufficiently Met-like, that's no problem either: Retire 24 in Giant orange-and-black. It would be a worthy companion to (and reverse-image of) Jackie Robinson's Dodger blue-and-red 42, acknowledging the club's other spiritual forefather, another Negro League pioneer who achieved greatness in New York, and at long last, free up blue-and-orange 24 for the future.

Casey Stengel's 37, Gil Hodges's 14, Tom Seaver's 41, and, as of 2016, Mike Piazza's 31 are the only numbers retired for the Mets. Robinson's 42 has been out of circulation since it was retired throughout organized baseball in 1997, but the club has seemingly been judicious about the reissue of other numbers over the years.

Whether the retirements are too few is a matter of fierce debate in some circles, with one faction believing that reissuing numbers like 1, 17, and 36 amounts to an affront to the dignity of Mookie, Keith, or Jerry, while the other side feels that uniform number retirement is the ultimate honor and only deserving for those rarest of athletes who spend the majority of their careers with the Mets and receive Hall of Fame enshrinement, or contribute to team history in profound or unique ways. As the Mets go, the Retired Numbers Club is about as exclusive as it gets, and unfortunately enough, those players just haven't come around often enough. Others, let's call them the Yankees, have slashed numbers out of existence like a Presidents Day mattress sale. What does it say about Babe Ruth that a multiple steroid offender like Andy Pettitte or a mercenary vagabond like Reggie Jackson receive the same ultimate esteem?

A look to pro soccer might provide the most satisfying resolution to this dilemma. In that game, tradition holds that recycling the number of a former great to a current or newly arriving player glorifies the former while sending wishes of success and confidence to the latter. Thus, Pele is reborn through Romario. Maradona through Riquelme. This keeps the standards for number retirement reassuringly high—while also honoring the heritage of the team.

#9: TODD, TODD, TORRE & TY

A prodigy whose clubhouse chemistry went nuclear. The veteran signee who couldn't quite replace his popular predecessor. A young power hitter lost amid inept veterans. The ornery catcher who went from the record books to the "Where are they now?" files in a flash. The inauspicious debut of a future Hall of Fame manager.

Your No. 9 Mets: slightly imperfect.

"I don't believe anyone can deny the fact that I have consistently taken it on the chin for the last three years," wrote **Gregg Jefferies,** in an infamous 1991 fax read aloud to listeners of WFAN, New York's influential sports radio station and then-broadcast home of the Mets. The open letter, an act of desperation from a player suffering effects of a chilly reception from teammates and fans, was recited amid roaring laughter and ultimately served only as another shot on the chin and further isolation to a would-be phenom.

Given a little more maturity, a little more humility, and a more supportive work environment, Jefferies (1987–91) might have been the great player he

Gregg Jefferies and his glove were not always the best of friends.

was pegged to be after tearing through the minor league system. The Mets had rarely produced a better hitting prospect. He arrived, however, to a clubhouse with a low tolerance for self-assured golden boys and quick to resort to derisive anonymous quotes and humiliating pranks. And in stark contrast to his hitting, Jefferies had shoddy defensive skills, assuring that wherever he was positioned, he replaced a more capable fielder. That eroded the confidence of his teammates. Only when he was installed at first base did his hitting come around; unfortunately, that was in St. Louis several years after leaving New York an unhappy casualty of his own hype.

Jim Hickman (1962–66) was the last Mets survivor of the expansion draft and the team's all-time leader in home runs when he was traded to the Dodgers with Ron Hunt, for Tommy Davis. Hickman's career until then included infrequent moments of greatness (he was the first Met to hit three home runs in one game and the first Met to hit for the cycle) amid frequent struggles with the strikeout. The Mets also wavered on finding him a permanent home in the field, using him in all three outfield positions and at third base. Hickman was also notable for having worn three different uniform numbers in his Mets career: Although he spent the majority of his time in No. 9, manager **Wes Westrum** took No. 9 in 1966, forcing Hickman to change to No. 27. And after returning from a midseason injury and seeing 27 redistributed, he became No. 6.

Westrum, Casey Stengel's choice to succeed him as manager, lacked the Ol' Perfessor's ability to charm his way through losing—a pretty unique trait. Westrum does hold the distinction of managing the Mets out of the cellar for the first time as well as its first sub-100 loss season, in 1966.

Baseball's all-time record for most games caught in a single season is 160, set by Cub Randy Hundley in 1968. Somewhere in the midst of that exhausting summer, Hundley and his wife Betty conceived a son, Todd, who'd grow up to be a Met, and prove that toughness was hereditary.

Although **Todd Hundley** (1992–98) began his Mets career wearing No. 49, he switched to 9 in 1992 so as to honor his dad. In time, he developed into the best power-hitting catcher the club ever produced. In 1996 Hundley set the Met standard for home runs in a single-season with 41 (since matched by Carlos Beltran) while also setting an all-time record for homers by a catcher (since surpassed by Javy Lopez). Hundley did it while squatting behind home plate 150 times (a club record that seems unassailable today).

Perhaps unsurprisingly, there were aches and pains. Hundley toughed out an elbow injury to hit 30 homers and draw a career-best 83 walks to lead the Mets' improbable but doomed run at the 1997 playoffs. That injury, though, essentially finished his career with the Mets, who acquired superstar Mike Piazza while Hundley was on the disabled list.

Hundley attempted to reestablish his career in left field—an experiment even shorter and uglier than the doomed tenures of outfielders Howard Johnson and Daniel Murphy. As backup to the league's best catcher, Hundley played sparingly before being shipped to Los Angeles following the 1998 season.

Todd Zeile's signature moment for the Mets came up one enormous inch too short. His drive in Game 1 of the 2000 World Series at Yankee Stadium hit the top of the wall and bounced back onto the field, where it transformed into an inning-ending, spirit-crushing, momentum-demolishing event that perfectly suited Zeile's tenure with the Mets. Given the unenviable challenge of replacing the popular John Olerud at first base, Zeile (2000–01) actually performed adequately in 2000 and especially well in the postseason. But Mets fans didn't want comparable, they wanted better. And that was something Zeile could not provide.

Zeile returned in 2004 for his final professional season, this time as a reserve wearing his more familiar No. 27. No. 9 by then belonged to **Ty Wigginton** (2002–04), a hardnosed product of the Mets farm system who filled in admirably in the absence of an actual third baseman in 2003. Wiggy was on borrowed time. Sure enough, Wigginton was traded only weeks after David Wright's 2004 arrival.

Although his Mets and major league careers were brief, gangly, free-spirited outfielder **George Theodore** is one of the most memorable Mets characters of all time. An accomplished minor league slugger who had only scant success in the big leagues, Theodore distinguished himself by expressing his thoughts on philosophy, poetry, and metaphysics, and his geeky appearance (tall, slim, eyeglasses, curly hair) endeared him to fans who recognized him as one of their own. Theodore, who debuted in No. 18 before switching to 9 early in the 1973 season as a tribute to boyhood idol Ted Williams ("I thought it might help my batting," he said), further proved his worth by overcoming a broken hip sustained in a frightening collision with Don Hahn.

Theodore's popularity extended to the minor leagues, where the Visalia Mets in 1974 dressed their mascot, a dog named Emerson Boozer, in Theodore's old No. 19 as a tribute to him.

Jacob Kanarek/From Worst to First

Joe Torre couldn't argue his way out of the lousy hand he was dealt in his first managaing job with the Mets.

Joe Torre, the one-time National League Most Valuable Player, batting champ, and Brooklyn native long coveted by the Mets, was finally acquired near the end of his playing career in 1975. Torre in 1977 transitioned to player-manager just as the front office was packaging Tom Seaver in a trade that would cripple the organization for as long as Torre would manage. As a result, Torre (who officially retired as a player weeks into his managerial tenure) oversaw one of the bleakest stretches in Met history and was fired after compiling a five-year record of 286–420. He'd go on to considerable success in Atlanta, St. Louis, the Bronx, and Los Angeles.

Memorable home runs by otherwise middling guys who wore No. 9? Yes, we have a few of those.

Reserve catcher **Omir Santos** (2009–10) entered into fan consciousness when he was curiously called on to pinch-hit for his more accomplished teammate, Ramon Castro, with two outs and the bases loaded in the 9th inning of a game the Mets were losing by one run. Santos, who made his way to the plate from the bullpen still in his shinguards, popped out to second.

Weeks later, Santos rewarded Jerry Manuel's faith when he popped a two-out, 2-run homer over Fenway Park's Green Monster off closer Jonathan Papelbon, lifting the Mets from the brink of death to a stirring 3–2 win. As in the prior play things developed slowly: Santos waited on second base, and Gary Sheffield at third, while umpires reviewed the video, prolonging Papelbon's humiliation at the hands of a Met for the first—but hardly the last—time in his career.

There was that time **Kirk Nieuwenhuis** (2012–15) did it. His solo shot off Papelbon, then a member of the 2015 Washington Nationals, provided the deciding run as the Mets rallied from a 7–1 deficit for an 8–7 September victory that all but assured Washington was destined to finish looking up at the Mets and down on themselves. Moments of high drama were nothing new for Nieuwenhuis, who over a truncated four-year tenure as a reserve outfielder, had more than his share.

There was the time he saved Father's Day. Two outs from a home sweep at the hands of a bad 2013 Cubs team, Nieuwenhuis blasted a Carlos Marmol delivery into the Pepsi Porch, driving in three runs to end the day with joyous 4–3 victory that seemed to briefly rejuvenate the struggling club. The home run got subsequent attention when sourpuss sportscaster Bob Costas informed a national television audience that celebrating such a win signaled "the decline of Western civilization." This just in: Shut up, Bob.

And there was the time he became the first Met in fifty-four years and three stadiums to hit 3 homers in a home game. On July 12, 2015, weeks after getting claimed on waivers and activated by the Angels, released by them, and subsequently claimed back by the Mets, Nieuwenhuis went yard thrice against the Diamondbacks—the only homers he had in '15 other than his bell-ringer against Papelbon.

Other Met 9s, slightly more imperfect: Catcher **J. C. Martin** (1968–69), best remembered for his creative base running in the triumphant 1969 World Series, as well as reserve catchers **Bill Sudakis** (1972), **Bruce Bochy** (1992), **Ronn Reynolds** (1985), **Mike DiFelice** (2007), and **Ronny Paulino** (2011); reserve infielders **Phil Mankowski** (1982) and **Craig Brazell** (2004); and outfielders **Mark Bradley** (1983), **Jerry Martin** (1984), **Ricky Ledee** (2006–07) and in his third and final Mets uniform, **Marlon Anderson** (2008–09). **Randy Bobb**, a reserve catcher, appeared on the active roster in September of 1970, but he never appeared in a Mets game. His 9 lives were used by quite a few other strays.

Number 9

Number of times issued: 23 (20 players, 1 DNP, 2 managers)

Longest tenured: Todd Hundley (8 seasons, 793 games), Joe Torre (as manager, 5 seasons, 706 games)

Best single seasons: Hundley, 1996 (.259/.356/.550, 41 HR, 112 RBIs, 32 doubles); Hundley, 1997 (.273/.394/.549, 30 HR, 86 RBIs)

Career statistical leaders: Home runs (Hundley 124, Jim Hickman 56, Gregg Jefferies 42); RBI (Hundley 395, Jefferies 205, Hickman 195); batting average (Jefferies .276, Ty Wigginton .270, Ronny Paulino .268)

The Constant 9

Lest any Mets fan forget, No. 9 stood for the television home for the Mets from the team's inception in 1962 through 1998. In the days before cable, WOR-TV was the only place to see the Mets unless you were at Shea Stadium or caught them on the road. The club's high and low

Dan Carubia

Ralph Kiner, Bob Murphy, and Lindsey Nelson together again at Shea for Old-Timers Day, 1987.

comedy was expertly described on Channel 9 by the trio of Ralph Kiner, Lindsey Nelson, and Bob Murphy through 1978, the longest-running broadcasting trio the game has seen. The trio is gone now, but turn off your phone, stare at the wall a moment with us, and you'll see and hear them again.

Channel 9 taught Mets history. Whether it was through the mouths of Kiner, Nelson, and Murphy—they alternated between TV and radio (what a concept!)—or via the highlight films that Channel 9 popped on the air the moment the tarp hit the field, a fan learned something new about the club with every broadcast, even when old stories were all there was to offer when the present club offered little worthy of note.

Channel 9 was busy. The station had broadcast the Dodgers and Giants—and even the Phillies during the baseball void—and filled the Mets-free hours with the Knicks, Nets, Rangers, Islanders, Cosmos, and pro wrestling when it

was the WWF (and WWWF). There was no local news we needed to stay turned for or hustle off the air to catch. Non-sports fixtures included Romper Room, the Million Dollar Movie, and racy Thames Television imports. About the only thing that could make a young fan smile after another Mets loss were the words, "And coming up after Mets baseball, it's The Benny Hill Show."

Kiner's Korner was named for the short porch in Forbes Field that Kiner the Pirate made famous with his numerous blasts, but in New York the name lived on long after the Pittsburgh park came down. The Mets postgame interview show featured a familiar set with the names of major league teams in a woodcut-like font behind the heads of the guests. You could tell that being on Kiner's Korner was often as big a thrill for the players as it was for those watching at home, loving every extra second of baseball exposure on TV. The show enabled fans to find out what the ballplayer was like beyond what could be conveyed in a newspaper story.

Casey Stengel set the standard when he literally brought the house down—à la Mr. Magoo—on the very first show when the Mets manager forgot to take off his microphone upon walking off the set. The anything-can-happen nature of live TV pervaded the show, even as technology became more sophisticated. After reading a few out-of-town scores, Kiner ended the show with, "And if you can't make it out to the ballpark, we hope to see you right back out there." As if any of us would dare disappoint him.

#10: THEY BROUGHT THE FUNK

He played every position except pitcher and catcher in 1962—and as things turned out, he could probably have done those at least as well as his teammates. **"Hot Rod" Kanehl** was the first Mets utility player, one of the first heroes of Mets fans, and the first to wear the No. 10 jersey.

Admired by manager Casey Stengel ever since he'd had him at a Yankee training camp in the late 1950s, Kanehl (1962–64) nearly didn't make it to the Mets. A dispute over the rights to his contract erupted as the minor league Syracuse franchise transitioned from control of the Twins to the Mets over the 1961–62 offseason, with each organization claiming the rights to Kanehl. Commissioner Ford Frick ruled in the Mets' favor in February of 1962.

Kanehl's grit, hustle, and versatility helped obscure meager statistical output: a .241 batting average and just 32 extra-base hits in nearly 800 at-bats over three seasons.

Poor stats, hidden or otherwise, happen to be a common characteristic of the No. 10 brotherhood. There has been flash and occasional sizzle from the 10-spot, but few have ever put together the whole package wearing that number. Out-making has generally been more prolific than output.

Rey Ordoñez (1998–2002) drove a hard bargain to be the franchise's most spectacular defensive player. Acquired by the Mets in a special lottery following a defection from the Cuban national team, Ordoñez came around at precisely the wrong moment for an all-glove, no-hit shortstop. Tantalized by a 60-RBI season in 1999, the Mets signed Ordoñez to a four-year contract that would turn disastrous. Injured in 2000, Ordoñez never developed any further as a hitter. In fact, he regressed. Later it was revealed that he was older by more than two years than the Mets had initially believed. Suddenly on the wrong side of thirty, he made the situation worse by badmouthing fans at the end of a bad season, and the Mets dealt him to Tampa Bay for two players to be named later.

Rey Sanchez (2003) succeeded Ordoñez and was expected to provide good defense and a steady bat and to mentor shortstop-to-be Jose Reyes. The new Rey failed miserably on all three counts and is best remembered today for receiving a haircut during a blowout loss early on in the Art Howe watch. This Rey's unreliability assured that Reyes would arrive ahead of schedule.

Rusty Staub wore No. 10 in Houston and in Montreal but patiently waited three seasons while backup catcher **Duffy Dyer** occupied the jersey for the Mets. Dyer (1968–74) might have been a better hitter than the man he understudied for, Jerry Grote. With Grote missing a good part of the 1972 season with an injury, Dyer reached career highs with 17 doubles and 8 home runs in 363 plate appearances; that's more homers than Grote ever hit in a single year and stood as the club record for catchers until John Stearns topped both marks five years later. On September 20, 1973, Dyer delivered a pinch-hit, game-tying double in the bottom of the 9th inning in the famous "Ball on the Wall" victory that marked the Mets' unlikely charge to the pennant.

Staub's move into No. 10 coincided with his best single season as a Met in 1975. He hit 19 home runs and 30 doubles and had a .382 on-base percentage while driving in 105 runs, a franchise RBI standard that lasted until Howard Johnson broke it in 1991. Staub was inexplicably traded following the season but reappeared as a free-agent acquisition in 1981 and began a second career as a beloved pinch hitter and local restaurateur.

Willie Randolph's controversial decision to "bring the funk," and Miguel Cabrera's subsequent bases-clearing double, all but killed whatever pennant hopes the 2005 Mets might have entertained. **Shingo Takatsu**'s ignominious Mets debut overshadowed the fact that the side-arming Japanese reliever also ushered in the lowest number in team history for a pitcher.

Dave Magadan sandwiched No. 10 (1989–91) between stints at 29. A slow-footed singles hitter with a poor glove and terrific plate discipline, the Mets seemed reluctant to play Magadan regularly despite obvious skills at reaching base. In 1990 he was second in on-base percentage and third in batting; rarified air indeed for any Met. In 1992, Magadan gave up No. 10 to accommodate new manager **Jeff Torborg.** A New Jersey native and one-time Manager of the Year with the White Sox, Torborg took over a faltering team and was fired with the franchise in shambles in 1993.

Torborg's habit of wearing No. 10 dated to his playing career as a Dodgers catcher in the 1960s. **Terry Collins** had a different reason to have chosen No. 10 when he was appointed Mets manager following the 2010 season: He chose 10, he said, as a tribute to Jim Leyland, who gave Collins his first major league coaching assignment in Pittsburgh. "Plus," Collins added, "my wife thinks I'm a 10."

Although his teams haven't always exhibited the fundamentals he preached, Collins has proven the Mets' best skipper at least since Bobby Valentine, popular with players and the press. And if he serves out the two-

Dan Carubia

Terry Collins keeps an even keel as baseball's oldest manager, with help from the game's best young rotation.

year contract extension received following 2015's World Series run, Collins will have managed more games than anyone in team history. He's already served as many years as the longest-tenured No. 10 in club history.

Endy Chavez (2006–08) capped one of greatest-ever seasons by a Met reserve with a catch that ranks among the best in playoff history. His soaring catch over the left-field fence in Game 7 of the 2006 Championship Series turned what should have been a two-run home run into an inning-ending double play. If he'd been only ten feet taller, Endy might have caught Yadier Molina's decisive blast a few innings later. Like Kanehl, Chavez played with an urgency and élan putting him among the pantheon of beloved bench guys.

Of all the tough-luck 10s, **Butch Huskey** (1993) had the worst debut: he struck out his first three times up in the major leagues and made an error as Darryl Kile no-hit the Mets at the Astrodome. **Greg Goossen** (1966–68) showed some promise, but it didn't stop Casey Stengel's alleged remark: "Goossen is only twenty, and in ten years he has a chance to be thirty." A hard-swinging right-handed hitting catcher/first baseman, Goossen was the first catcher to receive Nolan Ryan, and in 1968, his 8th-inning single broke up a perfect game bid by Larry Jaster of the Cardinals. After his baseball career, he later became an actor and personal stand-in for Gene Hackman.

Also in the 10-spot: Regular-Joe backstops **Joe DePastino** (2003), and **Joe Heitpas** (2004) and clock-punchers **Kevin Collins** (1965), **Mike Jorgensen** (1968), **Kelvin Chapman** (1979), **David Segui** (1994), **Gary Thurman** (1997), **Kevin Morgan** (1997), **Roberto Petagine** (1997), **Jeff Duncan** (2004), **and Brian Buchanan** (2004).

Another 10 finally arrived before it was all over. Though often rumored to be coming to Queens, being Dwight Gooden's nephew was as close as **Gary Sheffield** got to the Mets through 21 seasons in the major leagues. Cut by the Tigers in spring training, he joined the Mets on the eve of the 2009 season as a forty-year-old in pursuit of his 500th career home run. He got that, plus nine more dingers, while taking that vicious swing around the league one last time.

Number 10

Number of times issued: 26 (22 players, 2 managers, 1 coach)

Longest tenured: Manager Terry Collins (5 seasons, 810 games); Rusty Staub (6 seasons, 573 games); Rey Ordoñez (5 seasons, 645 games),

Best single seasons: Staub, 1975 (.282/.371/.448, 19 HR, 105 RBIs); Dave Magadan, 1990 (.328/.417/.457, 6 HR, 72 RBIs)

Career statistical leaders: Home runs (Staub 32, Dyer 16, Magadan 10, Gary Sheffield 10); RBI (Staub 207, Ordoñez 197, Magadan 123); batting average (Magadan .295, Endy Chavez .288; Staub .279)

Teen Idols: Lowest Numbers for Pitchers

Although known in his native Japan as "Mister Zero," Shingo Takatsu was "Mister One-Zero" during his stay with the Mets in 2005. Takatsu succeeded Cory Lidle (No. 11 in 1997) as the pitcher with the lowest uniform number in club history (not counting position players such as Desi Relaford, who pitched a scoreless inning wearing No. 8 in 2001).

Al Jackson, the diminutive left-hander, was the Mets' original teen idol, wearing No. 15 in 1962. Roger Craig donned No. 13 in an attempt to end his bad luck in 1963 and wound up holding a Mets record for lowest number for a pitcher for eighteen years and then sharing it with flaky reliever Neil Allen, who, like Craig, took on 13 seeking a change in fortune.

Ron Darling set a new low in 1985 when he switched from No. 44 to No. 12, the best of all three of Darling's Mets uniforms. Near the end of the 1986 season Darling suggested that Mets starters Rick Aguilera (38) and Sid Fernandez (50) join him, Dwight Gooden (16), and Bob Ojeda (19) in what would be an all-teen starting five.

The Mets reported for spring training in 1987 to find that equipment manager Charlie Samuels had followed through on the suggestion, issuing Aguilera No. 15 and Sid Fernandez No. 10. But the plan went awry when Fernandez couldn't get comfortable in No. 10, preferring the 50 he wore not only for his home state of Hawaii but for the cop show set there, Hawaii Five-0, also his favorite. Book 'em, Bobby O.

Following is a list of the lowest uniforms in Mets pitching history through 2015:

10: Shingo Takatsu, 2005

11: Cory Lidle, 1997

12: Ron Darling, 1985–89

13: Roger Craig, 1963; Neil Allen, 1981–83; Jeff Musselman, 1989–90; Jonathan Hurst, 1994; Matt Ginter, 2004; Billy Wagner, 2006–09; Jerry Blevins, 2015

15: Al Jackson, 1962–65; Dave Roberts, 1981; Rick Aguilera, 1987–88; Ron Darling, 1989–91

16: Dwight Gooden, 1984–94; Hideo Nomo, 1998; David Cone, 2003; Daisuke Matsuzaka 2013–14

#11: MAGNIFICENT TRANSIENCE

Like that reliever who scares fans to death, or a rough West Coast trip, a No. 11 is one of those things that seems a part of every Mets season. It's not always pleasant, but it's always there.

Despite just a handful of longtime occupants, the Mets have had a No. 11 on the

field in all but four of their seasons (1967, 1968, 1997, and 2002). The Mets experienced a decade of magnificent transience between 1991 (Tim Teufel)

Chapter and verse sums up Mets finances.

and 2001 (Jorge Velandia) when the jersey was worn by thirteen different men, none for more than a single year. No other number has appeared as consistently—if not so reliably—through the Mets' first fifty-four seasons.

The most prominent No. 11 was probably redheaded infielder **Wayne Garrett** (1969–76), who lasted eight seasons in New York despite the team's best efforts to find someone else to do his job. Garrett arrived as a twenty-one-year-old Rule 5 selection from the Braves in 1969 and surprised observers by making the team and staying with it as a platoon mate for Ed Charles. In the 1969 NLCS, Garrett's double in Game 1 and home run in Game 3 helped bury his former organization. Although Charles retired following the 1969 season, Garrett did not inherit third base but rather waited to step in while over the next three years the team tried (and failed miserably) to fill third base with Joe Foy, Bob Aspromonte, and Jim Fregosi. Gritting their teeth and sticking with Garrett might have kept Amos Otis and Nolan Ryan in blue and orange . . . at

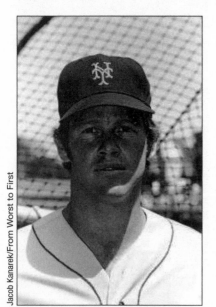

The Mets learned too late that the solution at third base had been in New York all along: Wayne Garrett.

least until the next troubled third sacker was made available by another team.

Garrett finally got a regular opportunity in 1973 and responded with 16 home runs and 20 doubles as the Mets visited the postseason again. And on a team devoid of speed, Garrett served as leadoff hitter and led the pennant winners with 6 steals. Yup, 6.

Garrett was traded to Montreal with Del Unser midway through the 1976 season for outfielders Jim Dwyer and **Pepe Mangual**, who immediately inherited the vacant No. 11 jersey. Mangual totaled just 20 hits in 109 at-bats in the uniform.

Like Garrett, **Ruben Tejada** (2010–15) became a longtime Mets fixture in spite of lukewarm support from the front office. A promising turn as a young reserve infielder in 2011 (.284 batting average and a .360 on-base percentage) won him an opportunity to supplant the departed Jose Reyes at shortstop, but he was only adequate there defensively and offensively and lacked the power and speed to prevent the club from experimenting with the likes of Wilmer Flores. Through 2015, he'd racked up more games at 11 than any Met except

Garrett. Ruben received more appreciation from Mets fans for walking out to Division Series introductions with a cane at Citi Field—after getting knocked off the postseason roster by a cheap Chase Utley rolling block—than he did for the first 583 times he actually took the field as a Met. The Mets put him on waivers in spring of 2016.

Connecticut native **Tim Teufel** (the name means "devil" in German) was brought in from Minnesota prior to the 1986 season to platoon at second base with Wally Backman. Never a great fielder, Teufel (1986–91) could swing the bat, hitting .308 with 14 homers doing part-time work in 1987. Teufel inherited the No. 11 jersey from **Kelvin Chapman**, who was Backman's platoon mate in 1984 and 1985. Chapman made his first appearance in 1979 (wearing 10) but disappeared into the minors for five long years before resurfacing in Davey Johnson's offense-first configuration.

The Mets by the 1990s had reduced Teufel's role to pinch-hitter, and seeking a backup for fragile shortstop Kevin Elster, traded Teufel to San Diego early in the 1991 season for **Garry Templeton**. Templeton then was thirty-five years old and playing (miserably) in what would be his final season as a major leaguer. Elster however was slow to return from offseason surgery, so the Mets in April of 1992 swapped with the Angels for another veteran shortstop, **Dick Schofield**. Schofield played 142 games in the No. 11 jersey, hitting just .205 in what would be his only season with the Mets.

Schofield's failure prompted the Mets to go with yet another veteran shortstop in 1993, Tony Fernandez, whose acquisition meant **Vince Coleman** would switch from No. 1 to the No. 11 jersey. The 1992–93 Mets spelled disaster for every 1.

Ancient ex-Yankee **Gene Woodling** turned out to be one of the best performers of the 1962 Mets, hitting .274 in 81 games. A deal to return as a player-coach in 1963 was scuttled, however, after Woodling went to bat for teammate Marv Throneberry in contentious contract negotiations. Woodling, it was decided, wasn't management material.

Roy McMillan (1964–66) spent the final years of his long and distinguished playing career as a defensive specialist for a Mets team that had never had one. McMillan, who could still play a mean shortstop and still couldn't hit (.226 and only 44 extra-base hits in 1,127 at-bats over three years) helped groom a successor in his own image: Bud Harrelson. McMillan later served as a Mets coach (1973–76) and as a mediocre interim manager who went 27–28 following the firing of Yogi Berra in 1975.

Len Randle was one of the few things that went right for the Mets in 1977, but even that had an ugly side. Randle was available only after being released by the Rangers when a spring-training confrontation with Texas manager Frank Lucchesi turned violent. In an otherwise chaotic year, Randle brought some stability to third base and led Mets regulars with a .304 batting average and 33 stolen bases (as well as 21 times caught stealing). Randle explained he wore No. 11 as a tribute to deposed Ranger manager Billy Martin (No. 1) and to God.

A singles-hitting shortstop with good speed and poor on-base percentage, **Frank Taveras** served three years hard time with the 1979–81 Mets. His 42 stolen bases in 1979 broke the club's single-season record set by Randle two years earlier.

Meaty catcher **Ramon Castro** (2005–09) was a longball threat while backing up starters Mike Piazza, Paul Lo Duca, and Brian Schneider over a five-year stint with the Mets. He clubbed eight home in 209 at-bats in '05 and added 11 bombs in just 144 at-bats two years later, but frequent back trouble limited his availability, as did friction with manager Jerry Manuel. Before 2009 was out, Castro would be traded to the White Sox and his No. 11 reissued twice: to backup infielders **Argenis Reyes** and **Anderson Hernandez**.

Former Brooklyn standout **Duke Snider** (1963) wore 11 while waiting for the Mets to trade Charlie Neal so he could reacquire his familiar No. 4. Bulletproof utility man **Joe McEwing** took No. 11 after Tom Glavine arrived to swipe his old No. 47 in 2003. McEwing (2003–04) settled on 11 by adding the digits on his old jersey.

The only pitcher to wear No. 11 for the Mets, **Cory Lidle** went 7–2 in a combination of starts and long-relief for the 1997 Mets.

Others (and there's a lot): **Ed Bouchee** (1962); **Tom Veryzer** (1982); **Mike Bishop** (1983); **Tucker Ashford** (1983); **Rick Parker** (1994); **Aaron Ledesma** (1995); **Tim Bogar** (1996); Mookie's nephew, **Preston Wilson** (1998); **Wayne Kirby** (1998), utility man **Shane Halter** (1999); leadoff hopeful **Jason Tyner** (2000); and backup infielder **Jorge Velandia** (2000–01).

Number 11

Number of times issued: 30 (all to players)

Longest tenured: Wayne Garrett (8 seasons, 883 games); Tim Teufel (6 seasons, 463 games); Ruben Tejada (5 seasons, 580 games);

Best single season: Garrett, 1973 (.256/.348/.403, 16 HR, 58 RBIs); Lenny Randle, 1977 (.304/.383/.404, 33 stolen bases); Teufel, 1987 (.308/.398/.545, 14 HR, 61 RBIs)

Career statistical leaders: Home runs (Garrett 55, Teufel 35, Ramon Castro 33); RBI (Garrett 295, Teufel 164, Tejada 148); batting average (Vince Coleman .279, Gene Woodling .274, Randle .272)

Hot Corner Roll Call: Third basemen by the Numbers

Over their fifty-four seasons the Mets have churned through third basemen at the rate of three per year, 157 in all (and counting), from Abbott to Zimmer, or more precisely, from Zimmer in 1962 to Johnson in 2015. That's Kelly Johnson, not be confused with predecessors Bob or Howard, who also manned the hot corner for the Mets.

Although third base was a running joke for the first twenty-five years of the team's existence, it has become a position of strength over the past two-plus decades: Ray Knight, Howard Johnson, Edgardo Alfonzo, Robin Ventura, and David Wright have been among the team's best players in that span. The following is a list of every Met to man the hot corner, when they first played there (with doubleheader games in parentheses), and the number they wore for their hot-corner debut. The most popular number for third sackers in their debut? It's 6, with fourteen members of that fraternity subset.

Third Baseman	Met 3B Debut	Uniform Number
1. Don Zimmer	April 11, 1962	17
2. Rod Kanehl	April 21, 1962	10
3. Felix Mantilla	April 23, 1962	18
4. Elio Chacon	May 5, 1962+	7
5. Cliff Cook	May 8, 1962	6
6. Frank Thomas	June 17, 1962	25
7. Rick Herrscher	August 2, 1962*	6
8. Sammy Drake	August 10, 1962	12
9. Charlie Neal	August 29, 1962	4
10. Ted Schreiber	April 14, 1963*	43
11. Chico Fernandez	May 12, 1963 (1st game)	7
12. Al Moran	May 12, 1963 (2nd game)	40
13. Larry Burright	May 12, 1963 (2nd game)	6
14. Ron Hunt	May 13, 1963	33
15. Jim Hickman	June 19, 1963	9
16. Pumpsie Green	September 5, 1963	18
17. John Stephenson	April 26, 1964*	49
18. Amado Samuel	May 8, 1964	7
19. Charley Smith	May 24, 1964	1
20. Wayne Graham	August 8, 1964	4
21. Bobby Klaus	August 15, 1964	6
22. Dan Napoleon	April 24, 1965*	16
23. Chuck Hiller	August 22, 1965	2

Third Baseman	Met 3B Debut	Uniform Number
24. Gary Kolb	September 1, 1965 (2nd game)	18
25. Kevin Collins	September 11, 1965	10
26. Ken Boyer	April 15, 1966	14
27. Eddie Bressoud	May 14, 1966	1
28. Jerry Grote	August 3, 1966	15
29. Sandy Alomar Sr.	April 15, 1967	5
30. Jerry Bucheck	April 23, 1967 (2nd game)	1
31. Tom Reynolds	April 29, 1967	16
32. Ed Charles	May 12, 1967	24
33. Bob Johnson	June 4, 1967 (1st game)	6
34. Phil Linz	July 19, 1967 (1st game)	2
35. Joe Moock	September 1, 1967 (1st game)*	18
36. Amos Otis	September 7, 1967*	28
37. Ken Boswell	September 18, 1967*	24
38. Bob Heise	September 25, 1967	23
39. Al Weis	May 1, 1968	6
40. Wayne Garrett	May 4, 1969 (2nd game)	11
41. Bobby Pfeil	June 26, 1969*	1
42. Joe Foy	April 7, 1970	5
43. Tim Foli	September 12, 1970	19
44. Bob Aspromonte	April 6, 1971	2
45. Ted Martinez	July 6, 1971	17
46. Jim Fregosi	April 15, 1972	2
47. Rich Puig	September 13, 1974 (2nd game)*+	6
48. Joe Torre	April 8, 1975	9
49. Jack Heidemann	May 7, 1975	12
50. Roy Staiger	September 12, 1975	35
51. Dave Kingman	September 15, 1975	26
52. Mike Phillips	May 16, 1976 (1st game)	5
53. Leo Foster	September 6, 1976	1
54. Len Randle	May 8, 1977 (1st game)	11
55. Doug Flynn	June 22, 1977	23
56. Joel Youngblood	June 24, 1977	18
57. Bobby Valentine	July 6, 1977	1

Third Baseman	Met 3B Debut	Uniform Number
58. Sergio Ferrer	April 30, 1978	3
59. Elliott Maddox	May 26, 1978	21
60. John Stearns	June 28, 1978	12
61. Alex Treviño	October 1, 1978	29
62. Richie Hebner	April 5, 1979	3
63. Kelvin Chapman	May 10, 1979	10
64. Phil Mankowski	April 15, 1980	2
65. Mario Ramirez	May 22, 1980	3
66. Jose Moreno	June 18, 1980	4
67. Bill Almon	July 27, 1980	25
68. Hubie Brooks	September 4, 1980	39
69. Wally Backman	April 18, 1981	6
70. Mike Cubbage	April 26, 1981 (2nd game)	3
71. Bob Bailor	September 24, 1981	4
72. Ron Gardenhire	September 27, 1981	19
73. Tucker Ashford	May 6, 1983	11
74. Clint Hurdle	September 12, 1983	33
75. Ross Jones	July 28, 1984	21
76. Ray Knight	August 29, 1984	22
77. Kevin Mitchell	September 13, 1984	32
78. Howard Johnson	April 9, 1985	20
79. Tim Teufel	April 12, 1986	11
80. Gary Carter	July 22, 1986	8
81. Dave Magadan	April 18, 1987	29
82. Mackey Sasser	May 11, 1988	2
83. Keith Miller	June 18, 1988	25
84. Gregg Jefferies	August 28, 1988*	9
85. Jeff McKnight	June 10, 1989	15
86. Craig Shipley	September 7, 1989	35
87. Tom O'Malley	September 7, 1989	27
88. Chris Donnels	May 7, 1991*	23
89. Garry Templeton	June 7, 1991	11
90. Bill Pecota	April 6, 1992	32
91. Junior Noboa	April 15, 1992	3

Third Baseman	Met 3B Debut	Uniform Number
92. Chico Walker	May 11, 1992	34
93. Steve Springer	August 20, 1992	13
94. Jeff Kent	September 26, 1992	39
95. Tim Bogar	May 29, 1993	23
96. Bobby Bonilla	June 25, 1993	25
97. Butch Huskey	September 8, 1993*	10
98. Doug Saunders	September 24, 1993	2
99. Fernando Viña	April 10, 1994	1
100. Edgardo Alfonzo	May 2, 1995	13
101. Aaron Ledesma	July 6, 1995	11
102. Bill Spiers	July 23, 1995	19
103. Carlos Baerga	July 30, 1996 (1st game)	6
104. Alvaro Espinoza	August 2, 1996	12
105. Matt Franco	September 8, 1996	15
106. Kevin Morgan	June 15, 1997*+	10
107. Jason Hardtke	June 21, 1997	19
108. Luis Lopez	July 12, 1997	17
109. Manny Alexander	July 13, 1997	6
110. Shawn Gilbert	September 24, 1997	12
111. Craig Paquette	May 3, 1998	18
112. Jim Tatum	May 16, 1998	19
113. Lenny Harris	July 12, 1998	19
114. Mike Kinkade	September 8, 1998	33
115. Robin Ventura	April 5, 1999	4
116. Melvin Mora	July 6, 1999	6
117. Shawon Dunston	August 8, 1999	12
118. Kurt Abbott	April 26, 2000	20
119. Joe McEwing	May 20, 2000	47
120. David Lamb	July 14, 2000	26
121. Jorge Velandia	September 8, 2000	11
122. Desi Relaford	April 22, 2001	8
123. John Valentin	April 14, 2002	4
124. Ty Wigginton	May 17, 2002*	9
125. Marco Scutaro	July 28, 2002	26

Third Baseman	Met 3B Debut	Uniform Number
126. Jay Bell	April 10, 2003	44
127. Todd Zeile	April 11, 2004	27
128. Ricky Gutierrez	April 22, 2004	6
129. David Wright	July 21, 2004*	5
130. Chris Woodward	April 13, 2005	4
131. Miguel Cairo	April 21, 2005	3
132. Jose Valentin	May 26, 2006	18
133. Eli Marrero	July 2, 2006	32
134. Julio Franco	September 10, 2006	23
135. Damion Easley	April 19, 2007	3
136. Ruben Gotay	September 7, 2007	6
137. David Newhan	September 29, 2007	17
138. Fernando Tatis	June 17, 2008	17
139. Andy Green	August 19, 2009	29
140. Wilson Valdez	August 25, 2009	4
141. Mike Hessman	July 29, 2010	19
142. Justin Turner	August 19, 2010	2
143. Luis Hernandez	August 31, 2010	3
144. Willie Harris	May 12, 2011	22
145. Daniel Murphy	May 31, 2011	28
146. Nick Evans	July 17, 2011	6
147. Josh Satin	September 28, 2011	3
148. Ronny Cedeno	April 10, 2012	13
149. Vinny Rottino	May 28, 2012	33
150. Zach Lutz	June 27, 2013	19
151. Wilmer Flores	August 6, 2013*	4
152. Omar Quintanilla	September 15, 2013	3
153. Eric Campbell	June 8, 2014	29
154. Anthony Recker	April 14, 2015+	20
155. Ruben Tejada	May 14, 2015	11
156. Danny Muno	May 25, 2015*	16
157. Juan Uribe	July 25, 2015	2
158. Kelly Johnson	October 3, 2015	55

*Major league debut in the field
+Only career appearance at 3B

#12: "IT'S A NICE NUMBER"

Although a long playing, coaching, and captaining career aligned **Willie Randolph** most closely with that other team in New York, a symbolic gesture at the beginning of his first spring training as Mets manager revealed he may have been one of us all along.

"I'm gonna wear No. 12. Why? You remember Ken Boswell? Second baseman on the '69 team? He was my favorite player growing up," Randolph told Bill Madden of the *Daily News.* "No. 12. It's a nice number."

While fans can drown in the empty platitudes spouting from athletes, there is something authentic about a **Ken Boswell** name

Ken Boswell, platoon and pinch hitting veteran.

check. Boswell indeed wore No. 12 (at least after shedding 24 for Art Shamsky in 1968), played the lefty-hitting second baseman in the strict Gil Hodges platoon system, and had a flair for the dramatic: Boswell clubbed home runs in two straight '69 NLCS games after homering 3 times all year. Although the arrival of Felix Millan in 1972 made Boswell a full-time backup, he excelled in that role. Boswell batted 1.000 (3-for-3, all in pinch-hit duty) in the 1973 World Series.

Randolph, by the way, also wore No. 12 in his last-gasp appearance as a player with the ill-fated 1992 Mets. The customary No. 30 he wore with the Yankees was unavailable then due to pitching coach Mel Stottlemyre. When Randolph was named manager in 2005, Cliff Floyd owned 30.

As a manager, Randolph was esteemed if not embraced. Replacing the bland Art Howe in 2005, he brought dignity to the role while exhibiting a gruff, fastidious charm that was equal parts Brooklyn street smarts and buttoned-up Yankee pomposity. His superb 2006 club faltered beneath injuries in the postseason before decaying in 2007 amid Randolph's growing detachment, denial, and paranoia. A wobbly start in 2008 famously resulted in an after-hours West Coast firing that set off days of recrimination while offering a glimpse inside a fracturing Met organization. Years later, the relationship between the Mets and Randolph hasn't healed.

If Randolph's firing raised the question as to who ran the Mets, the next man in the No. 12 jersey was a "gift" from the man who ran the Mets ragged from the other dugout: Bobby Cox. The Atlanta manager, who spent more than a decade torturing the Mets, gave New York the gift of Frenchy. **Jeff Francoeur** was the kind of tantalizing package of raw ability that Omar Minaya couldn't resist, but whose chronic and incurable flaws assured the Mets would continue spinning their wheels. Francoeur had a cannon for an arm, a terrible eye, a big smile, and bad timing. His liner on a ninth-inning hit-and-run created a new way to lose when Phillies second baseman Eric Bruntlett turned it into an unassisted triple play. By the end of 2010 the Mets had had enough of the gregarious, enthusiastic .237 hitter and flipped him to Texas for journeyman reserve infielder **Joaquin Arias**, who finished out 2010 hitting an even .200 in the No. 12 jersey. Frenchy ended the year in the World Series. Maybe his timing wasn't so bad after all.

Jeff Kent (1993–96) was never much for uniforms, baseball or otherwise. As a Mets rookie in 1992, he petulantly refused to engage in the customary freshman ritual of wearing an outlandish costume for a Mets road trip. The joke was ultimately on the Mets, who paid too much to get Kent (David Cone) and took too little in return for him four years later (Carlos Baerga and forgettable No. 12 **Alvaro Espinosa**). In between, Kent showed traces of the skill that would one day make him a National League MVP, hitting 21 home runs and driving in 80 in 1993. During a post-career stint on the television reality show *Survivor*, Kent's single-minded competitive nature represented a threat, but a lousy relationship with cast mates was his downfall. We weren't surprised. Sorry, Jeff. The tribe has spoken.

Fans looking for a counterpoint to Kent might find one in **Tommy Davis**, who was acquired prior to the 1967 season for longtime Mets Jim Hickman and Ron Hunt and flipped afterward in a deal that brought the Mets 1969 mainstays Tommie Agee and Al Weis. Davis led the '67 Mets in virtually every statistical category.

Jeff Kent launched more home runs and "what might have beens" than any Mets No. 12.

With four All-Star appearances, **John Stearns** (1977–84) makes a good case as the Mets' all-time No. 12. Nicknamed "Bad Dude," Stearns was a star defensive back at the University of Colorado who brought the same hard-hitting intensity to the baseball field. Acquired from Philadelphia in the Tug McGraw deal, Stearns in time would prove to be a stronger offensive contributor than predecessor Jerry Grote. His .264-15-73 performance in 1978 included a National League record for stolen bases by a catcher, 25. The mark stood until Jason Kendall broke it for the 1998 Pirates.

Pittsburgh's Dave Parker once left a collision with Stearns with a broken jaw; Atlanta's Chief Nok-a-Homa absorbed an open-field tackle from Stearns and thought better about dancing too close to the Mets' side of Fulton County Stadium ever again; and when an Expo threw a pitch near Mike Jorgensen's head in the wake of a long home run, there was Stearns dashing from dugout to mound faster than you can say, "Ralphie the Buffalo." Stearns would eventually discover he was not indestructible, spending much of his final years with the Mets nursing injuries on the sidelines.

Stearns wore No. 16 for his maiden appearances with the Mets in 1975 and 1976. He and **Lee Mazzilli**, who wore 12 for his first 24 games of his career,

All Big Eight in football and baseball at University of Colorado, John Stearns brought gridiron intensity to Mets.

Jacob Kanarek/From Worst to First

switched jerseys prior to the 1977 season so that Stearns could inhabit the same digits he'd worn in college.

Stearns finally got to wear 12 in a winning situation as a coach for ex-teammate Bobby Valentine in 2000–01.

When informed of the principals in the 2001 trade that made **Roberto Alomar** a Met, manager Bobby Valentine reportedly had one question: "What's wrong with him?" The answer, Mets fans would learn, was a sudden and irreversible decline in skills that made the trade for the Cooperstown-bound second baseman one of the most disappointing in club history. The twelve-time All-Star spent a listless season and a half in New York. The Mets seemed eager to erase his memory after his trade to the White Sox by issuing his No. 12 to rookie second baseman **Danny Garcia** (2003–04). Garcia, the first Met who was also a Brooklyn Cyclone, was a marginal talent, but his hustle got him through the following season.

In the middle of this family of second basemen and catchers was pitcher **Ron Darling**, who decided in 1985 that he preferred 12 to the No. 44 he'd worn the first few years of his career. Darling was the first and still the only Mets pitcher to wear No. 12. At the time, it set the mark for the lowest number worn by a hurler in club history.

Of the three uniform numbers Darling wore (15 was the third, which he changed to in August 1989), he was most successful in No. 12, going 68–38 with a 3.38 ERA. Darling was a first-round draft choice of the Texas Rangers out of Yale and was acquired along with Walt Terrell for Lee Mazzilli in one of the most lopsided trades in team history. Darling not only had a brighter future than Mazzilli, but he filled out his uniform every bit as well, succeeding Maz as a new favorite of Shea's female fans and copping the cover of *GQ*, too.

Juan Lagares, like Darling, brought a Gold Glove to No. 12. A stealth prospect from what was then a lightly regarded farm system, Lagares took over center field at Citi Field in 2013, but only after Collin Cowgill and Rick Ankiel had the first cracks at it. Lagares proved he belonged defensively, earning his Gold Glove in 2014 and the love of most advanced metrics. His hitting, then as now, is a work in progress.

The Mets debuted No. 12 on the back of veteran catcher **Joe Ginsberg**, who would appear in just two games with the '62 Mets. Expansion draftee **Sammy Drake** also wore 12 that year. Neither played in the majors ever again.

Was **Scott Hairston** the best reserve outfielder in Mets history or was the "first string" he backed up notoriously bad? A little of both. The veteran Hairston ripped a career-high 20 home runs in 2012 as a part timer, third-best on the team and the most of a group of alleged full-time outfielders including a washed-up Jason Bay, a disinterested Andres Torres, and a badly misplaced Lucas Duda.

Others: power-hitting catcher **Jesse Gonder** (1963–65); **Cleon Jones** (1965) with the right numbers in the wrong order; backup catcher **John Stephenson** (1966); mutton-chopped reserve infielder **Jack Heidemann** (1975–76); just-passing-through outfielder **Keith Hughes** (1990); **Shawn Gilbert** (1997–98), a Bobby V. special who made the Mets as a 32-year-rookie reservist; catcher (and hitter) in name only, **Jorge Fabregas** (1998); and **Shawon Dunston,** the free-swinging, late-season, bench-strength acquiree who made the most of a short stay (and a long NLCS at-bat) in 1999.

Number 12

Number of times issued: 22 (20 players, 1 coach, 1 manager)

Longest tenured: John Stearns (8 seasons, 718 games), Ken Boswell (7 seasons, 670 games), Ron Darling (5 seasons, 158 games)

Best single season: Jeff Kent, 1994 (.292/.341/.475, 14 HR, 68 RBIs); Stearns, 1978 (.264/.364/.413, 15 HR, 73 RBIs, 25 stolen bases); Darling, 1986 (15–6, 2.81, 184 strikeouts); Tommy Davis, 1967 (.302/.342/.440, 16 HR, 73 RBIs)

Career statistical leaders: Home runs (Kent 64, Stearns 41, Boswell 30), RBI (Stearns 302, Kent 264, Boswell 189), batting average (Kent .281, Stearns .265, Roberto Alomar .265)

Mets Uniform History: All Right, Pull Over

By March 1978, Tom Seaver was gone, Dave Kingman was on his fifth team in nine months, Jerry Grote had been dumped, Felix Millan had been sold (to Japan), Jon Matlack and John Milner had been dealt, and Bud Harrelson was about to be shipped to Philadelphia. All of this was hard to fathom as spring training brought the threat of another season from hell. Even those so helplessly attached to the club that they vowed to just root for the uniform were in for a rude awakening. The Mets pullover had arrived.

The 1978 pullover featured blue and orange bands on each sleeve and similar piping around the neck (two blue bands surrounding an orange band). The club retained the home pinstripes and road gray, both with the skyline logo patch on the left sleeve. The two buttons around the collar of the new threads were as superfluous as the neatly stacked bats in the dugout of what would be the worst team in the National League.

The new look followed a trend that transported the audacious and multicolored outfits of the period from the stands onto the field. The National League seemed especially afflicted as the new style resulted in dizzying orange stripes in Houston, the McDonaldland look in San Diego, and road grays turned blue in Montreal, Philadelphia, St. Louis, and Chicago (the American League had six blue-road-fever victims but still had to answer for the Cleveland Indians' mono- chromatic maroon softball look). True, the Mets didn't have zippers on their uniforms like the Phillies; they weren't stuck in 1976—or 1876—like the Pirates with their disturbing combina- tion of tops, bottoms, stripes, and pillbox hats; and the Mets hadn't lost all sense like the White Sox with their perpetual pajama party. But the Mets had dipped a toe in the fetid water of trendi- ness while others kept their shirts buttoned at home and on the road. The Mets would retain a pullover uniform, in varying styles, until 1991.

#13: LUCKY US

Traditionally considered bad luck, No. 13 is rarely issued by the Mets unless specifically requested, which often indicates one of two things about the requester: They're either a Venezuelan infielder or a relief pitcher with something to prove.

The first category includes **Jorge Velandia** (2003), **Ronny Cedeño** (2012), presumed 2016 wearer **Asdrubal Cabrera**, and the most accomplished Met to have worn No. 13, **Edgardo Alfonzo**. Like many of his Venezuelan countrymen, Alfonzo preferred to wear No. 13 in honor of Reds great Dave Concepcion. (Ozzie Guillen and Omar Vizquel are other noted Venezuelan wearers of 13 for the same reason, and their wearing of it has inspired additional followers).

Alfonzo (1995–2002) began his career as a twenty-year-old fill-in infielder with the Mets in 1995 but didn't truly arrive until he was inserted as the everyday third baseman in 1997 and revealed himself to be among the best all-around players the team had ever developed. He hit well, ran the bases smartly, and was an exceptional fielder at third base and second base, where he moved to accommodate Robin Ventura when he arrived in 1999. Alfonzo shifted back to third in 2002 to make room for Roberto Alomar.

In 1999 the Fonz hit .304-27-108, not to mention a scorching a 6-6-6 night in the closing days of the Astrodome, going 6-for-6 and crossing the plate half a dozen times to set club records in each category. He launched some of the biggest hits that October—a two-run home run in the 1st inning of the loser-goes-home Wild Card play-in game with the Reds and a pair of home runs in Game 1 of the Division Series against Arizona, including a tie-breaking grand slam in the 9th. Several all-time club standards were in reach for Alfonzo when the Mets abruptly let him go as a free agent in 2002. At the time, he ranked third in doubles, runs, and hits, fourth in total bases, and seventh in RBIs, but

Fonzie had faded from being a great player to a merely good one. Alfonzo's subsequent performance—if not the performance of those who replaced him on the Mets—indicated this unpopular decision was also a prudent one.

Neil Allen: The man who broke in both 13 and 46 at Shea Stadium, with all the luck and goodwill that came with those numbers.

After establishing himself as a budding relief ace wearing No. 46, **Neil Allen** sought to distinguish himself by changing to the No. 13 jersey as the 1981 season began. He was the first Met to boldly wear 13 at Shea and the first at all since the **Roger Craig** exorcism of late 1963 (see sidebar). In time, Allen's role would be usurped by a succession of more reliable men, including the maligned Doug Sisk and revered Jesse Orosco. Allen eventually brought good luck on the trade market, being the principal guy shipped to St. Louis in the 1983 Keith Hernandez heist.

Billy Wagner (2006–09), who was always a little more about Billy Wagner than he was about the Mets, arrived as a free agent in 2006 with an eye on adding to a Cooperstown-worthy résumé having distinguished himself wearing 13 over 11 seasons as a fearsome closer in Houston and Philadelphia. His 40 saves in 2006 helped the Mets comfortably win their division, although a poor League Championship Series allowed the underdog St. Louis Cardinals to steal their way into the World Series. Wagner had an excellent campaign in 2007, but was not immune to the team-wide September swoon that cost that club a playoff spot. Things got worse in 2008 when Wagner issued a public tirade against teammates, blew a save in the All-Star Game, and suffered a season-ending injury in August that proved a crucial loss in another late season collapse. Wagner would return a year later only long enough to be traded to Boston. He achieved that elusive 400th save in 2011 as a member of the Braves.

Bad luck arrived by trade in 1989 when the Mets foolishly sent Mookie Wilson to Toronto for left-handed reliever **Jeff Musselman**, a Harvard grad who'd be ineffective for the Mets and out of professional baseball in a little more than a year.

Lee Mazzilli went to the Blue Jays the same day as Mookie, only Maz went over the waiver wire. Mazzilli had gotten three more years out a career that seemed over in July of 1986, when he was let go by the last-place Pittsburgh Pirates. The Mets reacquired him and dressed him in No. 13 (his familiar 16 belonging to Dwight Gooden). No longer the fleet handsome outfielder of the disco age, the late-model Mazzilli (1986-89) was an accomplished veteran pinch-hitter and a steely, been-there, done-that presence on a team with a lot of strong personalities. The only Met to see both the '77 Seaver trade and the '86 parade, Maz later managed the Orioles wearing 13.

Other 13s: **Clint Hurdle** (1985), who like Mazzilli continued wearing 13 as a manager (Rockies and Pirates); tough-guy catcher **Rick Cerone** (1991); **Rodney McCray** (1992), still crashing through a minor-league outfield fence on a highlight reel somewhere; **Steve Springer** (1992); **Jonathan Hurst** (1994); **Matt Ginter** (2004); **Brian Daubach** (2005); **Alex Cora** (2010); **Mike Nickeas** (2010–11); **Josh Satin** (2013–14); and **Jerry Blevins** (2015).

Blevins, a quirky lefty specialist acquired on the cusp of the 2015 season in a trade from overconfident rival Washington, helped the 2015 Mets off to a great start but bad luck found No. 13 in the form of a hard line drive off the bat of Marlin Dee Gordon, fracturing his forearm in April. Shortly before he was to have returned to the club, Blevins fell and re-fractured the same bone, ending his season. Upon resigning with the Mets for 2016, Blevins conceded 13 to the newly arriving Cabrera, saying he'd find something else to wear. Better luck next time, Jerry.

Number 13

Number of times issued: 20 (19 players, 1 coach)

Longest tenured: Edgardo Alfonzo (8 seasons, 1,086 games), Neil Allen (3 seasons, 114 games), Lee Mazzilli (4 seasons, 243 games), Billy Wagner (4 seasons, 183 games)

Best single season: Alfonzo, 2000 (.324/.425/.542, 25 HR, 94 RBIs); Alfonzo, 1999 (.304/.385/.502, 27 HR, 108 RBIs); Wagner, 2006 (3–2, 40 saves, 2.24 ERA)

Career statistical leaders: Home runs (Alfonzo 120), RBI (Alfonzo 538), batting average (Alfonzo .292), ERA (Wagner, 2.37)

Very Superstitious, Nothin' More to Say

The de facto ace of the early Mets, Roger Craig, did nothing so well as lose. He lost close games and he lost blowouts. He lost because his team didn't support him with their gloves, and he lost because they didn't support them with their bats. Often, he lost because of both. Frequently, he lost because of his own mistakes. He lost as a starter, and because Casey Stengel trusted him most, he lost as a reliever. He lost and lost.

After fashioning a record of 10 wins and a league-leading 24 losses for the 1962 Mets, Craig got off to a 2–2 start in 1963 before a loss May 4 to the Giants started a mind-bogglingly luckless streak. Between May 4 and August 4 he lost 18 decisions in a row. (It was the kind of streak only another Met(s) could break: Craig Anderson topped it in 1964 (19), and Anthony Young shattered both marks three decades later with 27 straight.)

At Wrigley Field on July 4, 1963, Craig was working the bottom of the 9th of a 1–1 game when Ernie Banks reached second on a throwing error by shortstop Chico Fernandez. Craig proceeded to throw a wild pitch to the following batter that catcher Norm Sherry collected only to throw into left field in an attempt to catch Banks advancing to third. He trotted home for consecutive loss No. 11.

Fourteen straight losses came due and Craig began to think about unconventional ways to change his luck. It began with borrowing teammate Tracy Stallard's No. 36 jersey for his July 19 start against the Phillies at Connie Mack Stadium (Stallard, a starter who did not appear in the game, presumably wore the No. 38 formerly belonging to Craig and caused no clubhouse fuss because there were no names on the back).

Craig was riding No. 36 to a three-hit shutout when with one out in the bottom of the 9th and the Mets ahead 1–0, Tony Gonzalez tripled and Roy Sievers followed with a game-ending two-run home run.

No. 36 went back to Stallard and Craig lost four more times before, on August 9, he wore a 2–20 record and the No. 13 jersey to the Polo Grounds mound to face the Cubs. Tied at 3 in the bottom of the 9th, and with two men on base, Stengel pinch hit Tim Harkness for Craig, and Harkness was intentionally walked. "I wouldn't care if he was my uncle," Stengel said, "he was out of the game."

Jim Hickman followed with a fly ball to left that ticked off the overhanging bleachers for a grand slam that could only have been hit in the odd dimensions of the Polo Grounds. An excited Craig left the dugout to make sure the runners touched the bases. Craig spent the rest of the season—two more wins and two more losses—wearing No. 13. In an act of mercy, over the offseason the Mets traded him to St. Louis, where he won a World Series ring while wearing No. 41.

Changing the number on the shirt doesn't always accompany a change in luck. Howard Johnson got more than he bargained for when he impulsively grabbed the No. 44 jersey David Cone left in May of 1991. Although Johnson thought the number change might put a charge into a slumbering bat, he admitted after a few days he felt "uncomfortable" in 44 and that his wife—whose jewelry bore the No. 20—didn't like it either. The Mets were on the road by the time Johnson came to this realization, so the team had a No. 20 jersey shipped out to San Diego for Johnson to wear.

Ron Darling twice changed his number for the Mets: once from 44 to 12, then from 12 to 15. The latter switch paid immediate dividends for Darling, who threw a complete-game victory over the Expos in his first appearance wearing 15.

"I'm not a superstitious guy," Darling protested after the second change, "but I thought I'd try something different. No. 12 hasn't been showing up this year."

Many years later, Darling would reveal the switch was more about playing a practical joke on team spokesman Jay Horwitz, whom Darling knew would panic when he couldn't explain who was wearing No. 15 on the mound that day.

#14: GOOD OLD GIL

The story of No. 14 literally begins and ends with the first and last man to wear the jersey for the Mets, **Gil Hodges**.

Hodges was nearing the end of his playing career when selected by the Mets in the expansion draft in 1961. A seven-time All-Star first baseman who to that point had spent his entire sixteen-year career with the Dodgers, Hodges was a beloved figure in New York, remarkable even among the bevy of ex–New York players who populated the Mets roster in their early years. Although an Indiana native, Hodges had married a local girl and lived year-round in Flatbush. His steadying influence and quiet power on the field and in the clubhouse had already begun speculation that he could someday manage the fledgling Mets.

This pin was given out in honor of Gil Hodges in 2000.

His playing highlights with the Mets included the franchise's first-ever home run, one of 9 contributed in just 127 at-bats in '62. But aching knees put an end to Hodges's career, so early in the 1963 season the Mets traded him to Washington, where he was immediately installed as the manager of the expansion Senators.

When Mets manager Wes Westrum resigned late in the 1967 season, the Mets board of directors was strongly in favor of retrieving Hodges from Washington, where he'd begun to turn around that team's fortunes. The Senators eventually took pitching prospect Bill Denehy and a reported $100,000 for Hodges.

Hodges helped improve the Mets by 12 wins in his first year at the helm and in 1969 did the impossible, leading a team that had never before played

Gil Hodges speaks with Ernie Banks before a 1969 Mets-Cubs game.

at .500 to a 100-win season and the world championship. To a man, players on those late 1960s teams speak reverently of Hodges's influence, and the results of 1969 are evidence of magnificent managerial maneuverings. Deploying limited resources skillfully, Hodges used platoons at several positions to complement an outstanding pitching staff en route to winning 41 games by a single run, one off of a major league record.

The Mets had disappointing 83-win seasons in 1970 and 1971. While players were striking during spring training of 1972, Hodges finished an afternoon of golf with his coaches and promptly collapsed dead of a heart attack at age forty-eight. The Mets formally retired his number 14 in 1973.

Between Hodges's departure in 1963 and his 1968 return, two men wore No. 14 for the Mets: **Ron Swoboda** (1965) and **Ken Boyer** (1966–67).

Swoboda was a twenty-one-year-old rookie in 1965 when he led the team with 19 home runs. Boyer, a veteran third baseman, requested his familiar No. 14 when he arrived in a trade from the Cardinals prior to the 1966 season, and Swoboda switched, eventually, to No. 4. But No. 14 was and will always be Gil's.

Number 14

Number of times issued: 4 (3 players, 1 manager)

Longest tenured: Ken Boyer (2 seasons, 192 games), Gil Hodges (as manager, 4 seasons, 648 games).

Best single season: Ron Swoboda, 1965 (19 HR, 50 RBIs)

Career statistical leaders: Home runs (Swoboda 19), RBI (Boyer 74), batting average (Boyer .258)

Retired: June 9, 1973

In Tribute: Remembering Lost Mets

Over their fifty-three years, many people with ties to the Mets have died suddenly. None, perhaps, has been as much of a shock as the death of Gil Hodges in 1972. In honor of their fallen skipper, the Mets wore black armbands just below the team logo on the left sleeve for that 1972 season, the first time a deceased Met had been so honored. His number was a retired a year later. Eddie Yost, third-base coach and close friend, still looked stunned in his 1973 yearbook photo.

Yost and the Mets wore black armbands again in 1976 after the franchise's matriarch and patriarch—owner Joan Payson and original manager Casey Stengel—died within a week of each other the previous autumn. The Mets have subsequently honored the passing of William Shea, who helped create the franchise and for whom the stadium was named; umpire John

McSherry, who died of a heart attack on the field during a game in Cincinnati; Tommie Agee, beloved hero of the 1969 Miracle Mets; Brian Cole, a twenty-two-year-old prospect killed in an accident at the end of spring training 2001; Tug McGraw, rally maker for the 1973 club and coiner of the catchphrase "Ya Gotta Believe"; Hall of Fame catcher Gary Carter, a key member of the Mets' 1986 world champions; beloved broadcasters Bob Murphy and Ralph Kiner, who entertained and informed generations of Mets fans; and GM Frank Cashen, who earned the everlasting admiration of the Mets faithful by creating a world championship team in Queens that would have to last a while, and make do for those not even born in 1986.

In Honor of	Season	Tribute
Gil Hodges	1972	Black armband on left sleeve
Casey Stengel, Joan Payson	1976	Black armband on left sleeve
William Shea	1992	*S* in pinstriped circle on left sleeve (the Mets wore no logo on the sleeve at the time)
John McSherry	1996	Home plate with crossed bats and "JM/NL Umpire/10" on right sleeve for native New Yorker
Tommie Agee, Brian Cole	2001 (Opening Day only)	A patch resembling a baseball on the right sleeve with the two players' numbers: 20 (Agee) and 60 (Cole)
Tug McGraw	2004	"Ya Gotta Believe" signed "Tug" under Shea fortieth anniversary patch on right sleeve
Bob Murphy	2004 (August to October)	"Bob Murphy" embroidered under Mets logo on left sleeve
Gary Carter	2012	A patch resembling home plate embroidered KID 8 for Carter's nickname and uniform number, worn on right sleeve
Ralph Kiner	2014	Round patch with microphone reading "Ralph Kiner: 1922–2014" worn on right sleeve
Frank Cashen	2014	Rectangular patch with initals "FC" right below Kiner tribute after Cashen died in July.

#15: METSMERIZED

The first in what has become a Mets tradition of acquiring catchers in lopsided trades was the 1965 deal that sent pitcher Tom Parsons and cash to Houston for **Jerry Grote** (1966–77).

Just twenty-three years old at the time, Grote was seen as something of a failed prospect for the Astros. He had struggled mightily in limited hitting appearances and fallen below catching prospects John Bateman and Ron Brand on Houston's depth chart. Above

Dan Carubia

all, however, Grote had a reputation as a "red ass." That is, he had an irascible personality the Astros feared might negatively affect relationships with teammates or management. He rarely had much more than a growl for the writers following the Mets.

Jerry Grote appeared in more games than any Mets catcher and No. 15.

Yet it was Grote's gruff demeanor that made him the valuable backstop he became with the Mets. His bat would come around only enough to turn him into a passable singles hitter: he reached career highs of 6 home runs and 40 RBIs in 1969. Grote blocked the plate and threw out runners with the very best of them, but he truly earned his keep by helping to develop an emerging group of young pitchers, including Koosman, Seaver, Gentry, McGraw, and Ryan. Teammates note Grote did this by force when necessary: he had a low tolerance for pitches that didn't go where he wanted them to go and often delivered that message with a hellacious return throw to the pitcher.

The tough love obviously had some effect. Seaver and Ryan thought enough of Grote to thank him by name at their respective Hall of Fame inductions.

Grote's acquisition may have flown under the radar at the time, but that was hardly the case with the Mets' two other most prominent 15s: **George Foster** and **Carlos Beltran**.

Foster had all the bona fides to perhaps become the last-ever 15 when the Mets traded for him in the winter of 1981 and subsequently signed him to a five-year, $10 million contract, the richest the team had ever given to that point. But Foster didn't have the kind of Mets career anyone had in mind.

The menacing black bat that once swatted 52 home runs in a season for the Reds was only good for 13 in 1982, Foster's first season as a Met. Foster cautioned pilots approaching LaGuardia not to fly too low, but that remark turned into a joke about pop-ups. Foster rebounded some in subsequent years—he knocked in 98 runs on 28 homers in 1983—a first step toward future glory for the team. Unfortunately for him, Foster wasn't around to taste champagne in 1986—he only rapped about it in the "Get Metsmerized" single—his unlistenable but lasting contribution to Mets lore. ("I live to play and that's my thing/This year we're gonna win the Series ring" rapped Foster in one of the song's better couplets). Struggling with a reduced role and hearing increasing boos, Foster was released midseason. So was "Get Metsmerized."

The "largest contract ever" label would later go to Beltran, whose performance over the course of his seven-year, $119 million contract would largely mirror that of the team: Valiently struggling in 2005; dominant in 2006; receding in 2007; rebounding in 2008; banged-up, controversial and largely unavailable in '09 and '10; and nearly relevant again in 2011. It was one hell of a ride.

Like Foster, Beltran's first year was underwhelming, but he got over it, posting one of the finest single seasons any Met ever had in 2006 (a team-record 41 home runs, 116 RBIs, 38 doubles and 18 stolen bases). He averaged 34 homers, 113 RBIs, and 112 runs scored between 2006 and 2008, but Beltran tasted pain with "the New Mets" as well: the face-first collision with Mike Cameron, watching Adam Wainwright's strike three to end the 2006 NLCS, and knees so bad Met fans learned more than they ever wanted to know about microfracture surgery. And if Beltran's signing kicked off a promising but ultimately unfulfilling era for Mets fans, his 2011 trade to San Francisco for pitching prospect Zack Wheeler helped to jump-start another.

The reconstruction that began with the Wheeler trade gained further momentum when the Mets swapped pitcher R. A. Dickey to Toronto in the winter of 2012 for a package of prospects including pitcher Noah Syndergaard and catcher **Travis d'Arnaud**, who took the No. 15 jersey upon his promotion from the minor leagues in 2014, though he switched to No. 7 in 2015. If he can stay on the field at least, d'Arnaud has a shot at becoming the Grote of this generation, while hitting that hopefully is closer to Piazza—or at least Stearns.

The first No. 15 in franchise history was diminutive lefty **Al Jackson** (1962–65), who lost 20 games twice but was probably the best young pitcher on the early Mets. Jackson held the franchise mark for most victories (43) until that record was broken by twenty-four-year-old Tom Seaver. Jackson was liberated to St. Louis for the 1966–67 seasons but returned in 1968 and 1969 for the last years of his playing career (wearing No. 38). Since then, Jackson has spent many years in the Mets' employ as a roving (or stationary) pitching instructor and is virtually the only remaining connection to the club's 1962 origins.

Pitcher **Rick Aguilera** (1987–88) switched from No. 38 to No. 15 in 1987; he'd move back to No. 38 as an All-Star closer with Minnesota. **Ron Darling** (1989–91) tried 15 after 44 and 12. It is the only number in which he had a losing record (18–20, 3.79 in 61 games). Shortstop **Kevin Elster,** who was close to Darling, requested he take over 15 after Darling was traded in 1991 but was convinced to wait until 1992, when he only got into six games before undergoing season-ending shoulder surgery.

One of the more underappreciated Mets was **Jose Vizcaino** (1994–96), the goggle-wearing middle infielder acquired from the Cubs for Anthony Young in 1994. Vizcaino in 1995 had perhaps the best offensive season by a Mets shortstop until Jose Reyes came along, but that was forgotten amid the eye-opening arrival of Rey Ordoñez in 1996. Vizcaino is probably better remembered by Mets fans for ending the nightmarish Game 1 of the 2000 World Series with a game-winning, 12th-inning single for the Yankees.

Shortly after Vizcaino was traded to Cleveland in 1996—a throw-in to "even out" the Carlos Baerga and Alvaro Espinoza for Jeff Kent fiasco—No. 15 went to minor league journeyman **Matt Franco** (1996–2000). Franco, nephew of actor Kurt Russell and a Bobby Valentine favorite, subsequently became one of the franchise's all-time pinch-hitting specialists, remembered still for the game-winning hit off Mariano Rivera in a 1999 interleague game.

Two short-burning, enigmatic outfielders arrived in June trades, wore No. 15, and quietly left town afterward. **Claudell Washington** (1980), who shortly after arriving hit three of his ten Met home runs in a single game against the Dodgers, ran away from the troubled Mets after the season. The arrival of **Richard Hidalgo** (2004) invigorated the franchise for as long as he was hot, which was one month and one month only (although it did help fuel the Mets' first-ever sweep of the Yankees).

The rest wore 15 for even shorter periods: **Butch Benton** (1978), the Mets' top draft in 1975 (sixth overall) was the first to succeed Grote in the 15 jersey but his career stalled in the high minors; journeyman southpaw **Dave Roberts** (1981) signed a two-year free-agent contract but lasted just two months; infielder **Brian Giles** debuted that September; **Jeff McKnight** made his Mets debut wearing No. 15 in 1989, the first of a record five number issues; reliever **Don Aase** made the Mets as a non-roster invitee in 1989 but wore 15 briefly before switching to No. 49; outfielder **Brady Clark** donned 15 in 2002, the first of two Mets stints; minor-league hitting legend **Val Pascucci** (2011) was the first to succeed Beltran in No. 15; and outfielder **Fred Lewis** passed through during 2012's garbage time, or, to be more specific about a trashed season, September 2012 garbage time.

Number 15

Number of times issued: 23 (20 players, 3 coaches)

Longest tenured: Jerry Grote (12 seasons, 1,235 games); Carlos Beltran (7 seasons, 839 games); George Foster (5 seasons, 655 games)

Best single season: Carlos Beltran, 2006 (.275/.388/.594, 41 HR, 116 RBIs); Beltran, 2007 (.276/.353/.525, 33 HR, 112 RBIs); Beltran, 2008 (.284/.376/.500, 27 HR, 112 RBIs); Foster, 1984 (.269/.311/.443, 24 HR, 86 RBIs).

Career statistical leaders: Home runs (Beltran 149, Foster 99), RBI (Beltran 559, Foster 361, Grote 357), batting average (Vizcaino .282, Beltran .280, Claudell Washington .275), wins (Al Jackson 40); ERA (Ron Darling 3.79)

Catch Them if You Can: Catchers by the Numbers

Catchers once all looked the same: shin guards, chest protector, glove, mask, and cap on backwards. Many catchers flipped up the bill on their cap to help keep the mask in place. That was about as stylish as it got. They all looked a lot like Jerry Grote and batted somewhere around seventh or eighth in the order, depending on how weak the weakest-hitting infielder was. Grote played 1,235 games as a Met, fourth-most in club history; it wasn't his fashion, his personality, or his hitting that got his name on the lineup card.

Grote was the antithesis of Cincinnati slugger Johnny Bench. While both were excellent receivers, Bench popularized the style of catching with one hand, using a hinged glove like Randy Hundley of the Cubs. Bench wore a helmet under his mask, an idea that resounded with catchers who didn't deem it a badge of courage to get a foul ball off the coconut with only a cloth cap for protection (helmets for catchers became mandatory in 1987). Grote still caught with both hands and without a helmet—there's even a yearbook photo of his young son in catching gear with a cloth cap—but Grote's backups kept their noggins protected.

J. C. Martin and Duffy Dyer were Mets trailblazers with batting helmets underneath their masks. Ron Hodges spent a dozen seasons at Shea wearing a catching helmet with no brim, resembling a bowl that might be used to cut an unkempt child's hair. Alex Treviño wore one just like it. John Stearns, always his own man, sometimes wore a brimmed helmet and sometimes not. (Stearns graced the cover of the 1978 Mets yearbook—the last edition that cost a buck—diving and missing a tag in his cloth-capped glory.) Dude's catching helmet—he wore one with an earflap while batting—sported his number 12 in orange on the back. Bruce Bochy's head was so large that he had to have a custom-made helmet that never seemed the right shade of blue (he arrived at camp in 1981 with a size 8 helmet in Astros orange: officials had to paint it blue).

Gary Carter provided stability and style at the position. The Kid used a mask with a built-in throat protector, and he wore the same headgear to both hit and catch. Todd Hundley, Mike Piazza, and Paul Lo Duca succeeded him as All-Stars at the position. Piazza made New Yorkers proud with his homemade "NYPD" batting helmet in the team colors in 2001. Piazza was an early advocate of Knee Savers, padding that fits over the back of the calves to help relieve some stress on the knees while crouching. If only Piazza, perhaps the best-hitting catcher ever, could have worn a full suit of armor to protect him from the dings and tips that constantly riddled him . . . it couldn't have hurt his throwing.

Backup backstops are often innovators of the tools of ignorance. Sourpuss Charlie O'Brien donned the first "hockey mask" in the majors with Toronto in 1997, four years after leaving the Mets. Alberto Castillo, a classic catch-and-throw guy—because he certainly wasn't a hit or run guy—first brought hockey to Shea. In late '97 he donned this newfangled tool of ignorance, complete with oversized baseball stitches painted white on blue and a big orange "NY" over the skull, perhaps half a foot of padding more than Jerry Grote ever had, or wanted. Kelly Stinnett, who'd replaced Charlie O. as backup catcher back in 1994, returned to the Mets briefly in 2006 and donned the hockey mask seven times.

Josh Thole got the out—and a concussion—on a collision with Ty Wiggington in 2012. In his first start after changing to a hockey mask, he caught Johan Santana's no-hitter. The most interesting part-timer may have been Jason Phillips. Not only did he wear those funky Bono-like glasses every game, day or night, but he wore his helmet forward, with the mask fitting over the brim. On your knees, boy.

The Mets through 2015 have employed 91 catchers, more than half of whom played fewer than 100 games. Following are the uniform numbers appearing most frequently on their catchers' backs:

Number	Catchers Appearing	Notes
9	8	Neither Joe Torre nor Todd Zeile count (Zeile's two catching appearances came while wearing No. 27).
5	7	The first four 5s in Met history were catchers (Hobie Landrith, Joe Pignatano, Norm Sherry, Chris Cannizzaro).
20	7	Mike Fitzgerald and Anthony Recker share record of 115 games each behind the dish.
33	6	All hail the obscure backstops of 33: Chuck Estrada, Barry Lyons, Kelly Stinnett, Tim Spehr, Mike DiFelice and Mike Kincade.
7	6	Digit of Jeff McKnight's lone inning behind the dish, 1993.
8	5	List includes Hall of Famers Gary Carter and Yogi Berra.

#16: OH, DOCTOR

As soon as **Dwight Gooden** arrived in 1984, the days of the downtrodden Mets seemed like a thing of the past. They were.

Everything about the young hurler was distinctive, including his age (nineteen) and his uniform number (the first Met pitcher to wear No. 16), but what set him apart from mere mortal Mets was what happened when he unleashed his electric right arm on the unsuspecting National League.

Gooden was something of a secret weapon when Davey Johnson took over as manager in 1984. Johnson had gotten a taste of Gooden's stuff during the 1983 Class AAA playoffs after Gooden was recalled to Tidewater from Class A Lynchburg, where all he'd done was whiff 300 batters in 191 innings. A strong proponent of promoting Gooden all the way to the big leagues in 1984, Johnson won a brief battle of wills with general manager Frank Cashen. It was a fight worth winning.

Doctor K electrified Shea Stadium, turning in a spectacular Rookie of the Year campaign and an even better season in 1985, when he went 24–4 with a club-record 1.53 ERA, 8 shutouts, and a Cy Young Award. The following year was not quite as dominant (17–6, 2.84), but the world championship was realized.

Dwight Gooden in his prime could get the crowd going at Shea Stadium, in spring training, or in a phone booth.

Although he reached mind-boggling heights in these early years, injuries and a recurring drug problem assured that Gooden spent much of his remaining days as a Met hiking the hills and valleys along the comeback trail. Struggling with an ERA of 6.31 in June 1994, Gooden was suspended by the league for violating his drug treatment program, a move that ultimately ended his Mets career in shame. He later compounded his sins by joining the Yankees, becoming a member of a world championship team there and throwing the no-hitter in the Bronx that every Mets fan who saw him in '84 and '85 assumed he would get in Flushing.

Gooden was a bit of uni number experimenter. He wore No. 64 in spring training of 1993 as a means of recapturing the focus of the 1984 training camp when he first won a job. He also spent some time wearing No. 00 as a means to cut the tension during the uptight spring training of 1989 (Roger McDowell joined Doc, wearing No. 0). At the same time, Gooden could be fiercely protective of his No. 16, swiftly squashing speculation that he might surrender it to Frank Viola when the latter pitcher was acquired in 1989. Viola had worn 16 in Minnesota for eight seasons, including a Cy Young year.

"I don't care how much money he makes. He can have my locker. I'll take him to the best restaurants and show him New York. He can even have my wife," Doc told *Newsday*. "But he can't have my number, no way."

Viola took another number, but that wasn't the case when the Mets acquired another one-time pitching sensation, **Hideo Nomo**, in 1998. Nomo took his old Dodgers number and became the first Met to wear 16 since Gooden's departure. He didn't do it much justice, going 4–5 and showing none of his Dodgers flash. Nomo's final appearance wearing 16 with the Mets was the last day of the season, a fine relief effort in a doomed game that dashed the club's blundered hopes of the postseason. He pitched for six other teams, including a triumphant return to the Dodgers in 2002, but Nomo wore 16 no more.

While Gooden was reportedly unhappy with the Mets issuing his number to Nomo, the next two wearers of the jersey asked for and received Doc's blessing.

Outfielder **Derek Bell** (2000), the booby prize in the Mike Hampton trade, had long worn No. 16 in other locales as a tribute to Gooden, who preceded him from Tampa to the big leagues and whom Bell considered a hero. Bell's most distinctive uniform characteristic belonged not his shirt, but to his pants, which were wide enough to serve as an auxiliary sail on the Hudson River–docked houseboat Bell lived on during his stay with the Mets.

Gooden's former teammate **David Cone** paid him tribute by wearing No. 16 during what proved to be the final days of his career in 2003.

Lee Mazzilli was a different kind of teen idol. The Brooklyn-born outfielder, who wore No. 16 for the majority of his time as a Mets regular, was about the best thing the Mets had during the disco era, and they never let their fans forget it.

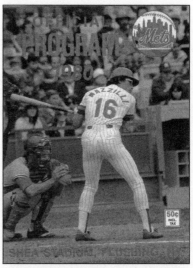

The handsome, 14th overall pick in the 1973 draft—literally made a poster boy in a 1978 Shea giveaway—was a capable, switch-hitting outfielder with some power, speed, and a good batting eye at a time when it was difficult to find a Met possessing any of those qualities. He wore his pants as tight as Bell's were loose. Beaten-up Mets fans of 1979 fondly recall Mazzilli's smashing performance in the All-Star Game at the Kingdome that year. He went 1-for-1 with a game-winning, bases-loaded

The tight No. 16 uniform that housed Lee Mazzilli's assets helped move programs for a 1980 team whose roster wasn't worth four bits.

walk against Ron Guidry, and a pop-fly of a home run to the left field corner that to Met fans looked like a 500-footer.

Mazzilli's trade to Texas following the 1981 season helped launch the Mets' mid-1980s glory years by bringing Ron Darling and Walt Terrell to New York, but Maz returned for a victory lap in 1986 (wearing No. 13 now that Gooden commanded 16).

Mazzilli, whose other exploits include youth speedskating titles, a big-league managing gig with the Orioles, a stint as studio analyst on SNY and starring role in an off-Broadway production of *Tony & Tina's Wedding* most recently has been watching the ascent of his son L.J., a second baseman in the Mets farm system last seen wearing No. 13 as a '15 Binghamton Met.

When the Mets failed to lure free agent Carlos Delgado in 2005, they settled for strong glove/weak bat **Doug Mientkiewicz**. His discount performance prompted the Mets to bench him and then trade for Delgado the following year.

Brooklyn-born (like Mazzilli), and a childhood fan of the Gooden-era Mets of the 1980s, **Paul Lo Duca** was an ideal No. 16. Acquired in a trade with the Marlins following the 2005 season, Lo Duca made the unenviable task of succeeding Mike Piazza look like a breeze. The catcher hit .318 with 39 doubles in his first season with the Mets and provided "red ass" intensity that fans appreciated and opponents didn't. He had trouble repeating the trick in 2007.

At his best, outfielder **Angel Pagan** (2008–11) was a kind of poor man's Carlos Beltran: With the latter missing parts of the 2009 and 2010 seasons with injuries, Pagan filled the void admirably, hitting .306 in a half-season in '09 and .290 in 2010, when he added 37 stolen bases, 31 doubles, 11 home runs, and 7 triples. Pagan struggled in 2011 and was shipped to San Francisco in what was easily Sandy Alderson's worst trade—netting Andres Torres—a very poor man's Angel Pagan—along with washed up reliever Ramon Ramirez. Pagan regained his winning form and earned two World Series rings.

A trio of inconsequential veterans followed Pagan in the 16 jersey: Catcher **Rob Johnson** (2012), and ex-phenoms **Rick Ankiel** (2013) and **Daisuke Matsuzaka** (2013–14). Matsuzaka was still seeking repossession of his once-famous gyroball when the Mets scooped him off the waiver wire. He eventually rounded into an acceptable swingman in 2014 (3–3, 3.89 in 34 games, including 9 starts).

The first wearer of the No. 16 jersey was reserve outfielder **Bobby Gene Smith**, who holds the distinction of being the first active player the Mets ever traded. The guy they received for him, catcher **Sammy Taylor**, inherited his No. 16 jersey. Catcher **Jesse Gonder** wore 16 briefly in 1963 but turned it over to **Dick Smith** in midseason. Smith (1963–64) and the man who followed him in the 16 jersey, **Danny Napoleon** (1965–66), were typical early Mets: free-swinging minor league sluggers whose power didn't translate to the big leagues. Following Napoleon were reserves **Tommy Reynolds** (1967), **Kevin Collins** (1968), and Queens native **Mike Jorgensen** (1969–71).

Crouching, choked-up slap-hitter **Felix Millan** wore No. 16 for 1973, his first year with the Mets. Millan switched to 17 a year later while reserve outfielder **Dave Schneck** switched into 16. Catcher **John Stearns** began his Mets career wearing No. 16 (1975–76).

Danny Muno, a 2011 draftee, was the first prospect acquired by the Alderson front office to reach the big leagues with the Mets but was unable to stick. A .148 batting average will do that. **Dilson Herrera** took 16 later in 2015 when his previously issued No. 2 went instead to Juan Uribe while Herrera was in the minors. No. 16 patiently awaits its next wearer of distinction.

Number 16

Number of times issued: 18 (18 players)

Longest tenured: Dwight Gooden (11 seasons, 305 games), Lee Mazzilli (5 seasons, 702 games)

Best single season: Dwight Gooden, 1985 (24–4, 1.53 ERA, 268 strikeouts in 278 1/3 innings, Cy Young Award); Gooden, 1984 (17–6, 2.60 ERA, 276 strikeouts in 218 innings, Rookie of the Year); Paul Lo Duca, 2006 (.318/.355/.428, 5 HR, 49 RBIs); Lee Mazzilli, 1979 (.305/.395/.449, 15 HR, 79 RBIs)

Career statistical leaders: Home runs (Mazzilli 59, Derek Bell 18); RBI (Mazzilli 296, Paul Lo Duca 103); batting average (Lo Duca .297, Felix Millan .290, Mazzilli .271); wins (Gooden 157), saves (Daisuke Matsuzaka 1, Gooden 1); ERA (Gooden 3.10)

The Whiff of Success: Strikeouts by the Numbers

On May 18, 2005, soon-to-be-released Mets relief pitcher Manny Aybar faced the Cincinnati Reds in the top of the 9th inning and the Mets leading, 10–3. And though Aybar surrendered a double, a single, and a two-run homer during the inning, when he caught Ryan Freel looking at strike three for the first out, it marked a momentous occasion in team history: The moment 36 surpassed 41 as the uniform number to produce the most strikeouts in Mets history.

That nobody had occupied the 41 jersey for twenty-three years speaks well of the greatness of Tom Seaver, who provided 2,541 strikeouts—roughly 96 percent of the strikeouts of all Mets to wear No. 41 (or close to the same number as his percentage of votes for Hall of Fame induction). Seaver by himself, in fact, struck out more batters than all the combined wearers of all Mets numbers but for 36, which draws most of its power from Jerry Koosman's 1,799 whiffs. No. 36 also has the advantage of twenty-four other guys on the job, including Tracy Stallard (228 Ks), Ed Lynch (223), and Greg McMichael (143). Thanks to retiring the 41 jersey in 1988, it is stuck at five wearers and 2,651 Ks forever.

But movement elsewhere is afoot: Heading into 2016, just 125 strikeouts separate the respective numerical-teams of Steven Matz, Matt Harvey, Noah Syndergaard and Jacob deGrom: Game on!

Following is a list of the most strikeouts by a Mets uniform number through 2015.

No.	Strikeouts	Notes
36	2,819	Koosman with 1,799; Tracy Stallard 228; Ed Lynch 223.
41	2,651	All but 110 Ks by Seaver (2,541).
45	2,177	Tug McGraw leads with 618; Pedro Martinez second with 464.
38	2,148	30 contributors led by Dave Mlicki with 402 Ks and reliever Skip Lockwood with 368.
16	2,094	Doc Gooden 1,875; blowout position player Rob Johnson with 1.
32	2,025	With 1,023 whiffs, Jon Matlack accounts for more than half.
33	1,915	Matt Harvey (449) on the doorstep of all-time leader John Maine (467.)
34	1,908	Mike Pelfrey leads with 506.
29	1,902	Steve Trachsel rang up 580 victims; Frank Viola 314.
48	1,900	Only a matter of time before Jacob deGrom (349) overtakes leader Aaron Heilman (395).
39	1,887	Gary Gentry leads with 563 followed by Bobby Parnell (293).
35	1,870	Dillon Gee departs with 101 fewer whiffs than leader Rick Reed (590).
27	1,859	Craig Swan leads with 671, but Jeurys Familia (177) should maintain consistent uniform dividends.
47	1,851	Leader Tom Glavine (516) overcame Jesse Orosco (506) in what looks to be the final indignity.
22	1,763	Al Leiter with 1,106; Fat Jack Fisher with 475.

#17: "I'M KEITH HERNANDEZ"

On July 4, 2010, in the top of the seventh inning of what was to be a 9–5 Mets win over the Washington Nationals, **Fernando Tatis** entered the game as a pinch hitter for Chris Carter. Tatis singled and advanced to third on a run-scoring double by Angel Pagan but was left on base when David Wright stuck out. Following the game the Mets placed Tatis on the 15-day disabled list with a right shoulder sprain from which Tatis never returned.

That was the last time a No. 17 appeared in a Mets game.

By then, the wonton reissuing of **Keith Hernandez**'s former number had become something of an annual indignity for Mets fans. Before Tatis, it was useless reserve **David Newhan** (2007), and before that, pitching disaster **Jose Lima** (2006). They joined a parade of lesser-lights in 17 going back a full decade: **Dae Sung Koo** (2005); **Wilson Delgado** (2004); **Jason Anderson** and **Graeme Lloyd** (2003); **Satoru Komiyama** (2002); **Kevin Appier** (2001); **Mike Bordick** (2000); **Luis Lopez** (1997–99) and **Brent Mayne** (1996).

The predictable handwringing from fans—and from Hernandez himself, who occasionally used the bully pulpit of the broadcast booth to bemoan the seeming carelessness with which his number was reissued—appeared to have finally gotten the attention of the Mets during the 2010–11 offseason. After infielder Chin-Lung Hu was acquired from the Dodgers in a December trade, an online version of the Mets roster listed Hu as having been assigned No. 17. A week later the Mets held a press conference introducing Hu and conspicuously presenting him with a No. 25 jersey. While on one level the press event served to publicize the acquisition of a Taiwanese-born player to Queens' diverse residents, it was a lot of effort for a reserve infielder with a career .191 batting average and no options destined for release weeks into the season.

The Wilpon-hears-a-Hu incident marked a stealth retirement for No. 17. Thanks to post-career *Seinfeld* appearances and a long-running gig as New York's most acerbic, honest, and entertaining sportscaster, Hernandez's stature continues growing long after six-and-a-half resplendent years in blue and orange.

Acquired from the Cardinals in June of 1983 at the bargain price of Neil Allen and Rick Ownbey, Hernandez (1983–89) was not unlike a lot of new arrivals to New York: He needed to fight it for a bit to see how he fit in. Mex was dealing with cocaine allegations that hastened his departure from St. Louis and struggling with the question of whether the Mets were the kind of team he would want to sign with again when his contract expired following the 1984 season.

For another thing, the uniform number he'd worn to a batting title and co-MVP award in 1979 (37) was unavailable, as it had been retired for Casey Stengel in 1966. And since the '83 Mets already employed a 7 (Hubie Brooks), a 27 (Craig Swan), and a 47 (Jesse Orosco), Hernandez had to adjust to 17.

Although the 1983 Mets were far from a success, Hernandez found just enough talent on the horizon—and excitement in the city—to commit to a five-year engagement in what he'd once considered "baseball Siberia." What the Mets got in return was one of the team's all-time performers: a revolutionary defensive player, a skilled hitter slotted comfortably in the No. 3 slot in the lineup, and the headstrong,

Keith Hernandez displays that sweet stroke that is just part of the Legend of Mex.

Dan Carubia

urbane, chatty, on-field general who'd guide the team through its best era.

Batting averages over his first four Mets seasons—.306, .311, .309, and .310—illustrate just how consistent Hernandez could be offensively, while

Gold Glove awards in eleven consecutive seasons (seven as a Met) only begin to describe the swashbuckling style with which Mex played first base. His aggressive, daring defense could change the opposition's strategy.

Mets teammates found Hernandez unforgettable as well. Pitcher **David Cone** switched from 44 to 17 midway through the 1991 season as a tribute to his departed teammate and brought the number to the All-Star Game in 1992. Ex-teammates Ron Darling (Oakland A's), Bobby Ojeda (Los Angeles Dodgers), and Roger McDowell (Dodgers, following Ojeda) all wore their respect for Hernandez on their backs after leaving the Mets. Cone wore 17 again with the Royals in 1993.

Whatever the recent past or future holds for No. 17, it should be noted that short-lived and insignificant players wearing 17 were a Mets tradition long before Mex arrived. **Rod Gaspar** (1969–70) and **Ted Martinez** (1970–73) were modest but useful role players for the '69 and '73 pennant-winning Mets; outfielder **Jerry Morales** (1980) wasn't so magical. **Ellis Valentine** (1981–82) was a one-time fearsome power hitter and possessor of the strongest right-field arm in baseball, but by the time he got to the Mets (from Montreal in a poor trade for fireballing reliever Jeff Reardon), aftereffects of a beaning rendered him harmless with a bat in his hands.

The lone exception to the pre-Keith hole at 17 was second baseman **Felix Millan**. Like Hernandez, Millan led his team in hits multiple times, played outstanding defense, and wore one of the more memorable mustaches in team history.

Millan (1974–77) rarely struck out and—very much unlike Hernandez—rarely walked. Choking up on the bat as though it were a dumbbell Millan slapped (and we mean slapped) 191 hits in 1975, a team record that stood for twenty-one years. All but 40 of those hits were singles. Millan that season also became the first Met to play 162 games in a single year, a team record matched by John Olerud in 1999.

Jacob Kanarek/From Worst to First

No Met has ever choked up on the bat as much (or as famously) as Felix Millan.

Millan had a fiery temper that inadvertently brought an end to his major league career. Following a collision at second base he foolishly threw a punch at massive Pirates catcher Ed Ott, who summarily body-slammed Millan to the Three Rivers Stadium turf, dislocating Millan's shoulder, sending him to Japan, and ushering in the **Gil Flores** (1978–79) era at 17. It would be a long wait indeed for Keith.

That 17 was going to be a frequently issued number was evident all the way back in 1962, when it debuted on the back of **Don Zimmer** and then went to infamous catcher **Choo Choo Coleman.** Zimmer, the first third baseman in team history, suffered through an 0-for-34 slump but rallied all the way to 4-for-52 before being released in early May.

Coleman (1962–63) was a speedy, left-handed hitting, defensively challenged catcher whose peculiarities made him a legend on the scale of a minor Marv Throneberry. Coleman made uniform number history when he reportedly welcomed roommate Charlie Neal back after the 1962 season by saying, "I know you. You're No. 4."

Veteran pitcher **Frank Lary** was the first two-time Met in team history and a curious one at that. Purchased from the Detroit Tigers in May 1964, Lary made thirteen forgettable appearances and was sent away to the Milwaukee Braves that August (in exchange for pitcher **Dennis Ribant**, who wore the 17 jersey the rest of the year). Lary, however, reported to Mets camp the following spring, leading to speculation there were under-the-table conditions to the deal the previous summer: was Lary only loaned to the Braves, or was he, like original Met Harry Chiti, traded for himself? The Mets explained, vaguely, that Lary was payment for certain debts owed in the aftermath of one or more of the fifteen "conditional" deals the Mets and Braves had engaged in over the past three seasons. Whatever. The first two-time Met in team history was more effective the second time around, going 1–3, 2.98 in fourteen appearances, including seven starts. But he'd be on the move again—for good this time—to the White Sox in July.

Dick Stuart (1966) wanted Ed Kranepool's number (7) and job (first base), but didn't get either. A prodigious slugger with an ego to match, Stuart had hit 28 home runs in 1965 with the Phillies but accounted for only 4 by the time the Mets released him in June of '66. Stuart wasn't a complete disappointment: With 6 errors in 23 games at first base, he lived up to his nickname, "Dr. Strangeglove."

Mets fans were titillated at glowing reports of the speedy switch-hitting minor league center fielder they'd acquired from Pittsburgh over the 1967 offseason and could hardly believe their eyes when he turned out to be slight, balding **Don Bosch** (1967–68). In parts of two seasons he hit only .157 and, needless to say, failed to solve the club's longstanding center field problem.

The Mets paid full retail—exciting young Melvin Mora—for summer rental Bordick when they needed an experienced shortstop for 2000's pennant run. He faltered come fall and by winter was back in Baltimore as a free agent. But Bordick was small beer when it came to lost free agents in 2000. After NLCS MVP Mike Hampton ditched the Mets for the Denver school system, it was a long step down to the next-best available free agent pitcher: veteran right-hander Appier (2001). The one-time Kansas City phenom got a great contract but was only so-so; so he and the balance of his contract went to the Angels in exchange for Mo Vaughn and a whole new set of expensive problems.

Talented but cold pitcher **Bret Saberhagen** (1994–95) wore 17 for two of his four years with the Mets, including an excellent '94 (14–4, 2.74 ERA, and a stunning 143:13 strikeout to walk ratio).

Explaining that his name was difficult to pronounce, Korean-born lefty relief pitcher Dae Sung Koo (2005) informed media and teammates he'd prefer to be referred to as "Mr. Koo." Mr. Koo's one and only career highlight was shocking the Yankees' Hall-of-Fame bound Randy Johnson by blasting a double to deep center field, and then completing the humiliation by brazenly scoring from second on a bunt with a swanlike, full-Met-jacketed dive on a subsequent sacrifice bunt. In a nationally televised game.

Bret Saberhagen was all about control–at least on the mound..

Lopez (1997–99) filled in for Rey Ordoñez at shortstop, out-hit Rey-Rey as a Met (.250 to .245), and once punched the Gold Glover on the team bus, which was something everyone wished they'd done when Ordoñez later called the Shea fans "stupid." Lopez was part of two shocking developments on September 14, 1997. First, he started the game wearing 17 on "Keith Hernandez Day" when many fans hoped the number might be put in storage to honor Mex (when the Mets honored Mookie Wilson the year before they had the sense to outfit his numerical successor, Lance Johnson, in a temporary number). Second, the banjo-hitting Lopez socked a homer for the only run in a 1–0 win that afternoon.

Who else? Backup catcher **Jim Schaffer** (1965); whiff-prone outfielder **Larry Elliot** (1966); utility man **Jeff McKnight** (1993) in the third of his five numerical stops. And we'll end where we began, with the last wearer of 17. Tatis (2008–10) came out of retirement to add pop off the bench, reuniting with GM Omar Minaya, who as a Texas scout had signed Fernando 15 years earlier. Tatis put up a .297/.369/.484 line with 11 home runs to earn both 2008 NL Comeback Player of the Year and accolades from Keith Hernandez, ever watchful in the booth.

Number 17

Number of times issued: 30 (20 position players, 10 pitchers)

Longest tenured: Keith Hernandez (7 seasons, 880 games), Felix Millan (4 seasons, 528 games)

Best single seasons: Hernandez, 1984 (.311/.409/.449, 15 HR, 94 RBIs); Bret Saberhagen, 1994 (14–4, 2.74 ERA); David Cone, 1991 (14–14, 3.29, 241 strikeouts in 232 2/3 innings)

Career statistical leaders: Home runs (Hernandez 80, Fernando Tatis 21, Ellis Valentine 13); RBI (Hernandez 468, Felix Millan 145, Tatis 101); batting average (Hernandez .297, Wilson Delgado .292, Tatis .279); wins (Cone 24); ERA (Saberhagen 2.98)

This One Goes Out: Numerical Tributes

As noted above, Keith Hernandez left such a strong enough impression on teammates like David Cone, Ron Darling, and Roger McDowell that they went on to honor him by wearing his number elsewhere. Worth noting is McDowell, who switched to 17 in 1993, left behind his old Dodgers number, 31, to be picked up by a young catcher named Piazza. That the Mets retired No. 31 therefore can be traced almost directly to Hernandez, who, of course, is an indirect numerical descendent of Casey Stengel.

From the obscure (Tito Fuentes, Ken Boswell, John Mabry) to the legendary (Ted Williams, Roberto Clemente, Jackie Robinson), following is a list of some Mets and the men they honored with their choice of uniform number:

No.	Player/manager	In honor of
9	George Theodore	Ted Williams
10	Terry Collins	Jim Leyland

No.	Player/manager	In honor of
12	Willie Randolph	Ken Boswell
13	Edgardo Alfonzo	Dave Concepcion
13	Jorge Velandia	Edgardo Alfonzo
17	David Cone	Keith Hernandez
20	Neil Walker	Tom Walker
21	Carlos Delgado	Roberto Clemente
23	Ted Martinez	Tito Fuentes
42	Butch Huskey	Jackie Robinson
42	Mo Vaughn	Jackie Robinson
45	John Franco	Tug McGraw
47	Joe McEwing	John Mabry
56	Darren Bragg	Lawrence Taylor

#18: DAR-RYL!

Darryl Strawberry is always going to be 18.

That was his age when the Mets drafted him, first in the nation, out of Crenshaw High in Los Angeles in 1980. At eighteen, all things were possible. "Best tools I've seen in thirty years," one scout gushed. "The black Ted Williams," others suggested.

That was just the beginning of the expectations heaped upon a kid who, just as expected, would become the greatest offensive player the organization had ever developed. At the same time, this Rookie

Strawberry Donut: Darryl Strawberry works with a weighted bat before a game at Shea.

Dan Carubia

of the Year, this shoulda-been '88 MVP, this seven-time Mets All-Star, this Game 7 homering right fielder would never escape suspicion that that his promise went unfulfilled.

Between arriving as a wide-eyed rookie in the May of 1983 and leaving as a bitter free agent in 1990, Strawberry hit more home runs (252), scored more runs (633), and drove in more runs (733) than any Met before him (his home run total still stands as the all-time mark as 2016 dawns, while he remains top-five in virtually all meaningful offensive categories). Somehow he did all of that while appearing at times that he wasn't trying very hard. Part of that was the illusion of his gracefulness—Strawberry took long, easy strides in the field and on the base paths and unfolded long, powerful arms when he swung—and part unreasonable expectations to meet. Strawberry, like no other Met, seemed to grasp that fan sentiment and through comments to the media, he fed it, always promising to have "a monster season" while providing only very good ones. He knew how to hurt fans, too, telling them "now you'll see the *real* Darryl Strawberry," while displaying a new uniform number—44—on a Dodger jersey after signing with his hometown team as a free agent.

If that were so, we'd take the unreal Strawberry. Over the next nine seasons Strawberry would encounter legal troubles, health scares, and drug scandals while toiling in 44 (Dodgers), 17 (Giants), and 26 and 39 (Yankees) while hitting only 83 home runs. He was 18 no longer.

Felix Mantilla (1962) was the first shortstop in Mets history, even though he spent most of 1962 as a third baseman. The Mets got three players for Mantilla in a trade with the Red Sox after the season, but the deal still blew up in their faces. One of the returnees was **Pumpsie Green** (1963), remembered as the first player to break the color barrier for the last team to integrate. Green was a switch-hitting, versatile infielder who reached base at a pretty good clip, but he arrived at Mets camp overweight and spent most of the year in AAA.

Lost in the twin tragedies of the Seaver and Kingman trades of June 15, 1977, was a third trade that sent reserve infielder Mike Phillips to St. Louis for **Joel Youngblood** (1977–82). That one didn't turn out all that bad.

Youngblood played some third base, second base, and all three outfield positions for the Mets, although his versatility might also have been a curse in that Joe Torre never found him a regular position. His strong arm was suited best for right field, but the Mets couldn't resist the temptation of trying power bats there. Youngblood didn't like third base and vice-versa but for his part hit nearly everywhere he was asked to play. He led the team in home runs (16) and doubles (37) in 1979 and was challenging for the league batting crown in 1981—his only All-Star season—when he got injured.

Youngblood is destined to be remembered for becoming the first man to get hits for two different teams in the same day: He singled for the Mets in a day game at Wrigley Field, was informed he was traded to Montreal,

Dan Carubia

Joel Youngblood had a cannon for an arm and showed it at six different positions.

and joined the Expos that night in Philadelphia, where he singled off Steve Carlton (wearing No. 25, by the way). The circumstances overshadowed the fact that the second Youngblood trade also turned out pretty well for the Mets, bringing pitcher Tom Gorman.

Youngblood was the last player to wear 18 before Strawberry; **Bret Saberhagen** (1992–93) was the first to receive No. 18 after him. Saberhagen had worn No. 18 to stardom (and two Cy Young Awards) in Kansas City, but the Mets didn't get a good season from him until he changed to No. 17 in 1994.

Moises Alou came to the Mets with a reputation for a strong bat, a weak glove, and shaky health, and he didn't disappoint on any count. The forty-year-old outfielder clobbered the ball at a .341/.392/.524 clip and fashioned a team-record 30-game hitting streak in 2007. He hit even better in 2008 but in only 15 games before injuries ended his season, and his career.

Alou's arrival in New York forced **Jose Valentin** to switch to No. 22. Wearing 18 in 2006, Valentin sat on the bench while two other men tried and failed to nail down the second base job: When he finally got his chance, he socked 18 home runs (including two grand slams) and hit .271 in a comeback year.

In what seemed like a deliberate attempt to sedate the manager's office after the frenzy of the Bobby Valentine era, the Mets hired low-key skipper **Art Howe** in 2003 and subsequently put fans to sleep. Probably remembered best for Mike Piazza's botched transition to first base, Howe appeared to be a quiet observer while a front-office leadership crisis (and to be sure, poor results on the field) led to his own firing late in 2004—an event the tabloid readers knew sooner than Howe did. Howe met this fate the way he always did, with quiet dignity, staying on as a lame duck until the end of the season.

The remaining 18s are almost entirely reserves of various skill. Pitcher **Dennis Ribant** wore 18 for the first part of 1965, was sent to the minors, and returned in September to see the jersey on the back of recently acquired utility man **Gary Kolb.** Ribant switched to No. 30, and Kolb, who hit just .167, was traded following the season. Diminutive outfielder **Al Luplow** and infielder **Joe Moock** shared 18 in 1967, the Summer of Love, when the Mets were giving anyone a chance. **Duffy Dyer** (1968) got the only one of his 440 Met hits while not wearing No. 10 during his major league debut as 18. It was also worn by reserve outfielders **Jim Gosger** (1969), **Dave Marshall** (1970–72), **George Theodore** (1973), and **Benny Ayala** (1974) whose Mets career peaked with a home run in his first turn at-bat.

Jeff McKnight (1994) took 18 when Saberhagen switched to 17. It would be McKnight's fifth and final number with the Mets. More short-lived scrubeenos followed in 18, including **Jeff Barry** (1995), **Kevin Roberson** (1996), **Craig Paquette** (1998) and **Todd Haney** (1998). Gangly starter **Jeff D'Amico** (2002) pitched some wonderful games early in the year but was out of the rotation by August and out of New York for good soon after.

In Japan, No. 18 has a long association with ace pitchers, a tradition dating back to the 1930s when top hurlers were often issued No. 8 (Eiji Sawamura, Japan's equivalent of Cy Young) or 18 (Japan Hall of Fame pitchers Masao Date, Motoshi Fujita, and Tsuneo Horiuchi). In the modern era, top pitchers like Hideki Irabu, Daisuke Matuzsaka and Masahiro Tanaka each wore 18 before arriving stateside. (Matsuzaka would wear 16 when he joined the Mets in 2013.)

The Mets' first Japanese player, **Takashi Kashiwada**, was a modest left-handed relief pitcher and not an ace. Kashiwada's 1997 debut was two months before Irabu splashed down, toadlike, in the Bronx, making Kashiwada New York's first Japanese import. Higher hopes accompanied **Ryota Igarashi** (2010–11) to New York but the would-be set-up man was more of a let-down man, pitching to a 7.12 ERA in his debut season while bouncing between the Mets and their farm clubs for two years.

No shame in being the second-best Darryl to wear No. 18 for the Mets: That was 1999 stretch-run pickup **Darryl Hamilton** (1999–2001), who hit .339 that year, helping the Mets into a postseason for the first time in more than a decade. Hamilton played out the remainder of his big league career as a Mets reserve.

Marlon Anderson (2005) had a fine year as a pinch hitter, highlighted by a 9th-inning pinch-hit, inside-the-park home run to tie what became the club's signature win of 2005. Anderson made the mistake of signing with the Nationals in 2006, but returned in 2007 (wearing 23 and later, 9) and still hitting.

That the 2009 Mets were destined to go nowhere was evident in all sorts of ways but maybe none so poignant as the site of **Jeremy Reed** playing first base at the same time Daniel Murphy patrolled left field. That happened. Reed, a reserve who came along in the reckless J. J. Putz trade, spent the entire year with the Mets making a single memorable contribution: demonstrating his inexperience at first base in a humiliating 11-inning loss to the Dodgers which seemed to cost him the trust of Jerry Manuel. Third-base coach **Tim Teufel** has worn 18 since 2012, keeping the memories of better days and better plays.

Number 18

Number of times issued: 26 (25 players, 1 manager)

Longest tenured: Darryl Strawberry (8 seasons, 1,109 games), Joel Youngblood (6 seasons, 610 games)

Best single seasons: Strawberry, 1987 (.284/.398/.583, 39 HR, 104 RBIs, 36 stolen bases); Strawberry, 1988 (.269/.366/.545, 39 HR, 101 RBIs); Moises Alou, 2007 (.341/.392/.524, 13 HR, 49 RBIs)

Career statistical leaders: Home runs (Strawberry 252, Youngblood 38), RBI (Strawberry 733, Youngblood 216), batting average (Alou, .342, Darryl Hamilton, .283, Felix Mantilla .275), wins (Bret Saberhagen 10), saves (Dennis Ribant 3), ERA (Saberhagen 3.38)

Great Runs: Teammates with Consecutive Numbers

On a clear night you can look to the stars and make out the Big Dipper, Orion the hunter, Sagittarius the archer, and the '86 Mets.

Aligned like a constellation of ascending uni numbers, the Mets of the late 1980s provided several of the most devastating straights in team history. Following are lists of notable Mets teammates who wore consecutive numbers.

6 numbers:

1986: Foster 15, Gooden 16, Hernandez 17, Strawberry 18, Ojeda 19, Johnson 20
1987–88: Aguilera 15, Gooden 16, Hernandez 17, Strawberry 18, Ojeda 19, Johnson 20
1989: Darling 15, Gooden 16, Hernandez 17, Strawberry 18, Ojeda 19, Johnson 20

5 numbers:

1989: Gooden 16, Hernandez 17, Strawberry 18, Ojeda 19, Johnson 20

3 numbers:

1968–71: Seaver 41, Taylor 42, McAndrew 43
1969–71: Agee 20, Jones 21, Clendenon 22
1975–77: Kingman 26, Swan 27, Milner 28
1986: Backman 6, Mitchell 7, Carter 8
1992: Gooden 16, Cone 17, Saberhagen 18
2015: Matz 32, Harvey 33, Syndergaard 34

#19: HE'S CRAFTY

The 1985 season ended about as painfully as it could for the Mets, who won 98 games only to see the NL East title flag fly over St. Louis and their left-handed junkballing ace, John Tudor, who in six assignments versus the 1985 Mets pitched to an eye-popping, soul-crushing, division-deciding ERA of 0.93.

The Mets were still smarting that offseason when they surrendered four prospects to Boston for **Bob Ojeda**, thereby securing a crafty soft-tossing lefty of their own.

Early reviews of the trade, which sent the Red Sox highly regarded pitching prospects Wes Gardner and Calvin Schiraldi, suggested the Mets paid too high a price for Ojeda, whose career record was just over .500 and who was viewed merely as a candidate to crack the '86 rotation. But Ojeda became perhaps the steadiest, if least spectacular, of the Mets' starters that year. He led the team with 18 wins and a 2.57 ERA, finished fourth in Cy Young voting, and was at his best in critical games during the postseason. He started and won Game 2 of the NLCS and Game 3 of the World Series with the Mets trailing in each case. He was also the starter in Game 6 of both the NLCS and World Series. The loser of the latter was Schiraldi, who also lost Game 7 for Boston.

Ojeda found it difficult to replicate his success in the coming years. He was injured in 1987 and a rebounding year in 1988 ended when, on the day before the Mets clinched the NL East title, Ojeda severed a portion of his middle finger with a hedge clipper in an accident

Dan Carrubia

Bobby Ojeda was all guile and offspeed—on the mound and in the broadcast booth.

at home. He bounced back from that to win 13 games in 1989 before finishing his Mets career as a reliever in 1990.

Ojeda's body of work with the Mets—51 wins and a 3.12 ERA over five seasons—qualifies him for the rather dubious honor of being the best of the thirty-five men who wore No. 19 for the Mets. Ojeda brought No. 19 with him from Boston: It is unlikely he'd choose to be associated with those other Mets 19s.

Like **Anthony Young**, for instance. Nobody ever doubted that the hard-throwing Young had plenty of ability, but in three years with the Mets nobody had worse luck. In two years wearing No. 19 (he wore No. 33 in his rookie year of 1991), Young went 3–30—including an excruciating 27 straight losing decisions to break Craig Anderson's club and major league record of 19, set over three seasons. All this while racking up 18 saves and fashioning a none-too-poor ERA of 3.98.

Balancing bad luck and bad decisions brought three players back to the 19 jersey after leaving the Mets.

Infielder **Tim Foli** was the first overall selection in the 1968 amateur draft: he spent parts of 1970 and '71 seasons with the Mets but was traded to Montreal in the Rusty Staub deal. The Mets reacquired Foli to be Bud Harrelson's successor in 1978 and then shipped him off again for short-stop Frank Taveras in a 1979 challenge trade won by the soon-to-be-world-champion Pirates.

Lenny Harris was a premier Mets pinch hitter in 1998, who bolted on a free-agent deal with the Rockies following the season. The Mets missed him, though, so reacquired him from Colorado in 2000. This time it cost them a young pitcher, Bill Pulsipher, once a prized possession of the Mets organization.

In between Harris's two stays with the Mets, the No. 19 jersey went to **Roger Cedeño**. His 66 steals in 1999 set a then-team record and gathered enough value for him to be a key figure in the Mike Hampton trade the following winter. Mets fans who witnessed Cedeño's misadventures in the outfield and his poor second half in '99 felt they dodged a bullet, only to be shot down when GM Steve Phillips wildly overestimating Cedeño's abilities as a leadoff hitter and outfielder, signed him to a four-year deal starting in 2001.

That announcement came just days after Harris was included in a typically convoluted Phillips trade involving three teams, eleven players, and a suitcase of cash. What was important was that it left 19 open again for Cedeño, who subsequently had two abysmal seasons.

The Mets acquired outfielder **Ryan Church** (2008–09) in a trade for exasperating prospect Lastings Milledge, only to wind up with a more severe kind of headache. Church suffered two concussions during his first season as a Met: one during a spring-training collision with teammate Marlon Anderson, and another while sliding into second base—and Yunel Escobar's knee— during a game in Atlanta that May. As Church's career suffered under extensive aftereffects, the Mets came under criticism for failing to treat the condition right away. Manager Jerry Manuel, some contended, added insult to injury by appearing to question Church's toughness as he struggled to make it back. Those events helped lead to the adoption of league-wide protocols regarding concussions including creation

Dan Carubia

Ryan Church prepares to hit what will be the last out ever recorded at Shea Stadium, September 28, 2008.

of a 7-day concussion disabled list introduced in 2011. It also contributed to David Wright donning that gigantic helmet following a 2010 beaning.

Left-handed reliever **Ken MacKenzie** (1962–63) was the first wearer of the 19 jersey for the Mets, and with a 5–4 mark in 1962, the first Mets pitcher to have a winning record. So he was traded to St. Louis for right-handed reliever **Ed Bauta** (1963) in a deal that helped neither team.

Hawk Taylor (1964–67) was among the bonus-baby rejects that populated the early Mets. A rugged catcher who signed with the Braves for a reported six-figure bonus in 1957, Taylor carved out a living as a light-hitting reserve over parts of four years with the Mets. Taylor briefly lost No. 19 in 1964 to utility man **John Stephenson**, who would later return in other numbers.

Tom "The Blade" Hall (1975–76), listed generously at 6 feet and 150 pounds, and **Daniel Ray Herrera** (2011), 5-foot-6, 165, with a soaking wet mullet—were two of the clubs' wispiest pitchers ever, and neither reliever made a big impression on the mound. Reliever **Heath Bell** (2004–06) by contrast wore 19 on a XXXL jersey. His best work would come following a trade to San Diego where he racked up three consecutive seasons of 40-plus saves and seemed to delight in blasting the Mets' king-sized mistake—Jon Adkins and Ben Johnson proved a very small return.

Veteran sinkerballer **Scott Erickson** (2004) made the Opening-Day roster against just about every fan's wishes, but he injured himself while warming for his first start. He finally joined the team in July, had one good and then one bad start for the Mets, and was traded to Texas.

Infielder **Ron Gardenhire** (1981–85) the first Met born in Germany, was the regular shortstop in 1982 and had a chance to play under four Mets managers in a five-season career (Joe Torre, George Bamberger, Frank Howard, and Davey Johnson). Injuries and a weak bat eventually did him in, but Gardenhire learned from his masters and went on to a successful run as the skipper of the Minnesota Twins.

That journeyman long shot reliever **Lino Urdaneta** (2007) made it all the way back from the Mexican League became easier to explain when it was revealed he'd failed a test for performance-enhancing drugs. Veteran catcher **Sandy Alomar Jr.** surfaced in 2007 while his namesake dad coached third. Alomar surrendered No. 19 to **Jeff Conine**, as the erstwhile Mr. Marlin who played the last weeks of his career as a wannabe Mr. Met.

Other product 19s: blue-collar reservists **Kevin Collins** (1967), **Brian Ostrosser** (1973), **Jim Gosger** (1973–74), **Leo Foster** (1977), **Luis Alvarado** (1977), **Butch Benton** (1978), **Jeff Gardner** (1991), **Shawn Hare** (1994), **Bill Spiers** (1995), **Jason Hardtke** (1996–97), **Jim Tatum** (1998); **Cory Sullivan** (2009); **Gary Matthews** (2010); **Zach Lutz** (2012-13); and **Johnny Monell** (2015). Last call goes to **Mike Hessman**, who announced his retirement in 2015 after hitting more home runs in the minor leagues than any player in history: 433 in 19 seasons. The last of his 14 major league homers—and his only big-league triple—came as a 2010 Met.

Number 19

Number of times issued: 40 (35 players)

Longest tenured: Bobby Ojeda (5 seasons, 140 games), Roger Cedeño (3 seasons, 453 games), Lenny Harris (3 seasons, 261 games)

Best single seasons: Ojeda, 1986 (18–5, 2.57 ERA); Cedeño, 1999 (.313/.396/.408, 66 stolen bases, 23 doubles)

Career statistical leaders: Home runs (Cedeño 18, Ryan Church 14; Hawk Taylor 11), RBI (Cedeño 114, Church 71, Tim Foli 52); batting average (Cedeño .279, Church .278); wins (Ojeda 51, Ken McKenzie 8), saves (Anthony Young, 18); ERA (Ojeda 3.12. Young 3.98).

Why Don't We Steal Away: Stolen Bases by the Numbers

Jose Reyes has run away with just about all stolen-base records the Mets own, but his departure to Miami after the 2011 season left one item on the shelf: The all-time uni-number crown.

That still belongs to the man whose individual records he swiped—Mookie Wilson—and his mates in the No. 1 jersey who have combined to out-steal every jersey in team history. Despite employing the Mets' one-time single-season stolen base king in Roger Cedeño (his 66 steals in 1999 broke Wilson's record of 58 in 1982, although Jose Reyes would subsequently surpass that total with 78 in 2007), No. 19 with 161 career steals ranks only 13th among the Mets' most stealingest numbers through 2015:

No.	Steals	Notes
1	536	Mookie Wilson with 281; Lance Johnson with 65; and Vince Coleman with 61.
7	486	With 370 career steals, Jose Reyes has stolen more bases himself than the combined efforts of every uni except No. 1. Juan Samuel ranks second with 31 steals wearing 7.
20	341	Did you know Howard Johnson (201) is third all-time? Tommie Agee is next with 92.
5	311	David Wright accounts for 193 of these.
11	285	Team effort of Frank Taveras (90), Len Randle (47), Vince Coleman (38), and Wayne Garrett (33).
18	273	Darryl Strawberry (191 steals) could run a little, too.
16	261	Lee Mazzilli styled to 134 steals. Angel Pagan adds 87; Dwight Gooden 1.
6	220	Wally Backman got his jersey dirty 104 times successfully via the stolen base.
12	216	Catcher John Stearns with 86; Juan Lagares caught Ken Boswell for 2nd with 26 career swipes.
4	212	Lenny Dykstra (116 steals) accounts for than half of these.
3	199	Bud Harrelson swiped 115.
22	193	Speedy Eric Young Jr. with a 1-steal lead over Kevin McReynolds (68 and 67 respectively).
19	161	Roger Cedeño's 105 steals are tops; Lenny Harris next with 15.

#20: THUNDER AND LIGHTNING

Two of the most notable Mets to combine power and speed have worn No. 20. For a franchise that often has often struggled to get it all together, **Tommie Agee** and **Howard Johnson** were standouts.

When Agee first arrived at Shea in 1968, he looked a lot like all the other candidates to become the team's first great center fielder. He was a bust.

The 1966 American League Rookie of the Year with the White Sox, Agee was acquired by the Mets in a trade for Tommy Davis in 1968 (Al Weis came, too). Agee's athleticism and strength had some observers comparing him to Willie Mays, but the newly dubbed "Shea Hey Kid" struggled badly. He encountered an 0-for-34 slump en route to hitting a paltry .217 with 5 home runs and 13 stolen bases on the year.

Displaying a new confidence steeled in lengthy talks with his skipper, Gil Hodges, Agee led the '69 Mets with 26 home runs and 76 RBIs, numbers that don't begin to describe his contributions. Agee's leadoff home run in Game 3 of the 1969 World Series was all but forgotten by the time the game ended, as the center fielder saved five runs with two Amazin' catches: the first reaching to rob Elrod Hendricks with two on in the fourth and the second a sprawling catch of Paul Blair's drive to right-center with the bases loaded in the seventh.

Agee twice more led the Mets in home runs, but his game deteriorated following the death of Hodges. Agee was traded to Houston after 1972, ironically making room for the "real" Willie Mays. Although his number wasn't retired, it was displayed prominently at Shea Stadium on the facing of the

The Tommie Agee marker at Shea for the only fair ball ever launched into the upper deck.

Dan Carubia

Howard Johnson switch hit and switch slugged—going big in odd-numbered years and small in even-numbered years.

concourse entryway near upper deck section 48: the spot where, on April 10, 1969, Agee blasted the only fair ball ever landed in the upper deck at Shea.

Howard Johnson had a familiar name but was otherwise an unknown quantity when he arrived from Detroit in a trade for pitcher Walt Terrell 1985. Although he too got his Mets career off to a slow start, in time it looked like one of the great steals the Mets ever made.

Featuring power from both sides of the plate, Johnson had a tendency to alternate great years with so-so ones. HoJo finished in the top ten in NL MVP voting in 1987, '89, and '91, but his respective averages in '88, '90, and '92 were .230, .244, and .223. Yet when the year was odd and HoJo was smoking the ball, few players were better. In 1991 he became the only Met to lead the league in RBIs and set a club mark (117) that lasted until 1999. He also led the NL with 38 homers and had his third of three 30-30 seasons for the club. When he finished his Mets career in 1993, HoJo ranked second all-time in home runs (192), RBIs (629), stolen bases (202), doubles (214), and runs (627); and third in total bases (1,823).

Expansion draftee **Craig Anderson** (1962–64) was the first player to wear No. 20 for the Mets. The tall right-handed reliever got off to a 3–1 start, including winning both games of a doubleheader against the Milwaukee Braves. He then lost his next nineteen decisions in a row (sixteen in 1962, two in 1963—including the last major league game ever played at the Polo Grounds—and one more in 1964) to break original Met Roger Craig's record for most consecutive losses and set a standard that would last until it was bested three decades later by another unlucky Mets hurler, Anthony Young.

John Pacella (1977, 1979–80) is better remembered for what he didn't wear—his hat—which flew off his head with nearly every pitch he threw. Pacella's violent delivery brought the Mets three wins over parts of three seasons.

All-or-nothing slugger **Jeromy Burnitz** (2002–03) returned to the Mets in 2002 and had a year even worse than his .219 batting average and 19 home runs suggested. Burnitz had a good enough comeback in 2003 to earn some value at the midseason trade deadline, when he brought back, among others, **Victor Diaz** (2005–06). Diaz, like Burnitz, wore No. 20, swung violently, and had impressive power. His iron glove, however, made every ball hit his way an adventure.

Journeyman role player **Kurt Abbott** was the Mets' last line of defense at shortstop in 2000—after Rey Ordoñez and Mike Bordick were hurt, and Melvin Mora was traded. His inability to corral Luis Sojo's 87-hopper in Game 5 of the World Series that year helped to seal the Mets' doom.

In a deflationary market and in need of a right fielder, the Mets somehow allowed free agent Vladimir Guererro to sign in Anaheim while settling for ex-Yankees troublemaker **Karim Garcia** (2004), who made bigger news in the police column than the sports pages and within months was swapped to Baltimore. Garcia's brief reign surpassed in disappointment the short Mets career of **Ken Henderson** (1978), the veteran right fielder who, seven games into his Mets tenure, ran into a wall and never appeared in a game for them again. If only fans could have escaped the '78 Mets so easily.

The Mets were searching for a right fielder again in 2006 when they arranged a deal for veteran slugger **Shawn Green** (2006–07), whom they hoped would rebound from a string of subpar seasons. Like Ken Henderson, Green was not the same player he'd once been; like Victor Diaz, he made fans wince every time a ball was hit near him; and like John Pacella, he just couldn't keep that hat on.

The 1980s Mets sacrificed consecutive No. 20s to help build a champion. **Rick Ownbey**, a flaky but talented young pitcher, was outbound freight in the Keith Hernandez deal in the summer of 1983. Later that year September call-up **Mike Fitzgerald** (1983–84) slipped into the No. 20 jersey and smashed a two-run homer in his first big-league at-bat. Fitzgerald ascended to No. 1 catching duties in 1984 only to be dealt to Montreal in the Gary Carter trade when the season was over.

Anthony Recker (2013–15) never hit better than .215 over parts of three seasons as a Met reserve catcher, but he was always a threat to hit one out. Even when he didn't, his chiseled features and boyish smile made him something to watch. And as a mop-up pitcher with an 18.00 ERA, A.R. technically qualifies as only No. 20 without a losing record (0–0). **Bob Friend's** 5–8 mark in 1966 was as good as it got in that department.

Other 20s: nineteen-year-old catcher **Greg Goossen** (1965) the second coming of **Choo Choo Coleman** (1966), utility man **John Sullivan** (1967), briefly visiting catchers **Jerry May** (1973) and **Ike Hampton** (1974), ambidextrous pitcher **Greg Harris** (1981), outfielder **Ryan Thompson** (1994–95), sabermetric heartthrob **Roberto Petagine** (1996), pinch hitter **Mark Johnson** (2001), outfielder **Prentice Redman** (2003), resurrected reliever **Ricky Bottalico** (2004), and outfielder **Jason Pridie** (2011).

Number 20

Number of times issued: 31 (29 players, 2 coaches)

Longest tenured: Howard Johnson (9 seasons, 1,154 games); Tommie Agee (5 seasons, 661 games)

Best single seasons: Johnson, 1991 (.259/.369/.559, 38 HR, 117 RBIs, 30 stolen bases), Johnson, 1989 (.287/.369/.559, 36 HR, 101 RBIs, 41 stolen bases); Agee, 1969 (.271/.342/.464, 26 HR, 76 RBIs)

Career statistical leaders: Home runs (Johnson 190, Agee 82); RBI (Johnson 626, Agee 265), batting average (Shawn Green .284, Agee .262), wins (Bob Friend 5); ERA (John Pacella 4.83)

I Got the Power: Home Runs by the Numbers

On April 11, 1962, leading off the fourth inning, Gil Hodges whacked a first-pitch fastball from Larry Jackson over the left-field fence at original Busch Stadium. It was his 362nd career home run, and the Mets' first. Through 2015 exactly 400 other men have combined to hit 6,817 home runs as Mets.

As the chart below illustrates, those homers have been fairly well distributed across the uni spectrum, with the most powerful numbers in club history through 2015—5 and 20—each contributing about 6 percent of the total home runs hit. But it's also a dynamic race. A view of the same leaderboard in the previous edition of Mets by the Numbers, updated through 2007, showed No. 20 as first, 18 second and 9 third—all have fallen since. And if this were the Billboard charts, No. 21 would be festooned with a bullet—it didn't rank in the Top Ten eight years ago.

Following is a list of combined home runs by uniform number, updated through 2015:

No.	HRs	Notes
5	420	David Wright's 235 round-trippers account for more than half.
20	408	Howard Johnson with 190; six in double figures led by Tommie Agee's 82.
21	389	Strong last decade behind Carlos Delgado (104) and Lucas Duda (101).
18	377	Darryl Strawberry still holding on as the team's all-time HR king (252), but last No. 18 to homer was Marlon Anderson in 2008.
15	351	Carlos Beltran with 149 belts; George Foster 50 back at 99.
9	342	Of the 20 men to wear 9, only Mike DiFelice and Ronn Reynolds have failed to homer in it. Todd Hundley leads with 123.
7	291	Ed Kranepool still on top with 106. Jose Reyes next with 81.
4	267	Seven players in double figures, led by Robin Ventura (77).
12	257	Jeff Kent paces a balanced attack with 64 taters.
22	242	Kevin McReynolds leads with 122 McHomers.
25	237	Bobby Bonilla with 95 bombs and 55,000 boos.
31	223	220 belong to Mike Piazza. Mike Vail has the other 3. And always will.

#21: BEAST MODE

Resembling something of a cross between a ballplayer and a furry woodland beast, **Lucas Duda** innocently wandered in from a distant forest and into left field late in the 2010 season but it would be a few years before he would find a more suitable habitat.

Ultimately, selecting the mysterious Duda over troubled incumbent Ike Davis to man first base in 2014 should go down as one of the defining trials of the Sandy Alderson administration, and through two years at least, it's been a triumphant one.

Duda Smash! Lucas Duda leans into one at Citi Field.

Duda speaks softly and carries a big stick. Easily one of the least competent pretend outfielders for a team that's tried more than a few over the years—

Daniel Murphy, Todd Hundley and Howard Johnson among them—the Dude abided at first base and in the Mets lineup where a natural patience-and-power approach clicked with organizational philosophy and at times punished opposition pitching, clobbering 30 home runs in 2014 and another 27 in 2015. And with a notable World Series throwing error aside, he's been a defensive plus as well.

The Mets never seemed shy about making an example of **Cleon Jones**, their talented and occasionally defiant outfielder.

There was the time in 1969 when Jones was led off the field by manager Gil Hodges after a fly ball fell in front of him for a hit. There was the awkward public apology the Mets had Jones give after an extramarital affair made the headlines. Finally there was a battle of wills between Jones and manager Yogi Berra over Jones's allegedly refusing Berra's order to pinch hit, an incident that hastened the end of both men's respective tenures with the Mets.

But Jones, who wore 21 for the last ten of his twelve years with the Mets, ought to be best remembered as an example of the kind of player the Mets developed far too few of in their formative years. The kind that could hit, catch, and run. Signed out of Alabama A&M in 1963, Jones was the

Cleon Jones was the everyday big righty bat for the 1969 and 1973 pennant winners.

first farm-developed everyday Mets player to approach superstar status and until Darryl Strawberry came along, was probably the best hitter in team history.

When he walked away from New York in 1975, Jones was the Mets' all-time leader in hits, home runs, and RBIs and the first Met to collect 1,000 hits. Although all those records have since been broken, his .340 average in 1969 (third in the NL that year) stood as the Mets standard for twenty-nine years, when it was broken by John Olerud. And his shoe-polish-on-the-baseball, kneel-down catch to end the 1969 World Series remain unforgettably Amazin'.

Kevin Elster was the anti-Duda. Handsome, smooth and outspoken, the farm-raised shortstop added 10-homer-a-year power to the Mets' tradition-al all-glove, no-hit shortstop model. A solid fielder who made everything look easy, Elster (1987–91) may have been too smooth for his own good. When he switched his uniform from No. 21 to 15 in 1992 he remarked to *Newsday* that he felt 21 was "a sissy number." He proceeded almost imme-diately to require major surgery on an injured shoulder and never played for the Mets again. Elster's best year as a Met was probably 1989, when he hit 10 home runs and drove in 55. During that season he ended his major league record 88 consecutive games without an error at shortstop.

Bill Pulsipher (1995, 1998) began his Mets career promisingly as the left-handed representative of the doomed pitching trio (alongside Jason Isring-hausen and Paul Wilson) known as "Generation K." Pulsipher was the first of the three to reach the majors, the first to go down to injury, and probably endured the weirdest trip back, overcoming elbow woes as well as anxiety issues to reappear briefly in 1998. The Mets traded Pulsipher away twice: once in 1998 and again in 2000 after they'd reacquired him (and dressed him in 25). But he never won more than the five games he got right out of the chute in 1995.

Dan Carubia

Calm and cool Kevin Elster relaxes in the Mets dugout.

Shortly after Pulsipher was traded in 1998, right-handed junkball artist **Masato Yoshii** (1998–99) slipped into his discarded No. 21 jersey. The first truly successful Mets import from Japan, Yoshii overcame first-half struggles to be a key contributor down the stretch in 1999, when he finished a respectable 12–8. Yoshii was traded to the Rockies following the season for pitcher **Bobby M. Jones** (2000, 2002), whose frequent injuries averted a lot of potential confusion with a teammate of the same name. Jones was one of three men to wear 21 in 2002: **Mark Little** arrived in a deadline trade just in time to play a small but crucial role in the season-killing doubleheader sweep by the Diamondbacks: Little interrupted a rally by reaching on a force play and immediately was picked off first. Little was traded away days later, and light-hitting reserve outfielder **Raul Gonzalez** (2002–03) took over No. 21.

Like Yoshii, first baseman/outfielder **David Segui** (1994–95) switched to 21 at his first opportunity. Segui's beloved No. 21 belonged to backup catcher candidate Joe Kmak, who was cut as the team broke camp. A well-traveled but nonetheless decent player most days, Segui's stint with the Mets (10/42/.241 in '94) was probably the worst of his eight major league stops.

Slugging first baseman **Carlos Delgado** (2006–09) famously rejected a contract offer from the Mets in 2005 to sign instead with Florida, but the tables turned when the Marlins traded him to the Mets the following season. Delgado, whose customary No. 25 belonged at the time to Kaz Matsui, proudly donned No. 21 instead as a tribute to Puerto Rican countryman Roberto Clemente. Delgado proved a critical addition to the 2006 club, smashing 38 home runs and driving in 114 for the division winners. A series of injuries—and what some perceived to be indifferent play—limited his productivity in 2007, but he was hammering away again in 2008 (38 home runs, 115 RBIs) before hip injury ended his season—and career—early in 2009.

Elliot Maddox (1978–80) wound down his career as a middling outfielder/third baseman for the Mets and a plaintiff in a suit against Shea Stadium and the city of New York. Maddox claimed sloppy field conditions caused him to slip in the outfield as a member of the Yankees when they shared Shea in 1975, nuking his career. Maddox lost. That's what Mets did then.

He spent the vast majority of a lengthy Mets career wearing No. 7, but **Ed Kranepool** (1962–63) debuted in No. 21—he was the first Met to wear it—and might never have changed had the Mets not acquired legendary lefty **Warren Spahn** (1965) in what was to be Spahn's final year. Hired as a pitcher-pitching coach and viewed then as a possible successor to manager Casey Stengel, the forty-four-year-old Spahn neither pitched nor coached with much effectiveness or enthusiasm. He was released midseason and finished his career as a Giant.

Husky veteran catcher **Rod Barajas** signed as a free agent in 2010 and in a pattern to be repeated by John Buck a few years later, collected a mess of early-season home runs before his engines quit and was out of Queens before August was up.

Others: reliever **Bob Moorhead** (1965), outfield reserves **Billy Baldwin** (1976) and **Pepe Mangual** (1977), power prospect **Gary Rajsich** (1982–83), utility man **Ross Jones** (1984), outfield prospects **Herm Winningham** (1984) and **Terry Blocker** (1985), veteran enemy **Kevin Bass** (1992), and ex-Yankees reserve **Gerald "Ice" Williams** (2004–05). Mysterious, fictional Met **Sidd Finch** wore 21 also.

Number 21

No. of times issued: 27 (25 players, 2 DNPs)

Longest tenured: Cleon Jones (10 seasons, 1,165 games), Kevin Elster (5 seasons, 512 games)

Best single seasons: Jones, 1969 (.340/.422/.482, 12 HR, 75 RBIs); Carlos Delgado, 2006 (.265/.361/.548, 38 HR, 114 RBIs); Lucas Duda, 2014 (.253/.349/.481, 30 HR, 92 RBIs)

Career statistical leaders: Home runs (Delgado 104, Duda 101, Jones 92); RBI (Jones 513, Delgado 339, Duda 318); batting average (Jones .284, Gary Rajsich .273, Kevin Bass .270); wins (Masato Yoshii 14); ERA (Bill Pulsipher 4.28, Warren Spahn, 4.36)

Big in Japan

About five minutes after the Mets traded Bill Pulsipher to the Brewers in 1998, Masato Yoshii claimed Pulsipher's No. 21 jersey. Notoriously superstitious, Yoshii said he made the switch for "good luck."

Japanese generally associate No. 4 with bad luck. Four is a homonym of shi, which means "death," and as a result is often issued to unknowing U.S. gaijin playing in Japan.

When Takashi Kashiwada became the first Met from Japan in 1997, he was issued No. 18, which in Japan is the jersey typically reserved for superstar pitchers. Pitchers in Japan tend to wear numbers between 11 and 19. But since Japan's major and lone minor league clubs share numbers, it's not unusual to see numbers over 50, with bullpen catchers and coaching staffs frequently appearing in triple digits. Field staff typically wear numbers in the 70s: in Bobby Valentine's first stint managing the Chiba Lotte Marines, he wore No. 81.

The Marines, by the way, never issue No. 26 to a player. That number belongs to the 26th man: their fans.

#22: WE COULD BE HEROES

The Mets have had two World Series MVPs in their history and both have worn No. 22. If a few things—OK, a lot of things—broke differently, they might have had three.

Donn Clendenon, **Ray Knight**, and **Al Leiter** each did the Mets proud in their postseason history. The Mets made the 1973 World Series without a 22 to lead them, while **Kevin Plawecki** made the 2015 World Series roster, but he didn't appear.

Clendenon was the only significant in-season addition the Mets made in 1969. They were nine games behind the Cubs on the day they made the trade and eight games up by the time the season ended. Teammates would later say the veteran's presence helped the team develop the character to win.

Slugging first baseman Donn Clendenon had the Mets' back after coming over in their only trade of the 1969 season.

Statistics made Clendenon's case for World Series MVP: He hit .357 against Baltimore, with 3 home runs and 15 total bases—the latter two figures were records for a five-game Series, and Clendenon only played four games against Baltimore. Amazingly, he did not bat even once in the Mets' NLCS sweep of Atlanta. (When Gil Hodges platooned, he meant it!) Clendenon stuck around for another two seasons in New York, setting what was then a team record with 97 RBIs in 1970.

Like Clendenon, Knight (1984–86) was a right-handed-hitting veteran corner infielder whose best years were with other clubs but whose signature moment came leading the Mets to postseason glory. But where the '69ers benefited from Clendenon's cool professionalism, the '86ers would absorb the emotional and at times bloodthirsty style of Knight.

The Mets thought enough of Knight when he arrived in a trade with Houston in 1984 that Bobby Valentine, then serving as third-base coach, gave up No. 22 for him. Knight nearly played his way out of a Mets jersey in 1985, hitting just .218 with 6 home runs amid injuries and boos. Knight fought his way back, bare knuckled, in 1986. With new acquisition Howard Johnson poised to take over third base, Knight blasted off to a furious start with 6 April home runs. His brawls with Dodger Tom Niedenfuer and Cincinnati's Eric Davis served as rallying points for the '86 team.

Knight finished off the year just as furiously. He drove in the tying run in the 9th inning of Game 6 in Houston. He hit .391 in the World Series, including the third of the three two-out singles to spark the miraculous Game 6 rally, scoring the winning run on Mookie Wilson's famous trickling ground ball. And his home run in the 7th inning of Game 7 provided the Mets with the last lead they'd need.

Yet Knight gracing the cover of *Sports Illustrated* with his foot crossing home plate was to be the last fans would see of him in a Mets uniform. Heartbroken, he finished his career quietly with two final seasons in the American League.

Al Leiter never won a sports car for being the World Series MVP. He didn't even win a postseason game for the Mets. But at the turn of the century, the hardworking lefty was the team's soul and the closest thing it had to a big-game pitcher. Leiter shut down Cincinnati to win the 163rd game of the season in 1999. His performance in the 2000 World Series—particularly the doomed final-game effort—should be remembered as one of the most courageous in team history.

Despite his Yankees pedigree, Leiter (1998–2004) grew up a Mets fan in New Jersey. Leiter never had a losing year as a Met, going 95–67 with a 3.42 ERA, though by the end fans found his outings as strenuous for them as for Leiter: They required maximum effort and grunts just to get through.

A rookie catcher thrust from Class AAA to No. 1 status when Travis d'Arnaud went down with a lengthy injury, Plawecki showed flashes of the bat that had made him an intriguing prospect, but struggled through a long summer before reinforcements arrived.

Kevin McReynolds (1987–91, 1994) was a true Catch-22: Despite numbers that might indicate greatness (27 home runs, 99 RBIs, and 21 steals without getting caught in 1988) the droll country slugger lacked the charisma to be a true superstar. Fans never forgave the indignity of McReynolds's remarks comparing playing in the postseason with fishing, but then they probably didn't understand how much he loved casting a line. Reacquiring McReynolds in 1994 after he'd demonstrated his laconic blandness was a curious decision, but it did rid the team of Vince Coleman.

Kevin McReynolds warms up in Port St. Lucie.

Workhorse **Jack Fisher** (1964–67) won 38 games and lost 73 over four long seasons with the Mets but was the team's de facto ace until Tom Seaver came along. Although "Fat Jack" was best known as the Baltimore pitcher who allowed a home run to Ted Williams in the Splinter's last turn at-bat, which was a better legacy than equaling Roger Craig's Mets record of 24 losses—despite a 3.94 ERA—during the 1965 season.

Bayside's own **Mike Jorgensen**, who made his Mets debut in the 1960s, had a return engagement in the 1980s (1980–83) while wearing 22. The reserve outfielder/first baseman had productive seasons as a part-time starter and pinch-hitter, especially in 1982, where he was always a threat to draw a walk.

When GM Sandy Alderson remarked "What outfield?" he was probably referring to speedy veteran reserve left-fielders wearing No. 22 and getting way too much playing time. **Willie Harris,** whose highlight-reel catches with the Braves and Nationals routinely tortured the Mets, provided too little of that magic in a Mets uniform in 2011. **Eric Young Jr.** (2013–14) spent two seasons in New York as a semi-regular, leading the team in stolen bases both years and winning the NL steals crown in 2013, with 38 of his 46 SBs after a trade with Colorado.

Speed killed other 22s. The 1995 Mets won a bidding war with the Dodgers for veteran free agent leadoff man **Brett Butler**, only to trade him to the Dodgers in a late-season housecleaning. That same summer the Mets sent Bobby Bonilla to the Orioles for prospect **Alex Ochoa,** who'd make his big-league debut in the Mets outfield that September. Ochoa (2005–07) had five tools but hardly had time to unpack them all: He would be traded eight times in eight years, including twice by the Mets.

Xavier Nady (2006) used a Kingman-like cut to slam 14 home runs in a half-season with the Mets, setting the pace for a dominant season, only to find himself sacrificed at the trade deadline: he went to Pittsburgh in the infamous Oliver Perez deal.

Backup catcher **Charlie O'Brien** (1992–93) would have preferred No. 22 when acquired from the Brewers in 1990, but didn't take it until McReynolds got out of the way. O'Brien in the meantime wore 33 until Eddie Murray got in the way, and 5.

The first Met to wear 22, right-handed reliever **Bob Moorhead**, punched a dugout door in St. Louis' Sportsman Park following an ineffective outing, breaking two knuckles and ending his season without a win or a save in 105 1/3 innings. Moorhead did not resurface until three years later in a different number (21). The Mets have since tried a number of bullpenners in 22 without making much more of an impression: **Jack Aker**, a one-time bullpen ace for the A's who collected two wins and two saves in 1974; **Dale Murray** (1978–79); flameout prospect **Royce Ring** (2005); and Cuban lefty **Raul Valdes** (2010). Then there was **J. J. Putz**, the so-called headliner in an 11-player, three-team trade with Seattle and Cleveland in which the Mets pissed away seven players, including Jason Vargas and Joe Smith, still winning and saving games for their respective clubs in 2015. Putz (2009) got blasted for a 5.22 ERA and an elbow injury in his only Met season.

The leftover 22s who didn't pitch—and didn't hit: reserves **Joe Hicks** (1963), **Bob Gallagher** (1975), **Jay Kleven** (1976), **Michael Tucker** (2006), and **Ramon Martinez** (2008). **Jose Valentin** wore 22 in 2007, the season the fairy godmother's spell wore off in Queens.

Number 22

Number of times issued: 29 (26 players, 1 coach, 1 DNP)

Longest tenured: Al Leiter (7 seasons, 213 games), Kevin McReynolds (6 seasons, 787 games), Mike Jorgensen (4 seasons, 363 games)

Best single seasons: McReynolds, 1988 (.288/.336/.496, 27 HR, 99 RBIs); Leiter, 1998 (17–6, 2.47 ERA, 174 strikeouts in 193 innings); Donn Clendenon, 1970 (.288/.348/.515, 22 HR, 97 RBIs)

Career statistical leaders: Home runs (McReynolds 122, Clendenon 45); RBI (McReynolds 456, Clendenon 171); batting average (Brett Butler .311, Alex Ochoa .273); wins (Leiter 95, Jack Fisher 38), saves (Dale Murray 9), ERA (Leiter 3.43)

Teamwork (to Make the Dream Work): Teams by the Numbers

Position for position, there may not be a better number than 22, at least as Mets go. It provides a speedy leadoff center fielder and a strong defensive catcher. A couple of power hitters, a five-tool prospect, and hardworking left-right combinations in the rotation and the bullpen.

Following are a few representative "teams" staffed only by players who wore the same number as Mets. In some cases, players have been placed in positions they didn't necessarily play, and certain players, due to number switches, are eligible to for more than one team (Jose Valentin, adept at several positions and strategically dressed in two numbers, fits both categories). The teams listed consist of only those numbers that qualified without massive or unimaginable switches (for example Teams 21 and 25 couldn't take the field without a catcher; Teams 27 and 29 hadn't enough middle infielders even to fake it).

Team 22

Scouting report: Considerable power and strong defense, although you might not want Ramon Martinez out there every day at shortstop. Leiter and Fisher need to go deep into games because the bullpen is shaky.

C: Charlie O'Brien
1B: Donn Clendenon
2B: Jose Valentin
SS: Ramon Martinez
3B: Ray Knight
LF: Kevin McReynolds
CF: Brett Butler
RF: Alex Ochoa
SP: Al Leiter, Jack Fisher
RP: Raul Valdes, Dale Murray

Team 17

Scouting report: Tough to beat the right side of the infield, but the outfield could use a few hitters. Starting pitching a plus.

 C: Choo-Choo Coleman
1B: Keith Hernandez
2B: Felix Millan
SS: Mike Bordick
3B: Don Zimmer
LF: Fernando Tatis
CF: Rod Gaspar
RF: Ellis Valentine
SP: David Cone, Bret Saberhagen
RP: Graeme Lloyd, Dae Sung Koo

Team 18

Scouting report: These guys will score some runs, but look for relief help at the deadline.

 C: Duffy Dyer
1B: George Theodore
2B: Jose Valentin
SS: Felix Mantilla
3B: Joel Youngblood
LF: Moises Alou
CF: Darryl Hamilton
RF: Darryl Strawberry
SP: Bret Saberhagen, Jeff D'Amico
RP: Takashi Kashiwada, Ryota Igarashi

Team 20

Scouting report: Anthony Recker's abrupt promotion from "emergency" to "everyday" at third base is worrisome, as is the starting pitching.

 C: Mike Fitzgerald
1B: Roberto Petagine
2B: Kurt Abbott
SS: Howard Johnson
3B: Anthony Recker
LF: Jeromy Burnitz
CF: Tommie Agee
RF: Shawn Green

SP: Craig Anderson, John Pacella
RP: Ricky Bottalico, Greg Harris

Team 23

Scouting Report: Pat Mahomes is the long man, and they're going to need him.

 C: Jason Phillips
1B: Julio Franco
2B: Doug Flynn
SS: Tim Bogar
3B: Chris Donnels
LF: Bernard Gilkey
CF: Joe Christopher
RF: Dave Schneck
SP: Kaz Ishii, Brian Rose
RP: Pat Mahomes, Blaine Boyer

Team 26

Scouting Report: Weak outfield production and Kingman at third base. Good thing the pitching looks strong.

 C: Jason Phillips
1B: Rico Brogna
2B: Marco Scutaro
SS: David Lamb
3B: Dave Kingman
LF: Bruce Boisclair
CF: Terrence Long
RF: Jon Nunnally
SP: Frank Viola, Orlando Hernandez
RP: Terry Leach, Alejandro Peña

Team 33

Scouting Report: Starring pitching a strength but the lineup is Eddie and the Losers.

 C: Barry Lyons
1B: Eddie Murray
2B: Mike Kinkade
SS: Ron Hunt
3B: Clint Hurdle
LF: Andy Tomberlin
CF: Dan Norman
RF: Bubba Trammell

SP: Matt Harvey, John Maine
RP: Ken Sanders, Anthony Young

Team 16

Scouting Report: Doc and Dude and somewhat crude. Derek Bell is also the long reliever.

 C: Paul Lo Duca
1B: Doug Meintkiewicz
2B: Felix Millan
SS: Kevin Collins
3B: John Stearns
LF: Dick Smith
CF: Lee Mazzilli
RF: Derek Bell
SP: Dwight Gooden, David Cone
RP: Hideo Nomo, Daisuke Matsuzaka

#23: SKIDOO

Bernard Gilkey brought No. 23 and a contract the Cardinals could no longer bear to pay from St. Louis in 1996. He summarily delivered what easily was the most impressive accomplishment of any Mets player ever to wear the No. 23 uniform and what might have been the best single season to that point in club history.

Without so much as a warning, the wide-eyed, right-handed slugger hit .317 with 30 home runs, 117 RBIs, and 44 doubles. The RBI total tied Howard Johnson's team record (since broken), but the 44 doubles through 2015 are still the all-time club standard. Gilkey added 17 stolen bases and 18 assists from left field.

The Mets were quick to reward Gilkey with a four-year contract only to see him transform back into an unwanted commodity. He slipped to 18 home runs in 1997 and just four in 1998 by the time the Mets finally unloaded him to the Arizona Diamondbacks.

One surprisingly strong season in otherwise mediocre tenures is a characteristic of several Met 23s. Call it the 23 Skidoo.

Original Met **Joe Christopher** (1962–65) turned in a 16/76/.300/.360/.466 performance in 1964; numbers that looked unimaginable for the smiling Virgin Islander, considering his first two seasons with the Mets; 1965 was back to same old, same old.

Well-traveled mop-up man **Pat Mahomes** (1999–2000) fashioned an unexpected 8–0 record in 1999 out of an uncanny ability to hold the fort while the offense fought back deficits, often massive ones, and was a key ingredient in the playoff push. Mahomes, who hit .313 in '99 after never batting in the AL, even singled in the go-ahead run in the top of the 13th and then held off the Cubs in the bottom of the inning in his most memorable Mets moment.

While bouncing between New York and the minor leagues, catcher **Jason Phillips** wore four different numbers for the Mets, but it was while wearing No. 23 in 2003 that Phillips surfaced to stay. Phillips made the Opening Day roster only because Mike Piazza was suspended for a spring-training fight with Guillermo Mota, but thanks to some pop in his bat and Mo Vaughn's career-ending injuries, Phillips took over at first base despite having no experience at the position. He promptly whacked 11 home runs, hit 25 doubles, and went .298/.373/.442 in 403 at-bats. That performance earned him a full-time gig in 2004, which turned into a total flop (7/34/.218/.298/.326 in 362 at-bats). Just prior to the 2005 season, Phillips turned over his jersey in a trade for **Kaz Ishii** (2005), a one-time Dodger phenom who never found his stuff again.

It would have been nice to have gotten just one great year from **Doug Flynn** (1977–81), but a Gold Glove award in 1980—and splendid defense generally—was about as good as it ever got. Flynn arrived in the Tom Seaver trade in 1977 in time to take over for injured and/or departing middle infielders Felix Millan and Bud Harrelson. He eventually settled in at second base but never hit any better than .255 or reached base at a .300 clip, he didn't steal much, and he rarely hit for power. He hit an inside-the-park grand slam in 1979, but Flynn's offensive signature was connecting for three triples in a single game on August 5, 1980: one each to left, center, and right in Montreal. Did we mention he could really pick it?

After Flynn departed, the Mets were optimistic that **Brian Giles** (1982–83) would also be a Gold Glover at second base. But a lack of a bat scorched his career when Davey Johnson took over in 1984 and reinstalled Wally Backman at second base.

Jacob Kanarek/From Worst to First

Doug Flynn is the only Mets second baseman to win a Gold Glove.

Reserve outfielder **Dave Schneck,** below the Medoza line in 23 (.189) and career (.199), was the pivot man in a three-way number swap prior to 1974 that saw Felix Millan switch from 16 to 17, **Ted Martinez** move from 17 to 23, and Schneck go from 23 to 16. Martinez selected 23 because it was the number worn by his contemporary and hero, Tito Fuentes.

That forty-seven-year-old pinch hitter **Julio Franco** was still playing in 2006 was nearly as big a shock as the fact he was playing effectively, and in the first year of a two-year contract. Franco, whose big-league career predated the birth of many teammates—and four franchises—by 2007 appeared to finally be acting his age, though he set or extended any number of "oldest player to" marks, including becoming the oldest active Met ever. His number and role as a pinch hitter for the 2007 Mets would be given to **Marlon Anderson**, who hit .319 with 25 RBIs in just 77 plate appearances.

The Mets might never have had a player whose profile-to-performance ratio was any more out of whack than **Brian Schneider** (2008–09). Acquired from the Nationals to replace Paul Lo Duca as the No. 1 catcher in 2008, Schneider pitched car dealerships, had his own wine (Schneider Scharnonnay), forced Marlon Anderson into a new uni number (9), and got the celebrity New York treatment despite doing very little offensively, spending considerable time on the disabled list and underdelivering on his defensive reputation. His mentoring of another left-handed hitting successor (Josh Thole) only resulted in more Schneiderness.

Michael Cuddyer, who in addition to a distinguished baseball résumé was an amateur magician, made a draft pick vanish upon signing with the club then—ala-kazaam!—made his own career disappear. A friend of David Wright and a solid citizen who served as a reliable clubhouse spokesman, Cuddyer amid a series of injuries did precious little else for the 2015 squad, and announced his retirement following the season despite a year to go on his contract—a rare trick indeed.

Mike Baxter (2011–13) will never have to buy a drink as long as Johan Santana is around. On June 1, 2012, Baxter made one of the club's most memorable defensive plays, racing to the warning track in left field to haul in a 7th-inning drive by the Cardinals' Yadier Molina, hitting the fence with such force it dislocated Baxter's shoulder and kept him off the field for nearly two months. But Baxter held the ball, and a determined Santana recorded the first—and through 2015, still the only—no-hitter in club history. Baxter grew up in nearby Whitestone, Queens—had the fence not been there he might have crashed onto his doorstep.

Outfielders **Matt Lawton** (2001) and ten years later, the intense-but-ineffective **Chris Carter** (2011) were disappointing trade returns for respective All-Stars Rick Reed and Billy Wagner, respectively. Utilityman **Chris Donnels** (1991–92) gave way to the even more versatile **Tim Bogar** (1993–95). Bogar switched to No. 11 when Gilkey arrived.

There's more where they came from: reserve outfielders **Bill Murphy** (1966); **Leroy Stanton** (1970–71); **Jesus Alou** (1975); **Jermaine Allensworth** (1998); **McKay Christensen** (2002) and **Esix Snead** (2002); back-up infielder **Bob Heise** (1967–68); catcher **Taylor Teagarden** (2014), and briefly visiting pitchers **Brian Rose** (2001) and **Blaine Boyer** (2013). And a final chorus for 23 for Joe Frazier's .214-hitting outfielder from 1976: *And he's bad, bad, **Leon Brown**, baddest Met in the whole damn town.*

Number 23

Number of times issued: 32 (29 players, 2 coaches, 1 DNP)

Longest Tenured: Doug Flynn (5 seasons, 636 games), Joe Christopher (4 seasons, 485 games), Bernard Gilkey (3 seasons, 380 games)

Best single seasons: Gilkey, 1996 (.317/.393/.562, 30 HR, 117 RBIs); Pat Mahomes, 1999 (8–0, 3.68 ERA); Christopher, 1964 (.300/.360/.466, 16 HR, 76 RBIs); Jason Phillips, 2003 (.298/.373/.442, 11 HR, 58 RBIs)

Career statistical leaders: Home runs (Gilkey 52, Christopher 28), RBI (Gilkey 223, Christopher 156, Flynn 155), wins (Mahomes 13, Kaz Ishii 3); ERA (Mahomes 4.74)

Chain, Chain, Chain: Linking Trades

Tim Bogar's boys can swim.

The reserve infielder and former No. 23 was traded away by the Mets nearly twenty years ago and has been retired since 2001, but Bogar DNA is still very much a part of the Mets ecosystem.

As of 2016, Bogar was the patriarch of the Mets' longest active "trade chain" connecting players in the organization via transactions. Here's how: In 1997 Bogar was traded to Houston for Luis Lopez, who was traded in 2000 to Milwaukee for Bill Pulsipher, who was traded to Arizona later that year for Lenny Harris, who was swapped in 2001 to Milwaukee for Jeromy Burnitz, whose 2003 trade to Los Angeles yielded Victor Diaz, who in 2006 was traded for catcher Mike Nickeas. Nickeas remarkably lasted long enough in the organization to make the Mets in 2010 and was included in the earthshattering R. A. Dickey trade to Toronto in 2012, a deal yielding not only burgeoning stars like Travis d'Arnaud and Noah Syndergaard but also Wuilmer Beccera, a sleeper outfield prospect, and second-base prospect Dilson Hererra (through John Buck, who also came in the Nickeas-Dickey trade).

That's a heck of a lot for little old Tim Bogar.

Follow a Mets trade chain and you'll find both diminishing returns and surprising successes. Roger Craig was turned into George Altman who became Billy Cowan who became Lou Klimchock. In three years and four regrettable trades, the Mets—Presto!—turned Len Dykstra and Roger McDowell into Paul Gibson. Yet twenty years of returns churned out of 1986 reserves Ed Hearn and Rick Anderson. They were traded together to Kansas City for David Cone; Cone was later traded for Ryan Thompson. Thompson went to Cleveland for Mark Clark, who went to the Cubs in the six-player deal that brought the Mets Brian McRae and Turk Wendell. Wendell went to Philadelphia for Bruce Chen, who went to Montreal in 2002 for Scott Strickland, who broke the chain when he was released by the organization in 2005.

A related chain begins with the 1984 debut of Kevin Mitchell, who went to San Diego for Kevin McReynolds, who went to Kansas City for Bret Saberhagen, who went to Colorado for Juan Acevedo, who went to St. Louis for Rigo Beltran, who (along with McRae), went to Colorado for Chuck McElroy, who went to Baltimore for Jesse Orosco, who went to St. Louis for Joe McEwing. That chain was snapped when McEwing was released in 2005.

Follow the acquirees of the 1977 Tom Seaver trade and you'll find Dave Kingman (via Steve Henderson), George Foster (through Doug Flynn and Jim Kern), Ellis Valentine (courtesy of Dan Norman) and Junior Ortiz (Pat Zachry to Jorge Orta to Steve Sentenay) and . . . ah the hell with it. Still a rotten deal.

#24: SAY HEY

While the fan base, and to a certain extent, the character of the early Mets can be traced most directly to their predecessors in Brooklyn, it should not be forgotten that the team's first owners were fans of the team in Upper Manhattan.

Joan Payson, the wealthy society matron who bankrolled the Mets, was a former minority owner of baseball's New York Giants and the most prominent of their shareholders to oppose club's move to San Francisco. Payson left running the Mets to an appointed board of directors. The most influential of these was her stockbroker, M. Donald Grant.

So it was no surprise the young Mets openly coveted Giants star center fielder **Willie Mays.** Speculation circulated throughout the 1960s regarding what it might take to corral Mays—a million dollars?—and how prepared Payson and Grant might be to part with such a sum. Obtaining the best player in the game by trade back then was, quite simply, impossible. Even if it were the early Mets hadn't enough talent to give back.

Finally in May of 1972, the Mets traded a young pitcher, Charlie Williams, and $100,000 to San Francisco for Mays in a deal many considered a Mother's Day gift from Grant to Payson. **Jim Beauchamp** was invited to surrender his No. 24 jersey as the Say Hey Kid returned to New York. Mays hit a home run in his first game—against San Francisco to boot—to provide the margin of victory.

It was understood the Mets weren't getting the same Willie Mays who last played in New York in 1957. Though even at the age of forty-one, Mays was still effective as a part-time first baseman/outfielder, pinch hitter, and clubhouse presence whose legendary instincts and hustle inspired his teammates. He was popular at the gate, too. Mays looked considerably creakier by the time he'd announced his retirement in 1973, but his victory-lap season continued when the Mets and Mays unexpectedly found themselves in the World Series.

Dan Carubia

Willie Mays said goodbye to America as a Met in 1973. Thirty-five years later, No. 24 led to way to say goodbye to Shea Stadium.

Mays occupied 24 as a coach from 1974 to 1979, at which point the jersey went into a kind of limbo. While Mays never achieved the impact of a Mets player whose number would be retired—though in a similar scenario, the 1970s Brewers did retire the No. 44 of Hank Aaron, who was a shadow of the legend he'd been as a Milwaukee Brave. The Mets, at least, seemed to acquiesce to Payson's wishes that the number not be issued again (Payson died in 1975).

So quietly into mothballs 24 went, and there it slumbered for more than ten years until the Mets issued it again to minor league journeyman **Kelvin Torve** upon his recall from AAA in August of 1990. While no official explanation for the screw-up ever emerged, fan and media outcry was swift. Years later, Torve confesses to being unaware of any controversy until asked to wear a different jersey.

"When I got to New York, I saw a locker with my uni in it, No. 24. I didn't give a second thought to it," Torve said in an interview from Davidson, North Carolina, where he works as a salesman for a packaging company and as a guest instructor at youth baseball camps. "I was just happy to be there. I'd have worn 2.4 if they asked me to.

"When we were on the road in California was the first I heard of any controversy," Torve continued. "[Equipment manager] Charlie [Samuels] came up to me and said, 'Listen, we made a mistake with your number. People have been calling. It was Willie Mays's number. So we'd like to change your number.' I said, 'Shoot, that's fine with me.' I didn't want to be a pain about it. And I guess they wanted to keep it low-key, not make a big deal about it. So I just started wearing No. 39 from that point on."

That he was issued No. 24 by accident—or perhaps, to clandestinely test fan sentiment—is virtually all that is recalled of Torve, a left-handed-hitting first baseman/outfielder who wasn't even the Mets' most memorable Kelvin. He came to the Mets as a free agent following stints in the Giants and Twins organizations and played two seasons with the Orix Blue Wave in Japan following his release by the Mets in 1991.

It should be noted that Torve hit .545/.615/.727 in 11 at-bats while wearing No. 24, with two doubles, including a game-winner. "I know Willie Mays did it proud too," he offered. Over parts of the 1990 and '91 seasons wearing No. 39, Torve hit a modest .263.

Until Mays came along, 24 was most closely associated with **Art Shamsky** (1968–71), the power-hitting outfielder and hero to countless area fans who identified with a Jewish star. Shamsky was swiped from Cincinnati after 1967 in a trade for utility man Bob Johnson. He overcame an early-season injury to post the best season of his career in 1969, providing 14 home runs and 47 RBIs in 303 at-bats as the left-handed-swinging member of three-way outfield rotation with Ron Swoboda (the righty) and Rod Gaspar (the switch-hitter who backed up both men).

Shamsky was part of the outgoing freight in an ultimately poor trade with St. Louis following the 1971 season; beefy pinch hitter Beauchamp was among the returnees. (Also going away were Jim Bibby, who would be a fine pitcher before long, and Rich Folkers, a decent reliever. In addition to Beauchamp, the Mets got back relievers Chuck Taylor and Harry Parker.)

Bob L. Miller (1962)—the L. distinguished him from teammate Bob G. Miller and also indicated his boxscore specialty—was the first wearer of the 24 jersey. Miller scuffled through a 1–12 season that belied his true ability: He'd be traded by the Mets following the season but lasted another twelve years in the majors, many of them as an effective reliever. He rejoined the Mets in 1973, wearing No. 30.

Art Shamsky was second in homers (14) and batting average (.300) on the 1969 Mets.

Johnny Lewis (1965–67) had speed, a strong arm, power, and wore No. 24—just like Mays. Lewis, however, didn't do those things nearly as well or as consistently as his Giants contemporary. That said, his 15-home run, .331 on-base percentage season in 1965 made him that years most accomplished Met. His greatest moment came that season when he broke up Jim Maloney's no-hitter in the 11th inning—his home run accounting for the only run as the Mets stole a win in Cincinnati.

Jerry Hinsley, one of the many early Mets without a career win, wore 24 in '64. **Ed Charles** wore it early in his Met career in '67, and **Ken Boswell** debuted in 24 later that year.

Although the Mets survived the Torve Insurrection, some were up in arms again in 1999 when future Hall of Fame outfielder **Rickey Henderson** insisted upon his customary No. 24. (Henderson was serious about No. 24. He once purchased it from Blue Jays teammate Turner Ward for $25,000). Rickey informed the Mets that he wanted 24 but would accept No. 35—his number as an A's rookie—in the event Mays rejected his entreaties (though Rick Reed may have had something to say about that). In the end, Henderson received Mays's blessing, then went out and had the last great year in a legendary career, hitting .315, reaching base at a .423 clip, and stealing 37 bases. Sulking over the Mets' refusal to renegotiate his contract, and smarting over his implication in the previous season's card-playing fiasco during the NLCS, Henderson was released in 2000. He worked his way back post-retirement, serving as a base-running instructor in spring training, then as first base coach in 2007.

Number 24

Number of times issued: 11 (10 players, 2 coaches)

Longest tenured: Art Shamsky (4 seasons, 404 games), Johnny Lewis (3 seasons, 226 games)

Best single seasons: Shamsky, 1969 (.300/.375/.488, 14 HR, 47 RBIs); Rickey Henderson, 1999 (.315/.423/.466, 12 HR, 42 RBI, 30 doubles, 37 stolen bases); Lewis, 1965 (.245/.331/.384, 15 HR, 45 RBIs)

Career statistical leaders: Home runs (Shamsky 42, Lewis 20); RBI (Shamsky 162, Lewis 67, Henderson 44, Willie Mays 44), batting average (Henderson, .298)

Mets Uniform History: The Mercury Mets

"Leading off . . . playing left quadrant . . . Rickey Henderson."

When Henderson dug into the plate to lead off the Mets' first inning on July 27, 1999, he looked up to the Diamond Vision screen to see a portrait of himself looking back, albeit one with slime-green skin and the long pointy ears of a Vulcan. Turning now to the evening's opposing pitcher, Pittsburgh's Kris Benson, revealed Benson wearing a shiny sleeveless jersey adorned with an oversize Pirates logo that made him look as though he were wearing a satin beach towel.

Henderson in his long career no doubt had seen some dumb things; he'd come up with Oakland when Charlie Finley still owned the team. "Turn Ahead the Clock" night had to be near the top.

The league-wide promotion dressed teams in futuristic uniforms and asked fans to imagine the games were taking place in the year 2021—a ham-handed reference to its sponsor, the real-estate company Century 21. Similar events took place that year at thirteen other parks. Eight clubs, including the traditionalist Yankees, Dodgers, and Cubs, wisely chose not to participate. The Mets were not only enthusiastic hosts but provided the signature moment of garish inelegance, the Mercury Mets.

For the Mets it wasn't enough to update their logo; they'd relocated the team to planet Mercury. (Perhaps the city, not to mention the planet, got to be too much to share with the Yankees.) Their uniform was a black, sleeveless v-neck pullover with silver graphics depicting a symbol casting its shadow onto a cratered planet. The same symbol—imagine the Prince logo designed by a preschooler—appeared on black Mets hats. On the uni backs, names appeared vertically alongside numbers in a futuristic font.

The doctored stadium graphics, renamed positions, and other details completed the very picture of future schlock; like a 1950s-era science fiction film so gloriously bad it was campy good. But that's only in retrospect. At the time it was just embarrassing.

"If we can't sell the product as it is, maybe we should give it a rest," Mets starting pitcher Orel Hershiser told reporters after the game (under a barrage of similar criticisms, Century 21 quietly dropped the promotion for 2000). The Mercury Mets lost their only game, 5–1, victims of a complete-game effort by Benson, or perhaps something worse, Mike Piazza speculated.

"We weren't beamed up to the proper coordinates," he deadpanned.

Gonna buy me a Mercury... and leave this uniform on another planet.

#25: BOBBY BOO

PROGRESSION:

Player	Years
Frank Thomas	1962–64 (to Aug. 7)
Gary Kroll	1964 (from Aug. 11)–1965
Larry Stahl	1967 (to May 10)
Bob W. Johnson	1967 (May 10–18)
Larry Stahl	1967 (from June 21)–1968
Amos Otis	1969
Don Hahn	1971–74
Del Unser	1975–76 (to July 21)
Jim Dwyer	1976 (from July 21)
Willie Montanez	1978–79
Bill Almon	1980
Randy Jones	1981 (to Aug. 9)
Charlie Puleo	1981 (from Sept. 11)–1982
Danny Heep	1983–86
Al Pedrique	1987 (to May 16)
Keith Miller	1987 (from June 16)–1991
Bobby Bonilla	1992–95
Yorkis Perez	1997
Jay Payton	1998
Bobby Bonilla	1999
Bill Pulsipher	2000
Alex Escobar	2001
Gary Matthews Jr.	2002 (to April 3)
Scott Strickland	2002 (from April 5)
Don Baylor (coach)	2003
Kazuo Matsui	2004–06 (to June 9)
Pedro Feliciano	2006 (from Aug. 4)–2010
Chin-lung Hu	2011
Ricky Bones (coach)	2012–15

When the Mets introduced **Bobby Bonilla** after signing him to what was then the richest contract in baseball history, they presented him with jersey No. 23.

It was their first mistake.

While Bonilla (1992–95, 1999) had some good seasons for the Mets, they weren't at the level that fans or the press demanded. And Bonilla's handling of criticism while the team struggled wrote an odd, and at times ugly, story of his years with his hometown team. Then again, signing Bonilla for considerably more money than they were willing to pay Darryl Strawberry a year before didn't exactly invite reasonable expectations.

Bonilla led the Mets in home runs, on-base percentage, and slugging percentage for three straight seasons beginning in 1992, but he's best remembered for a thin skin and a thick wallet. He offered to fight beat writers who wrote critically of him, he appeared preoccupied with official scorers when charged with an error, and he once tried to tune out the boo-birds by conspicuously wearing earplugs on the field. The volume was always tuned to high when Bobby Boo stepped up.

Bonilla's ascension to the most reviled player in team history wasn't complete until the Mets curiously reacquired him in 1999. Unhappy with a reserve role, Bonilla, who hit .160 in '99, feuded with manager Bobby Valentine, often complained of injuries, and was exposed for playing cards in the clubhouse as the Mets lost in excruciating fashion in the National League Championship Series.

Dan Carubia

Bobby Bonilla as a Met, the smile not yet wiped off his face.

Bonilla had one year and $5.9 million remaining in his contract when the Mets arranged a buyout prior to the 2000 season. Then obliviously swimming in double-figure returns from what would turn out to be Bernie Madoff's phony investment schemes, the Mets arranged to invest his salary in a Madoff account with the idea that interest from a deferred payment would make everyone rich. When the Madoff scandal became public in 2008 the club was left holding the bag—and on the hook for 25 consecutive annual payments of $1.2 million to Bonilla. The Mets will be cutting those annual checks until the year 2036, when Bonilla will be seventy-three years old and, likely, relaxing on a private tropical island. Even today it is a higher annual salary than many players earn for the cash-poor Mets. Shoulda just signed Strawberry, you think?

Met fans booed themselves hoarse over another 25: **Kaz Matsui**. Matsui was more of a patsy than a criminal, though, and he hadn't an ounce of Bonilla's contempt or arrogance. Like Bonilla, however, Matsui was an expensive mistake and out of position in more ways than one.

Seemingly lusting after the same new marketing revenue streams the Yankees had tapped into with Hideki Matsui in 2003, the Mets outbid several suitors for the services of Kaz Matsui that offseason, despite already having a terrific young shortstop in Jose Reyes. The Mets gave him Reyes's position (shortstop) and lineup slot (leadoff) but stopped short of taking the shirt off Jose's back. Matsui wore No. 7 in Japan and would have favored it with the Mets. Even we are dubious whether it would have helped.

Matsui hit the first pitch he saw in the majors over the fence in right-center at Turner Field. Then things started getting weird. By the end of his first season in New York, the Mets could see Matsui was miscast as a shortstop, though it was Matsui who had trouble seeing and probably needed eyeglasses. He also suffered from a recurring back problem, a language barrier, and general dislocation. Yet they also knew he could hit some. Attempts at second base in 2005 and 2006 started promisingly when Matsui, remarkably, hit home runs in his first plate appearances those two years as well (his 2006 lid-lifter was an inside-the-park job). But recurring injuries slowed his progress, frustrated management, and brought out a meanness in fans normally reserved for Bonilla. He was traded away in 2006 for his own good.

For all the futility of the 1962 Mets, it certainly took a while for anyone to match the power production that year of **Frank Thomas** (1962–64). His 34 home runs stood as the team record until Dave Kingman bashed his way to 36 in 1975; his 94 RBIs lasted until Donn Clendenon knocked in 97 in 1970. Acquired from the Braves for $125,000 worth of George Weiss's post-expansion draft "mad money" in the first big trade the Mets ever made, Thomas had a swing tailor-made for the Polo Grounds and its inviting deck in left field. Thomas slumped to 15 home runs in 1963 as age and competitors for an outfield job began catching up with him.

When Thomas was traded to Philadelphia and their doomed pennant drive late in the 1964 season, one of the players that came in return, 6-foot-6 pitcher **Gary Kroll**, could fit only into the No. 25 jerseys Thomas left behind. One in a string of strapping young projects of the early Mets, Kroll (1964–65) never got his act together despite having what observers agreed was outstanding raw material. He threatened to retire upon a 1965 demotion and eventually would be surrendered to Houston as a fallen star.

Flashy first baseman **Willie Montanez** (1978–79) was always fun to watch, even when the Mets weren't. Montanez brought style to acts as mundane as catching a pop fly, holding a runner on base, taking a warm-up swing, and famously, circling the bases after a home run. He drove in 96 runs for an awful 1978 Mets team but had little to style about in 1979. Montanez was one of the lucky ones: he was traded to Texas in August. One of the returnees was minor-league righty Ed Lynch, who'd go on to a fine career as a Met.

In May of 1967, the Mets purchased the contract of journeyman reserve infielder **Bob W. Johnson** from Baltimore; after the season they'd trade him straight-up for Art Shamsky. In between, Johnson (1967) had the best four months of his career, batting .348/.377/.474 in 230 at-bats.

Center fielder **Don Hahn** (1971–74) came to the Mets with a great reputation for his glove, perhaps because the Mets feared his bat wouldn't make

Dan Carubia

Danny Heep on the field at Shea before fateful Game Six of the 1986 World Series.

Dan Carubia

It really was hard to wipe the smile off the face of hustling Met Keith Miller.

much of an impression. Hahn's triple in Game 5 of the 1973 World Series chased Vida Blue from the game and drove in the insurance run in a 2–0 win. The heart of a Mets reserve squadron known as the "Scum Bunch," **Danny Heep** (1983–86) provided a dangerous left-handed bat off the bench and proved to be a capable, if slow, everyday player in case of injury. Heep was acquired in exchange for future Mets enemy Mike Scott.

Del Unser (1975–76) became an excellent pinch hitter later in his career, but he was yet another short-term center-field solution for the Mets. A first-round pick in Washington when Gil Hodges managed the Senators, Unser landed in New York—along with John Stearns and Mac Scarce—in the Tug McGraw deal. Unser batted .294 with 10 home runs, mostly out of the leadoff spot in his one full season at Shea in 1975, but he was sent to Montreal at the trading deadline the next year in one of the many bad Met trades involving center fielders (and third basemen). **Jim Dwyer** (1976), another future bench specialist, was part of the paltry return from the Expos that also cost Wayne Garrett; Dwyer was later traded for a handful of beans a mere fourteen seasons before he played his last game.

Young outfielder **Amos Otis** (1969) got on Gil Hodges's bad side while moping though a trial at third base and was subsequently traded to Kansas City in a move the Mets would regret for years and years and years. By contrast, nobody ever questioned the desire of **Keith Miller**

(1987–91), even if his talent wasn't up there with the best. Miller went on to a career as a sports agent representing among others, David Wright.

Sandy Alderson's first offseason press conference as Mets general manager—thank Bonilla and Madoff for making this day necessary—included an interrogation from a reporter for a local newspaper in Flushing asking whether he intended to sign Asian players. Within weeks, Alderson was introducing Taiwan-born infielder Chin-lung Hu at another press event, a move he was careful to frame was about baseball first, local fans second. Hu are you kidding? He hit .050 as a Met.

Over the course of his professional career, **Pedro Feliciano** has belonged at one time or another to the Dodgers, Reds, Tigers, Yankees, Fukuoka Daiei Hawks of the Japan Pacific League, Cardinals and Cubs but through 2015 he's only thrown a major league pitch for the Mets. Lost from and reacquired by the Mets on three separate occasions, the diminutive lefty sidewinder suited up 55, 39, 25, and again in 55 over a truncated nine-year career. His two-year stint with the Yankees was spent entirely on the disabled list but the signing granted the Mets the draft pick (Michael Fulmer) they used to acquire Yoenis Cespendes in 2015, proving even when Perpetual Pedro wasn't a Met, he was one of us.

Feliciano's best years came wearing No. 25, the jersey he switched to from 39 when Roberto Hernandez joined the Mets bullpen during the 2006 campaign. He wore No. 55 upon his initial appearance with the Mets in 2005 when he was one of four minor leaguers acquired for Shawn Estes from Cincinnati, and again in September of 2014 in what was his most recent Met appearance. We're not necessarily counting out another engagement.

A peek at Feliciano's matchup statistics is essentially akin to listing the National League's East's most feared hitters—in order, Utley, Howard, McCann, Dunn, Rollins, Victorino, LaRoche, (Chipper) Jones, (Adrian) Gonzalez, and Abreu—most of whom Feliciano reduced from MVP candidates to the likes of your remaining 25s: outfielders **Larry Stahl** (1967–68), **Jay Payton** (1998), **Alex Escobar** (2001), and **Gary Matthews Jr.** (2002); infielders **Bill Almon** (1980) and **Al Pedrique** (1987); and pitchers **Randy Jones** (1981), **Charlie Puleo** (1981–82), **Yorkis Perez** (1997), **Bill Pulsipher** (2000) and **Scott Strickland** (2002).

Number 25

Number of times issued: 28 (25 players, 2 coaches)

Longest tenured: Bobby Bonilla (5 seasons, 515 games); Pedro Feliciano (5 seasons, 364 games); Danny Heep (4 seasons, 395 games); Frank Thomas (2 seasons, 342 games)

Best single seasons: Thomas, 1962 (.266/.329/.496, 34 HR, 94 RBIs); Bonilla, 1993 (.265/.352/.522, 34 HR, 87 RBI); Willie Montanez, 1978 (.256/.320/.392, 16 HR, 96 RBIs); Feliciano, 2009 (6–4, 3.03, 59 strikeouts in 59 1/3 innings)

Career statistical leaders: Home runs (Bonilla 95, Thomas 52, Montanez 22); RBI (Bonilla 295, Thomas 173, Montanez 143); batting average (Del Unser .271, Bobby Bonilla .270); Wins (Feliciano 17, Charlie Puleo 9); Saves (Feliciano 4, Scott Strickland 2); ERA (Pedro Feliciano 3.24)

Uni Swaps

Uniform numbers and transactions are practically blood relatives. Following is a list of Mets trades in which the acquiree took the place—and uniform number—of the guy he was traded for. Some of these trades were multiplayer deals, but this list includes only those whose unis were swapped, and only those in which the new player took over the number at the first available opportunity. We might also call these Del Unser Deals (DUDS), in honor of the former No. 25 who arrived, and departed, via the Uni Swap.

Date	Met Traded	Team	In exchange for	Number
April 26, 1962	B. G. Smith	Cubs	Sammy Taylor	16
Aug. 5, 1963	Ken MacKenzie	Cardinals	Ed Bauta	19
Aug. 7 1964	Frank Thomas	Phillies	Gary Kroll	25
Aug. 8, 1964	Frank Lary	Braves	Dennis Ribant	17
Oct. 15, 1964	Dick Smith	Dodgers	Larry Miller	16
April 1, 1967	Ed Bressoud	Cardinals	Jerry Buchek	1
July 11, 1967	Chuck Hiller	Phillies	Phil Linz	2
Oct. 18, 1971	Art Shamsky	Cardinals	Jim Beauchamp	24
Dec. 3, 1974	Don Hahn	Phillies	Del Unser	25
July 21, 1976	Del Unser	Expos	Jim Dwyer	25
July 21, 1976	Wayne Garrett	Expos	Pepe Mangual	11
Sept. 10, 1982	Tom Hausman	Braves	Carlos Diaz	32
July 31, 1989	Kevin Tapani	Twins	Frank Viola	26
May 31, 1991	Tim Teufel	Padres	Garry Templeton	11
Jan. 22, 1992	Mark Carreon	Tigers	Paul Gibson	45

Date	Met Traded	Team	In exchange for	Number
July 29, 1996	Jeff Kent	Indians	Alvaro Espinosa	12
Sept. 14, 1999	Dan Murray	Royals	Glendon Rusch	48
Dec. 11, 2000	Bubba Trammell	Padres	Donne Wall	33
July 23, 2001	Todd Pratt	Phillies	Gary Bennett	7
Aug. 15, 2002	Shawn Estes	Reds	Pedro Feliciano	55
March 20, 2005	Jason Phillips	Dodgers	Kaz Ishii	23
Jan. 21, 2006	Kris Benson	Orioles	Jorge Julio	34
Dec. 5, 2006	Brian Bannister	Royals	Ambiorix Burgos	40
Aug. 31, 2010	Jeff Francoeur	Rangers	Joaquin Arias	12

#26: KONG

On July 19, 1976, in the top of third inning, Phil Niekro of the Atlanta Braves hit a soft, sinking liner to left field off Craig Swan of the Mets. **Dave Kingman,** playing left field instead of his usual right, hustled in toward it, stuck out his glove, and went into an awkward slide on his backside.

Kingman wore No. 26 on his back but the significant numbers on this night were 91 (the number of games Kingman had appeared in, of 93 played), 32 (the number of home runs Kingman had registered in those 91 games), and 56 (both the number of home runs Kingman was on pace to hit for the season and Hack Wilson's then National League record). He was averaging a home run every 12.2 trips to the plate.

Dan Carubia

A Dave Kingman swing usually resulted in either a ball in the parking lot or in the catcher's mitt.

Niekro wound up on second base as Kingman's lanky frame landed awkwardly on his glove hand. Kingman wound up on an operating table having torn thumb ligaments repaired.

The most serious threat any Mets hitter had ever made on the all-time record books was over.

With the Mets a safe distance from the pennant race, Kingman's injury also effectively eliminated the best reason anyone would show up at Shea, hastened the eventual departure of manager Joe Frazier and inspired, forty-eight hours later, the insipid Unser/Garrett for Mangual/Dwyer trade. Before you knew it, it was 1977 and things were really falling apart.

Kingman returned to the '76 lineup in late August and gave Mike Schmidt a challenge for the National League home run title, but "Sky King" lost by a single dinger, 38–37. He'd settle instead for a new club home run record that he'd tie in 1982, and Darryl Strawberry would break five years later.

Over two rocky tenures with the Mets (1975–77 and 1981–83), Kingman was at once impossible to ignore and maddeningly flawed. He was a strapping power hitter who might send the next pitch through a bus window in the parking lot but more likely would swing ferociously and miss by a lot. He couldn't field at four different positions. Described as aloof with teammates and often icy to the press, Kingman had a kind of stardom that looked good only from a distance. He left the Mets for good following the 1983 season as their leading career home run hitter with 154 (he has since fallen to fifth all time). Kong never batted higher than .238 (1976) and reached base at a .300 clip only once (1981) as a Met.

Though he never took the mound as a Met, Kong went 11–4 with a 1.38 ERA at USC, so it's perhaps fitting that No. 26 is the first Mets number where pitchers outnumber hitters. Side-arming swing man **Terry Leach** (1985–89) fulfilled Kingman's legacy of the one freaky season when, in 1987, he started 10–0 and finished 11–1.

Leach hung around the fringes of the organization for seven seasons (the last five wearing No. 26). Acquired and traded away twice by the Mets, Leach didn't make an Opening-Day roster until age thirty-three in '88. (Read more about him Chapter 43.)

Any list of poorly timed Mets injuries should include the right calf strain suffered by **Orlando Hernandez** (2006–07) prior to his scheduled start of Game 1 of the National League Division Series in 2006. El Duque injured himself while jogging, a testament to his advanced age—he was listed at forty but his actual age no one may ever know. Hernandez won 18 games for the Mets over two years, remaining a reliable strikeout man until retiring.

Lefty **Frank Viola** wore 26 upon his arrival from Minnesota in 1989, becoming the third Met that season to do so: Leach and pitcher **Kevin Tapani** proceeded him. **Rico Brogna** (1994–96) had a respectable .289-22-76 campaign in 1995 but was traded when John Olerud arrived. **Alejandro Peña** (1990–91) was John Franco's first setup man and not a bad one at that. Journeyman right-hander **Bob Shaw** (1966–67) was one of three 11-game winners on the 1966 Mets. Enigmatic fifth starter **Jae Seo** (2004–05) and his array of good and bad spent two seasons in 26. Only the bad seemed to follow him upon being sent away.

Galen Cisco (1962–65) took a sound beating along with the rest of the early Mets. His 3.62 ERA led the 1964 Mets even though he lost 19 games, second most in the league to teammate Tracy Stallard's 20. Cisco was the third 26 on the '62 Mets: the first two, **Herb Moford** and **Wilmer "Vinegar Bend" Mizell**, threw the last pitches of their respective careers in the jersey. Combined, they were 0–3 with a 7.30 ERA.

The Mets dropped like stones in 2009. In May alone the Mets went through three shortstops, with a severe drop in quality along the way: Jose Reyes to Alex Cora to **Ramon Martinez**. Hastily summoned from Class AAA

Super prospect Fernando Martinez waits on a spring training pitch, just as Mets fans waited on him—in vain.

Buffalo, he took the field wearing a jersey reading, MARTINEZ 26. The next day, Ramon Martinez wore No. 6. The week after that, outfielder **Fernando Martinez** made his major league debut, he too wearing a MARTINEZ 26 jersey. Pure speculation on our part but the circumstances and suddenness of the switch suggests the Mets simply gave Ramon a jersey they'd intended to give to Fernando.

As things turned out, the latter Martinez (2009–2011) might not have belonged in uniform, either. At one time the club's most prized prospect, Martinez made sporadic appearances and few contributions over parts of three seasons with the Mets, hitting .183 with one home run.

Others made less painful turns in 26: pitchers **Bill Graham** (1967), **Ray Burris** (1979), **Scott Holman** (1980), and **Kevin Tapani** (1989); the debuting **Bruce Boisclair** (1974); and reserves **Ced Landrum** (1993), **Ralph Milliard** (1998), **Terrence Long** (1999), **Jon Nunnally** (2000), **David Lamb** (2000), **Jason Phillips** (2001), and **Marco Scutaro** (2002–03).

A Queens native and son-in-law of Gil Hodges, right-hander **Mike Bruhert** (1978) might have been born to be a Met, but his 4–11 record assured his stay was brief. Relievers **Barry Manuel** (1997) and **Billy Taylor** (1999) became familiar with Shea boo-birds in their respective, short-lived tenures. Barry, Billy, Bruhert (and let's not forget No. 25 Bonilla)—there's always a B to boo.

Number 26

Number of times issued: 33 (29 players, 2 coaches)

Longest tenured: Dave Kingman (6 seasons, 664 games), Galen Cisco (4 seasons, 126 games)

Best single seasons: Terry Leach, 1987 (11-1, 3.22 ERA); Kingman, 1976 (.238/.286/.506, 37 HR, 86 RBIs)

Career statistical leaders: Home runs (Kingman 154, Rico Brogna 34); RBI (Kingman 389, Brogna 126); batting average (Brogna, .291); wins (Leach 21, Cisco 18); saves (Alejandro Peña 9, Leach 4); ERA (Peña 2.98, Leach 3.02)

Spring Training and Other Untrustworthy Things

Not including Viagra-related spam, the most common e-mail received over seventeen-plus years at MBTN.net headquarters comes from fans who recall Dwight Gooden wearing No. 64 and wondering why it isn't listed.

That happened all right, just not during a regular-season or postseason game: it was during spring training. And rules of the project state that what happens in St. Lucie stays in St. Lucie (or St. Petersburg, as the case may be).

That yearbook and baseball-card photographers for years made spring training sites their home helped spread the confusion. This was especially true as Gooden became a sensation in 1984 and pictures of the phenom wearing 64 from 1984's spring training were widely distributed. Dave Kingman was on the cover of the 1981 Opening Day program in a spring No. 5 before wearing familiar 26 for his whole second term.

For some players spring training offers the opportunity to work on a new stance or learn a new pitch. Others give new uniforms a tryout. Gooden donned No. 00 (along with Roger McDowell, who wore 0) in an attempt to lighten the mood in 1989, but both were back in their respective 16 and 42 when the games started counting. John Franco wore No. 00 during some 1993 workouts (along with 76, 77, and 92).

Seeing players wearing uniform numbers usually suited for linemen or wide receivers is a sure sign that spring has arrived. Although as chaotic as it looks, the Mets appear to apply some logic to their spring assignments, often using uniform numbers to group their invitees into certain loosely defined categories.

Dan Carubia

Don't believe everything you see in spring training. Ruben Tejada, No. 11 for every game as a Met, wore 79 to make the team in March of 2010.

Which is why you'll often see players newly arrived from other organizations wearing numbers in the high 50s. This group includes minor-league free agents, trade throw-ins, and Rule 5ers (players picked from other teams with a chance to either make the big-league club or be returned from whence they came). Young prospects who have earned invitations to big-league camp through promising play in the minors typically follow with numbers in the 60s. The most promising members of this group could find themselves upgraded to a lower number.

Organizational prospects—or the likely denizens of that season's AA and AAA rosters—populate the 70s. Catchers are as essential to spring training as sunblock, floppy caps, and loud shirts. Backstops are put to good use with all the arms in camp, and they tend to get their own designation in the 80s and 90s. But their specialized skill may earn them a future spring training invite while low-numbered flash in the pans may get burned from too much exposure too soon.

#27: IN THE FAMILIA WAY

Craig Swan deserved better. He made his debut appearance just as the Mets were winning a division and his last one just as they became contenders again. The decade between might be called the Craig Swan Era, a period that bridged the gap between the Mets of Seaver, Harrelson, and Kranepool and those of Mookie, Darryl, and Gooden and featured all of two winning seasons: 1975 and 1976.

Swan (1973–84) would be the last in long line of successful farm-raised starters of the '60s and '70s. On his best days Swan was a worthy successor to Tom Seaver, but injuries cost him consistency, and a poor supporting cast cost him victories.

Being the best pitcher on a bad team in an ugly era was Craig Swan's lot in life.

With Seaver gone in 1978, Swan won the National League ERA title at 2.43 to go along with a 9–6 record. He won a team-high 14 games for the putrid 1979 Mets—the next closest finisher had 6—and finished 11–7 for a 1982 squad that lost 97 games.

If Swan provides a lesson for Met 27s, it is, perhaps, that the numbers just don't matter. Writing in the *New York Times* in 1976, Murray Chass relayed how Swan miserably failed a pop quiz regarding uniform numbers administered by equipment manager Herb Norman. Swan, Chass reported, whiffed when asked to identify No. 17 (Felix Millan) and No. 6 (Mike Vail), guessing that neither number was occupied. No. 55? "Don't be silly. There is no 55," Swan remarked, forgetting that the digits belonged to his manager, Joe Frazier.

Carlos Gomez (2007) was one of several prospects of the Omar Minaya/Tony Bernazard Era to be aggressively promoted to the big leagues way ahead of schedule. The abilities that would one day make Gomez one of the league's best power-and-speed men were evident, but the results were not, and Gomez would the centerpiece of the outgoing package in the Johan Santana trade that winter. Nearly a decade later the Mets nearly reacquired Gomez in a deal that would have cost them another promising young hitter in Wilmer Flores.

Jeurys Familia grunts as Pedro Feliciano looks on, among others.

Had the deal come off as drawn up (which would also have kept Yoenis Cespedes out of Flushing), there may have invited speculation as to the rightful wearer of 27: Gomez, or up-and-coming closer **Jeurys Familia** (2012–15). The Mets brought Familia along slowly but when they needed a new closer early in 2015 season, he was more than capable. Taking over for suspended Jennry Mejia the first week of the year, Familia tied the Armando Benitez 2001 team record of 43 saves in a season to go with a 1.85 ERA and 86 strikeouts in 78 innings.

As the year progressed so too did the Mets faith in Familia to whom 4- and 5-out saves became just as automatic as the 3-out variety. Betrayed by a poorly-timed quick pitch and bad fielding behind him, Familia blew 3 saves in the World Series after blowing none in his last two months of the season.

Dennis Cook (1998–2001) was the most accomplished reliever to have worn No. 27 before Familia. An intense competitor who wanted the ball in the worst way, the lefty Cook teamed with righty Turk Wendell to give the Mets one of the game's best contemporary setup tandems. Cook won 10 games and saved 3 in relief in 1999 and didn't allow a run over ten appearances in postseason play. In 2006, another Mets postseason run was fueled in part by an excellent season out of the bullpen from veteran lefty **Darren Oliver**, who was 4–1 with a 3.44 ERA in his only Mets season.

Pete Harnisch (1995–97) briefly assumed No. 1 starter duties, but he was no Tom Seaver. He was no Craig Swan, even. The Long Island native battled depression and tobacco withdrawal while clashing with manager Bobby Valentine.

At age thirty-three and in his thirteenth professional season, **Don Cardwell** (1967–70) was the oldest pitcher on the 1969 pitching staff. Cardwell redeemed some early-season shakiness by winning five consecutive decisions starting in August '69 as the Mets caught, then surpassed, the Cubs to clinch the Eastern Division. The streak, which included six straight starts allowing two runs or fewer, lowered Cardwell's season ERA by nearly an entire run.

Rookie call-up **Mike Jacobs** (2005) was ticketed to return to AAA when he walloped a pinch-hit, three-run home run in his first major league at-bat, which led to more at-bats and more home runs: a torrid pace of 11 in his first 100 at-bats.

Jacobs was the fourth man to homer in his first plate appearance for the Mets. The uniform numbers of the players go in ascending order: Benny Ayala 18, Mike Fitzgerald 20, Kaz Matsui 25, and Jacobs 27. Never living up to the promise of their first at-bats in blue and orange, the Mets traded away all four players, selling high on Jacobs to obtain his replacement, All-Star upgrade model Carlos Delgado.

Others to wear 27 are notable in strange ways. Pitcher **Tom Parsons** (1964–65) went 1–10 in 1965, but Houston deemed him acceptable trade fodder for Jerry Grote. Reliever **Mark Corey** (2001–02) is best remembered for a pot-related freakout that ended his Mets career and would be cited by critics as justification for manager Bobby Valentine's firing after the season. Utility man **Tom O'Malley** (1989–90) was no great shakes as a Met but was a future MVP in Japan. **Dallas Green** (1966) spent two weeks as a reliever for the Mets but would return as the team's manager twenty-six years later.

Overmatched infielder **Mike Glavine** (2003) had better connections (yes, he's Tom's brother) than skill.

Righthanded spot-starter **Nelson Figueroa** had just enough ability to hang at the fringe of the Met roster in 2008 and 2009. A graduate of Abraham Lincoln High in Brooklyn—the same school that produced Lee Mazzilli—Figueroa, like Mazzilli, was originally a Mets draft pick (2005) and also like Maz, followed his playing career with an analyst gig on SNY, the Mets' TV network.

Others: pitchers **Larry Foss** (1962), **Wes Gardner** (1984–85), **Bob McClure** (1988), **Jason Middlebrook** (2002–03), **Mike Matthews** (2005), and **Pedro Beato** (2011–12). Also, reserves **Stan Jefferson** (1986), **Randy "Moose" Milligan** (1987), **Chuck Carr** (1991), **Ced Landrum** (1993), **Frank Catalanotto** (2010) and **Jesus Feliciano** (2010).

Jim Hickman (1966), **Bruce Berenyi** (1984), and **Todd Zeile** (2004) did their most memorable work in other uniform numbers. Though Zeile homered in his final career at-bat to send out 27 in style.

Number 27

Number of times issued: 25 (24 players, 1 coach)

Longest tenured: Craig Swan (12 seasons, 229 games), Dennis Cook (4 seasons, 225 games), Don Cardwell (4 seasons, 101 games)

Best single seasons: Swan, 1978 (9–6, 2.43 ERA); Swan, 1979 (14–13, 3.29 ERA); Cook, 1999 (10–5, 3 saves, 3.68 ERA, 68 strikeouts in 63 innings)

Career statistical leaders: Home runs (Mike Jacobs 11); RBI (Todd Zeile 35); batting average (Jacobs, .310); Wins (Swan 59, Cook 25); Saves (Jeurys Familia 49, Cook 6); ERA (Familia 2.42, Don Cardwell 3.31).

Mets Uniform History II: Clothes Make the Mets, 1982–1996

When you're winning, you look good in anything. When you're losing, the hope is that the uniform might take your mind off what you're watching. Or so the thinking goes.

In 1982 the Mets added George Foster, George Bamberger, and blue alternate road tops. The blue shirts with the orange and white trim on the neck and sleeves made a nice change at the time, but this marked a recurring theme of modifications to what had been a consistent look over the club's first two decades. And those blue tops were about the only time the Mets looked good during their second half tanking. The '82 yearbook had (over)optimistically proclaimed, "Every game may be Fireworks [Night] at Shea this summer." Tellingly, Fireworks Night was rained out.

The next year the Mets went to thick striping from the neck to the socks on both home and road jerseys. The two-button crew neck was replaced by a pullover v-neck. The previous year this look had only been worn on the road. No one much noticed until the Mets acquired Keith Hernandez in June of '83 and he spent the next seven seasons aligning the stripes on his uniform, and helping change how the Mets looked on the field—and not just their clothes.

The twenty-fifth anniversary patches set the '86 Mets apart stylistically, as did their exemplary play during their Sherman-like march through the National League, followed by unforgettable battles in the NLCS and World Series (for more on patches, see the ends of chapters 38–39). In 1987 the club switched their road uniforms back to "New York." This was written in script instead of the traditional block lettering that they'd worn until switching to "Mets" on the road unis after the '73 World Series. As much as people loved the Mets after '86—unless you rooted for another NL team, and then you tended to hate them—the script "New York" was ditched after one year. Pro-block lettering, different (and uglier) than the 1960s and 1970s road uniform lettering, was added in 1988 and worn though 1990.

In 1991 the Mets not only lost Darryl Strawberry, they lost the pullover uniform they'd worn during his entire Mets tenure. The pullover was gone and the button down returned—so did the team's losing ways, ending a record run of seven straight winning seasons. But the Mets looked good. Until 1993, when the uniform and team were shot to hell simultaneously.

That year the racing stripes came off the sides, replaced by a thinner stripe on the pants. The jersey lost the stripes on the arm but picked up a tail, which ran underneath "Mets" on the home jersey and "New York" on the road duds. It was a different script than the '87 road look yet was still unappealing—though not as much as the 103-loss debacle of '93. Mets hats would have the mark of Cain from that year forward as well. The MLB logo was placed on the back of hats, following a trend of inserting manufacturer's logos on major league uniforms beginning in 1987, according to Mets uniform historian Michael Cesarano.

#28: "#IMWITH28"

Whether he was butchering a play in the field, or taking the league's best pitcher deep, inventing a new way around the bases, making a blind behind-the-back flip, smashing a double down the line, making the third out at third base, suffering a knee injury or overcoming one, he was, in a word, so very Murphy—a verb, an exclamation, an adjective. An improviser, as versatile as he was limited, reliably unpredictable, a resilient klutz, a savant, a hero, a goat, a provocative quote, and a hashtag. Above all he was a Met. That was **Daniel Murphy**. They don't make 'em any Murphier.

By the time his Mets career came to an end—he signed with the rival Washington Nationals as a free agent in the 2015–16 offseason—Murphy had accounted for more than one-fourth of all games ever played by a Met wearing No. 28—nearly 40 percent among position players. His lead over the second busiest 28, **John Milner**, is exactly 162 games and almost 1,000 at-bats.

No Met 28 had more hits, runs scored, doubles, triples, RBIs, and stolen bases than Murphy (Milner had more home runs and walks); none had more errors; none made more outs; none were a bigger force in the postseason; no player made you crazier behind brilliant and brilliantly awful plays than Murphy.

Murphy began and ended his Mets career in pennant races, but there wasn't a much winning in between. When called up for the first time in August of 2008, Murphy was slotted in left field and shot out of the gate by hitting better than .400 over his first 18 games, helping the Mets briefly overtake Philadelphia for the National League East title—a lead they'd infamously blow in late September for a second straight year.

Murphy adapted. Though miscast as a left fielder, he adequately replaced two different injured first basemen—Carlos Delgado (in 2009 when Murphy's 12 home runs led a sorry club in an enormous new ballpark), and then Ike Davis. Murph also subbed at third base for David Wright. Murphy found a home at last at second base, where we can agree he was a pretty good hitter.

A pretty good hitter, but never a feared slugger until an astonishingly sizzling postseason run in 2015. Murphy homered seven times including a record six in consecutive postseason games spanning the Division and League Championship series. His tiebreaking home run off Dodgers Zack Greinke provided the deciding run in the Division Series (two other homers in that series victimized Clayton Kershaw). Murphy homered in all four games of the convincing NLCS sweep of the Cubs, hitting .529 and deservedly collecting series MVP honors.

Jacob Kanarek/From Worst to First

The Hammer takes a mighty cut. John Milner led the Mets in home runs four times in six full seasons.

The performance made it all the more difficult to cut ties with Murphy following the 2015 season, an outcome assured when he rejected a qualifying offer. The Nationals presented Murphy with a No. 20 jersey. Met fans can still say #ImWith28.

A wiry power hitter with fast hands, menacing sideburns, ultra-high stirrups, and a head of steam, Milner (1971–77) led the Mets in home runs for three straight seasons beginning in 1972, and again in '77, when his 12 was the fewest by a team leader until . . . Murphy in 2009.

Nicknamed "The Hammer" for a resemblance to Hank Aaron, Milner lacked none his namesake's power, just his consistency and good health. Milner pulled everything, and when he got a hold of one it made first basemen nervous, and maintenance crews install new scoreboard light bulbs. His five Met grand slams—three in 1976 alone—held up as the club record until Mike Piazza broke it. Milner could take a walk, invited the HBP with an aggressive crowding stance at the plate, and was an adequate fielder at first base and right field. His snare of a soft liner and two-step to the bag clinched the unexpected '73 division title.

Other hitters in 28 include **Amos Otis** (1967), **Bob Heise** (1969), **Wally Backman** (1980), **Darren Reed** (1990), **Jeff Conine,** and **Sandy Alomar** (2007)—all of whom spent time in other Mets uniform numbers. In '07 Conine and Alomar had to be first duo of forty-one-year-olds in baseball history to trade jerseys, as Conine took Alomar's 19 in exchange for 28. **Tommy Herr** (1990–91) was a veteran of the mid-1980s Cardinals teams that Mets fans had always hated, and their feelings didn't change much as Herr's career sputtered ineffectively toward an end in orange and blue.

Bobby Jones (1993–2000) was never going to be the best Fresno-born pitcher in Mets history, but he was about as far ahead of fellow Fresnonians Jaime Cerda, Dennis Springer, and Rick Baldwin as he was behind Tom Seaver.

Guilty of unglamourousness and, even, at times, dullness, Jones over eight seasons complied 74 wins, ninth in team history through 2015. And just when fans expected a struggle, he tossed a one-hit, complete-game shutout on a sunny and brisk October afternoon to eliminate the Giants in the 2000 Division Series. Like Murphy, it was a resplendent swan song from an outgoing homegrown player.

Coming out of nowhere to record 9 wins and a team-best 3.10 ERA, lantern-jawed Mainer **Carl Willey** (1963–65) emerged as the Mets' best starting pitcher of 1963. Willey was poised to assume Opening-Day pitching duties for the Mets in 1964 when a line drive by Gates Brown in a spring training game broke Willey's ample jaw. When he returned in June, Willey was assigned to the bullpen and never regained effectiveness as a starter.

The Mets most often called on 28 in relief: **Sherman "Roadblock" Jones** (1962) returned in 28 after an earlier stint in 36; bonus baby **Jim Bethke** (1965) began and ended his major league career at age eighteen and was perfect (2–0); hard-throwing but wild lefty **Bill Hepler** (51 walks in 69 innings in 1966); shaggy **Dwight Bernard** (1978–79); maverick philosopher and well-past-his-prime fireman **Mike Marshall** (1981); **Scott Holman** (1982–83); **Scott Strickland** (2003); goggle-wearing reliever/magician **Juan Padilla** (2005); and **Brandon Knight** (2008), who wore 28 a week before Murphy's debut.

Number 28

Number of times issued: 24 (21 players, 3 coaches)

Longest tenured: Daniel Murphy (7 seasons, 903 games), Bobby Jones (8 seasons, 193 games), John Milner (7 seasons, 741 games)

Best single seasons: Murphy, 2015 (.281/.322/.449, 15 HR, 73 RBIs); Jones, 1997 (15–9, 3.63 ERA); Carlton Willey, 1963 (9–14, 3.10 ERA, 4 shutouts); Milner, 1973 (.238/.340/.423, 23 HR, 72 RBIs).

Career statistical leaders: Home runs (Milner 94, Murphy 62); RBI (Murphy 401, Milner 338); batting average (Murphy .288, Milner .245), wins (Jones 74); saves (Juan Padilla 1); ERA (Willey, 3.29, Scott Holman 3.45).

The Namesake Series

Luggage and fan mail may have been another story, but fans rarely had trouble distinguishing Bobby Jones from Bobby Jones when they were Mets teammates in 2000.

Bobby J. Jones was white, right-handed, wore No. 28, and started games; Bobby M. Jones was black, left-handed, wore No. 21, and pitched in relief. Bobby M. Jones relieved Bobby J. Jones three times in 2000. The highlight came on September 28 when the Joneses combined to defeat Greg Maddux, 8–2. Atlanta, as the saying goes, couldn't keep up with the Joneses.

More difficult to distinguish were the Bob Millers of 1962, perhaps because they were so undistinguished themselves. Bob L. Miller, a right-handed starter, finished with a 1–12 record. Bob G. Miller, the left-hander reliever acquired from the Reds in midseason, went 2–2 with a 7.20 ERA. The Millers appeared in the same game on five different occasions, the lone win coming on a 14th-inning home run by Frank Thomas. Bob L. went the first seven innings; Bob G. pitched a scoreless 14th for the win.

The Mets have had five pairs of same-named players who weren't teammates: the Bob Johnsons (one a pinch-hitting whiz of 1967; the other a rookie pitcher who'd be a throw-in the Otis-Foy deal in 1969), the Mike Marshalls (the legendary reliever, 1981; and the Go-Go's-dating outfielder, 1990), the Pedro Martinezes (the obscure lefty reliever from 1996 and the greatest right-handed pitcher of his era), the Sean/Shawn Greens (reliever/outfielder) and the Chris Youngs (the pitcher who struck out too few, and the outfielder who struck out too often). Ike Hampton (obscure catcher of 1974) and Mike Hampton (mercenary lefty of 2000) form the honorary battery of this group.

Pedro A. Martinez (that's the first one) is one of several famous names that weren't. The Mets had the weak-hitting infielder Brian Giles, not the power-hitting All-Star outfielder. The Kevin Brown who played briefly for the 1990 Mets wasn't the dominant strikeout pitcher of the era but wasn't, that we know at least, a complete jerk, either.

The Mets have had several sets of relatives who share a name: the Alomars (Sandy Sr., and sons Roberto and Sandy Jr.), the Alous (Jesus, nephew Moises, and Moises's cousin Mel Rojas), and the Wilsons (Mookie and stepson Preston). Ron Hodges and Gil Hodges were not related, but Gil Hodges and Mike Bruhert were (Bruhert married Gil's daughter).

Related by blood, by marriage, or merely by alphabetical proximity, following are the most populous player surnames in Mets history, through 2015:

No. of Players	Surname	Roster
8	Jones	Barry, Bobby J., Bobby M., Chris, Cleon, Randy, Ross, Sherman
8	Johnson*	Ben, Bob L., Bob W., Howard, Kelly, Lance, Mark, and Rob
7	Hernandez	Anderson, Keith, Livan, Luis, Manny, Orlando, and Roberto
5	Miller	Bob G., Bob L., Dyar, Keith, Larry
5	Smith	Bobby Gene, Charley, Dick, Joe, Pete
5	Taylor	Billy, Chuck, Hawk, Ron, Sammy
5	Wilson	Mookie, Paul, Preston, Tom, Vance
4	Anderson	Craig, Jason, Marlon, Rick
4	Bell	Derek, Gus, Heath, Jay
4	Marshall	Dave, Jim, Mike A., Mike G.
4	Martinez	Fernando, Pedro A., Pedro J., Ramon
4	Phillips	Andy, Jason, Mike, Tony
4	Young	Anthony, Chris B., Chris R., Eric

*-Not counting manager Davey

#29: BANG THE METS SLOWLY

Slow to recover, slow around the bases, slow curves, slow to deliver: These are your Met 29s.

The only thing **Ike Davis** did quickly was age. He looked and played like a veteran when he was only a rookie, but he only got older from there.

The son of former Yankees reliever Ron Davis, Ike stepped into the Mets lineup for the first time in April of 2010—he wasn't wearing No. 29 that night, but 42 as everyone was in honor of that year's Jackie Robinson remembrance. Ike looked very much like a Major Leaguer from the start. He had a steady glove at first base, a whiff-heavy but patient approach at the plate, and light-tower power from the left side. If he wasn't quite Keith Hernandez with home runs, he was **Dave Magadan** with home runs, and as such an appropriate inheritor of the No. 29 jersey.

Davis unfortunately showed other characteristics of a veteran: Most significantly, a tendency for injuries and slow recoveries from them. Building upon a promising rookie season (19 home runs, .351 on-base percentage), Davis stumbled into teammate David Wright while settling beneath a popup near the pitcher's mound at Coors Field early in 2011. What appeared to be a benign twisted ankle became months of baffling setbacks that cost him the rest of the year. Davis put up a 32-homer season in 2012—only Carlos Delgado had more among Mets first basemen in history—only to suffer in 2013 with chronic flu-like conditions later diagnosed as Valley Fever, an affliction even more mysterious and difficult to heal than his ankle troubles.

The Mets finally gave up on Davis in 2014, shortly after his twenty-seventh birthday, and he's floated around seeking his old form ever since.

The aforementioned Magadan (1986–89, 1992) drew a lot of walks, hit some doubles, and always plodded slowly around the bases. Magadan had a career .292 batting average as a Met; his .391 career on-base percentage was second only to another noted slowpoke left-handed hitting first baseman: John Olerud, and 4 points above a predecessor he was most often compared to (if often unfavorably), Keith Hernandez.

Dan Carubia

A student of hitting, Dave Magadan was a future hitting coach and the first Met to finish in the top three in batting.

Speaking of slow, no Mets player wore No. 29 longer than **Steve Trachsel** (and no, we don't mean in a single game). Trachsel's career as a Met began terribly (he accepted a demotion to AAA after starting 2–10, 6.72 in 2001) and ended ugly (reportedly begging out of NLCS Game 2 in 2006, having surrendered five runs in an inning-plus). Between those extremes, Trachsel was a slow-working model of moderately priced consistency who by 2006 was the team's longest-serving player. Trachsel led the Mets in ERA in 2002–03, won 16 games in '03 (one of four times he led or tied for the team lead), and his 66 wins overall rank tenth in team history, through 2015. Trachsel wore 29 because he preferred not to wear the No. 28 initially assigned to him: That number belonged to Bobby Jones, a Cal State-Fresno college rival to Trachsel's Cal State-Fullerton squad.

Until R. A. Dickey pulled the feat in 2012, **Frank Viola** (1989–91) served 22 years as the last Mets 20-game winner. With 19 wins in mid-September 1990, the lefty whiffed in three attempts to get No. 20 while the Mets fell from a half-game behind division-leading Pittsburgh to mathematical elimination. He nailed down No. 20 in the final game of the season.

Now a long-term coach in the organization, it was reasonable to have expected more of Viola as a pitcher. A New York native and St. John's grad, he was at the top of his game when a blockbuster summer trade brought him home from Minnesota in 1989: New York surrendered five pitchers, including Rick Aguilera and Kevin Tapani, who'd combine for 198 wins and 311 saves over their careers (plus a Twins world championship in 1991).

While the pitching-infused Twins went from last to first in '91, the Mets dropped from second to fifth. Viola suffered an infected fingernail and lost 10 of his final 12 decisions. Viola may also have been dissatisfied with his uniform number. With 16 belonging to Dwight Gooden, Viola wore 26 in 1989 and then tried 29 in deference to his assigned number at St. John's. He was back in 16 at his earliest opportunity, when he signed with the Red Sox in 1992. (Viola's switch to 29 in 1990 forced Magadan to take No. 10. Mags would transition back to 29 when manager Jeff Torborg took No. 10 in 1992).

Copiague's own **Hank Webb** (1974–75) wore 29 when he entered in the 25th inning at Shea on September 11, 1974. He allowed a single to the first Cardinal he faced, Bake McBride, and then chucked a pickoff throw into right field. Ron Hodges, who'd entered after Duffy Dyer caught the first 23 innings, dropped the throw at home plate as McBride scored the first run by anyone in fifteen innings. And that's how the longest night game in National League history was decided.

Rookie **Octavio Dotel** (1998–99) had better luck in extra innings at Shea. He was set to take the loss in the 15th inning of Game 5 of the 1999 NLCS, but the "Grand Slam Single" made a winner of us all. Dotel played for a record 12 more franchises—starting with Houston, where the Mets sent him that winter in the Mike Hampton deal.

Walrus-sized southpaw **Mickey Lolich** was a two-time 20-game winner and World Series hero for Detroit, but the trade that made him a Met was a jumbo bust. Out went Rusty Staub, who had just set the season RBI mark as a Met and would drive in 318 runs over the next three seasons in the AL. In came the thirty-five-year-old Lolich, who posted a 3.22 ERA in '76, but lacking run support, won only 8 games and retired following his lone season in New York.

Staub initially arrived in a trade for **Ken Singleton** (1970–71), a young outfielder from Hofstra who'd grow into a hitter the Mets could have used for years to come. "Poor trade" is about all the comes to mind with the mention of **Rich Chiles** (1973), who arrived from Houston in the Tommie Agee deal and hit .120 in eight games.

Like Lolich, **Frank Tanana** (1993) was a veteran American League lefty strikeout artist who retired after a year with the Mets. By 1993, however, Tanana had long lost his strikeout stuff, but he had one last stop. The Mets traded Tanana to the contending Yankees in mid-September.

Junk-throwing lefty swingman **Tom Gorman** (1982–85), whom Keith Hernandez called "Gorfax" in a needling reference to the lefty fireballer of Dodgers fame that Gorman clearly was not, posted a 6–0 record in 1984. Gorman's claim to fame was as the winning pitcher on July 4, 1985, despite allowing a game-tying home run to Atlanta pitcher Rick Camp in the bottom of the 18th inning (the Mets won in the 19th).

Not so lucky in extras was lefty **Rob Gardner** (1965–66). He pitched the first 15 innings of a 0–0 game against Philadelphia interrupted by a curfew in 1965. Although the game started from scratch the next day, Gardner's epic no-decision is far more noteworthy than the portsiding trio that combined for a single win as Mets: **Willard Hunter** (1962), Rule 5 draftee **Don Rowe** (1963), and **Nick Willhite** (1967).

The Mets had high hopes for catching prospect **Alex Treviño** (1978–81). So did the Reds, who insisted on him in the George Foster trade to succeed Johnny Bench. Treviño got raves for his defense and filled in admirably for an injured John Stearns in 1980, but he holds the Mets record for most turns at-bat without ever hitting a home run (733). He returned briefly for a nine-game cup of coffee with the Mets in 1990 (wearing No. 6), his final major league season.

Then there's expansion draftee **John "Thumper" DeMerit** (1962); luckless **Craig Anderson** (1963); relievers **Danny Frisella** (1967–69) and **Bob D. Johnson** (1969); infielders **Tim Corcoran** (1986) and **Jim Lindeman** (1994); starter **Robert Person** (1995–96); utility man **Steve Bieser** (1997); and pitchers **Masato Yoshii** (1998) and **Eric Cammack** (2000).

Lastly, a glimpse at roster malfunction in the closing year of Shea and the first season of Citi. The Mets issued 29 to eight different players over 2008–09, in each case 1 pitcher, 1 outfielder, 1 infielder and 1 catcher. It started with swingman **Jorge Sosa** (2007–08), who lost his effectiveness and the jersey went to outfielder **Chris Aguila**, to infielder **Andy Phillips**, back to Aguila, and finally to catching suspect **Gustavo Molina**. In 2009 the uni wasn't even worn until June, but then came outfielder **Emil Brown**, infielder **Andy Green**, catcher **Robinson Cancel**, and pitcher **Tobi Stoner**, who wore it until the day Ike Davis arrived in 2010. None were ever Mets again.

Number 29

Number of times issued: 38 (35 players, 1 DNP)

Longest tenured: Steve Trachsel (6 seasons, 160 games), Ike Davis (5 seasons, 454 games), Dave Magadan (5 seasons, 433 games), Tom Gorman (4 seasons, 98 games)

Best single seasons: Frank Viola, 1990 (20–12, 2.67, 182 strikeouts in 249 2/3 innings); Davis, 2013 (32 HR, 90 RBIs); Magadan, 1989 (.286/.367/.393 in 374 at-bats); Trachsel, 2003 (16–10, 3.78 ERA, 111 strikeouts in 204 2/3 innings)

Career statistical leaders: Home runs (Davis 68, Ken Singleton 18); RBI (Davis 224, Magadan 131); batting average (Magadan .290); wins (Trachsel 66); ERA (Mickey Lolich, 3.22, Viola 3.29)

Decisions, Decisions: Wins and Loses by the Numbers

Statisticians and other astute observers understand that a pitcher's winning percentage is a poor indicator of his quality or lack of it. Especially over time, a player's winning percentage tends to resemble the overall record of his team, which is why the chart below is full of results at or near a .47955 winning percentage, which happens to be the Mets' overall record through 2015 (4,128–4,480). Consider this: the Mets enter the 2016 season needing eighteen consecutive 90-win seasons to reach .500 as a franchise. Out-winning your team overall is a feat for the lucky or exceptionally good. But it couldn't hurt to wear 16.

Following is a list of winning percentages by uniform number in Mets history through 2015. Only numbers with more than 100 wins or losses were considered.

No.	Wins	Losses	Pct.	Notes
16	168	99	.629	Thanks to Doc, no other jersey comes close.
41	203	129	.611	Seaver's four predecessors combined to go 5–5.
50	115	98	.540	Sid Fernandez (97–78, .554), Duaner Sanchez (10–2, .833).
44	107	99	.519	David Cone (56–28, .667) won two-thirds of his decisions while wearing 44.
35	157	153	.503	Rick Reed (59–36, .621) was a winner, but it took Dillon Gee (40–37, .519) to push the 35s over .500.
33	136	140	.493	Matt Harvey (25–18, .581) and John Maine (39–32, .549) determined to turn 33 from a loser to a winner.
34	165	177	.482	Mike Pelfrey (50–54, .481) is the winningest and losingest 34.
49	121	131	.480	Jon Niese (61–61, .500) accounts for half the wins and almost half of the losses.
29	170	184	.480	Best percentage winner: Octavio Dotel (8–3, .727).
39	149	162	.479	Consider: Doug Sisk (17–16, .515) is the winningest 39 above .500.

No.	Wins	Losses	Pct.	Notes
45	151	165	.478	Pedro Martinez (32–23) second to Tug McGraw (47–55) in victories.
36	235	258	.477	Winningest and losingest number in team history.
22	151	166	.476	Al Leiter (.586) nearly makes up for Jack Fisher (.342). Nearly.
40	139	155	.473	Stragglers include .333-averaging relievers Jeff Innis (10–20) and Braden Looper (6–12)
32	154	175	.468	Jon Matlack (82–81) leads the way. Steven Matz (4–0) perfect for starters.
43	109	125	.466	R. A. Dickey (39–28, .582) flutters to the top.
26	103	122	.458	Terry Leach rocks a flashy .750 winning percentage (21–7); Galen Cisco (18–43, .295) the other extreme.
47	163	194	.457	Appropriately, Jesse Orosco went 47–47. Tom Glavine (61–56) is winningest. Devastating.
48	118	148	.444	17 pitchers, just 3 better than .500 (Julio Machado, Jacob deGrom, Randy Myers).
27	138	167	.434	Craig Swan's winning percentage will make you rolf (59–71).
30	83	112	.426	Nolan Ryan (29–37, .439), Mike Scott (14–27, .341), and Mike Torrez (11–22, .333) all won elsewhere.
38	146	220	.399	33 pitchers, only 3 with winning records: It all starts with Roger Craig (12–43, .218).

#30: NOLAN RYAN: THE ONE WHO GOT AWAY

PROGRESSION:

Player	Years
Dennis Ribant	1965–66
Nolan Ryan	1967 (did not play); 1968–71
Hank Webb	1973 (to May 11)
Bob L. Miller	1973 (from Sept. 22)–1974
Hank Webb	1976 (to May 27)
Jackson Todd	1977 (from May 2)
Mike Scott	1979–82
Mike Torrez	1983–84
Mel Stottlemyre (coach)	1985–93
Doug Linton	1994
Alberto Castillo	1995–98
Allen Watson	1999 (to June 18)
Jorge Toca	1999 (from Sept. 1)–2001
Cliff Floyd	2003–06
Aaron Sele	2007
Raul Casanova	2008
Josh Thole	2009–12
David Aardsma	2013
Andrew Brown	2014
Michael Conforto	2015

The Mets traded **Nolan Ryan** for Jim Fregosi. Okay? Can we move on now?

It's hard to imagine how things might have been different had the Mets ever been able to resist the urge to upgrade their third basemen in the wake of 1969. It cost the Mets a fine outfielder, Amos Otis, in 1970. In 1971, coming off a year of Bob Aspromonte at the hot corner, it cost the Mets an erratic but hard-throwing right-hander who would become the greatest strikeout pitcher of all-time (plus three prospects!) It cost them a pitcher who not only

Dan Carubia

Nolan Ryans' back... The Ryan Express put on Mets jersey No. 30 for the first time in 37 years to celebrate the 1969 world championship in 2009.

could have complemented Seaver-Koosman-Matlack in the '70s, but Gooden-Darling-Fernandez in the '80s, and maybe even Gooden-Cone-Fernandez in the early '90s. It cost them a pitcher whose number would be retired by three other organizations.

Hey, at least we got an aging injured infielder playing out of position for a year-and-a-half out of it.

It doesn't excuse them for taking so little in return, but the Mets were losing patience with Ryan (1968–71), who suffered from recurring blisters, allowed way too many base runners via the walk or HBP, and threw too many wild pitches. He'd won a career-high 10 games in 1971 but lost 10 of his final 12 decisions. The upside was always there—he pitched seven innings in relief to win the decisive game of the 1969 NLCS and struck out batters even more prolifically than he walked them—but the Mets needed more offense and decided Ryan, the least-realized of the pitching staff, was the one who had to go.

For the Angels, the Ryan trade was all the more remarkable because it replaced the Greatest Angel of All-Time with the succeeding Greatest Angel of All-Time. They would not only retire No. 30 for Ryan but also No. 11 for Fregosi. Both were deserving—in Anaheim.

The Astros, who would retire No. 34 for Ryan, obtained the player for whom they would retire No. 33 from the Mets in **Mike Scott** (1979–82). Scott (14–27, 4.64 as a Met) had shown little of the ability or treachery that would turn him into a force for the 1986 Astros and nearly eliminate the Mets from World Series contention. The Mets received outfielder Danny Heep in return for Scott—but the deal attracted little notice because the Mets also reacquired Tom Seaver the same week.

There's no un-doing the Ryan or Scott trades, but another trade of a No. 30 could yield riches. That wasn't on anyone's radar when left-handed hitting catcher **Josh Thole** (2009–12) was thrust into action as a rookie. Learning on the job, Thole acquitted himself well, hitting .277 with a .366 on-base percentage in 2010, but he couldn't reach those levels as the starter in 2011 or 2012. However, all those batted-down R. A. Dickey knucklers came in handy when he, caddy Mike Nickeas, and Dickey all went to Toronto in the blockbuster offseason trade bringing the Mets a Ryan-esque power pitcher, Noah Syndergaard, as well as Thole's next two successors: John Buck and Travis d'Arnaud.

The Mets in the meantime have high hopes that a subsequent left-handed-hitting rookie wearing No. 30 and making a sudden ascent from Class AA will continue to improve: **Michael Conforto**. As might be expected of the offspring of a Penn State linebacker and a three-time Olympic synchronized swimmer, Conforto hits hard and his timing couldn't be better. He raced from Oregon State to the big leagues in about a year—arriving in time to help the Met lineup transform from feeble to formidable, slugging .506 with nine home runs and 14 doubles in 194 plate appearances, and homering twice in Game 4 of the World Series.

In 1966 **Dennis Ribant** was the first Mets starting pitcher to fashion a winning record (11–9) and the first Met to wear number 30. He was subsequently traded to Pittsburgh.

Battle-scarred veteran **Mike Torrez** (1983–84) slogged toward the end of his career as a Met. Among the lowlights: a team record for most men walked in one game (10), lasting only 1 1/3 innings to end the Mets 10-game Opening Day win streak in 1984, and the frightening beaning of Dickie Thon.

Banished after a 1–12 record in 1962, **Bob L. Miller** (1973–74) returned to the Mets to play a small role in the 1973 stretch drive, temporarily taking the uniform number of perpetual prospect **Hank Webb** (1973, 1976). Pitcher **Jackson Todd** overcame a battle with cancer to make the Mets in 1977.

Jacob Kanarek/From Worst to First

Pitching coach **Mel Stottlemyre** (1985–93) came around just as the Mets had pitching prospects blos-

Jackson Todd at Wrigley Field in the lost season of 1977. (For more on hair, see Nino Espinosa, Chapter 39.)

soming everywhere. He coached under four managerial regimes (Johnson, Harrelson, Cubbage, and Torborg), wearing No. 30 for all but his first year with the Mets.

Defense-first catcher **Alberto "Bambi" Castillo** (1995–98) was the first non-pitcher to don the No. 30 jersey. Castillo's 14th-inning pinch single drove in the lone run in a 1–0 Opening-Day win over Philadelphia in 1998. **Andrew Brown** could have been an Opening-Day hero himself. The surprise starter in left field for the 2014 opener when Chris Young came up lame, Brown shocked fans—not to mention Washington starter Stephen Strasburg—with a first-inning, three-run home run to left center. Alas the Mets found a way to lose that game, and eventually, they lost Brown.

Reliever **Doug Linton** (1994) was the first post-Stottlemyre 30. Lefty swingman and Queens native **Allen Watson** visited home briefly in 2009. Chubby first base prospect **Jorge Luis Toca** (1999–2001) saw brief duty in three seasons. Veteran hurler **Aaron Sele** (2007) made more news as the longest holdout in the club's San Francisco head-shaving episode than for his infrequent long relief outings. **Raul Casanova** (2008) closed out a long career of infrequent catching with his best batting line: .273/.344/.364. **David Aardsma** (2013) provided nondescript relief work but jumped to the top of the Mets all-time list—alphabetically.

Fans applauded the bravery of **Cliff Floyd** (2003–06) when he limped off the field for the last time in 2003, having put up productive numbers in spite of a painful Achilles tendon injury that required surgery. But fans eventually grew tired of waiting for Floyd to get healthy. Signed to a four-year free-agent deal, the plain-speaking, left-handed-hitting slugger had just one injury-free season as a Met, 2005, when he clubbed 34 home runs. But his lasting memory will be that of a player compromised: given a chance to be Kirk Gibson in Game 7 of the 2006 NLCS, he turned out instead to be Cliff Floyd.

Number 30

Number of times issued: 21 (19 players, 1 coach)

Longest tenured: Cliff Floyd (4 seasons, 468 games), Josh Thole (4 seasons, 308 games), Nolan Ryan (4 seasons, 105 games), Mike Scott (4 seasons, 84 games)

Best single seasons: Floyd, 2005 (.273/.358/.505, 34 HR, 98 RBIs); Ryan, 1970 (7–11, 3.42 ERA, 125 strikeouts in 131 2/3 innings); Dennis Ribant, 1966 (11–9, 3.20 ERA, 10 complete games)

Career statistical leaders: Home runs (Floyd 81, Michael Conforto 9); RBI (Floyd 273, Thole 87); batting average (Conforto .270, Floyd, .268); wins (Ryan 29); saves (Scott 3, Ryan 2); ERA (Ribant, 3.11, Ryan 3.51)

Dirty 30 and the Unpopular Numbers

As Lotto players and roulette junkies might tell you, certain numbers just don't come up that often. In the case of Mets uniforms, the unpopular uniforms are often those boasting popular, long-time players. They also encompass the semi-retired (8, 24) and the stigma-laden (13).

Following is a list of the jersey numbers, between 1 and 49, least frequently issued to players in Mets' history through 2007. For a list of the most frequently issued numbers, see Chapter 6.

No.	No. of Players	Notes
24	9	Technically still in mothballs for Willie Mays, but reissued in 2007 for coach Rickey Henderson.
31	13	Scheduled to go out of circulation permanently in 2016. But after John Franco (9 years) and Mike Piazza (8), had few wearers anyway.

No.	No. of Players	Notes
8	13	Unissued since Gary Carter's Hall of Fame induction; last Wearer was Desi Relaford in 2001.
13	19	Another number taken out of mothballs by Neil Allen—he was the first to wear it in eighteen years in '81.
30	19	Belonged longest to a coach, Mel Stottlemyre; would've been nice if Nolan Ryan had kept it warm longer.
46	19	Not worn by a player until 1979 by Neil Allen.
47	19	Jesse Orosco kept it tied up for nine years; Tom Glavine for five.
9	20	Two managers wore 9 (Wes Westrum and Joe Torre).
28	21	Three players (John Milner, Bobby Jones, Daniel Murphy) with 7-year hitches.
4	24	Coaches Mike Cubbage, Cookie Rojas, and Matt Galante combine for eleven years occupancy.

#31: MIKE PIAZZA: THE ONE WHO CAME TO SHEA

Mike Piazza is the guy who changed everything.

Piazza's arrival in a 1998 trade brought a sudden boost in attendance and a new, higher profile for the Mets overnight. His signing of a seven-year deal following the season completed a philosophical shift of direction within the organization that had begun in 1997. No longer were the Mets practicing the McIlvainian discipline of patiently building a franchise of well-scouted prospects from within. The new mission, ready or not, was this: get this team into the World Series as often as possible while this guy is still in his prime.

With Steve Phillips on the cell phone and Bobby Valentine in the dugout, they pulled it off once, in 2000. The rest of the time Piazza simply did his thing, which was to hit the ball harder than any Met ever had, stir the emotions of Mets fans like no other player, and do it all with a stoic languidness that would withstand whatever absurd fates destiny had planned for him.

Piazza remained a hard competitor and a gentleman, for instance, when fans booed him shortly after his arrival in 1998; when a certain Yankees thug hurled dangerous objects at him—twice—in 2000; when forced to hold a news conference to discuss his sexual orientation; when sandbagged with the revelation he was the team's

Mike Piazza, the final No. 31, made the black uniforms and the Mets lineup look intimidating.

Dan Caribia

new first baseman; and so on. Even legitimate issues, such as Piazza's inability to control the opposition's running game, probably attracted more attention than it should have—not that the 2004 switch to first base solved anything.

Piazza hit 220 home runs as a Met—third all-time entering 2016—but is arguably the club's all-time leader in unforgettable home runs, gasp-inducing home runs, home runs that humiliated the opposing pitcher, and heroic home runs: September 21, 2001, the Trevor Hoffman game, the Billy Wagner game, the Ramiro Mendoza game, John Smoltz in Game 6, to name just a few. He hit so many, so hard, he whacked No. 31 clear out of existence. The Mets announced the retirement of No. 31 in 2016 to commemorate his induction into the Baseball Hall of Fame, the only Met besides Tom Seaver with the team insignia on his plaque.

The trade that brought Piazza to the Mets was discussed enough beforehand that there was time to settle the looming collision between Piazza, who wore 31 with Los Angeles and Florida (briefly), and **John Franco**, then the senior Met and occupant of the 31 jersey for eight years. Franco, to his credit, volunteered to step into a new jersey (45) and welcome Piazza aboard.

Franco (1990–98) to that point had appeared in 394 games, winning 35 and saving 221, numbers that made him the all-time Mets 31, and by a longshot. What he hadn't done in his career was reach the postseason, and so he gave up his number for the chance.

Franco in 1990 became the first Met ever to lead the league in saves and narrowly edged the man he was traded for, "Nasty Boy" Randy Myers, for the Rolaids Relief Man Award. Myers won a World Series that year. When both players' careers were through, Franco had an edge of 57 saves. Both men then ranked in the career top ten.

When Franco gave up 31 he chose 45 in honor of legendary Mets fireman Tug McGraw. What he may not have known was that No. 31 previously belonged to the Mets' very first relief ace, **Larry Bearnarth**, who like Franco was a product of St. John's University.

A burly right-hander, Bearnarth (1963–66) led the team with 58 appearances as a twenty-one-year-old rookie in 1963. Along with Al Jackson and Ron Hunt, Bearnarth was also among the few early Mets coveted by other teams.

The Mets spent their first draft pick ever on Montana schoolboy **Les Rohr** (1967–68), who made brief appearances wearing No. 31. **Jack DiLauro**, a 1969 Mets rookie, threw 63 2/3 innings (mostly in relief) from the left side in his only season with the club. As the most valuable member of the 1973 bullpen not named McGraw, **Harry Parker** (1973–75) picked up 8 wins and 5 saves in his best season with the Mets.

Freak rookie success **Mike Vail** (1975) fashioned a 23-game hitting streak in 1975 that somehow convinced the Mets they could trade Rusty Staub. Vail wrecked his ankle playing basketball that offseason and returned (wearing No. 6) as a shadow of his former self. Hard-throwing righty **Bruce Berenyi** (1985–86) had electric stuff but couldn't overcome injuries. At 29, Berenyi had been brought over from Cincinnati in June 1984 as elder statesman to New York's young yet surging rotation. He went 9–6 but was pedestrian compared to rookies Dwight Gooden, Ron Darling, and Sid Fernandez.

Iguana-eating reliever **Julio Machado** (1989) was assigned 31 before Franco arrived; he reappeared in 1990 wearing the No. 48 most recently belonging to Myers.

Others include pitchers **Ron Herbel** (1970), **Don Rose** (1971), **Roy Lee Jackson** (1977–80), and **Gene Walter** (1987). **George Bamberger** wore 31 as a Mets manager in 1982 and '83, but Bambi's heart was never really into it.

Number 31

Number of times issued: 14 (13 players, 1 manager)

Longest tenured: John Franco (9 seasons, 394 games), Mike Piazza (8 seasons, 972 games)

Best single seasons: Franco, 1996 (4–3, 28 saves, 1.83 ERA); Franco, 1990 (5–3, 33 saves, 2.53 ERA); Piazza, 1999 (.303/.361/.575, 40 HR, 124 RBIs); Piazza, 2000 (.324/.398/.614, 38 HR, 113 RBIs)

Career statistical leaders: Home runs (Piazza 220, Mike Vail 3), RBI (Piazza 655, Vail 17); batting average (Vail .302, Piazza .296); wins (Franco 35, Harry Parker 14, Larry Bearnarth 13); saves (Franco 221, Parker 11); ERA (Franco 2.73, Bearnarth 3.43)

9/11/01: A True Tip of the Cap

The Mets were in Pittsburgh the morning of September 11, 2001. They had crept back to the fringes of the National League East race and were a few hours away from heading to the new PNC Park for the first time. Then the world changed. The tragedies that day at the World Trade Center, at the Pentagon in Washington, and just 64 miles south of Pittsburgh—in Shanksville— created profound sorrow and made just about every American not involved in an emergency service or the military feel utterly helpless.

Following six days of national mourning, the Mets took the field in Pittsburgh with heavy hearts. The Pirates, who were supposed to be at Shea Stadium on that date, hosted the series because Shea was still being used as a staging area for supplies to reach rescue workers.

Pittsburgh, where commercials for games against the Mets a decade earlier had featured the tagline, "The Mets: Another reason to hate New York," now cheered the players who represented the city that had been so shaken.

The Mets wore their emotions on their sleeves, and they expressed their feelings on their heads as well. The Mets wore hats to honor the service personnel who had risked all to save others: FDNY (fire), NYPD (police), PAPD (Port Authority), EMS (paramedics), and OEM (emergency management). The Mets wore the hats before the first game in Pittsburgh on September 17 before putting on their black and blue Mets caps. Manager Bobby Valentine, who'd worked tirelessly coordinating volunteer efforts and donations, continued wearing his NYPD hat. The next night the Mets followed suit and they played in the hats honoring the services the rest of the season. Mike Piazza's black and blue catching helmet read "NYPD." An American flag was affixed to all batting helmets and uniforms for the Mets and every club (including the majors' two Canadian teams).

The Mets swept the Pirates and headed to Shea to play the city's first professional outdoor sporting event since the tragedy. Security was tight but throats were tighter as no one seemed sure they should go to something that had suddenly become, well, trivial in the grand scheme. The emergency services that had responded so quickly and given so much in a time of tragedy were at Shea in force. The Mets lined the field before the game representing them with the hats. A roll call of some players' representation that night:

Edgardo Alfonzo	FDNY
Kevin Appier	FDNY
Armando Benitez	FDNY
Bruce Chen	FDNY
John Franco	NYPD
Al Leiter	PAPD
Joe McEwing	FDNY
Jason Phillips	NYPD
Desi Relaford	FDNY
Tsuyoshi Shinjo	FDNY
Robin Ventura	PAPD
Rick White	NYPD
Todd Zeile	NYPD

There were plenty of hugs to go around. The Mets and Braves hugged before the game, fans embraced emergency personnel at every turn, and Liza Minnelli hugged Jay Payton after the first version of "New York, New York" that didn't make anyone think of the Yankees. Fittingly, it was Piazza who rose to the momentous occasion.

With the Mets down by a run in the 8th inning, Piazza launched a long two-run home run against Steve Karsay. New York had regained just a tiny bit of its swagger, even if its heart was still broken. The Mets also won the next night—their fifteenth victory in seventeen games—to pull within three and a half games of the first-place Braves. The Mets faded, but their volunteerism, compassion, and emotion remained in the minds of the faithful. The Mets played for free that Friday night, donating a day's pay, some $440,000, to Rusty Staub's Widows' and Children's Benefit Fund. Mets fan and songwriter Terry Cashman even wrote a song about what may have been Piazza's greatest moment.

Joe McEwing proudly wears the FDNY hat during a game on September 11, 2003.

David G. Whitham

The Mets continued the tradition for several Septembers following the event until Major League Baseball, inexplicably citing league uniform guidelines, put an end to the tribute in 2011, relegating the sartorial tribute to batting practice. We won't forget.

#32: ORNERY LEFTIES

Jon Matlack (1971–77) won in double-figures for his first five full seasons, picking up a Rookie of the Year award in 1972 and the win and co-MVP honors (with Bill Madlock) in the 1975 All-Star Game. A big left-hander with bat-shattering stuff, Matlack stepped into a rotation with Tom Seaver and Jerry Koosman and held his own.

Despite it all, you could say Matlack had Met luck. Over seven seasons and 204 games, Matlack's career record was a deceptively mediocre 82–81, the result of poor run support—a characteristic of every Mets team to employ Matlack.

Jacob Kanarek/From Worst to First

Jon Matlack had a big kick—and an even bigger arm.

The Mets' first-round draft pick in 1967, Matlack was brought along slowly until debuting with

15 victories and a 2.32 ERA—fourth-best in the National League—to earn 1972 NL Rookie of the Year. His sophomore season was literally more painful. Pitching to Marty Perez of the Braves that May, Matlack took a screaming line drive off his forehead and hit the ground like an empty uniform. Despite a fractured skull, Matlack was back in just eleven days. His gutsy two-hit, complete-game shutout of the favored Reds in Game 2 of the NLCS evened the best-of-five series. Matlack got three starts in the 1973 World Series and pitched to a 2.16 ERA, but lost twice, including the decisive Game 7 on two-run homers by Bert Campaneris and Reggie Jackson.

Unhappy with the organizational strife in 1977, Matlack slumped to his worst year as a Met—7–15 with a 4.21 ERA—and went to Texas in the strenuous but ultimately pointless Willie Montanez deal. He remains the gold standard for Mets 32s, particularly the lefties who followed.

Trading for **Mike Hampton** in his walk year was a risky strategy that paid off in predictable ways: Hampton led the Mets to the World Series, and then he walked.

An ornery lefty, Hampton at his best could be a diminutive version of Matlack. He walked too many guys, but Hampton went 15–10, 3.14 in 2000 and was named MVP of the NLCS after twice beating the Cardinals, including a complete-game shutout in the Game 5 clincher. But his meek opposition to Roger Clemens's World Series bat-throwing tantrum would be a dissatisfying final appearance for the Mets. His parting remarks about the quality of Colorado schools struck Mets fans as a particularly vile strain of malarkey.

As 2016 dawns it's a little soon to consider **Steven Matz** in the company of Matlack or Hampton, but don't blame us for dreaming.

A lefty starter with similarly nasty stuff, Matz, like Matlack, was a top Mets draft pick (he was the team's first selection in 2007); and like Hampton, he was a key figure in a National League championship squad during his first season in New York. The product of Long Island's Ward Melville High, Matz's development was slowed by Tommy John surgery. When he finally arrived in 2015, Matz looked very much like the real deal: 4–0 with a 2.27 ERA over six starts, including a major league debut for the ages: a 7–2 victory over the Reds powered by 7 2/3 innings of six-hit ball, and at the plate, three hits, and four RBIs in front of ecstatic friends and family on a glorious July afternoon. Here's to more of the same.

In all, the Mets have suited up eight different left-handed pitchers in 32 (plus **Mark Carreon**, an outfielder who batted right but threw left).

Jim Singer

Steven Matz warms up before his spring 2016 debut in Jupiter, Florida.

Once-and-future Yankee setter-upper **Mike Stanton** (2003–04), set a then-team record with 83 appearances for the 2004 Mets, despite the fact that fans so seldomly wanted to see him. Reliever **Carlos Diaz** (1982–83) had an outstanding season out of the bullpen in 1983 (3–1, 2.05 ERA in 54 games), which Frank Cashen alertly parlayed into a trade for Sid Fernandez.

Southpaw starter **Bruce Chen** (2001–02) arrived in a midseason trade for fan favorites Turk Wendell and Dennis Cook, but helped the Mets in their ultimately unsuccessful drive for the East crown in 2001. He was the starting pitcher on the emotional night of September 21, 2011, but got a no decision. Like Matz, **John Lannan** (2014) was a left-handed product of Long Island (Chaminade High in Mineola), and a short-lived predecessor in 32. Like Lannan, **Dave Williams** (2006–07) was a middling lefty vet who made the final appearances of his big-league career as a Mets spot-starter.

Fourteen right-handed pitchers have worn 32 with far less panache than the southpaws. **Paul Wilson** (1996) was considered the surest bet of the Generation K pitchers, but injuries limited the former No. 1 overall draft pick to just 26 games for the Mets. Ageless veteran and quick pitch advocate

LaTroy Hawkins had a terrific season for a bad team: 3–2, 2.63, and 13 saves in 2013 as a forty-year-old closer.

Few teams in baseball embraced the player-rights movement more insincerely than the Mets, whose tradition-bound ownership found free agency particularly abhorrent (and expensive). But to send a signal they were trying, they signed free agent **Tom Hausman** (1978–82), an underwhelming right-handed swingman who amassed a 12–17 record over five seasons in New York. The Mets dealt Hausman to Atlanta in 1982, bringing back the aforementioned Diaz.

Jack Hamilton (1966–67) was the first wearer of the 32 jersey, leading the Mets in appearances in 1966 while walking nearly as many men as he struck out (a ghastly 93–88 strikeout-to-walk ratio). Hamilton tossed the second one-hitter in team history, allowing only a fourth-inning bunt single to the opposing pitcher, Ray Sadecki of St. Louis, in May of 1966.

Remaining righties: **Hal Reniff** (1967), **Dick Tidrow** (1984), **Rick Anderson** (1986), **Tom Edens** (1987), **Pete Smith** (1994), **Brent Hinchcliffe** (2001), **Danny Graves** (2005), **Jeremi Gonzalez** (2006), **Carlos Muniz** (2008), and **Jenrry Mejia** (2010, 2012).

Kevin Mitchell (1984) debuted as the first Mets position player to wear No. 32. Veteran spare-part **Eli Marrero** was one of three 2006 Mets to wear No. 32—yet the Mets made the postseason anyway. But 32 has always come down to pitching; even overhyped infielder **Bill Pecota** (1992) made his only contribution as the first Mets position player to take the mound.

Number 32

Number of times issued: 29 (26 players, 2 coaches 1, DNP)

Longest Tenured: Jon Matlack (7 seasons, 203 games), Tom Hausman (5 seasons, 125 games)

Best single seasons: Matlack, 1972 (15–10, 2.32 ERA, 169 strikeouts in 244 innings, Rookie of the Year); Matlack, 1974 (13–15, 2.41 ERA, 195 strikeouts in 265 1/3 innings); Mike Hampton, 2000 (15–10, 3.14, 151 strikeouts in 217 2/3 innings)

Career statistical leaders: Home runs (Mark Carreon 7); RBI (Bill Pecota 26); batting average (Carreon, .318); wins (Matlack 83); saves (LaTroy Hawkins 13, Mike Stanton 5); ERA (Matlack 3.03, Hampton 3.14)

1967 by the Numbers

The 1967 Mets were a fascinating, if disappointing, club. Built, torn down, and rebuilt by general manager Bing Devine in his one and only full year on the job, the '67 Mets used a team-record 54 players (55 if you count Nolan Ryan, who was on the roster in September but did not appear in a game). They were the ultimate team in transition.

The group featured twenty-seven position players and twenty-seven pitchers. They had nine different second basemen, eleven third basemen, and twenty different pitchers would make at least one start. There were also two different managers: skipper Wes Westrum resigned in September and was replaced by interim Salty Parker.

At the time, the team was the largest in National League history, breaking the record of fifty-three players set by the 1945 Brooklyn Dodgers (thanks to all the men discharged after World War II) and second only to the dreadful 1915 Philadelphia Athletics, who used fifty-six men when Connie Mack pulled a Huizenga and disbanded a pennant winner. The '67 Mets would be the largest roster in all of baseball for another twenty-nine years. (The current record belongs to the 2014 Texas Rangers, who used 60 men).

As the saying goes, you can't tell the players without a scorecard, but even that was difficult with the '67 Mets, considering they had fifteen sets of like-numbered teammates (including four-of-a-kind at No. 38, who, unfortunately, weren't Aces):

No.	Players
2	Chuck Hiller, Phil Linz
5	Sandy Alomar, Ed Charles
6	Bart Shirley, Bob W. Johnson
18	Al Luplow, Joe Moock
19	Kevin Collins, Hawk Taylor
24	Johnny Lewis, Ken Boswell
26	Bob Shaw, Bill Graham
29	Danny Frisella, Nick Willhite
30	Dick Selma, Nolan Ryan
32	Jack Hamilton, Hal Reniff
33	Chuck Estrada, Bob Hendley
34	Jack Lamabe, Cal Koonce
35	Don Shaw, Billy Wynne
38	Ralph Terry, Dennis Bennett, Billy Wynne, Billy Connors
44	Bill Denehy, Al Schmelz

Although the crowded clubhouse combined to lose 101 games in the Summer of Love, the news wasn't all bad. Tom Seaver arrived with a 16-win, Rookie of the Year campaign. And behind the scenes, Devine's roster gymnastics were unearthing more good than bad. Between the time Devine was named GM in November of 1966 and the time he resigned in December of 1967 to return to the Cardinals, Devine made twenty-five trades, not including drafts or deals that didn't include major league players, gathering in Tommie Agee, Cal Koonce, Ron Taylor, Ed Charles, Al Weis, J. C. Martin, and Art Shamsky, among others. Devine also hired and then promoted third-base coach Whitey Herzog, later a Hall of Fame manager (not of the Mets, lamentably). As a director of amateur scouting, Herzog led drafts during 1967 that would produce Ken Singleton, Dave Schneck, Jon Matlack, Rod Gaspar, and Gary Gentry.

Nobody might have guessed, but by the time Devine left town in '67, the vast majority of the '69 world champion Mets were already in the organization. Only two players of significance from that team—Wayne Garrett and Donn Clendenon—would be added after Devine's departure. And his successor in the GM chair, Johnny Murphy, made no trades at all in 1968. The cupboard was full.

#33: PAIN RELIEF

PROGRESSION:

Player	Years
Ron Hunt	1963–66
Chuck Estrada	1967 (to June 12)
Bob Hendley	1967 (from June 12)
Billy Connors	1968
Les Rohr	1969
Ray Sadecki	1970–74
Ken Sanders	1975–76
Ray Sadecki	1977 (to May 2)
Dan Norman	1977 (from Sept. 12)–1978
Pete Falcone	1979–82
Clint Hurdle	1983
Bill Latham	1985
Barry Lyons	1986–90 (to May 18)
Charlie O'Brien	1990 (from Aug. 31)
Anthony Young	1991
Eddie Murray	1992–93
Kelly Stinnett	1994–95
Andy Tomberlin	1996–97
Tim Spehr	1998 (to May 5)
Mike Kinkade	1998 (from Sept. 4)–2000 (to July 28)
Bubba Trammell	2000 (from July 28)
Donne Wall	2001
Mike Bacsik	2002–03
Tyler Yates	2004
Mike DiFelice	2005 (to June 2)
Jose Santiago	2005 (July 25–Aug. 17)
Mike DiFelice	2005 (from Aug. 21)
John Maine	2006–10
Taylor Buchholz	2011
Vinny Rottino	2012 (to June 25)
Matt Harvey	2012 (from July 26)–15

He's got the stuff of Seaver, the swagger of Strawberry and, often, the common sense of Spencer (Shane, that is). He's **Matt Harvey**, the Dark Knight of Gotham who occasionally confuses himself with Superman.

Matt Harvey: Mix parts superhero with generous portions of superego and you have a must-watch Met ever ready for prime time.

Twenty-three-year-old Harvey arrived on July 26, 2012, and in a short while was inspiring comparisons to Joe Namath for his success on the field and his downtown lifestyle off it. Outstanding results in 2013, including the starting assignment at the All-Star Game at Citi Field, inspired Mets fans to rally around #HarveyDay and don Batman masks in the crowd. Looking back, it was a key step in the team's climb from a beaten-up laughingstock to World Series contender by 2015.

It's occasionally been difficult to determine whether Harvey's ultimate loyalty is to the Mets, to Qualcomm, to agent Scott Boras, or just to Matt Harvey, but it's already clear he's the Mets' most iconic No. 33 ever.

He took that honor from **Ron Hunt**, who like Harvey, was a maximum-effort performer who represented the Mets as a sophomore starter at the only other All-Star Game they ever hosted, in 1964.

A cocksure and enthusiastic infielder, Hunt (1963–66) hustled his way into Casey Stengel's plans and became the club's first farm-raised star. Hunt led the Mets in runs, hits, doubles, batting average, and on-base percentage while finishing second in Rookie of the Year voting to a guy named Rose. Hunt missed half of 1965 with an injury but rebounded to a second All-Star appearance in 1966.

Hunt is best remembered for his willingness to absorb a fastball in the ribs. He took 41 for the team as a Met—a record that lasted 50 years before David Wright and Lucas Duda surpassed it.

Grouchy first baseman **Eddie Murray** added to his Cooperstown résumé at Shea but it happened during the "Worst Team Money Could Buy" era, when tensions between writers and the Mets were at an all-time high. Murray, who rarely spoke to the press, let his bat do the talking and it had plenty to say, especially in 1993 when he drove in 100 runs. But it couldn't save that team from 103 losses.

The San Francisco Giants gave up Hall of Famer Orlando Cepeda to acquire **Ray Sadecki**, a former 20-game winner whom they shipped, four years later, to the Mets for minor leaguers Jim Gosger and Bob Heise. Sadecki (1970–74, 1977) provided valuable service as a left-handed swingman for the early '70s Mets and would eventually be traded back to the Cardinals for Joe Torre. The Mets reacquired Sadecki for a final go-round in 1977 but released him in early May.

Between Sadecki's two stints, No. 33 went to **Ken Sanders** (1975–76), a one-time relief ace of the Brewers who did some effective late-career work for the Mets. His 1975 season was interrupted by a scary injury when a return warm-up throw from catcher John Stearns struck Sanders square in the eye. Ouch.

Brooklyn-born lefty **Pete Falcone** (1979–82) battled for four years in orange and blue, but a tendency toward wildness and the gopher ball was his undoing.

One of the great revelations of 2006 was that it was rookie **John Maine**, and not Anna Benson, or even Jorge Julio, who was the central figure in the

Kris Benson trade. While several veterans dropped to injury, Maine (2006–10) thrust himself into the Mets rotation. He made three solid postseason starts as a rookie in 2006, and was probably the club's best starting pitcher by 2007, with 15 wins. Recurring shoulder injuries cut Maine's career short, but through 2015 he's the winningest 33 in club history.

The rest of the 33s are backup catchers **Barry Lyons** (1986–90), **Charlie O'Brien** (1990), **Kelly Stinnett** (1994–95), **Tim Spehr** (1998), and **Mike DiFelice** (2005); lunchbucket pitchers **Chuck Estrada** (1967), **Bob Hendley** (1967), **Billy Connors** (1968), **Les Rohr** (1969), **Bill Latham** (1985), **Anthony Young** (1991), **Mike Bacsik** (2002–03), **Tyler Yates** (2004), **Jose Santiago** (2005), and **Taylor Buchholz**

Dan Carubia

Remember the Maine? The enigmatic John Maine started the NLDS opener as a rookie in 2006.

(2011); and bench players **Dan Norman** (1977), **Clint Hurdle** (1983), **Andy Tomberlin** (1996–97), **Mike Kinkade** (1998–2000), and **Vinny Rottino** (2012). Outfielder **Bubba Trammell** (2000) had more World Series RBIs (3) than any Met besides Mike Piazza against the Yankees, so of course he was immediately dispatched for worn-out reliever **Donne Wall** (2001).

Number 33

Number of times issued: 32 (30 players)

Longest tenured: Ray Sadecki (6 seasons, 165 games) Ron Hunt (4 seasons, 459 games), Pete Falcone (4 seasons, 145 games), John Maine (5 seasons, 97 games).

Best single seasons: Matt Harvey, 2013 (9–5, 2.27 ERA, 191 strikeouts in 178 1/3 innings), Harvey, 2015 (13–8, 2.71, 188 strikeouts in 189 1/3 innings), Hunt, 1964 (.303/.357/.406, 6 HR, 42 RBIs, 11 HBP); Eddie Murray, 1993 (.285/.325/.467, 27 HR, 100 RBIs); Sadecki, 1971 (7–7, 2.92 ERA); John Maine, 2007 (15–10, 3.91 ERA, 180 strikeouts in 191 innings)

Career statistical leaders: Home runs (Murray 43, Hunt 20); RBI (Murray 193, Hunt 127); batting average (Hunt .282, Murray .274), wins (Maine 36, Sadecki 30, Falcone 26); saves (Ken Sanders 6); ERA (Harvey 2.55, Sanders 2.60)

Mets Uniform History: Gotto's Logo

In November 1961 a lot of people had no idea who or what the Mets were. Joan Payson favored Meadowlarks as the expansion club's name, but she demurred to public opinion when fans chose "Mets" in a contest. Mets seemed to fit. Tired of typing out "Metropolitan Baseball Club, Inc.," the company name certified by the National League eight months earlier, newsmen had already dubbed the new club "Mets." That had also been the name of an American Association club in the 1880s housed in the original Polo Grounds, just north of Central Park on 111th Street. (The "new" Mets were set to play in the fourth incarnation of the place, at 155th Street and Eighth Avenue.) But even as everyone agreed on the name, what exactly was a Met and what did one look like? Ray Gotto decided that with a flourish of his pen.

Gotto, a cartoonist who created the syndicated strip "Ozark Ike" about a hillbilly four-sport star, submitted the winning design out of five hundred entrants. Noted illustrator John Groth of *Sports Illustrated* was part of a three-man selection committee, as were representatives of two New York dailies that have long ceased to exist. Gotto was paid $1,000, while the three runners-up received 1962 season tickets. (Insert joke here.)

Gotto's iconic design featured the New York skyline, including such landmarks of the day as the Empire State Building, the Williamsburg Savings Bank, the Woolworth Tower, and the United Nations. The buildings were silhouetted in Dodger blue and "Mets" was colored Giant orange—the Mets have never had a problem borrowing from their predecessors, as the team's initial roster would prove—and the bridge in the foreground was white, as was the sky behind the city. Lest anyone forget it was a baseball club, orange stitches tied together the ball motif. In case anyone wondered where it was based, "NY" was tucked in just above the "M" in "Mets," or on the side of the Williamsburg Savings Bank building.

The logo remained virtually unchanged until 1999, when "NY" was dropped and "TM" added to the right of the UN Building, lest anyone forget the logo was trademarked (a Register mark had appeared in that spot since the early 1990s). The club still had the "NY" on the logo in 1999 spring training, but "NY" was gone in the regular season. Mets exec Mark Bingham told Uni Watch at the time, "The 'NY' on the logo never matched the one on the caps. The one on the logo was more primitive looking, sort of a stick-figure 'NY.'" So the Mets got rid of it. By then, the skyline was black with "Mets" in blue and outlined in orange on the black uniforms. It remained its original color on the white and pinstriped uniforms.

If only everything stood the test of time like the Mets logo. Gotto's script "Mets" has appeared on countless items from ashtrays to underwear. Meanwhile, that first beer at the Polo Grounds cost 45 cents and a box seat was just $3.50. Add a zero to each and you're still not in the ballpark today. Times have changed, but so have those 120-loss Mets.

#34: THE GOOD HANDS PEOPLE

PROGRESSION:	
Player	Years
Dave Hillman	1962
Jimmy Piersall	1963 (to July 27)
Cleon Jones	1963 (from Sept. 1) –1965 (to May 6)
Dennis Musgraves	1965 (from July 7)
Gerry Arrigo	1966 (to Aug. 16)
Nolan Ryan	1966 (from Sept. 9)
Jack Lamabe	1967 (to July 16)
Cal Koonce	1967 (from Aug 2)–1970 (to June 8)
Danny Frisella	1970 (from June 26)–1972
Phil Hennigan	1973 (to July 16)
Bob Apodaca	1973 (from Sept 9)–1977
Ray Burris	1980
Ed Lynch	1981
Rusty Tillman	1982
Junior Ortiz	1983–84
Sam Perlozzo (coach)	1987–89
Mario Diaz	1990 (to Aug. 28)
Julio Valera	1990 (from Aug. 30)–1991
Chico Walker	1992–93
Frank Seminara	1994
Blas Minor	1995–96 (to June 9)
Rick Trlicek	1996 (from Sept. 8)
Bob Apodaca (coach)	1997–99 (to June 5)
Mac Suzuki	1999 (June 18–22; did not play)
Chuck McElroy	1999 (from July 31)
Dennis Springer	2000 (to April 27)
Jerrod Riggan	2000 (from Aug. 28)
Tom Martin	2001
Pedro Astacio	2002–03
Ricky Bottalico	2004 (to July 30)
Kris Benson	2004 (from July 30)–2005
Jorge Julio	2006 (to May 24)
Mike Pelfrey	2006 (from July 8)–2012
Brandon Lyon	2013
Noah Syndergaard	2015

It just feels good to be a Mets fan when your team's got a deck of young aces, and maybe safer still that two of them happen to be superheroes.

We discussed Batman in Chapter 33; here we meet Thor.

Noah Syndergaard was one of three minor leaguers the Mets received in the transformative trade of R. A. Dickey following Dickey's Cy Young campaign of 2012. Listed at 6-foot-6, 240-pounds, Syndergaard possesses the long golden locks, build, and Nordic heritage of his mythical nicknamesake, and hurls a 98-mile-per-hour fastball for a hammer. He debuted for the Mets in May of 2015 and by year-end was profiling as something of a White Knight to Harvey's Dark Knight: Fearsome but fun-loving, visible but accessible. He won nine games—another two in the postseason—and whiffed 166 in 150 innings. It's early, but it looks like we're in pretty good hands.

Bob Apodaca felt like he was in good hands after he closed out the Mets' home-opening win in 1974. With stopper Tug McGraw unavailable due to illness, the twenty-one-year-old rookie entered with two Cardinals on base, one out and the Mets clinging to a 3–2 lead, but induced Tim McCarver to bounce into a game-ending 1-6-3 double play to save the game for Jerry Koosman. Afterward, Apodaca told the *New York Times* that shaking Jerry Grote's hand afterward felt better than anything, "Except maybe sex."

Jacob Kanarek/From Worst to First

Danny Frisella: A "Bear" of a Met and a righthanded compliment to Tug McGraw.

Dan Carubia

Tongue out, armed, and anxious, Mike Pelfrey has more wins than any No. 34 in Mets history–for now.

Undersized and undrafted, Apodaca used an effective sinkerball to collect 16 wins and 26 saves while posting a 2.86 ERA over four-plus seasons as a Met before elbow injuries curtailed his career. He returned as the club's pitching coach (1997–99) to lead a team of similar overachievers, before moving onto the same role with Rockies, who under his guidance surprisingly reached the 2007 World Series.

Apodaca was the last in a string of quietly successful setup relievers to have worn 34 for the Mets. A scrap-heap pickup from the Cubs, **Cal Koonce** (1967–70) won 6 games in relief, and saved 7, for the 1969 Mets.

Danny Frisella (1970–72) played with Tom Seaver in both Fairbanks and Flushing (as did Al Schmelz, briefly). Frisella's right-handed forkball complemented madcap McGraw's screwgie from the left side. Bear and Tug combined for 19 wins and a 1.82 ERA in '71, with Frisella earning 12 of the pair's 20 saves. Frisella was traded to Atlanta in the Felix Millan deal. He tragically died in an offseason dune buggy accident while still an active player at age thirty. Even his short time as a Met—and on earth—Frisella had more wins (21) than any 34 for thirty-seven years.

Then along came strapping righthander **Mike Pelfrey** (2006–12). The Mets' top draft pick in 2005, Big Pelf amassed more than twice the wins (50)—and losses (54)—as any Met No. 34, but let's just say his career in orange-and-blue was a little less gratifying than a Jerry Grote handshake. It was an Omir Santos high-five, maybe.

Veteran pitcher **Dave Hillman** was the first wearer of the 34 jersey in 1962, but many would follow. **Jimmy Piersall** ran the bases backwards after cracking his 100th career home run with the 1963 Mets and was summarily traded to California. Later that year, outfielder **Cleon Jones** (1963–65) made his earliest Mets appearances. **Nolan Ryan** (1966) also debuted in 34 (2 games, 15.00 ERA). He would switch to 30, which, along with 34, would be retired by three teams in his honor—in case you didn't get the message earlier, none of those teams were the Mets.

Julio Valera (1990-91) got off to a promising start as a twenty-one-year-old rookie in 1990 but he wasn't the same after suffering a crucial late-season loss in Pittsburgh. Successor **Chico Walker** (1992–93) was a versatile reserve and the only .300 hitter on the 1992 Mets. Walker, who as a Cub in 1986 made the out that clinched the division title, ended his Mets career with a home run in 1993.

Other 34s were less intriguing: **Dennis Musgraves** (1965), **Gerry Arrigo** (1966), **Jack Lamabe** (1967), **Phil Hennigan** (1973), **Ray Burris** (1980), who led Joe Torre's team in innings pitched and starts—not to mention losses and home runs allowed; **Ed Lynch** (making his Mets debut in 1981); outfield reserve **Rusty Tillman** (1982); beloved-but-ineffectual backup catcher **Junior Ortiz** (1983–84); **Mario Diaz** (1990); **Frank Seminara** (1994); **Blas Minor** (1995–96); **Rick Trlicek** (1996); and **Chuck McElroy** (1999); knuckleballer **Dennis Springer** (2000), and relievers **Jerrod Riggan** (2000), **Tom Martin** (2001), **Ricky Bottalico** (2004), and **Brandon Lyon** (2013).

Pedro Astacio (2002–03) came to the Mets with a reputation as a talented injury risk and lived up to those expectations spectacularly. He was very good until his shredded shoulder finally gave out, at which point he was awful. **Kris Benson** (2004–05) arrived at the bloody trade deadline of 2004, but his accomplishments never lived up his reputation as former No. 1 overall draft pick. And his wife, Anna, wasn't exactly Nancy Seaver. Some believe Anna's outfit, or lack of it, during the Mets Christmas party in 2005 hastened Benson's surprise trade to Baltimore weeks later. That deal brought John Maine and **Jorge Julio** (2006), who was traded for Orlando Hernandez, so nobody much complained . . . besides Anna.

Number 34

Number of times issued: 33 (30 players, 2 coaches, 1 DNP)

Longest tenured: Mike Pelfrey (7 years, 153 games), Bob Apodaca (5 seasons, 184 games), Cal Koonce (4 seasons, 119 games).

Best single seasons: Noah Syndergaard, 2015 (9–7, 3.24 ERA, 166 strikeouts in 150 innings); Pelfrey, 2008 (13–11, 3.96 ERA), Frisella, 1971 (8–5, 1.99 ERA, 12 saves), Apodaca, 1975 (3–4, 13 saves, 1.49 ERA); Chico Walker, 1992 (.308/.369/.423, 4 HR, 36 RBIs, 14 stolen bases)

Career statistical leaders: Home runs (Walker 9, Syndergaard 1, Jimmy Piersall 1); RBI (Walker 55, Junior Ortiz 23); batting average (Walker .268, Ortiz .236); wins (Pelfrey 50, Frisella 21, Apodaca 16); saves (Apodaca 26, Frisella 22); ERA (Frisella 2.70, Apodaca 2.86)

Mets Uniform History: The Pillbox Cap

The 1976 bicentennial made a lot of people go a little bit loopy. Maybe it was the tall ships, maybe it was the heat, or it could have been the striped polyester pants. The summer of '76 marked the 200th anniversary of our nation as well as the 100th anniversary of the National League, so party hats were ordered for the occasion. Pillbox caps like the ones ballplayers wore back in the day were worn by the Mets, Phillies, Reds, Cardinals, and, of course, Pirates, who kept them on for a decade. (The only franchises that had existed continuously since 1876, however, were the stovepipe-free Braves and Cubs.) The National League, featuring Dave Kingman in right field, wore special white pillbox caps with red stripes and with a script "N" for the All-Star Game festivities in Philadelphia.

Pillbox fever started at Shea a few weeks shy of the Fourth of July. The Mets broke them out for the Memorial Day doubleheader against Pittsburgh. The three orange stripes that wrapped around the squared-off blue cap looked surprisingly good as the Mets pounded out a 13–2 win in the opener. When the Mets predictably lost the nightcap, 2–1, despite a rare yet fine start by No. 34 Bob Apodaca, the new hat looked sillier than the short pants sported by the '76 White Sox. The Mets split the July 4 twin-bill against the Cubs wearing the funny caps, and the oldtimers were forced to wear them later that month.

The next year's yearbook left no photographic evidence that the Mets ever wore such chapeaus at Shea. If only the countless other fashion sins of the '70s could have vanished so easily.

#35: IRREPLACEABLE

Rick Reed (1997–2001) was a thirty-two-year-old journeyman, a veteran of four franchises, and a one-time strike replacement player with all of ten major league victories when he was invited to the Mets spring training camp in 1997.

He'd go on to win 59 games and lose 36 over the next four and a half years, becoming the kind of success the Mets had never quite had in No. 35, despite considerable efforts to find one. Among a crowd of longshots and even longer shots, Reed was a bullseye.

Relying on remarkable control and consistency, Reed at once was a revelation and a quiet guy seemingly content to slide behind higher-profile teammates even as he outperformed them. There was some ill will about Reed's replacement player past—his mom had really needed the money—but Reed ignored the slights and performed his job outside the union and inside the strike zone. Reed went 13–9, with a 2.89 ERA in 1997, walking just 31 guys in 208 1/3 innings. He cut that rate slightly in 1998, when he won a team-high 16 games and made the first of two trips to the All-Star Game.

Reed pitched in five postseason games and the Mets won four of them, including their only victory in the 2000 World Series. Reed's constant strike-throwing left him vulnerable to the home run, and he was less effective as he battled injuries later in his career, but he probably should have been given a chance to finish that career as a Met. Instead he was shipped to Minnesota in 2001

Sharon Chapman

Not overpowering, but 2011's biggest winner. Gee, what a concept.

for a dud outfielder, Matt Lawton, in a deal that did more to fuel tensions between Steve Phillips and Bobby Valentine than it did to help the Mets catch the Braves. Reed was also probably the best hitter who ever wore the Mets 35 jersey.

At his best, **Dillon Gee** was something of a poor man's Reed. The farm-raised Texan never possessed overpowering stuff, or an iron grip on a roster slot, yet hung in there for parts of six seasons a fifth starter. Gee led the 2011 Mets with 13 wins, and his 40 as a Met 35 is second only to Reed.

When the Mets were ready to move on from Gee, you knew it. Days after Gee was outrighted in 2015, rookie righthander **Logan Verrett** was up, wearing the same 35 jersey. Verrett meant no disrespect—he'd worn 35 in the minors and preferred to retain it—and given the fact that the Mets' farm product over the past six months had ridden the Rule 5 shuttle from the Mets, to the Orioles, to the Rangers, and then back to the Mets, he probably had bigger things to worry about. Verrett acquitted himself well, notching a win and a save in 14 appearances including four starts.

Joe Smith (2007–08) had only weeks of minor league experience when he made the Mets as a sidearming groundball specialist, and did not allow an earned run over his first 17 appearances. Smith would be one of seven—seven!—Met products sent away in a three-team trade amounting to about two months of J. J. Putz. Smith has since had seven consecutive years of excellent relief work in the American League.

Chunky reliever **David Weathers** (2002–04) led the Mets in appearances twice and pitched to a respectable 3.22 ERA as the Mets faded from relevancy. After trading Weathers in 2004, they got **Mike DeJean** (2004–05) to take his innings. DeJean had a brief encounter with success before it was revealed that he was pitching with a broken leg.

Dock Ellis once pitched a no-hitter on acid as a Pirate, but the Mets needed painkillers when he threw in 1979 (3–7, 6.04). Ellis was a Yankee before he was a Met, and the same poison may have infected lefty **Lee Guetterman** in 1992. Guetterman was all the Mets had to show for Ron Darling within a year of Darling's departure. Reliever **Doug Henry** (1995–96) led the Mets in appearances in 1996 and got the occasional save.

Billy Beane (1985) was the one-time first-round draft pick of the Mets who would become the influential general manager of the Oakland A's and tragic hero of *Moneyball*. As Michael Lewis's bestseller relates, Beane was a magnificent athlete whom the Mets had considered selecting ahead of Darryl Strawberry in the 1980 draft (the Mets had two first-round choices that year, including the overall top choice). Beane, however, would reject the notion of toolsy athleticism necessarily indicating baseball success based on his own truncated career with the Mets (3 hits over 18 September at-bats spanning two seasons).

M. Donald Grant's weakness for left-handed reliever **Don Shaw** interrupted, and nearly scuttled, the trade that brought Tommie Agee to the Mets. Shaw (1967–68), who pitched effectively before injuries intervened, wound up being lost to the Expos in the expansion draft. Omar Minaya's weakness for veteran infielders as bench help was sated briefly by **Jose Offerman** (2005).

Southpaw **Randy Jones** (1981–82) had No. 35 retired for him—in San Diego—where he starred for the Padres. He finished second to Tom Seaver in the 1975 Cy Young voting and beat out Jerry Koosman for the trophy a year later. By the time the soft-tossing Jones got to New York, he was battling injuries that would end his career at age thirty-two. **Pat Tabler** (1990) arrived as late-season help for the 1990 stretch drive. Tabler had a freak talent for hitting with the bases loaded, batting .489 in those situations over his career. In his final game as a Met, Tabler came up with the bases loaded . . . and got hit by a pitch. It didn't help the Mets win the division but it enabled Frank Viola to win his 20th game.

Other pitchers to don 35: **Ray "Frenchy" Daviault** (1962), **Larry Miller** (1965), **Billy Wynne** (1967), **Charlie Williams** (1971), **Randy Sterling** (1974), **Ed Lynch** (1980–81), **Joe Sambito** (1985), **Kenny Greer** (1993), and **Lance Broadway** (2009).

The reserve catcher wing houses **Joe Nolan** (1972), **Luis Rosado** (1977), **John Gibbons** (1986–87), and **Orlando Mercado** (1990). Position players include prospects **Roy Staiger** (1975), **John Christensen** (1984), and **Craig Shipley** (1989). In a return engagement in 2010, first baseman/catcher **Mike Jacobs** fit both categories.

Number 35

Number of times issued: 34 (32 players, 1 DNP, 1 coach)

Longest tenured: Rick Reed (5 seasons, 140 games), David Weathers (3 seasons, 180 games), Dillon Gee (6 seasons, 180 games)

Best single seasons: Reed, 1997 (13–9, 2.89 ERA, 113 strikeouts, 31 walks in 208 1/3 innings); Reed, 1998 (16–11, 3.48 ERA, 153 strikeouts, 29 walks in 212 1/3 innings); David Weathers, 2002 (6–3, 2.91 ERA in 71 appearances); Gee, 2013 (12–11, 3.62 ERA, 142 strikeouts in 199 innings)

Career statistical leaders: Home runs (Orlando Mercado 3, Reed 2); RBI (Reed 21, Gee 11, Pat Tabler 10, Jose Offerman 10); batting average (Tabler, .279); wins (Reed 59, Gee 40); saves (Doug Henry 13, Weathers 7); ERA (Weathers 3.22, Reed 3.66)

Mets Uniform History: Snow White and the '97 Mets

The 1997 season began strangely and kept getting stranger. The Mets opened on the West Coast, with every game seemingly held late at night. After stumbling to a 3–6 start with little sleep for the home folks, the Mets took Friday off; another bizarre move, but they didn't want to open at the same time the Yankees raised their newest championship flag. (And silly us, thinking it was because of Good Friday). So Saturday came and fans huddled under the Grand Central Parkway overpass, grilling while it poured until officials finally called the thing off. That led to an Opening Day doubleheader. On Easter Sunday.

Not only was the doubleheader crowd of 21,981 the smallest to watch a Shea opener since 1981, but the fans were blinded as well when the Mets took the field dressed in white from head to toe. Well, their spikes weren't white, but everything else was. For the first time in franchise history, the pinstripes were off the home uniform. It was called an "alternate" uniform, and many teams did this.

Mets players didn't like the white hats with the blue brim one bit, though. The term "ice cream man" came up often, and the white hats were discreetly shelved in favor of the blue hats, which now featured an orange button on top.

The '98 Mets would go *Mad* magazine—"Spy vs. Spy," white spy against black spy—as they changed uniforms willy-nilly. They wore white or black (that year's hot "alternate") almost every home game; they occasionally donned pinstripes just to throw everyone off. The Mets even pretended the whole white cap thing never happened. The 1998 yearbook used one photo of a player in a white cap: Butch Huskey on Jackie Robinson Night, with his 42 suddenly meaning more. Black or white, it was still baseball.

#36: THE KOOZ

As the story goes, **Jerry Koosman** might have been released as a minor leaguer were it not for the fact that he owed the club some money. So there was a time when Jerry Koosman was indebted to the Mets and not the other way around.

Five-plus decades into Mets history, Jerry Koosman remains the go-to lefty in a big game.

The hard-throwing lefty joined sophomore Tom Seaver in 1968 to form a one-two punch atop the Mets rotation that would last for a decade. Kooz won 19 games in '68 with 7 shutouts and a 2.08 ERA, finishing second to Johnny Bench in Rookie of the Year balloting. Koosman had 17 wins for the 1969 Mets and stepped up in the postseason, winning crucial Game 2 and decisive Game 5 of the World Series, allowing just 7 hits and 4 earned runs in 17 2/3 innings. Koosman pitched six postseason games between 1969 and 1973, and the Mets won them all.

Injuries in 1970 and 1971 robbed Koosman's career of some momentum—he never made the All-Star Game again after 1969—but he re-crafted his game to rely less on power on more on control. A 21-win season in 1976 was his best since his rookie year, but Koosman decayed along with the franchise in the years that followed, going 8–20 as the Mets dismantled in 1977 and a very un-Koosmanlike 3–15, 3.75 in 1978. The best lefty starter in franchise history ended his Mets career in Joe Torre's brutal bullpen.

Koosman was traded to Minnesota that winter, then as now, ranking second in franchise history to Seaver in starts (346), complete games (108), innings pitched (2,545), and shutouts (26).

Indelicately, the Mets issued 36 the following spring to **Wayne Twitchell** (1979), a lanky veteran reliever with exceptionally poor control. The sight of Twitchell in 36 was nearly as disturbing as encountering Koosman five years down the road in Phillies jersey No. 37 (the Phils had retired 36 for Robin Roberts). Although the Mets figured Koosman was close to being finished after '78, he hung around the Twins, White Sox, and Phillies through 1985, collecting another 86 victories, including 20 in 1979 for Minnesota.

Sherman "Roadblock" Jones (1962) was the first wearer of the 36 jersey. His nickname described dominating performances as minor-league stopper in the Giants system, but injuries blocked his opportunity to contribute to the Mets. The most notorious of these involved Jones burning his own eye in a cigarette-lighting mishap shortly before his first scheduled start.

Tracy Stallard (1963–64) was famous for having surrendered Roger Maris's 61st home run, but like most Mets pitchers of the Polo Grounds era, he was vulnerable to giving up the longball to anyone. Stallard in fact ranked tenth in the National League in home runs allowed in 1963—but fifth on his team!

The leader in gopher balls was Stallard's hapless teammate **Roger Craig**, who famously ended his losing streak by switching from 38 to 13 in 1963 after trying and failing, on July 19, 1963, while wearing Stallard's No. 36 uniform.

Cerebral right-handed junkballer **Ed Lynch** (1982–86) toiled through the early '80s for the Mets as a swingman and fifth starter before the talent of the staff surpassed him and he was traded to the Cubs during the triumphant 1986 season. Despite appearing in just one game in '86, his teammates voted him a full share of the World Series bonus. Lynch, lauded for his wit, later became general manager of the Cubs. As he said at that time, "I wouldn't have pitched seven years in the big leagues throwing 81 miles per hour if I couldn't get the most out of my abilities."

When the Mets were in need of a starter in 1998, they sent setup man **Greg McMichael** (1997–98; 1998–99) to the Dodgers in a trade for Hideo Nomo. A month later, looking for relief, the Mets dealt with the Dodgers to get McMichael back. Between McMichael's two stints the Mets issued 36 to **Jeff Tam**. McMichael was a change-up artist whose best season was 1997 when he won 7 games and saved 7.

Grant Roberts (2000–04) was a big-time prospect who made headlines for all the wrong reasons. Embarrassing photos of him mowing down a bong surfaced in the middle of what would be his best season in 2002.

Reliever **Darren O'Day** (2009) was adeptly acquired by the Mets in the Rule 5 draft but clumsily fumbled away within weeks. They wouldn't make the same mistake with lefty swingman **Sean Gilmartin**, a 2015 Rule 5er who provided valuable service to the eventual league champions. Like O'Day, short-time Mets hurlers **Dale Thayer** (2011) and **Collin McHugh** (2012–13) had better days in front of them after they departed the Mets.

Reliever **Willie Collazo**, who arrived late in the 2007 season, suffered the indignity of having his name spelled improperly on his home jersey (the road jersey, in which he made his debut, had it right: Two *L*'s, one *Z*, not the other way around). But perfection in the 36 jersey is possible if the timing is right. **Manny Hernandez** (1989) pitched one inning as a Met allowing no hits, walks, or errors. Reserve catcher **Dave Liddell** (1990) had just one turn at bat in the majors, a pinch-hit single. Liddell was acquired for Lynch way back in 1986.

Others, far from perfect: pitchers **Bob G. Miller** (1962), **Jim Bethke** (1965), **Mark Bomback** (1980), **Dan Boitano** (1981), **Tony Castillo** (1991), **Mike Birkbeck** (1995), **Don Florence** (1995), **Manny Aybar** (2005), **Henry Owens** (2006), **Ken Takahashi** (2009), and **Manny Acosta** (2010). Then there's infielders **Kevin Baez** (1990, 1992) and **Tito Navarro** (1993), catchers **Kelly Stinnett** (2006) and **Juan Centeno** (2013–14), and outfielder **Chip Ambres**, whose lone hit as a 2007 Met was a game-winner.

Number 36

Number of times issued: 27 (25 players)

Longest tenured: Jerry Koosman (12 seasons, 376 games), Ed Lynch (5 seasons, 145 games)

Best single seasons: Koosman, 1968 (19–12, 2.08 ERA, 17 complete games, 7 shutouts, All-Star); Koosman, 1976 (21–10, 2.69 ERA, 17 complete games); Lynch, 1985 (10–8, 3.44 ERA, 6 complete games)

Career statistical leaders: Home runs (Koosman 2); RBI (Koosman 39); batting average (Tracy Stallard .142, Koosman .121); wins (Koosman 140, Lynch 33), saves (Greg McMichael 8, Koosman 5), ERA (Koosman 3.09)

Two-Timing Mets

Robert Frost wrote "Nothing Gold Can Stay" almost forty years before the Mets first took breath. If he'd lived beyond the Mets' first year of existence, Frost, a noted baseball fan, might have said, "Everything Blue and Orange Shall Return" . . . or perhaps not.

There is little literary merit concerning the second helpings of the forty-one once-and-again Mets. To put it bluntly, few have been better the second time around, but there is something poetic about the rebirth of a player in a new form. Some have returned to New York to add a gentle flourish to a distinguished career: Rusty Staub as a part-time player and the game's best pinch hitter in the early 1980s; Kevin McReynolds coming back as a live body in a trade for villainous Vince Coleman and calling it quits with class during the strike; and Todd Zeile, freed from the shackles of everyday playerhood, capping off an interesting career with a home run in his last at-bat, as a catcher no less (and fans gasping in horror that an out-the-door Art Howe might spoil the last line by making Zeile bat one more time).

Pedro Feliciano wasn't so good in his comeback with the 2013 Mets, but it was great to see him back after spending the entirety of his two-year, $8 million hitch with the Yankees on the disabled list. Feliciano cost the Yankees more in two years not to pitch than he made in seven seasons with the Mets when he led the National League in appearances three straight years. Now that's a Met.

There's also been a few career-ending clunkers: early favorite Al Jackson coming back after so much good pitching for bad clubs, being a 1969 Met and . . . stinking up the joint with a 10.64 ERA before the Reds bought him; Ray Sadecki, a versatile pitcher for Yogi Berra's believers, made the '77 club out of spring training and was released not long before manager Joe Frazier got the axe; and David Cone, who left too soon in 1992 and stayed too long in 2003, returning from retirement to allow 37 baserunners in 18 innings before getting hurt and quitting for good.

Kirk Nieuwenhuis left and came back so quickly you might have missed it. Secreted to Anaheim when the Mets couldn't sneak him through waivers, he came back when the Angels tried to the same thing two weeks later. The Mets hadn't even had time to reassign No. 9. And he ended up being a hero just enough times to still be playing for the Mets in the '15 World Series. Just call him the Homecoming King.

Constrasting Nieuwenhuis's lickety-split reunion were original Met Bob L. Miller and backup catcher Kelly Stinnett, who each went twelve seasons between games for the club.

If there is any poetry in second acts at Shea, it is written by one George Thomas Seaver. And even those verses turn bitter. The Franchise was in Big Red limbo for more than five years, returning to a Mets club that wasn't much better than the one he left, but at least it was near the terminus of the club's enduring rebuilding project. Then, after a handful of pleasant reminiscences at Shea, he was gone again in a free-agent compensation snafu. Imagine Seaver on the same staff as young Dwight Gooden, giving lessons in pitching and life. As John Greenleaf Whittier wrote a century prior, "For all sad words of tongue and pen, the saddest are those 'It might have been.'"

Below are the once-bitten, twice-shy Mets, listed chronologically from when they became two-timers. And a one, and a two . . .

Player	1st Tour	2nd Tour	Number(s)
Frank Lary	1964	1965	17
Al Jackson	1962–65	1968–69	15/38
Jim Gosger	1969	1973–74	18/19, 5
Bob L. Miller	1962	1973–74	24/30
Ray Sadecki	1970–74	1977	33
Tim Foli	1970–71	1978–79	19
Mike Jorgensen	1968, 1970–71	1980–83	16/22
Dave Kingman	1975–77	1981–83	26
Rusty Staub	1972–75	1981–85	4, 10/10
Tom Seaver	1967–77	1983	41
Bill Almon	1980	1985	25/2
Lee Mazzilli	1976–81	1986–89	12, 16/13
Clint Hurdle	1983, 1985	1987	33/13/7
Alex Treviño	1978–81	1990	29/6
Hubie Brooks	1980–84	1991	62, 39, 7/7
Jeff McKnight	1989	1992–94	15/5, 7, 17, 18
Kevin McReynolds	1987–91	1994	22
Greg McMichael	1997–98	1998–99	36
Bobby Bonilla	1992–95	1999	25
Josias Manzanillo	1993–95	1999	39

Player	1st Tour	2nd Tour	Number(s)
Jeff Tam	1998	1999	38, 36/36
Bill Pulsipher	1995, 1998	2000	21/25
Lenny Harris	1998	2000–01	19
Pete Walker	1995	2001–02	49/43
Roger Cedeño	1999	2002–03	19
Jeromy Burnitz	1993–94	2002–03	5/20
Tsuyoshi Shinjo	2001	2003	5
David Cone	1987–92	2003	44, 17/16
Todd Zeile	2000–01	2004	9/27
Roberto Hernandez	2005	2006	39/49, 39
Kelly Stinnett	1994–95	2006	33/36
Marlon Anderson	2005	2007–09	18/23, 9
Brady Clark	2002	2008	15/44
Anderson Hernandez	2005–07	2009	1, 4/11
Mike Jacobs	2005	2010	27/35
Gary Matthews	2002	2010	25/19
Jason Isringhausen	1995–99	2011	29, 44/45
Omar Quintanilla	2012	2013–14	6/4, 0
Pedro Feliciano	2002–10	2013	55, 39, 25/55
Kirk Nieuwenhuis	2013–15	2015	9/9
Eric Young Jr.	2013–14	2015	22/1

Note: *The / delineates the number(s) worn from first tour from second.*

#37: THE ONE AND ONLY CASEY

Because there was only one **Casey Stengel**, No. 37 is the only number to be issued once and only once in team history.

Managing a team to a .302 winning percentage isn't the typical route to numerical immortality, but Stengel wasn't a typical manager, and the situation he entered into in 1962 wasn't typical either. Presented with a collection of rejects as the result of a cruelly uncharitable expansion draft, Stengel embraced the role as ambassador of the Mets to help sell the team even as he led to it to new depths of futility.

Stengel had plenty of experience with bad teams, enduring managing stints with the talent-poor Brooklyn Dodgers (1934–36) and Boston Braves (1938–43) as well as a string of minor league franchises. These assignments helped Stengel develop a managing style that drew on the mentors of his playing days (Wilbert Robinson, the clown, and John McGraw, the master strategist). His break came when he was unexpectedly named manager of the Yankees in 1949 and subsequently led them to ten pennants in twelve years. His firing, along with Yankees general manager George Weiss, in the after-math of the Pirates' surprise victory in the 1960 World Series, freed both men up to lead the new New York franchise.

The Ol' Perfesser had plenty of managerial tricks—he had a good eye for talent, and he used the bullpen and platoons effectively—but it was insufficient weaponry to fight a dearth of talent. Instead Stengel sensed an opportunity to create an attraction. His stream-of-consciousness ramblings and unique turns of phrase were enthusiastically received by writers. His calls for the "Youth of America" to join his "Amazin' Mets" helped sell the franchise to a new generation. He even called for the club's ballparks to be decorated with "placards," to express their joy and sorrow at being

We'll take their word for it this is supposed to look like Casey Stengel, given out on the final day of 2014.

part of something new. The Mets in no time were outdrawing Casey's former employers in the Bronx.

Following the game of July 24, 1965 (a 5–1 loss to the Phillies) Stengel entertained attendees for the Old Timer's Game scheduled the next day at Toots Shor's restaurant, and at some point, he fell and broke his hip. He officially retired shortly afterward, and the Mets retired jersey No. 37 on September 2 of that year.

Although Stengel is associated closely with No. 37—it was retired for him by the Mets and the Yankees—that association developed rather late in his career. Stengel never wore a number as a player—his playing career ended seven years before numbering became standard practice in 1932. His coaching and managerial career saw him dressed in 31 (Brooklyn, 1932–36), 36 (Brooklyn, 1936), 31 again (Boston Braves, 1938–39), and 32 (Boston Braves, 1940–43) before taking 37 with the Yankees in 1949.

When the Mets acquired Jimmy Piersall, a career-long wearer of No. 37, in 1963, there was some discussion of how the Mets would handle a veteran player whose favored number belonged to the manager. Among the considerations were 37A—a nod to owner Joan Payson's affinity for horse racing—and 73, before they eventually settled on 34, the *New York Times* reported. Some in the organization felt using two 37s would be acceptable, the *Times* added. "If the fans can't tell the difference between them, they don't deserve to be Met fans."

Stengel brought personality to the Mets with a capital *P*. Writers couldn't stop writing when he opened his mouth. Even after he finally put away the uniform, Stengel remained in the club's employ for the last decade of his life. He was a goodwill ambassador and his own translator of Stengel-ese, a language in which sentences rambled on forever without a point but always with a punch line:

"We got some very excellent fellows that we selected them 'cause they were college men," he said of that first met team in spring training. "We figured if we couldn't find them that was good, we'd get them that was smart, and we checked on the college men and we selected 'em very carefully 'cause they was from Johns Hopkins, which is a very brilliant place, except we found our men was from the clinic instead of the college, and our most valuable man was the orthopedic surgeon which, thank heavens, we did not pick up in the expansion draft but got him on Park Avenue."

Casey reminded fans of the club's humble past at the 1969 World Series and celebrated in the locker room he helped break in. He continued coming to Shea for Old-Timer's Day festivities, even as his body was ravaged by cancer. He died at in 1975 at 85, just a week before Joan Payson.

Number 37

Number of times issued: 1 (1 manager)

Longest tenured: Casey Stengel, 1962–65

Best single season: Stengel, 1964 (53–109)

Career statistical leader: Stengel 175–404 (.302)

Retired: September 2, 1965

Mets Uniform Controversies

When Kenny Rogers was traded to the Mets in 1999, he was presented with a problem: his favorite uniform number, 37, was retired by the club. Following the lead of players like Carlton Fisk, who reversed his 27 to 72 upon jumping from the Red Sox to the White Sox, Rogers suited up in 73.

Following is a list of similar cases in Mets history, when a player the Mets acquired had some equity in a number already occupied—or retired—by the club, and their resolutions.

Player	Year	# request	But it was taken by	So instead he settled for
Antonio Bastardo	2016*	59	Dan Warthen	59; Warthen switched to 38
Yoenis Cespedes	2015	52	Carlos Torres	52; Torres switched to 72
Juan Uribe	2015	2	Dilson Herrera	2; Herrera switched to 16
Tyler Clippard	2015	36	Sean Gilmartin	46
Manny Acosta	2011	46	Dale Thayer	46; Thayer switched to 36
Francisco Rodriguez	2009	57	Johan Santana	75
Moises Alou	2007	18	Jose Valentin	18; Valentin switched to 22
Carlos Delgado	2006	25	Kazuo Matsui	21
Kazuo Matsui	2004	7	Jose Reyes	25; coach Don Baylor switched to 52
Braden Looper	2004	41	Retired for Tom Seaver	40; Jae Seo switched to 26
Tom Glavine	2003	47	Joe McEwing	47; McEwing switched, to 11
Don Baylor (coach)	2003	25	Scott Strickland	25; Strickland switched, to 28

Player	Year	# request	But it was taken by	So instead he settled for
John Valentin	2002	13	Edgardo Alfonzo	4
Jeff D'Amico	2002	13	Edgardo Alfonzo	18
Roger Cedeño	2002	19	Lenny Harris	19; Harris was traded a week later in the offseason
Jeromy Burnitz	2002	20	Mark Johnson	20; Johnson switched to 5
Mike Hampton	2000	10	Rey Ordoñez	32
Todd Zeile	2000	27	Dennis Cook	9
Kenny Rogers	1999	37	Casey Stengel	73
Mike Piazza	1998	31	John Franco	31; Franco switched to 45
Tony Fernandez	1993	1	Vince Coleman	1; Coleman switched to 11
Jeff Torborg (mgr.)	1992	10	Dave Magadan	10; Magadan switched to 29
Garry Templeton	1991	1	Vince Coleman	11
Vince Coleman	1990	29	Dave Magadan	1
John Franco	1990	31	Julio Valera	31; Valera switched to 48
Frank Viola	1989	16	Dwight Gooden	26
Lee Mazzilli	1986	16	Dwight Gooden	13
Keith Hernandez	1983	37	Casey Stengel	17
Felix Millan	1974	17	Teddy Martinez	17; Martinez switched to 23; Dave Schneck switched to 16 to accommodate Martinez
Willie Mays	1972	24	Jim Beachaump	24; Beauchamp switched to 5
Bob Aspromonte	1971	14	Gil Hodges	2; (Aspromonte, a Brooklyn native, wore 14 previously as a tribute to Hodges)
Tommy Davis	1967	12	Johnny Stephenson	12; Stephenson switched to 19
Ken Boyer	1966	14	Ron Swoboda	14; Swoboda switched to 17 (spring training), then to 4 see Stuart, below)
Dick Stuart	1966	7	Ed Kranepool	17; Stuart was assigned No. 10 upon his arrival just prior to spring training; later that spring, he arranged to take 17 from Swoboda, who was also in uni-number limbo as the result of the newly arrived Ken Boyer
Yogi Berra	1965	8	Chris Cannizzaro	8; Cannizzaro switched, to 5

Player	Year	# request	But it was taken by	So instead he settled for
Warren Spahn	1965	21	Ed Kranepool	21; Kranepool switched, to 7
Jimmy Piersall	1963	37	Casey Stengel	34
Duke Snider	1963	4	Charlie Neal	11; Snider would switch to 4 following Neal's trade, July 1
Gene Woodling	1962	14	Gil Hodges	11

*2016 assignment

#38: COFFEE IS FOR CLOSERS

Number 38 in Mets history has often been a reliever's number. Many times, however, it hasn't provided nearly enough relief.

New York is especially tough on its relievers. Fans are often quick to dismiss a ho-hum 9th inning in a close win, preferring to remember the three-run home run or the starter who got them there; a 9th-inning meltdown is recalled far differently. Often forgotten is the 5th-inning error that allowed a crucial run to score or a bases-loaded strikeout by the Mets cleanup hitter—although in New York, it won't take long for these to be second-guessed. The brunt of the blame usually falls on the man who threw the last pitch.

If you're familiar with the epic 1978 Mets highlight film (dubbed *Turning It Over*) that hit the airwaves every time Pete Flynn's crew unrolled the tarp in '79, you'll recall a poignant scene of Joe Torre removing Jerry Koosman in a 1–0 game in the 9th in favor of **Skip Lockwood** (1975–79). Lockwood then allowed a two-run home run to San Diego's Derrel Thomas, who would hit just three homers all year. No wonder Kooz won only three times in '78 while Lockwood set the franchise record with 13 losses in relief.

Lockwood, a bespectacled Bostonian who started his major league career as an infielder, was actually better than dramatized. In five seasons with the Mets, he blew just 18 of 83 saves. He had a 2.80 ERA in 227 career appearances for the Mets. Lockwood led the team in saves for four straight years, something no Met reliever did until John Franco

If you thought the late 1970s were a bad time to be a Mets fan, you were right. But think how much worse it could have been without Skip Lockwood to close out victories.

came along (two of Ron Taylor's four years as leader came when saves were still an "unofficial" statistic, pre-1969).

Rick Aguilera (1985–86, 1989) began his career in the rotation but won one of the most memorable games in Mets history in relief. Aggie got the win in Game 6 of the 1986 World Series after allowing two Boston runs in the top of the inning. He switched out of 38 after the Series before jumping back in for the '89 season. By then he'd made the conversion to the pen and showed the stuff of an excellent reliever. He was a great one . . . only it was with Minnesota after he became part of the package that landed Frank Viola.

Nondescript pen men included **Bob Gibson** (1987), **Blaine Beatty** (1989–91), **Dave Telgheder** (1993–95), **Jeff Tam** (1998), and **Jerrod Riggan** (2001).

Roger Craig (1962–63) started the first Mets game ever and was rewarded for his pioneering efforts by leading the league in losses in both his years with the Mets (24 and 22). He set a losing precedent for 38s that lasted through **Ed Bauta** (1963), **Willard Hunter** (1964), **Dave Eilers** (1965–66), **Ralph Terry** (1966–67), **Dennis Bennett** (1967), **Billy Connors** (1967), **Al Jackson** (1968–69), **Jesse Hudson** (1969), and **Rich Folkers** (1970). **Buzz Capra** (1971–73) finally managed a winning mark in 1972 (3-2). **Jerry Cram** (1974–75) never started (or won) a game as a Met, but he pitched eight scoreless innings one night in September 1974—from the 17th to the 24th against St. Louis—and the Mets promptly lost in the 25th.

Tim Leary debuted in 1981 as perhaps the club's most highly touted young pitcher since Tom Seaver, but Leary hurt his arm in the Chicago chill after three innings and returned as damaged goods in '83 and '84. His post-Mets career was healthier, if not successful.

On most days **Dave Mlicki** (1995–98) was an unremarkable mid-rotation starter, but he will always be remembered as the surprise star of the first ever Mets-Yankees regular-season game in 1997, throwing a complete-game shutout over Andy Pettitte in the Bronx. A dozen years later at the same address, an anonymous Venezuelan waiver-wire pick making his first Mets start, **Fernando Nieve**, would also beat Pettitte and the Yankees, throwing 6 2/3 innings of 4-hit ball. Nieve (2009–10) won his first three starts as a Met, but had less success out of the bullpen in 2010.

Victor Zambrano (2004–06) could never outlive the legacy of who he wasn't. In a trade that appeared like a mismatch the day it was made and then only got worse, the Mets acquired Zambrano (and, don't forget, Bartolome Fortunato) from Tampa Bay for top prospect Scott Kazmir (and not-so-top prospect Joselo Diaz) on July 30, 2004. Zambrano's time in New York can best be described as a lab experiment of mad scientist pitching coach Rick Peterson, whose offhanded remark that he could fix Zambrano's mechanical issues "in ten minutes" is still remembered. Peterson kept his job; GM Jim Duquette did not, though whether Duquette was a patsy for grey-haired "superscouts" hired to oversee him is still murky. Following that fateful trade, Zambrano won only 10 games; Kazmir, a three-time All-Star, has won 98 and counting.

The 2007 bullpen was reeling amid a massive September swoon when the Mets reached all the way to AA to call up **Carlos Muniz** on September 21. But the sickness was contagious. Muniz made his debut mopping up after a rotten Tom Glavine start in Washington, giving up two seemingly meaningless tack-on runs that loomed large when the Mets rallied for 6 in the 9th only to fall, 10–9.

Desperate for affordable pitching, the threadbare post-Madoff Mets issued 38 to three wobbly former Milwaukee Brewers: **Matt Wise** in 2010; **Chris Capuano** in 2011, and **Shaun Marcum** in 2013, with only Capuano lasting a whole year, and barely so. **Garrett Olson**, lasted only one-third of inning with the 2012 Mets, leaving the club with career ERA of 108.00. **Jae Seo** (2002) and **Pat Strange** (2002) each made their major league debuts in 38. **James Baldwin** (2004) made two ineffective starts before being asked to leave. **Vic Black** (2013–14) showed promise as a young reliever before injuries derailed him.

Pat Howell, like Mets predecessors Tommie Agee, Cleon Jones and Amos Otis, hailed from Mobile, Alabama, where they make terrific outfielders. Howell, the only position player ever to wear No. 38 for the

Mets, was so dazzling a center fielder his mid-season callup abruptly moved Howard Johnson from center field to left, although Howell didn't hit enough to stay.

Number 38

Number of times issued: 39 (36 players)

Longest tenured: Skip Lockwood (5 seasons, 227 games), Dave Mlicki (4 seasons, 122 games), Rick Aguilera (3 seasons, 85 games), Roger Craig (2 seasons, 71 games)

Best single seasons: Lockwood, 1976 (10–7, 2.67 ERA, 19 saves, 108 strikeouts in 94 1/3 innings); Aguilera, 1985 (10–7, 3.24 ERA, 74 strikeouts in 122 1/3 innings); Aguilera, 1986 (10–7, 3.88 ERA, 104 strikeouts in 141 2/3 innings)

Career statistical leaders: Wins (Aguilera 26, Lockwood 24, Mlicki 24); saves (Lockwood 65), ERA (Lockwood 2.80)

Mets Uniform History: Patches (Part I): From Fair to Foul

The Mets wore a patch on their left sleeve for their first game in the major leagues. For their second game, they didn't wear any. The Mets wore the patch with the familiar Mets skyline logo only on their road uniforms from 1962 to '66. At the Polo Grounds their sleeves were as bare as their cupboard was of talent.

The Mets moved to Shea Stadium in 1964, coinciding with the New York World's Fair. The club commemorated the event with a patch that featured the fair's icon: the "Unisphere," a twelve-story, twenty-ton, space-age globe made by U.S. Steel. The left side of the patch was blue and the right side orange with a diagonal white line splitting the image. It was the first patch worn by the Mets at home. It was worn on the road as well—on the left sleeve—with the skyline patch moving to the right sleeve on the road uniforms.

By 1966, the World's Fair was over and the Unisphere patch disappeared (the actual Unisphere remains a half-mile south of Citi Field), and for the first time the Mets put the skyline logo patch on the left sleeve of their home uniform. That changed in 1969. A 100th anniversary patch with the now well-known MLB logo of a silhouetted batter (said to be modeled after Twins slugger Harmon Killebrew) was worn on the left sleeve of every team in 1969 to commemorate a century of acknowledged professional baseball. The Mets ditched the skyline logo during their signature '69 season but brought it back for the World Series. The Mets wore the skyline logo on their left sleeves and shifted the MLB logo to the right on their pinstripe uniforms.

The Mets wore no skyline logo patch at Baltimore's Memorial Stadium (they hadn't worn it on home or away uniforms against Atlanta in the first NLCS). But the skyline logo patch worked wonders at Shea. How else could anyone explain Agee's catches, Swoboda's dive, the ball glancing off J. C. Martin's wrist, the shoe polish incident, or the miraculous culmination?

For the next dozen years, the Mets kept the skyline patch on the left sleeve of their home and away uniforms. All National League clubs were required to wear a red, white, and blue National League patch that included a handlebar mustache and pillbox cap, plus stars and stripes on their right sleeve to honor the NL's centennial, which coincided nicely with America's bicentennial in 1976. The left sleeve was crowded with the skyline logo along with a black armband for departed Joan Payson and Casey Stengel. The skyline logo remained on the left sleeve through the Joe Torre years, even as players and fans disappeared in droves. Despite slogans to the contrary, the magic had presumably run dry by 1982. The skyline logo came off.

#39: RISK MANAGEMENT

The Mets have had some great rookies in their history, but no rookie arrived in a great season and enjoyed it quite like **Gary Gentry**. Gentry was in the middle of everything in 1969. His major league debut was the game Tommie Agee hit his one-of-a-kind blast into the upper deck at Shea; he pitched the NL East clincher against St. Louis; he started the pennant-clincher

Gary Gentry sporting facial hair in his later Mets years.

Jacob Kanarek/From Worst to First

against the Braves; and was twice bailed out in Game 3 of the World Series by Agee's miraculous catches. That first year proved impossible to top.

Drafted by three different teams, Gentry spurned them all, and some felt he got what he deserved when the lowly Mets selected and signed him out of baseball factory Arizona State in 1967. He made the Mets out of spring training less than two years later. Gentry (1969–72) couldn't have picked a better place to be than Shea Stadium, making 37 starts (including two in the postseason) and winning 14 for the world champs. He remained steady, if unspectacular, through '72. Yet he still cast a large enough shadow to net Felix Millan and George Stone from Atlanta on his way out of town.

Jacob Kanarek/From Worst to First

Ladies and gentlemen, Nino Espinosa.

Nino Espinosa (1975–78) brought back playoff-fixture Richie Hebner just before the '79 season. Little did anyone realize how quickly Nino and his frilly 'fro would be missed. A 200-inning, double-digit winner on the worst team in the league was worth his weight in gold compared to a hacking, grave-digging malcontent who'd played in seven NLCS and reached one World Series.

From 1982 to 1987, tuning in a Mets game and seeing 39 on the mound usually meant the Mets were in trouble or soon to be there: **Doug Sisk** was pitching. A hard-throwing sinker-baller, Sisk (known as Doug "Risk" in his day) routinely created chaos out of order. His numbers weren't bad (33 saves, 3.10 career ERA), but rarely was there a dull moment achieving them. Believe it or not, he pitched once in the 1986 NLCS *and* World Series—both losses—and allowed no runs.

Dick Selma (1966–68) paid his dues on lousy Mets teams only to wind up getting traded to the Cubs and seeing the Mets celebrate. **Dan Wheeler** (2003–04) enjoyed it the opposite way. A bargain-bin pickup, Wheeler had been one of the few pleasant surprises of 2003, but he was dealt days before the September 2004 deadline to be on a team's postseason roster. And when the Astros finally won a postseason series after forty-two years of existence, who was on the mound to get the last out? Wheeler.

Josias Manzanillo (1993–95, 1999) was probably the Mets' most reliable and enthusiastic reliever in 1994 (3–2, 2.66, 48 whiffs in 47 1/3 innings) but not in any of his other campaigns including a return engagement in 1999. **Roberto Hernandez** traveled a similar path: He won a bullpen role in 2005 and did well enough in New York so that Pittsburgh threw money at him in '06. After reliever Duaner Sanchez was injured in a cab accident—wear your seat belts, people!—the Mets swiftly reacquired Hernandez. Bert, however, lost his effectiveness at age forty-one. He had also lost his number to **Pedro Feliciano** (2006), but Feliciano obligingly changed digits within a week.

The son of a fireman, skinny righty **Bobby Parnell** (2008–15) generated four-alarm heat on the mound—his fastball occasionally registered in the triple-digits—igniting a slow ascension to closer by 2013, when he racked up 22 saves by midseason. Then it all burned to the ground: Neck surgery ended his 2013 campaign, and Parnell returned in 2014 only long enough to blow an Opening-Day save and his elbow in the same inning. He was patched up again by late 2015, but had lost the spark.

Others: **Steve Dillon** (1963–64), **Tommy Moore** (1972–73), **John Strohmayer** (1973–74), **Phil Lombardi** (1989), **Kelvin Torve** (1990–91), **Rich Saveur** (1991), **Josias Manzanillo** (1993–95, 1999), **Juan Acevedo** (1997), **Rick Wilkins** (1998), **Jim Mann** (2000), **Dicky Gonzalez** (2001), **Steve Reed** (2002), **Vic Darensbourg** (2004), **Jon Adkins** (2007), and **Claudio Vargas** (2009).

The number has also served as a staging area for better times ahead for a handful of Mets hitters. **Hubie Brooks** donned 39 briefly in 1980. **Jeff Kent** wore it for a month after coming to the Mets from Toronto in the David Cone trade in 1992. And before his overpriced Kona concession ever arrived at Shea, **Benny Agbayani** was a warm body in 39 in '98.

Number 39

Number of times issued: 27 (24 players)

Longest tenured: Bobby Parnell (8 seasons, 329 games); Doug Sisk (5 seasons, 263 games), Gary Gentry (4 seasons, 131 games), Dick Selma (4 seasons, 105 games)

Best single seasons: Gentry, 1969 (13–12, 3.43 ERA, 154 strikeouts in 233 2/3 innings); Espinosa, 1977 (10–13, 3.42 ERA, 105 strikeouts in 200 innings); Sisk, 1983 (1–3, 2.24 ERA, 11 saves, 67 games), Parnell, 2013 (5–5, 2.16, 22 saves).

Career statistical leaders: Home runs (Kent 3, Brooks 1); RBI (Kent 15, Brooks 10); batting average (Brooks .309, Kent .239); wins (Gentry 41, Espinosa 25); saves (Parnell 37, Sisk 33), ERA (Roberto Hernandez 2.65, Sisk 3.10, Selma 3.16)

Mets Uniform History: Patches (Part II): Racing the Skyline

The development of patches on Mets uniform sleeves in the 1980s was directly related to substantial changes in the uniform. A blue alternate uni plus road grays with a racing stripe led to the banishment of the skyline logo from the sleeve for eleven years.

The Mets did wear a patch on their left sleeve for one year during that period: 1986. A twenty-fifth anniversary patch featured the skyline logo as the centerpiece with crossed bats set inside a diamond on a blue field. The edges of the diamond were trimmed in orange and white. The diamond had "1986" at first base and "1962" at third, and the home plate area read "25th Anniversary." This was placed on top of the racing stripe. Oh, it was busy, but so were the Mets. Garment care instructions? For best results, douse repeatedly with chilled champagne.

The Mets eliminated the racing stripe and resurrected the skyline logo on the left sleeve in 1993, just in time for their worst season in twenty-eight years. The Mets wore two patches a year later. The one on the right sleeve commemorated the 125th anniversary of professional baseball. The Mets boxed the skyline logo on their left sleeve for the twenty-fifth anniversary of the "Miracle Mets." The strike wiped out two commemorative pin giveaways as well as everything else on the professional baseball landscape in year 125.

The skyline logo returned, along with the players, in 1995. Despite all the changes and additions to the uniform, the logo has remained on the left sleeve every year since. All major league teams honored Jackie Robinson with a right-sleeve patch in 1997. A home plate with an extended rectangle featured Robinson's signature, along with his debut year, the current year, and "50th Anniversary" marked his landmark breaking of baseball's color barrier. Shea Stadium was the sight for the national ceremony fifty years to the day of his debut.

For the Mets' 2000 season opener in Tokyo, a patch was worn on the right sleeve of both the Mets and Cubs for the first two major league games ever played in Japan—in addition to various advertising patches giving the two-game series a vaguely NASCAR feel. A World Series logo was stitched on team hats that October.

September 11, 2001, was one of the most heartrending days in history. In the wake of the terrorist attacks, American flag patches were sewn on the back of every uniform and placed on hats and batting helmets as well. The sleeves simply read, "9-11-01." The Mets wore this remembrance with an American flag on each side of the date on the right sleeve in 2002, along with a patch commemorating the club's forty years in the National League. The gold and green patch, with "Mets" in orange and blue, featured the years 1962 and 2002 along with "40th Anniversary." The '02 season ended a lot more like '62 than anyone could have imagined.

Two years later, Shea Stadium celebrated its longevity. The images of the neon pitcher and batter from the exterior of Shea were placed side by side, separated by a diagonal line reminiscent of the Unisphere patch of forty years earlier. The southpaw pitcher started his motion on the left side of the patch with a blue background, while the lefty-swinging batter took a cut on the opposite side with an orange backdrop. The years 1964–2004 as well as "40th Anniversary" and "Shea Stadium" appeared in white lettering. Underneath the patch was the catchphrase "Ya

Gotta Believe," signed "Tug" in honor of deceased reliever Tug McGraw. (Black armbands and special patches to honor other fallen Mets are featured in Chapter 14). At the 2004 All-Star Game in Houston, the Shea patch was replaced on the right sleeves of Tom Glavine and Mike Piazza with a 2004 All-Star Game logo. Tug's motto remained, just as it always will in fans' hearts.

The final year of Shea, 2008, featured a tribute patch. A circle shows two sides of Shea: the gray "classic" Shea complete with the colored aluminum siding on the left, and the "modern" blue version with the neon catcher on the right. Above both is a classy yet slightly different version of the familiar skyline.

Citi Field's 2009 birth was commemorated with a rectangular logo worn on the right sleeve positioned so as to resemble a blue baseball diamond reading "Inaugural Season" with an orange stripe along the first-base line reading "2009"—a design roundly criticized both for its lack of imagination and uncomfortably corporate feel reflecting the multimillion "naming rights" deal for the bank in the wake of the financial crisis. Led by influential ESPN columnist Paul Lukas, fans by midseason were fighting back with T-shirts reading "I'm Calling It Shea," still a common sight at whatever you want to call the park.

The Mets turned fifty in 2012. A patch on the left sleeve overlayed a gold-lettered "50th Anniversary" over the familiar skyline logo. The following year, the skyline—sans the Mets wordmark—was overlayed with orange letters in the "Tuscan" road-jersey font reading "All-Star Game" positioned just below the bridge, celebrating the first mid-summer classic hosted by the Mets since 1964.

Who hustled onto the Mets sleeve in 2014? None other than a smiling Mr. Met—a symbol of the team from its earliest days finally made it to the left jersey sleeve of the blue alternate wear—and somewhat less aesthetically pleasing, to batting-practice caps. Home pinstripes included the skyline logo and in 2015, for the first time in fifteen years, a World Series patch.

#40: STONE COLON

Nobody likes turning 40. Naturally, that carries over to the Mets. While they've had some good seasons from players' age forty, they've had relatively few by anyone wearing that number. Until the arrival of **Bartolo Colon** in 2014: number 40, age forty, waistband 40. He was baseball's first 40-40-40 man.

Bartolo Colon has been great for fans and for young pitchers watching how a professional succeeds and has fun.

For a team that was supposed to be brimming with young pitching talent, signing Bartolo Colon was some kind of a joke, right? Most Mets fan knew little about Colon since he'd spent almost his entire 16-year career in American League outposts from Cleveland to Anaheim, donning both Sox, with a lone National League stop for a few months as a Montreal Expo—at the cost of Cliff Lee, Brandon Phillips, and Grady Sizemore. Then Expos GM Omar Minaya traded him for Orlando

"El Duque" Hernandez. Colon's career seemed petering toward its inevitable end in Oakland when, in 2012, he had his best season since he'd won the 2005 AL Cy Young season as an Angel. He finished second in the AL in wins (19), ERA (2.65), and fewest walks (1.371) per nine innings. Still, at his age, free agent offers were minimal. Suddenly the Mets, with barely enough money to pick up the check at an IHOP, signed Colon to a two-year, $20 million deal through his age forty-two season. It was insane. Brilliantly insane.

Colon not only took the pressure off the young pitchers, he took the pressure off everybody. The second oldest player in the National League, he responded to jams by tossing the ball in the air a few times and then throwing a fastball that the batter knew was coming and striking him out. He whiffed four batters for every walk, and though he gave up plenty of hits (Bartolo allowed more hits than any major league pitcher in 2014–15), he averaged 14 wins and almost 200 innings per year for a team always in need of both. And then he stepped up to bat.

Gary, Keith, and Ron pontificate at length about this phenomenon every fifth day—plus continued awe after the Mets opted to *Live Más* with another helping of Bartolo in 2016—but Deadspin summed up Bartolo at the bat perhaps as well as anyone: "We should treasure every time Mets pitcher Bartolo Colon has to take an at bat. Baseball's giving us a present." The helmet falling over his face, the mighty cut (at anything), the midswing smile, and then the stunning, blessed contact! One outfielder falls into a black hole, the other two run the other way for help—and Bartolo still stops at second base. If you can't enjoy Bartolo brand baseball, you're doing it wrong.

Everybody else who has worn No. 40, did it wrong—whether they meant to or not.

George Stone (1973–75) came over in a heist from Atlanta with Felix Millan and helped the Mets win the NL pennant by going 12–3, 2.80 in '73. Yet he remains among the more obscure "What Ifs" in franchise history. What if he'd pitched Game 6 of the '73 World Series in Oakland and Tom Seaver was rested in case they needed him for Game 7? People have not let that rest for 40 years, but few of them ever bring up the fact that the A's pitchers they faced—Catfish Hunter and Ken Holtzman—each allowed one run in those starts in Oakland. And if Stone *had* pitched and been beaten in Game 6 and the Mets still lost the Series, he wouldn't be George the Obscure, he'd be known in Queens as George #$%*&@! Stone.

There was cursing and sobbing aplenty in the wake of the Midnight Massacre. Like Tom Seaver, **Pat Zachry** (1977–82) was a right-handed pitcher and a former Rookie of the Year (Zachry shared the award in 1976 with the Padres' Butch Metzger). That's where the similarities ended. Even as the longest tenured of the four players returned in the Franchise-annihilating deal of 1977, the giraffish Zachry never tempted anyone to forgive M. Donald Grant or forget Tom Seaver.

Zachry's best season at Shea came in 1978, when he made the All-Star team after starting out 10–3 with a 2.90 ERA for a team that was 13 games under .500 at the midway point. But on July 24, with the shine already coming off the All-Star, Zachary allowed a single to Pete Rose in the 7th inning to push the loathed one's hitting streak to 37 straight and tie the twentieth-century NL mark set by Tommy Holmes (on the premises at Shea, because he was a Mets employee). Zachry was so incensed about the hit—and that he'd been yanked against his former team—that he kicked the dugout step, fractured his left foot, and was done for the season. Those 10 wins were the most he had in any of his six seasons as a Met. Number 40 won 41 times as the replacement for the irreplaceable 41—ain't that a kick . . . in the step.

Armando Reynoso (1997–98) seemingly came out of nowhere to lead a postseason drive in 1998, but the drive and Reynoso's Mets career petered out one game too early. His loss against Atlanta in the season finale cost the Mets a tie for the Wild Card and did little to redeem a strong 7–3 record. It's hard to blame the team's collapse on Reynoso, whose Musketeer-like mustache and arsenal of off-speed stuff helped compile a 13–6 career mark as a Met.

When multiple competitors all pitched worse in 2003 spring training, rookie **Jae Seo** got the last available seat on the charter to Flushing and responded with a surprisingly strong campaign (9–12, 3.82) despite the media ignoring his request to be called Jae Weong Seo. Oddly, he didn't pitch well enough to go north again in 2004. And that was after surrendering his number to newly acquired closer **Braden Looper** (2004–05). Looper did just fine for a team going nowhere. Yet fans still mastered the tricky feat of turning the "Loop" chant into old-fashioned boos during his second Shea season, when he failed to tell anyone that he was pitching with a shredded shoulder.

Calvin Schiraldi (1984–85) did little of note while wearing a Mets uniform, but the prized prospect helped bring Bob Ojeda to Shea in trade and delivered the Mets' second world championship by suffering losses in the final two games of the '86 World Series for Boston. Mercifully, there was no sign of 40 for the Mets outside of the celebratory pilings-on in the

'86 postseason. That would have meant **Randy Niemann** was in the game. As designated mop-up man, you want to keep that guy warming up coffee— not his arm—in the pen. He remained in that vicinity as bullpen coach under several Mets regimes.

Sidearmer **Jeff Innis** (1987–93) was a beguiler in the Mets bullpen and a good clubhouse interview. He was the first Met whose last name began with *I*, and while, of course, there's no "I" in team, there was plenty of team in Innis, who gamely led the Mets in appearances during the sorry seasons of 1991–93.

Brian Bannister (2006) had the ability to fill the bases and then somehow pitch out of it, but it was running the bases that did him in, putting him on the disabled list, knocking him off the depth chart, and banishing him to Kansas City for reliever **Ambiorix Burgos**. Burgos got hurt after just 17 Mets appearances, but Bannister won AL Rookie of the Year in K.C. The Royal son a pitch (his dad, Floyd, a former first overall pick, spent 15 years as a major league southpaw) used baseball analytics to make up for what his right arm lacked in velocity. He learned well because the Red Sox created a special analytics position just for him in 2015. Now that's two jobs in baseball we'd kill for.

Anyone still complaining about Rey Ordoñez's weakness at the plate ought to take a gander at the stats of shortstop **Al Moran** (1963–64), who managed a sickly .193 batting average (and 27 errors) in 119 games as a rookie for the '63 club. His sophomore season was brief.

Other 40s: **Dick Rustek** (1966), **Jerry Hinsley** (1967), **Bill Short** (1968), **Brent Strom** (1972), **Eric Gunderson** (1995), **Dave Telgheder** (1995), **Mike Fyhrie** (1996), one-game right fielder **Ryan McGuire** (2000), one-win pitcher **C. J. Nitkowski** (2001), and dreadlocked pot-smoking outfielder **Tony Tarasco** (2002), the all-time offensive leader in the 40 crowd (which isn't saying much).

Two recent Mets are worth mention because they made the game a little more fun. Backup catcher **Robinson Cancel** (2008) didn't liven things up much in 28-game, three number Mets tenure (he also wore 4 and 29), but it was fun to mispronounce his name and make Chris Berman-esque pronouncements in the last days of Shea such as a Doors infused, "Robinson Cancel my subscription to the resurrection" or more fittingly, "Robinson Cancel my season tickets."

Tim Byrdak (2011–13) could have easily packed it in after his left shoulder gave out following 128 trips from the bullpen in the first two years of the Terry Collins regime. Byrdak came back from surgery at age thirty-nine and pitched eight September games for the middling Mets (they lost each of his last eight major league appearances in 2013). He came back not because the games were important, but because the game is.

Number 40

Number of times issued: 21

Longest tenured: Jeff Innis (6 seasons, 288 games), Pat Zachry (5 seasons, 135 games)

Best single seasons: George Stone, 1973 (12–3, 2.80 ERA in 148 innings); Bartolo Colon, 2014 (15–13, 4.09 ERA in 202 1/3 innings, 24 walks in 33 starts); Zachry, 1978 (10–6, 3.33 ERA in 21 starts); Jae Seo, 2003 (9–12, 3.82 ERA in 188 1/3 innings)

Career statistical leaders: Home runs (Tony Tarasco 6, Al Moran 1, Robinson Cancel 1); RBI (Moran 27, Tarasco 15); batting average (Tarasco .250, Cancel .244, Moran .195); wins (Zachry 41, Colon 29); saves (Braden Looper 57, Jeff Innis 5); ERA (Innis 3.05, Looper 3.15, Zachry 3.62),

---

Mets Uniform History: Out of the Blue and into the Black

Mets uniforms got a lot more complicated in the 1990s. In 1998, a year after the introduction of the "snow white" home uniform—and the failed white cap experiment—the Mets made black the new blue. New alternate hats were black with blue brims. Black became the primary shading color on both home and away uniforms as well as the skyline patch (now minus an "NY"). A black alternate jersey that read "Mets" was worn at home and on the road. The plot darkened.

The next year an all-black third alternate hat was introduced, as was a new black road uniform that read "New York." These changes were made without abandoning the old uniforms, so the Mets, who'd never worn more than one uniform at Shea Stadium in any of their first thirty-five seasons, now had three different uniforms and three different hats for home games, not to mention two road uniforms plus a new batting practice jersey and hat. The Mets also removed names from the backs of the home uniforms in 1999, the first time players had gone nameless at Shea in twenty-two seasons. That experiment ended after one year.

But why all the new uniforms? Why black? "The black was added as a style element based on some degree of research of fans in terms of what was popular in the marketplace," Mets VP Dave Howard told the New York Times in 2006. The Mets created new inventory—as the Milwaukee Brewers had done repeatedly—and it sold better than the old items. Of course, the Mets had improved dramatically on the field, inter-league play with the Yankees created even more area interest in the team, and there were 1.5 million more fans at Shea in 1999 than there had been five seasons earlier when pinstriping and blue had been the rule. They came, they saw, they bought merchandise.

Reaction to the black uniforms was mixed. While younger fans inclined to spend big money on replica jerseys bought in—literally—to the color scheme, fans whose allegiance traced back to prior eras tended to be less enthusiastic. Opposition caught fire online behind the efforts of Paul Lukas, the ESPN columnist and "UniWatch" founder, as well as MetsPolice.com, which righteously issued virtual citations to the violation of club traditions.

Lukas dug deeper into the causes of the black uni movement, and found that manufacturer rep Bob Halfacre, who'd been to New York, "three or four times in my life," sent a black shadow sample to the team. It soon became the team's preferred look, and took on its own shadowy life. The last vestiges of the black color scheme remained until 2012, coinciding with the fiftieth anniversary of Mets baseball.

Lukas, ever the investigator, did a followup interview in 2015, in which Halfacre admitted, "I don't think they ever needed black in the first place. Frankly, I thought the whole idea was kinda silly to start with." We could have told you that back in the '90s.

#41: TOM TERRIFIC

Tom Seaver was serious. Serious about pitching. Serious about winning. Serious when he said to lay off his family.

A signing snafu by the relocating Braves in 1966 enabled the Mets to win a three-team lottery against the Indians and Phillies for the rights to George Thomas Seaver. He was on the Mets roster a year later and helped pitch them to a world championship two years after that. While a lot of things had to align for the heretofore horrific Mets to actually become amazin', there would have been no chance for a miracle in Flushing, or much of anything to believe in in '73, without Tom Terrific. He won the Cy Young both years and should have won in '71, too. He made up for it by winning the award in '75 to become the first right-hander with three Cy Youngs.

Seaver didn't think losing was funny and as a rookie shunned the cutesy-poo image of the stumbling expansion club, the worst team since the nineteenth-century Cleveland Spiders (at a time when your great-grandfather might have remembered seeing that team name in the bottom of the standings in the paper). For an organization that had produced zip as far as legitimate pitching prospects at the major league level, Seaver was a revelation. In his first three years he accumulated 57 wins, or more than the entire team had won in any of its first four seasons of existence. Not even Dwight Gooden's remarkable 1985—with Tom still logging innings in an ugly White Sox uniform—could surpass Seaver's '69 mark for wins (25), his '70 record for innings (291), or his '71 marks for complete games (21) and strikeouts (289). Seaver's career marks may last as long as the Mets exist. If those records ever are surpassed, including his marks for starts (395), complete games (171), shutouts (44), and innings (3,045), we hope to live long enough to see it.

A malicious 1977 *New York Daily News* column by Dick Young sparked Seaver's demand for a trade, although the deterioration of the franchise around "The Franchise" may have made such a deal inevitable. Young was booed at the Hall of Fame later that horrible summer when he spoke in Cooperstown. Seaver returned triumphantly in 1983 (9–14 record for a last-place team aside) and received the most thunderous applause Shea Stadium had heard since he left. One of the great moments in uniform number recognition took

Jacob Kanarek/From Worst to First

Tom Seaver in 1976: Not yet a decade in the league and fresh off his third Cy Young Award.

place at Shea that afternoon. PA announcer Jack Franchetti, after introducing the mostly forgettable starters on Opening Day, simply said at the end, ". . . and pitching, number 41 . . ." The fans never forgot that number.

A front-office error allowed him to go to the White Sox in '84, but let's be real: it was another team's screw-up that let Seaver become a Met in the first place. He won his 300th in the Bronx for Chicago, but his plaque in Cooperstown has the right "NY" on the cap.

Seaver's number 41 was the first—and until 2016's Mike Piazza ceremony, the only—number retired for a Mets player. While many complain that the Mets should retire other numbers for players, no one has surpassed Seaver's legacy.

Unfortunately, 41 couldn't be retired retroactively. But at least 41 was never worn by any Mets other than pitchers. One-time Brooklyn ace **Clem Labine** (1962) was the first wearer of the 41 jersey but didn't last through April of the Mets' inaugural campaign. **Grover Powell** (1963) became an overnight sensation by throwing a four-hit shutout in his first start but quickly lost his way. He was struck in the face by a Donn Clendenon line drive in his next start and never won another game.

Relievers **Jim Bethke** (1965) and **Gordon Richardson** (1965–66) followed. They combined for a 4–4 lifetime record.

Number 41

Number of times issued: 5

Longest tenured: Tom Seaver (11 seasons, 401 games)

Best single season: Seaver, 1969 (25–7, 2.21 ERA, 208 strikeouts in 273 1/3 innings, Cy Young Award); Seaver, 1971 (20–10, 1.76 ERA, 289 strikeouts in 286 1/3 innings); Seaver, 1973 (19–10, 2.08 ERA, 251 strikeouts in 290 innings, Cy Young Award); Seaver, 1975 (22–9, 2.38 ERA, 243 strikeouts in 280 1/3 innings, Cy Young Award)

Career statistical leaders: Home runs (Seaver, 6), RBI (Seaver, 60), batting average (Seaver, .150), wins (Seaver, 198), ERA (Seaver, 2.57), strikeouts (2,541)

Ed Lynch Called Them Earnies: ERA by the Numbers

Although expressing a pitcher's efforts over nine-inning increments has become a bit of quaint notion in an era of relief specialists and pitch counts, the earned-run average has withstood the scrutiny of baseball's quantitative revolution better than most stats of its age.

Anything below 3? That's very good. Over 4? Not so much. In the 1s? Extraordinary. Over 5? Send him back to Lynchburg. It may seem overly simple, but it's a fairly accurate gauge of pitching performance.

Sure, ERA+, which sets the runs allowed to league averages at baseline of 100 and expresses the number as a percentage above or below that, is useful (Tom Seaver's 166 ERA+ in 1969 was 66 percent better than the league average) but who can figure that out? The formula for ERA (earned runs times nine divided by innings pitched) is about as complicated as a stat needs to be, which is to say, it was the only thing to inspire us to learn multiplication and long division in elementary school.

With that in mind, here's a list of earned-run average over Mets history as arranged by uniform number. Stats are current through 2015 and include only numbers with 1,000 innings pitched. As with strikeouts and wins, the performances of a few extraordinary performers tend to weigh the top:

No.	ERA	Notes
41	2.64	Seaver, of course (2.57).
16	3.25	Dwight Gooden (3.10) carrying Larry Miller (5.02), Hideo Nomo (4.82), and David Cone in 2003 (6.50).
50	3.35	Sid Fernandez (3.14) does almost all the work here.
12	3.38	Ron Darling and Ron Darling alone.

No.	ERA	Notes
36	3.50	Jerry Koosman (3.09) leads an otherwise shaky pack.
17	3.54	Bret Saberhagen (2.98) and David Cone (3.07)
31	3.56	John Franco (2.73) the last and best pitching inhabitant of this number.
32	3.61	Lefties Matz (2.27), Matlack (3.03) and Hampton (3.14) among the stingiest.
43	3.63	R. A. Dickey flutters in with a 2.98 mark.
39	3.64	Relievers Steve Reed, Pedro Feliciano and Roberto Hernandez are all sub-3 men.

#42: ROGER MCDOWELL AND MEMORIES OF JACKIE

In 1997 Major League Baseball officially retired 42 from every team in honor of groundbreaking Brooklyn Dodger Hall of Famer Jackie Robinson. Bud Selig's stunning decree occurred at Shea Stadium on April 15, the fiftieth anniversary of Robinson's legendary debut. President Bill Clinton and Rachel Robinson looked on, completely unaware that they were doing the Mets a favor in discontinuing a number that had seen its share of flops and fops at Shea.

What's a fop? A dictionary definition might lean toward a "dandy" or "trickster," and **Roger McDowell** (1985–89) managed to fill both roles during his Mets career. Memories of McDowell range from the man who was a zen master of hotfoots (another dictionary definition: the affixing and subsequent lighting of a book of matches to the heel of an unsuspecting teammates' spikes) to his role as the "second spitter" in his *Seinfeld* cameo, but McDowell was one of the most effective right-handed relievers the Mets have ever had. While Jesse Orosco got the deserved kudos for his yeoman's

work in 1986, McDowell had more saves, became the first Met to surpass 70 appearances in a season, and won a club record 14 times in relief. He threw a somewhat forgotten five scoreless innings preceding Messy Jesse's appearance in Game 6 of the NLCS. (Billy Hatcher's game-tying home run off Orosco blew the victory for McDowell.) Who got the win that clinched the world championship? It was McDowell (despite getting clubbed in his second inning of work), although Orosco's final glove fling is the enduring image of the Game 7 triumph.

Even after throwing 127-plus innings in relief in each of his first two years in the majors, McDowell remained extremely effective. His career-best 25 saves were overshadowed by the season-crushing home run he allowed to Terry Pendleton in 1987. McDowell was a setup guy who threw multiple innings and still racked up lots of saves (notching 29 more in a Mets uniform than Randy Myers, one of the guys he set up). And he knew plenty about pitching, as evidenced by his long-term role as Atlanta Braves pitching coach.

Alas, the clownish McDowell left New York not with a hot-footed bang but with a whimper. As if the 1989 Lenny Dykstra/Juan Samuel trade wasn't a big enough joke, the Mets threw Roger in, too. No one was laughing.

With a 9–4, 2.74 ERA bullpen performance in 1969, **Ron Taylor** (1967–71) played a role similar to McDowell's for the first world championship club. A member of the 1964 world champion St. Louis Cardinals, Taylor was the only man on the '69 staff with postseason experience. He came on to record the final out for the first World Series win in club history. Tug McGraw, who wasn't even used in that Series, soon superseded Taylor's role as game-ending savior, but Taylor was already working toward a new career as a doctor.

The Canadian-born right-hander became team physician of the Blue Jays in 1979 and remains with the team almost four decades later as physician emeritus. His career was chronicled in the documentary, *Dr. Baseball*, produced by his sons, Drew and Matt.

Chuck Taylor (no relation) followed in 42 in '72, with **Hank Webb** debuting in the number later in the year and **Tom Hall** giving it a one-day test drive in 1975. Hall was acquired while the team was on the road, likely carrying the 42 jersey for catcher **Ron Hodges** if they needed an emergency backup. Hodges (1973–84) was in the minors at the time but had worn it before and would wear it afterward. A long time afterward.

Hodges had his greatest moment as a Met in his first few months on the job. On September 20, 1973, with the hard-charging yet still sub-.500 Mets a game and a half behind Pittsburgh, he entered a tie game in extra innings and was the recipient of the throw after "the carom" that nailed a shocked Richie Zisk at the plate in the 13th. Hodges then singled in the winning run in the bottom of the inning. "The Ball on the Wall" was the definitive moment during the team's climb from the basement to the division title in the final month of the 1973 season, and it was the biggest moment for the "Virginian gentleman" (as Bob Murphy often called him). He punched the clock after that, outlasting sixteen other backstops while only catching 100 games once over a dozen seasons. Lefty-hitting catchers are indeed worth their weight in gold.

Grandfathered into the 42 clause was big, freckled outfielder **Butch Huskey** (1995–98), who hinted at greatness in '97 but didn't quite get there: he switched to 42 (from 10) deliberately as a credit to Robinson. His first major league game saw the Mets get no-hit, and good luck never seemed to find him after that, although the Oklahoma kid could hit the ball a country mile . . . especially in spring training.

Although the Mets assured fans that **Mo Vaughn**, a former American League MVP who'd missed the entire 2001 season with a torn left bicep, would be healthy, they apparently made no promises he'd be in shape. The first baseman clubbed 26 home runs in 2002, but he could be seen from space. His 2003 campaign was an even bigger disaster, partly because

Dan Carubia

Butch Huskey wore 42 for Jackie Robinson and was in the lineup the night it was retired across baseball at Shea.

Vaughn had only gotten larger, slower, and more fragile over the offseason and partly because of the fiasco of keeping him on the roster all year as an insurance dodge.

You would think the Mo Vaughn experience would have been the end of the line for a number that got off to a questionable start with .220-hitting outfielder **Larry Elliott** (1964), whose claim to fame in Mets annals is that he was traded for Ed Charles. But it lives on, if only for a night each year. MLB decided to have all players wear 42 on 4/15 for the Jackie Robinson debut anniversary. Confusing to those at the ballpark? Maybe, but easy enough to follow if fans pay attention to the game instead of their phones. But is it fitting? You bet your Jackie Robinson rotunda it is.

Number 42

Number of times issued: 10 (9 players)

Longest tenured: Ron Hodges (12 seasons, 666 games)

Best single seasons: Roger McDowell, 1986 (14–9, 3.02 ERA, 22 saves), Ron Taylor, 1969 (9–4, 2.72 ERA, 13 saves)

Career statistical leaders: Home runs (Butch Huskey 55); RBI (Huskey 211); batting average (Huskey .268); wins (McDowell 33, Taylor 21); saves (McDowell 84, Taylor 28), ERA (Ron Taylor 3.04, McDowell 3.13)

Retired: April 15, 1997

Days of Remembrance

With the retiring of Mike Piazza's 31 in 2016, the Mets officially removed a uniform number from circulation for a player for the second time—and the first since Tom Seaver in 1988. Jackie Robinson, who played for Brooklyn but was a pioneer on and off the baseball diamond, had his number was retired throughout baseball in a surprise announcement at Shea during a 5–0 win over the Dodgers in 1997.

This book is about numbers, but it is certainly worth noting the two names hanging with the five numbers at Citi Field. Bill Shea's name was hung on the stadium for getting New York its own team after the Dodgers and Giants skipped town, and Shea's name was hung on the wall on Opening Day of the final year at Shea in 2008. Kiner, the Hall of Fame slugger who broadcast games in each of the franchise's first 52 seasons—and gave both New York and Pittsburgh completely different and splendid versions of Kiner's Korner—was posthumously honored on Opening Day 2014 when his name was hung in left field above the Party City Deck.

Following is a closer look at the circumstances surrounding the retirement of the three longest hanging numbers in Mets annals.

37: Retired in a ceremony prior to a Thursday afternoon game against the Astros on September 2, 1965, attended by only 11,430 fans. Although the Mets rallied late, they lost to the Astros that day, 4–3. The bigger event for Casey Stengel was a press conference at the Hotel Essex three days prior, when the seventy-five-year-old manager formally announced his retirement at the advice of doctors who recently treated Stengel's broken hip. Stengel explained he couldn't manage any longer if he couldn't walk to and from the dugout to change pitchers. Motioning with his cane he remarked, "You don't expect me to go onto the mound and take a pitcher out by putting this around his neck, do you?"

14: The Mets were criticized for acting too quickly to name a replacement manager when Gil Hodges died suddenly prior to the 1972 season. They chose an appropriate time to memorialize him before an Old-Timer's Day crowd of 48,000 a year later. A home run from Willie Mays—himself an old-timer—provided the difference in a 4–2 win on June 9, 1973. The opponent, fittingly, was Hodges's old club, the Dodgers.

41: Retired in a Sunday afternoon pregame ceremony on July 24, 1988, two years after Seaver's last game in baseball and twenty-two since he began his career with the Mets. Seaver asked the crowd to indulge him as he said thanks "in my own way" and proceeded to the pitcher's mound, where he turned and bowed to each section of the crowd, drawing thunderous applause from the throng of 46,000. The Mets went out and lost the game that afternoon 4–2 to the Braves, the organization that originally signed Tom Terrific but lost him on a technicality.

#43: THE LOST NATION NO MORE

For a long time, number 43 left a blank when it came to memorable Mets. Appropriately, Lost Nation, Iowa-born hurler **Jim McAndrew** (1968–73) was the only name that rang a bell, and even that had grown faint with time.

Drafted out of the University of Iowa, McAndrew won at least 10 games under both Gil Hodges and Yogi Berra and was in the rotation for much of the pennant-winning 1969 and 1973 seasons, but he never pitched in the postseason. The club infamously stood

Lost Nation, Iowa's Jim McAndrew was sort of lost in the shuffle among the superb pitching staff of the late 19760s and early 1970s.

pat after their very exciting but very fortunate "Ya Gotta Believe" 1973 pennant, with one minor exception: Sending McAndrew to the Padres for Steve Simpson, who never made it out of the minors for New York.

Unlike McAndrew, **R. A. Dickey** never pitched for a winning team in New York, but you never forgot he was around. Dickey overcame numerous obstacles—including abuse at the hands of a female baby sitter—and used his talent in athletics and the classroom to major in English and star on the mound for the University of Tennessee. But his pro career was the stuff of novels and epic poems about tragedy and adversity assigned by English professors. The Mets were the fifth team in as many years to sign the peripatetic—Prof. Dickey would love that dollar word—knuckleballer before the 2010 season. In a Triple-A game broadcast on SNY from Buffalo, the thirty-five-year-old Dickey threw a one-hitter. Fans weren't the only ones saying, "Why isn't this guy pitching in Flushing?" He soon was and he was killing it. Just two of his 27 appearances were shorter than five innings and one of those was a relief outing during the final weekend to lower his ERA to 2.74,

R.A. Dickey ordering up another knuckler on his way to winning the 2012 Cy Young Award.

seventh lowest in the National League. He won the Branch Rickey Award for community service (Al Leiter and Bobby Valentine were Mets who previously won the award).

His 8–13 season in 2011 made it seem like, "Oh, well, it was a nice story." And it was. Dickey's book, *Wherever I Wind Up*, came out as he became the first Met in twenty-two years to win 20 games and the first Met in twenty-seven years to claim a Cy Young Award. No Met had ever thrown back-to-back one-hitters—and only George Thomas Seaver exceeded Robert Allen Dickey's three complete-game one-hitters in a Mets uniform. Dickey was so hot . . . he was traded.

The classic bad team scenario/harsh reality is that your best player is also your most valuable trading chip. And it is a tribute to Dickey that two players the Blue Jays traded to get him—Noah Syndergaard and Travis d'Arnaud—turned the December 2012 coal-in-the-stocking deal that bummed out fans into the 2015 pennant that elated those same fans. And Dickey's AL East 2015 champion Blue Jays came just two game shy of making a book-worthy World Series ending.

The decision in the deciding game of the 2015 World Series went to number 43, but **Addison Reed**, like his club, ran out of gas in extra innings against the relentless Royals. Up until then, Reed had been superb since coming over from Arizona at the August trade deadline. He had a 1.17 ERA in 17 games and then held the Cubs scoreless in two outings in the NLCS. The five runs he gave up in the 12th against Kansas City were more than he'd allowed, total, in his Mets career. If not for one bad inning . . .

No other 43 had ever pitched in a postseason game as a Met, though many others had solid experience with multiple bad innings. **Rigo Beltran** (1998–99), **Jaime Cerda** (2002), **Royce Ring** (2006), and **Sean Henn** (2013) were lefties whose pitches were buried in the backs of bullpens just enough to make their time in the pen rather short. **Brian Stokes** (2008–09) was one of many overused, ineffective righty relievers during the maddening closing weeks of Shea Stadium's existence. Stokes allowed 50 percent of inherited runners to score in the final two months of 2008 as the bullpen blew what could have been a fun final fling in Flushing.

Buddy Carlyle saved Opening Day of 2015 in Washington. It was his first day in 43 and his first save in a major league career that began in 1999. A good news story, Carlyle overcame diabetes, injuries, and bad luck to have success as a Mets reliever. The 2014 Mets just needed a fresh arm during a run of extra-inning games in Philadelphia. Carlyle donned 44, won his Mets debut, and finished 2014 with a 1.45 ERA in 31 innings. But injuries again knocked out Caryle after just eight innings in 2015. Baseball can be cruel.

Terry Leach wore the number in 1981–82, before carving out a solid Shea career in a uni number a few blocks north of this bad 43 neighborhood. Still, Leach had his best game—and one of the top performances in team history—wearing 43: a ten-inning, one-hitter against the Phillies in the final weekend of 1982 in what was just his second career start.

Former Yankee **Shane Spencer** made the Mets in 2004 and then proceeded to make an Art Howe–led club look more taken advantage of than usual. Whether it was urinating outside a pizza joint and then beating someone up about it, walking through a bar barefoot and being amazed about a foot getting cut on broken glass, or getting a DWI on a subsequent rehabilitation assignment, Spencer made you forget he was just about the best 43 with a bat the Mets have ever had. He later took his tired act on the road to Japan. Sayonara, Shane.

A promising young pitcher acquired in the Roger Craig trade, **Bill Wakefield** (1963) made a team-high 62 appearances in 1963 but never made it back to the majors again. **Dick Rusteck** (1966) fired a complete-game, four-hit shutout of the Reds in his major league debut in June of 1966 that turned out to be the only win in his career.

Then there were those youngsters whose success came only after leaving the Mets' No. 43 jersey behind. **Juan Berenguer** (1978–80) eventually found control of his wicked fastball as an American League setup man. Lefty bullpenner **Mike Remlinger** (1994–95) and slowball ace **Paul Byrd** (1995–96) earned livings as useful ballplayers long after leaving the Mets.

The Lost Nation: **Ted Schreiber** (1963), **Darrell Sutherland** (1965–66), **Joe Grzenda** (1967), Midnight Massacre acquiree **Paul Siebert** (1977–78), future sabermetric centerfold **Billy Beane** (1984), **John Mitchell** (1986–89), the **Kevin Brown** (1990) who was not the one you're thinking of, **Dan Schatzeder** (1990), **Doug Simons** (1991), **Mark Dewey** (1992), **Mickey Weston** (1993), the horrendous **Toby Borland** (1997), pre-heroic **Todd Pratt** (1997), **John Hudek** (1998), **Pete Walker** (2001–02), **Bartolome Fortunato** (2004, 2006), and **Jason Vargas** (2007)—yes, the Jason Vargas, who has made a nice living in the rotations of the Mariners, Angels, and Royals since leaving the Mets in the aggravating J. J. Putz deal.

Number 43

Number of times issued: 35 (33 players, 1 DNP)

Longest tenured: Jim McAndrew (6 seasons, 146 games); John Mitchell (4 seasons, 27 games)

Best single seasons: R. A. Dickey, 2012 (20–6, 2.73 ERA, Cy Young Award—league-leading 33 starts, 5 complete games, 3 shutouts, 233 2/3 innings, 230 strikeouts); Dickey, 2010 (11–9, 2.84 ERA, 104 strikeouts in 174 1/3 innings); McAndrew, 1972 (11–8, 2.80 ERA, 81 strikeouts in 160 2/3 innings); McAndrew, 1970 (10–14, 3.56 ERA, 111 strikeouts in 184 1/3 innings); Bill Wakefield, 1964 (3–5, 3.61 ERA, 62 games)

Career statistical leaders: Home runs (Spencer 4, Todd Pratt 2); RBI (Spencer 26, Pratt 19); batting average (Pratt .283, Spencer .281); wins (Dickey 39, McAndrew 36); saves (McAndrew 4, Terry Leach 3); ERA (Dickey 2.95, McAndrew 3.54, Wakefield, 3.61)

Styling Mets

Style is hard to define. It's especially difficult when everyone wears the same outfit. Still, any longtime follower of the Mets must admit that there have been a few players whose dress has made them stand out above the crowd, even as the team has endured more costume changes than a high school production of Gilbert and Sullivan's Mikado. What follows are a few prime examples in terms of individual dress. Check local listings for more.

Player	Digression	Style analysis
Lee Mazzilli	Uniform tighter than the rest	It was the '70s; Maz was the "Italian Stallion"; a screaming female teenager might buy a hot dog, a pretzel, and an RC Cola.
John Pacella	Hat several sizes too small	It flew off after almost every pitch, and he had a handlebar mustache; both more memorable than his pitching in 1980.
Roy McMillan	Nerd specs	Wait, that wasn't an ironic display of cool but actual nerdiness.
Ron Swoboda	Love beads	Leader of the 1960s Mets counterculture reportedly had his snatched away by conservative veteran teammate Don Cardwell on a team flight, nearly leading to fisticuffs before peace triumphed, man.
Bruce Bochy	Gargantuan helmet	After arriving in New York in 1982, his extra-large cranium would not fit in any Mets helmet and he had to wait until his was rushed up from Tidewater before he could play.
Rusty Staub	High socks	Many have tried this, but the '80s Rusty flew in the face of the trend of low stirrups on the way to no stirrups.

Player	Digression	Style analysis
Jose Cardenal	Afro hairstyle	Mid-'70s Mets like Nino Espinosa and Billy Baldwin wore afros when they carried more heft as a signal of racial pride, but they couldn't match Cardenal for volume.
Keith Hernandez	Racing stripes perfectly aligned	A few '80s Mets may have been guilty of this level of fastidiousness, but he's admitted a mild obsession about it; he's also Keith Hernandez.
John Olerud	Batting helmet in the field	A brain aneurysm in college didn't alter his sweet swing, but he thereafter wore a flapless helmet in the field for protection—and as a message to his mom.
Turk Wendell	Necklace of animal teeth on mound	He was getting national press for quirkiness while still in the minors, what did you expect? Turk forever rules the rosin slam!
Tsuyoshi Shinjo	Triple-wide orange sweatbands	The Jim Palmer of Japan, Shinjo was a noted underwear model in his home country. He took to wearing argyle-patterned sweatbands during his final baseball season there.
Derek Bell	Mr. Baggy Pants	Was he too big for his britches, or was it the other way around? Either way, that's just style, man.
Lastings Milledge	Enormous crucifix necklace	Useful in the event of broken bat. Or vampire attack.
Jason Phillips	Helmet facing forward under mask	Really, this is just an excuse to mention those Bono glasses again.
Tom Wilson & Jose Parra	Wearing wrong Met uniform at Yankee Stadium in 2004	Donned the black "Mets" jersey instead of the "New York" road jersey worn by the rest of the team; we know there are too many jerseys, but couldn't they have made this faux pas in Montreal?
Noah Syndergaard & Jacob deGrom	Flowing Locks	Thor's long blond locks do indeed look Norse god-like as he throws bolts from a 6-foot-6, 240 frame. Now deGrom is a couple of inches shorter and 60 pounds lighter—yes, 60—but these young guns, plus a couple of other studs with more traditional coiffures, makes every day a good hair day.
Yoenis Cespedes	Canary-yellow compression sleeve	An odd fashion choice but he made it sing.

#44: POWER OUTAGE

Forty-four is a slugger's number. The Yankees had Reggie Jackson, the Giants had Willie McCovey, while the Braves—and even the Brewers—laid claim to Hank Aaron. The Mets had . . . **Jay Payton**?

That Mets fans had to wait a long time for the oft-injured Payton (1999–2002) to arrive was even more aggravating, but he finally showed up, injury-free at last, as the only groomed member of Bobby Valentine's ragtag outfield. Payton won the starting center field job in 2000 and made a case for Rookie of the Year. His career stalled amid yet more injuries in 2001. Finally getting it together in 2002, he was shipped off to Denver as part of the final Steve Phillips trading deadline fiasco.

The same day that Payton was traded to Colorado, a minor league outfielder was sent to San Diego along with the other Bobby Jones for must have middling relievers Steve Reed and Jason Middlebrook. The one that got away was **Jason Bay**. Seven years, a Rookie of the Year Award, three All-Star Games, and 185 home runs later, Bay signed with the Mets as a free agent at age thirty-one, traditionally the most expensive years of any slugger and often the least productive. In parts of three years Bay hit 26 home runs—he hit more homers than that in five different seasons with the Pirates and Red Sox. Blame the Great Wall of Flushing, or injuries, or some Mets free agent curse, or bad feng shui away from Fenway, but the man who was once traded for Manny Ramirez in Boston, hit like the second coming of Manny Alexander in New York. The Mets terminated Bay's contract two years ahead of schedule. And it was still too late.

Since this book was first published in 2008, 44 has turned over 12 times. Of those dirty dozen Mets, Bay was the only one who started and ended the year on the active roster in 44. And that was just **John Buck**'s luck. Buck took over 44 from Bay as the retinue of the present in a trade for the future with Toronto: reigning Cy Young winner R. A. Dickey and two catchers who could corral his knuckleball in exchange for Buck plus high end prospects Travis d'Arnaud, who would soon render Buck obsolete, and Noah Syndergaard, who would do the same to a few veteran pitchers in the organization. Buck started out like a house afire, drilling nine home runs and 25 RBIs in his first month as a Met in 2013. But before you could say "Da-da," Buck slumped, went on paternity leave, and was replaced by d'Arnaud even as he awaited the arrival of Master Bentley Buck. John Buck was soon traded to the Pirates, his third trade in nine months. He joined a fourth team that winter, signing with Seattle, and was designated for assignment on his 34th birthday. Births and birthdays are supposed to bring joy, not hardship, but such is the baseball life.

Though **Mike Cameron**'s Mets tenure (2004–05) also ended unhappily, he had a few of the moments a team might expect from an outfielder clad in 44. He arrived as a free agent from Seattle with a reputation for great play in center field and prolific strikeout numbers. Cameron saw his position taken away by Carlos Beltran as 2005 dawned. In fairness, Cammy managed 30 home runs and solid play once he recovered from an early-season injury in '04. Although he was unhappy about moving to right field the following year, he showed great natural ability at the position until he ran smack-dab into Beltran in what may have been the scariest collision in club history. Cameron was fortunate to recover fully from the facial injuries sustained in the collision and wind up patrolling center field in sunny San Diego, where the gruesome scene had occurred.

For five games in May of 1991, **Howard Johnson** tried to channel Hank, Reggie, and Willie in 44 as he battled a slump. He switched back to 20 after admitting he felt "uncomfortable" in his new number, and that his wife disapproved. It was a wise choice, as HoJo wound up having his best season. (While it's not our place to suggest numbers, it would have been intriguing if HoJo had gone orange-roof crazy with 28—made famous as the number of the ice cream flavors available at his namesake restaurant and hotel chain—but that might have made him feel like an advertising tool, or worse, hungry.)

A Mets outfielder wearing 44 once made the cover of *Sports Illustrated*. Unfortunately, it was diminutive **John Cangelosi** (1994) about to be punched by ex-Met Charlie O'Brien after an ill-advised mound charge. The Cangey-man, with 135 homer-free trips to the plate as a Met, was released shortly after creating his own version of the "*SI* Cover Jinx."

Lastings Milledge (2006–07) had more than enough magnetism and style to fill the No. 44 jersey, but his mouth got in the way. He managed to annoy the veterans almost immediately and maybe that was why he was left off the 2006 postseason roster. Or maybe it was because the Mets front office saw that he wasn't good enough to justify a spot. The former GM is bashed plenty—even in these pages—but it is to Omar Minaya's credit that he conned Washington into sending two everyday starters, Brian Schneider and Ryan Church, for a fifth outfielder. That pair had their own flaws as players, but they lasted longer than Milledge.

Devoid of true sluggers in the 44 slot, the Mets did have an honest-to-goodness power pitcher in that jersey. **David Cone** (1987–91) was at his Mets best in 44: as a brief rookie sensation in '87 before getting hurt, going a sterling 20–3 the next year, and then winning his first NL strikeout crown before heading for the teens during the 1991 season.

Coney was clearly the best of a group of arms that also included **Al Schmelz** (1967), **Bob Rauch** (1972), **Mac Scarce** (1975), **Bob Myrick** (1976–78), **Andy Hassler** (1979), **Ray Searage** (1981), **Bill Latham** (1985), **Tim Burke** (1991–92), **Tom Filer** (1992), **Kevin Lomon** (1995), **Tim Redding** (2009), **Kyle Farnsworth** (2014), **Buddy Carlyle** (2014), and **Eric O'Flaherty** (2015), who wasn't any tougher on lefties than the man he replaced in the 44 jersey, outfielder **John Mayberry Jr.** (2015).

In 2008 the Mets threw four 44s at the wall: end of the line outfielder **Brady Clark**, plus pitchers **Tony Armas Jr.**, **Eddie Kunz**, and **Brandon Knight**. None stuck, with the Mets or anyone else.

Jim Bibby had a long pitching career, but as a young man recently back from driving trucks through the jungles of Vietnam, he wore 44 for stints in 1969 and 1971 without ever pitching in a game for Gil Hodges. **Aaron Harang** spent the last month of 2013 as a Met—and deserved battle pay.

Other Mets wore the number for a time and had a lot on the ball: **Jeff Reardon** (1981)—traded for a man with a tremendous right arm, Ellis Valentine, who had become, sadly, a pitch-shy outfielder who had started hitting like a pitcher—and a young **Ron Darling** (1983–84). Darling led the

NEIL ALLEN and JEFF REARDON

The Mets traded No. 44, Jeff Reardon too soon, but picked the perfect time to deal Neil Allen.

charge of Mets hurlers to lower numbers when he switched to 12; he was stylish and gifted enough to pull it off with aplomb.

Another talented young Met pitcher was **Jason Isringhausen** (1995–97, 1999). Izzy was issued No. 29 when he joined the team in 1995, but he switched to 44 prior to his first start as a reminder of the lowly round in which the Mets drafted him: no Met draftee, in fact, had ever made the major league roster from such a low pick. While he didn't get the win in his debut against his homestate Cubs, Izzy did go 9–2 with a 2.81 ERA that year, allowing even hardened Met fans to believe Generation K was more than a PR myth. Alas, it was a pipe dream that even Eugene O'Neill would have thought too cruel for production.

After sticking with Isringhausen through seemingly endless injuries and confounding behavior, Steve Phillips traded the twenty-six-year-old to Oakland just in time for him to blossom as a short reliever. After a few loops around both leagues, the two-time prodigal All-Star returned to Flushing in another century and another number.

Human power failures **Harry Chiti** (1962), **Leroy Stanton** (1972), **Tom Paciorek** (1985), **Ryan Thompson** (1992–93), and an end-of-the-line **Jay Bell** (2003) also wore 44. Chiti, a veteran reserve catcher, was acquired from Cleveland in April of 1962 for a player to be named later. Chiti hit just .195 in 15 games for the Mets, who farmed him to Jacksonville on June 15 before quietly returning him to Cleveland to complete the trade. The Mets, as often pointed out, got fleeced in the Chiti-for-Chiti deal. No Met dared put on the jersey again until **Bill Denehy** (1967), a twenty-one-year-old with a 1–7 record and a drinking problem, who was sent to Washington—along with $100,000—for manager Gil Hodges.

Number 44

Number of times issued: 26 (25 players, 1 DNP)

Longest tenured: David Cone (4 seasons, 127 games), Jason Isringhausen (4 seasons, 60 games), Bob Myrick (3 seasons, 82 games)

Best single seasons: Cone, 1988 (20–3, 2.22 ERA, 213 strikeouts in 231 1/3 innings); Cone, 1990 (14–10, 3.23 ERA, 233 strikeouts in 211 2/3 innings); Isringhausen, 1995 (9–2, 2.81 ERA, 55 strikeouts in 93 innings); Mike Cameron, 2004 (.231/.319/.479, 30 HR, 76 RBIs, 22 SB); Payton, 2000 (.291/.331/.447, 17 HR, 62 RBIs)

Career statistical leaders: Home runs (Cameron 42, Payton 33); RBI (Payton 128, Jason Bay 124, Cameron 115); batting average (Payton .277, Lastings Milledge .257); wins (Cone 56, Isringhausen 18); saves (Andy Hassler 4, Kyle Farnsworth 3); ERA (Cone 3.09, Bob Myrick 3.48)

Mets Uniform History: What's in a Name?

When the Mets came into the National League in 1962, it had been thirty years since the requirement that every major leaguer be numbered. As time passed, a public watching baseball games at football stadiums craved additional information that the National Football League had already acquiesced to: names on the back of the uniforms.

Bill Veeck, not surprisingly, was the first to do so with the White Sox, but the Mets had kept the same uniform with the number and no name through 1977. After a horrific season in which nothing went right on the field, the Mets started tinkering with the tailoring. The pullover with piping on the sleeves and neck arrived in '78; a year later came the names. If the names had been "Schmidt" or "Bench" or heaven help us, "Seaver," Mets fans certainly would have volunteered to do the stitching.

Instead, the Mets had "Youngblood." That was the first name with double-digit letters on the back of the uniform. Longer names, like harder times, were bound to come. The style with which the Mets displayed those names has changed over the years. Letters initially were affixed onto a swath of fabric that was then stitched to the back of a jersey. That style was dropped by the Mets in 1988. (Incidentally, when the Mets presented Tom Seaver with a retired jersey that year it was unplated—a style of jersey Seaver never wore in his playing days with the club.)

The font also slimmed from thick, boxy letters used in 1981 to a leaner style in 1982, although some players holding over were never refitted with the new style, leading to non-uniform uniforms. They would also get more sophisticated as time went on. Although Willie Montanez qualified, Alex Treviño in 1980 was the first Met to sport a tilde on his nameplate. The Mets even got tricky with specialty lettering, taking a capital "P" and turning upside down; not once, not twice, but thrice in 2014 for d'Arnaud, de Grom, and den Dekker. They corrected that issue with a proper small "d" in 2015, though by then den Dekker was Washington's uniform problem.

Following are the lengthiest statements ever made on the back on a Mets uniform, including a nod to names that were long before stitching them on the back became a necessity:

Length	Name (Met Debut)	Debut Uni Number
12 letters	Isringhausen, Jason (1995)	44
	Mientkiewicz, Doug (2005)	16
11 letters	Christensen, John (1984)	35
	Allensworth, Jermaine (1998)	23
	Hinchcliffe, Brett (2001)	32
	Christensen, McKay (2002)	23
	Middlebrook, Jason (2002)	27
	Darensbourg, Vic (2003)	39
	Schoeneweis, Scott (2007)	60
	Nieuwenhuis, Kirk (2012)	9
	Quintanilla, Omar (2012)	6
	Leathersich, Jack (2015)	51
	Syndergaard, Noah (2015)	34
10 letters	Washington, Claudell (1980)	15
	Gardenhire, Ron (1981)	19
	Strawberry, Darryl (1983)	18
	Winningham, Herm (1984)	21
	McReynolds, Kevin (1987)	22
	Candelaria, John (1987)	45
	Whitehurst, Wally (1989)	47
	Schatzeder, Dan (1990)	43
	Saberhagen, Bret (1992)	17
	Guetterman, Lee (1992)	35
	Manzanillo, Josias (1993)	39
	Strickland, Scott (2002)	25
	Catalanato, Frank (2010)	27
	Granderson, Curtis (2014)	3
Managers	None	

Length	Name (Met Debut)	Debut Uni Number
Coaches	Monbouquette, Bill (1982)	56
	Stottlemyre, Mel (1984)	48
	Stephenson, John (1992)	51
Pre-1979	Cannizzaro, Chris (1962)	8
	Throneberry, Marv (1962)	2
	Christopher, Joe (1962)	23
	Stephenson, John (1964)	49
	Sturvidant, Tom (1964)	47
	Richardson, Gordon (1965)	41
	Aspromonte, Bob (1971)	2
	Strohmayer, John (1973)	39
Coach	McCullough, Clyde (1962)	54

#45: TUG MCFRANCO AND SIR PEDRO

In recent years you can make the claim that 45 has become the pitcher's number for the Mets. Two members of the Mets Hall of Fame wore 45, and, as a way to break the tie with 31, a third Met in the National Baseball Hall of Fame in Cooperstown donned 45 in Flushing, though his Hall of Fame plaque has a "B" on it (and by all rights should be the funky Montreal "M" stuck on Gary's Carter plaque).

Pedro Martinez (2005–08) brought the swagger back to Shea. Fans squealed when Pedro took the mound in 2005. He danced when the sprinkler went off mid-game. He threw the most complete games by a Met in seven years. He shrugged off Braden Looper's blown saves. He made fans think no-hitter when he took the mound, although even Pedro could only do so much.

Pedro made one of Omar Minaya's biggest gambles pay off, if only for a year. Injuries quieted him after that, but what he did in 2005 for the franchise—and to opponents—cannot be downplayed. Pedro came as close as anyone of living up to the tradition set forth by the first man to wear the uniform number. **Ron Locke**? No, not him. (Locke won once in 25 games as a '64 Met.) Make that the man who owned that number the longest.

Tug McGraw (1965–67, 1969–74) was one of the true characters (and best pitchers) in the history of the Mets. He was a starter for Casey Stengel, a trusted reliever for Gil Hodges, and he brought the Mets from the dead to the pennant in '73. His rallying cry of "Ya Gotta Believe!" lives on whenever teams are counted out but there are still games on the schedule and pages on the calendar.

Jacob Kanarek/From Worst to First

Tug McBlur: Lover, lefty, leprochaun–Frank Edwin McGraw brought his own unique spirit to the Mets uniform.

Dan Carubia

The long Mets career of John Franco was split between No. 31 and 45, closer and setup guy, lightning rod and captain.

The club's first true stopper, Tug collected 85 saves with the Mets and averaged two innings per outing over a five-season span. He was a perfect 12-for-12 in save opportunities for the 1969 club. He was 11–4 in 1971. The next year he was the winning pitcher in the All-Star Game, saved 27, and finished with a 1.70 ERA for the second straight year. He pitched a career-high 118 2/3 innings in '73, plus 18.2 more in the postseason. The Mets dealt their king of hearts to the rival Phillies after the 1974 season in a head-scratcher of a deal that netted John Stearns, and the Flushing faithful were forced to watch his thigh-slapping and screwgie through many a close contest with that annoying *P* on his hat.

The downgrading of the save by the sheer increase in its volume makes for invariable and complicated comparisons between McGraw and **John Franco** (1998–2001, 2003–04). Let's just say these different era closers both showed plenty of spunk. The Franco that gave up the No. 31 he'd worn at Shea since 1990 for Mike Piazza's 1998 arrival had only about a year left as a compiler of saves. Yet the 45 Franco may have actually been more valuable—and more like Tug—than the one that set the standard for career saves by a southpaw.

He still was in big trouble if teams ignored his sinking stuff, but he began compiling big outs in earlier innings like Tug, whose uniform number he took as a tribute. Franco opted for Tommy John surgery at age forty-one, stayed around a little too long, and was booed a little too harshly in his Shea return as an Astro, but he looked like a one-eyed jack beating a flush when he threw his high-school-speed fastball past Barry Bonds with all the cards on the table in the 2000 Division Series.

Number 45 even has a few milestones on its ledger. Pedro Martinez became the first pitcher to reach his 3,000th career strikeout in a Mets uniform. Though John Franco hit save 300 wearing 31, **Jason Isringhausen** hit that number as a Met during his 2011 return. Ironically, Izzy had just one save in parts of four Mets seasons (wearing 44), but the prodigal son returned a dozen years later and got his 300th—which turned out to be his final career save—after he was thrust into the closer's role in the first year of the Terry Collins regime.

Zack Wheeler hopes to add to that 45 milestone chain, but so far he is best known for being traded for Carlos Beltran and nearly being dealt for Carlos Gomez. Beyond his memorable debut when his win finished a double-header sweep in his Atlanta hometown in June 2013, Wheeler has heard the names Matt Harvey and Tommy John mentioned far more often than his own.

A wild card is the only non-pitcher in the group: pinch-hitting stalwart **Mark Carreon** "Luggage" (1990–91), who wore the number in tribute to his father, Cam Carreon. Mark was the club's all-time pinch-hitting power specialist. His 8 career pinch-hit homers are still the club record, and his 4 bench blasts for the 1989 Mets (wearing 32) tied Danny Heep's 1983 mark, which was eclipsed by Jordany Valdespin in 2012.

Rick Baldwin (1975–77) was dealt a tough hand as follower of Tug in 45, but Baldwin left behind good numbers: 3.60 ERA, 105 games, 182 2/3 innings, and 7 saves, though he blew 8 saves, helping usher in the Skip Lockwood bullpen era.

John Candelaria was a Met for three starts in the closing weeks of the 1987 season and won twice. He was ineligible for the postseason, but his

Jacob Kanarek/From Worst to First

It was hardly fair to Rick Baldwin (or to Mets fans) to replace the beloved fireman Tug McGraw with a rookie in the late innings.

teammates made sure that wasn't a problem. The Candy Man went to the sugar daddy in the Bronx after the season, but he was never able to regain the form that made him a 20-game winner and All-Star for the 1977 Pirates. He stuck around to gain 177 wins in the bigs; 2 as a Met.

Two Gibsons wore 45: **Paul Gibson** (1992–93) and coach **Bob Gibson** (1981). The latter Gibson should not to be confused with the Bob Gibson who spent his last week in the majors as a 1987 Met (wearing 38). One of the most intense competitors of his era, Bob Gibson the Cardinal (in fearsome 45) started nine times in the World Series, completed eight, and won seven, not to mention garnering two Cy Young Awards and carrying a 1.12 ERA in 1968 that would have made Christy Mathewson blush. Gibson wore 45 when he joined old pal Joe Torre's staff in 1981 as a co-pitching coach with Rube Walker. While Gibson was inducted into the Hall of Fame upstate in Cooperstown that summer, the downstate New York experience (complete with cataclysmic strike) went so well that the whole staff was fired after the season. Torre, Gibson, and Walker, plus Joe Pignatano, reemerged with a division title in Atlanta in 1982.

Discounting the first two years from hard-throwing **Jeff Reardon** (1979–80), the rest of the 45 deck has been stacked with face cards and forgettable pitchers: **Darrell Sutherland** (1966), **Billy Connors** (1968), **Butch Metzger** (1978), **Brent Gaff** (1982–84), **Edwin Nuñez** (1988), **Mauro Gozzo** (1993–94), **Jerry Dipoto** (1995–96), and **Justin Hampson** (2012).

Number 45

Number of times issued: 23 (19 players, 2 coaches)

Longest tenured: Tug McGraw (9 seasons, 361 games), John Franco (6 seasons, 302 games), Rick Baldwin (4 seasons, 105 games)

Best single seasons: Tug McGraw, 1973 (5–6, 3.87 ERA, 25 saves, 81 strikeouts in 118 2/3 innings); McGraw, 1972 (8–6, 1.70 ERA, 27 saves, 92 strikeouts in 106 innings); McGraw, 1969 (9–3, 2.24 ERA, 12 saves, 92 strikeouts in 100 1/3 innings); Pedro Martinez, 2005 (15–8, 2.82 ERA, 208 strikeouts in 217 innings); John Franco, 2000 (5–4, 3.40 ERA, 56 saves, 55 2/3 innings); Zack Wheeler, 2014 (11–11, 3.54 ERA, 187 strikeouts in 185 1/3 innings)

Career statistical leaders: Home runs (Mark Carreon 14); RBI (Carreon 47); batting average (Carreon .256); wins (McGraw 47, Martinez 32); ERA (Jeff Reardon 2.47, McGraw 3.17, Wheeler 3.50); saves (McGraw 85, Franco 56)

Somebody Save Me: Saves by the Numbers

Nolan Ryan recorded the first official save in Mets history on April 9, 1969. At the behest of Chicago newspaper writer Jerome Holtzman—later named MLB grand poobah of history—baseball adopted the save as an "official" statistic that year. Baseball historians have generally taken the rules of the save (getting the last out with a three-run lead or less, pitching the last three innings regardless of score, or coming in with the tying run on deck) and applied them retroactively.

If you go by that logic, the real first save in Mets history belongs to Roger Craig, who came out of the bullpen to nail down the first Mets extra-inning win (for otherwise luckless Craig Anderson) on May 6, 1962. Imagine the modern-day Mets waiting until May for their first save of the year—or the twentieth game, for that matter—and bringing in a starter to get the last outs? Lucky for the Mets there was no WFAN to rail about their 4–16 start. Comedy Central might've helped, though.

Because we can, we are mixing old and new, the official and the unofficial, to provide the uniform numbers in Mets history with the most saves through 2015. You may want to avert your eyes upon seeing names like Armando Benitez and Braden Looper . . . and you may also be surprised to see how many times these names came through.

Number	Saves	Notes
31	233	Love him or hate him, John Franco racked up the saves: 221 wearing this number and 56 more for Team 45.
45	167	Two wily lefties: Tug McGraw (85 saves) and Franco (56).
49	162	Maligned Armando Benitez closed the door 160 times.
13	140	Billy Wagner racked up 101 saves as a Met; Neil Allen had 39.
47	126	Jesse Orosco with 107 of these.
42	114	Roger McDowell rode that sinker to 84 saves.
48	100	Randy Myers with 56 nasty saves; Frank Francisco with 24.
75	83	Francisco Rodriguez the only occupant and sole owner of 75's saves.
38	80	Don't skip Lockwood: He had 65 saves in the '70s.
39	79	Bobby Parnell raced to 37 before injuries did him in; Doug Sisk collected 33.
34	60	Underrated Bob Apodaca (26) and tragic Danny Frisella (22) showed guile and guts for the '70s Mets.

#46: RICKEY, DON'T USE THAT NUMBER

Number 13 is generally considered unlucky, but **Neil Allen** figured it had to be better luck than 46. The first wearer of 46, Allen got his big break in the big leagues when he got hurt in May of 1979. The Mets then had to put the rookie on the disabled list instead of sending him to Tidewater, as his 7.06 ERA and 0–5 record demanded. When Allen came back, he was one of the very few pleasant developments in an otherwise horrific '79 season. He went 6–5 with a 2.45 ERA after the injury. Allen was fourth in the NL with 22 saves in 1980—a remarkable achievement given the team he was pitching for—before rolling the dice with 13.

The saga of **Oliver Perez** was like a bad Mexican soap opera. All that was missing was a busty nurse who made you forget your high school Spanish. Perez, from the farm heavy Mexican state of Sinalao, arrived in New York and donned 46 because someone else got hurt. Duaner Sanchez, the club's top setup man in 2006, was lost for the year after being injured in a cab ride from hell in Miami during the early hours of the July 31 trading deadline. The resulting trade was a knee-jerk grab into the team's recent past to rescue Roberto Hernandez from the Pirates. But Omar Minaya also pulled Perez, a fireballing left-handed prospect turned bust at age twenty-four, out of that deal. To do so, Minaya surrendered likeable, hard-hitting

Enigmatic lefty Oliver Perez was a wild card in more ways than one, and once in a while, an ace.

Sharon Chapman

right fielder Xavier Nady, the only man in club history with a first name that started with an *X*.

Hernandez wasn't close to filling Duaner's shoes, but Perez spent a few weeks in Norfolk and showed flashes of promise. He averaged more than a strikeout per inning with the Mets, but his combined major league totals for the year were 3–13, 6.55 ERA. *Ay, chihuahua!* Injuries to yet other pitchers put him on the NLCS roster, where fate intervened. With the Mets down to the Cardinals in the series, he won Game 4 in St. Louis. Four nights later he was called on to start the deciding game, making Perez the pitcher with the worst record of any Game 7 starter in major league history. He then joined Al Leiter (Game 5, 2000 World Series) among the great wasted efforts in franchise postseason history.

He won 15 games and whiffed 174 in 2007, all while leaping over foul lines in a single bound and excelling against enemies like Atlanta and the Yankees. The next year he went 10–7 and fanned 180 in 34 starts, including the last game ever at Shea. Like Game 7 against St. Louis, Perez kept his team in the game, Endy Chavez made an amazing catch . . . and the Mets lost after Ollie exited. Once again, the season was over.

If both parties had walked away then, this chapter might be named "Oliver," but it's not. In February of 2009 Omar Minaya gave Perez a three-year, $36 million deal. *Ay Dios Mio!* He pitched in the World Baseball Classic for his home country and was never the same. Wilder than a mad bull in the midday sun, he walked 100 batters in his last 112 innings as a Met, including his final batter as a Met to force in the winning run in the 14th inning of the 2010 season finale. New GM Sandy Alderson finally cancelled *Ollie*, la telenovela. Perez went on to be a situational lefty, which always seemed to be what would suit him best.

If Jason Isringhausen made **Dallas Green** crazy, what do you think Oliver Perez would have done to the man? Green wore 46 for parts of four seasons as manager of the Mets, surviving the 103-loss season in '93, the strike in '94, plus a brutal start in '95 before Generation K collapsed right over his head in '96. Dallas could have used big **Brian Bohanon** (1997–98), but then Bohanon was a Bobby Valentine/Apodaca reclamation project who hit hard (.255 batting average) and threw soft (3.57 ERA).

Tyler Clippard logged a 0.60 ERA in August 2015 after coming from Oakland. September brought a 6.14 ERA, but by then the Nationals were helping the Mets more than Clippard—though he summed up his former team early in his Mets tenure with the simple (and accurate) statement about the Nats: "They're beatable." Clippard got hit hard in the postseason but averted disaster until the roof fell in during Game 4 against the Royals, as a chance to even the World Series slipped away.

Tyler Clippard was right: The 2015 Nationals were beatable, but so too was he before it was over.

Others: future coach material **Randy Neimann** (1985); highly touted trade bait **David West** (1988–89); **Chris Jelic** (1990), whose lone major league hit was a homer; towering bust **Terry Bross** (1991); washed-up fireman **Barry Jones** (1992); brief visitor **Willie Blair** (1998); Norfolk shuttler **Jermaine Allensworth** (1999); and **Rich Rodriguez** (2000), who pitched poorly for eight teams but was at his absolute worst for a top-notch Mets club (props to his old roommate Steve Phillips for the free-agent contract).

Tyler Walker tempted fate in 2002 and got claimed by the Tigers on waivers. Rookie spot-starter **Jeremy Griffiths** (2003) fit right in with this motley group. Days after Griffiths was traded in '04, his uni number was taken over by **Jose Parra**, who continued the bad luck streak by suffering a freak injury—a line drive breaking a finger—during a rehab appearance for a minor injury. Among the rest in the conga line of 21st century bullpen fodder—**Dale Thayer** (2011), **Manny Acosta** (2011–12), and **Greg Burke** (2013)—lefty **Tim Hamulack** (2005) stands out. Hamulak's Mets ERA of 23.14 was more than half that of his high uniform number. Don't try this at home, kids.

Number 46

Number of times issued: 21 (all to players)

Longest tenured: Oliver Perez (5 seasons, 101 games), Neil Allen (2 seasons, 109 games), Brian Bohanon (2 seasons, 44 games)

Best single seasons: Allen, 1980 (7–10, 3.70 ERA, 22 saves, 79 strikeouts in 97 1/3 innings); Oliver Perez, 2007 (15–10, 3.56 ERA, 174 strikeouts in 177 innings); Perez, 2008, 10–7, 180 strikeouts in 194 innings, NL leader with 34 starts—and 105 walks); Bohanon, 1997 (6–4, 3.82 ERA, 66 strikeouts in 94 1/3 innings)

Career statistical leaders: Home runs (Jermaine Allensworth 3); RBI (Allensworth 9); batting average (Bohanon .255, Allensworth .219); wins (Perez 29); saves (Allen 30); ERA (Bohanon 3.57, Allen 3.61)

Managing to Get By

The Mets have often been a team defined by their managers: that it took until 2016 for there to be as many numbers retired for players as for managers should say as much.

There were the clownish-but-endearing early 1960s Mets and their clownish-but-endearing manager, Casey Stengel. As a Mets manager, Stengel was probably well beyond his prime as a strategist but at the peak of his abilities to create an attraction. The Mets stopped being a laughingstock and started to gain respect when manager Gil Hodges possessed the same qualities.

The Mets at other times in their history were young and made mistakes (Joe Torre), were brash and offensive-minded (Davey Johnson), strategic and conniving (Bobby Valentine), or passionless and distracted (Art Howe).

Two Mets managers have worn No. 9 (Wes Westrum and Joe Torre), 10 (Jeff Torborg and Terry Collins), and 55 (Joe Frazier and Frank Howard). Nine were former Mets players, with Hodges (14), Berra (8), Torre (9), Bud Harrelson (3), and Willie Randolph (12) wearing the same numbers they wore as players to the manager's office. Following is a chronological list:

No.	Manager	Years	Notes
37	Casey Stengel	1962–65	Zany but endearing.
9	Wes Westrum	1965–67	Stengel-like results without the charisma.
54	Salty Parker	1967	Strictly interim.
14	Gil Hodges	1968–71	Made the Mets respectable, then more than respectable.
8	Yogi Berra	1972–75	Ya gotta believe . . . or underachieve.
51	Roy McMillan	1975	Interim, and not really even cut out for that.
55	Joe Frazier	1976–77	No match for Seaver or Grant.

9	Joe Torre	1977–81	Players loved him, but . . . Hall of Fame managing careers have to start somewhere.
31	George Bamberger	1982–83	Heart wasn't in it.
55	Frank Howard	1983	Enormously interim.
5	Davey Johnson	1984–90	Created a monster.
3	Bud Harrelson	1990–91	Not cut out for it.
4	Mike Cubbage	1991	Strictly interim.
10	Jeff Torborg	1992–93	Worst manager money could buy.
46	Dallas Green	1993–96	Too much tough, not enough love.
2	Bobby Valentine	1996–2002	Charisma, excitement, ego to spare.
18	Art Howe	2003–05	Caretaker of organization in chaos.
12	Willie Randolph	2005–08	Efficient, businesslike, but lost ship with all hands aboard.
53	Jerry Manuel	2008–10	Deserves credit for reviving team in '08, but players did not respond in the final two weeks or the two years that followed.
10	Terry Collins	2011–15	Looked like he couldn't win and then he won the pennant. Changed his approach and Mets mindset.

#47: JESSE

Even after starting off their inaugural season 0–9, it was inevitable (on paper, at least) that the original Mets would win a game. That it fell to **Jay Hook** (1962–64), an engineer from Northwestern with a strong right arm, was proof that in baseball every team will beat every other team, even if one team has a 9 ½-game lead on the other on April 23. The great baseball writer Leonard Koppett said of Hook, "He could throw as hard as anyone, and he was intelligent and eager, and he could even show with diagrams and equations why a ball curved." He beat the Pirates that night, and of Mets pitchers with 10 or more decisions, his .296 winning percentage topped the '62 club. At 8–19, you didn't have to be an engineer to calculate that Hook was responsible for 20 percent of the club's wins and only 16 percent of its losses. The Mets won 15 of his 56 career starts for the club.

They should have retired 47 right then and there.

If they had, however, maybe the Mets would not have become the first expansion team to win multiple world championships. Reliever **Jesse Orosco** (1979, 1981–87) made it happen, getting the final outs for the pennant and World Series while most Mets fans were contorted into whatever "lucky" position had worked to that point. Orosco was acquired for Jerry Koosman in what became a trade of the pitcher on the mound for the final out of both the Mets' World Series clinchers. Messy Jesse saved 107 games as a Met, second only to John Franco, and had a career ERA of 2.74, second only to Tom Seaver. His best season, though, turned out to be the team's fifth last-place finish in seven years. In 62 games for the '83 Mets, Orosco tossed 110 innings and had a ridiculous 1.47 ERA with 17 saves and 13 wins for a team that couldn't even get Seaver into double digits in the victory column.

Orosco was reacquired in the 1999 offseason, only to be traded again before the season began. That was probably for the best since Orosco's career record of 47–47 confirmed his place as the Met most deserving of the number. All in favor, fling your gloves skyward.

The second Orosco deal actually netted the best 47 with the bat: **Joe McEwing** (2000–02). Super Joe was nothing super as a hitter—until **Andrew Brown** arrived in 2013, McEwing was the only 47 who wasn't a pitcher—but versatility, humility, and random bursts of offense kept him employed.

McEwing knew his place on the club, and he willingly surrendered 47 when veteran enemy lefty **Tom Glavine** (2003–07) signed on board. The future Hall of Famer deserved better than to walk into an Art Howe rebuilding project (although no one twisted his arm). The team's terrible bullpen seemed to pick Glavine starts for every blown save. He went 9–14 his first year with the club twenty years after another Hall of Fame-bound Tom struggled through the same record for an equally inept club. Working diligently at his craft, Glavine persevered and earned two berths as a Mets All-Star and increased his win total by two each of his first four years with the club. And in 2007, he finally notched win 300.

But no sooner had fans finally warmed up to Glavine—some were referring to him as Tom, by George—than the relationship soured again. Glavine was booed off the mound before the first inning was complete in what would be the final Mets game of 2007.

Despite Glavine's inglorious exit, Mets lefties have taken a liking to 47 in recent years. **Casey Fossum** (2009) and **Aaron Laffey** (2013) wore it for a combined three weeks, but **Hisanori Takahashi** made the most of his year as a Met. He served as starter, long man, setup man, and closer in 2010, his first year in America after a decade as a Yomiuri Giant. He tied for second on the Mets in appearances with 53, saved 8, won 10, and started 12.

Jose Valverde (2013) wasn't nearly as useful, but he did take over as closer after Bobby Parnell went down on Opening Day. By Memorial Day Papa Grande was out after allowing four home runs and blowing two of four save chances.

Dan Carubia

Hisanori Takahashi only pitched one year in New York, but did a little of everything and did it well.

And the rest: knuckleballer **Tom Sturdivant** (1964), **Darrell Sutherland** (1964), **Mardie Cornejo** (1978), **Wally Whitehurst** (1989–92), Rule 5 pick **Mike Draper** (1993), **Jason Jacome** (1994–95), **Reid Cornelius** (1995), and **Derek Wallace** (1996), whose career was cut short by a blood clot, but he still became the first Met with four strikeouts in an inning (while earning a save against the Braves).

It is too early to say if **Hansel Robles** is a reliever more in the mold of Jesse Orosco or **Miguel Batista** (2011–12), but the latest 47 appeared in 57 games as a rookie in 2015. He made a lot of friends among Mets fans and a few enemies among hitters who took exception to his quick pitch. At number 47, you're either quick or dead.

Number 47

Number of times issued: 19 (all to players)

Longest tenured: Jesse Orosco (8 seasons, 370 games), Tom Glavine (5 seasons, 164 games), Wally Whitehurst (4 seasons, 127 games), Joe McEwing (3 seasons, 308 games), Jay Hook (3 seasons, 81 games)

Best single seasons: Orosco, 1983 (13–7, 1.47 ERA, 17 saves, 84 strikeouts in 110 innings); Glavine, 2006 (15–7, 3.82 ERA, 131 strikeouts in 198 innings); Hisanori Takahashi (10–6, 3.61 ERA, 114 strikeouts in 122 innings); McEwing, 2001 (.283/.342/.449, 8 HR, 30 RBIs)

Career statistical leaders: Home runs (McEwing 13, Andrew Brown 7); RBI (McEwing 75, Brown 24); batting average (McEwing .242, Brown .227); wins (Glavine 61, Orosco 47); saves (Orosco 107); ERA (Orosco 2.74, Takahashi 3.61, Hansel Robles 3.67).

Mets Uniform History: Out of the Black and Into the Blue

Like a stubborn stain, the black took a while to scrub away for good.

The depressing color of Citi Field's walls weren't their only issue—they were impossibly tall and ridiculously distant—and so when the club pulled them down-and-in for the first time in 2012, they also changed the color of them from black to blue "which many of our fans have wanted," COO Jeff Wilpon acknowledged in a press statement. The change, the club added, was among those it was making so as to celebrate its fiftieth birthday that season, an event for which it also "retired" No. 50 for the year so as to celebrate the fans. (Sorry not sorry, Frank Francisco).

The other gift the Mets gave that year was removing all the black detail from the home jersey for the first time in fourteen years. Black faded out from the hats and road jerseys by 2013.

Of course it wasn't the just the end of an era, it was the beginning of a new one.

In 2012 the home uniform included a "heritage white" or cream-colored home pinstriped jersey (pinstripes since 2010 had been referred to as an "alternate" jersey). In 2013 came a new alternate jersey appropriating the style of the "snow white" jersey in blue, with orange lettering. The road version introduced (or re-introduced) silver-grey lettering, an element added to the "NY" symbol on alternate road caps in 2015.

Cream got creamed by 2014 when well-intentioned but (let's be honest here) fugly camouflage jerseys and hats were added as a "Military Monday" alternate for 2014 and 2015 and the white pinstripes regained official status. The Marines are on hold for 2016, when the planned alternate is based on the "racing stripe" pullover commemorating the thirtieth anniversary of the 1986 champions.

These changes have been increasingly influenced, or test-marketed, by one-off commemorative jerseys that can be seen as a kind of runway for the coming seasons: The current alt blue owes part of its momentum to well-received "Los Mets" alternates worn in 2011; that style morphed to an arresting solid orange version in 2013 that still hasn't seen an official designation.

In fashion, says Heidi Klum, one day you are in, and the next day you are out. Snow whites, creams, camo and black: Auf wiedereshen. See you around, probably.

#48: HOT DOG

Number 48 was first issued to a Mets player (Joe Nolan) who didn't play in a game. Then **Nino Espinosa** (1974) pitched twice and abandoned it. **Juan Berenguer** (1978) wore it for a few weeks without winning.

Randy Tate (1975) was the first to wear 48 and win a game, but it didn't happen often for him. His 5–13, 4.45 season—including going 0-for-41 at the plate—was his only year in the major leagues and included a heartbreaking loss to the Expos on August 4. The twenty-two-year-old rookie had a no-hitter, a 3–0 lead, and 12 strikeouts through 7 1/3 innings when Jim Lyttle slapped a single to left to break up the no-hitter.

A cruel progression of future Mets followed: Pepe Mangual walked. Jim Dwyer struck out. Gary Carter singled. And Mike Jorgensen whacked a three-run homer to left. Mets and Randy Tate lose, 4–3.

In a special pregame ceremony on May 25, 1980, the Mets presented reliever **Ed Glynn** with a hot-dog steamer bearing his No. 48. The gift recalled the Flushing-born Glynn's first career—as a vendor at Shea.

Glynn (1979–80), a lefty known as the "Flushing Flash" could cut the mustard out of the bullpen, too, as his 7 saves in 1980 attest. He lasted with the Mets for two seasons, or about as long as the average hot dog remains in the bottom of a steamer box.

Randy Myers (1985–89) might have been called a hot dog, but no one wanted to incite someone whose off-field interests were headlined by camouflage and gun magazines. Randall K. Myers, as Tim McCarver always called him (the K stood for Kirk, if you're dying to know), saved 56 games in his too-brief Shea career, averaging well over a strikeout per inning. His best year was 1988, when he saved 26 and compiled a 1.72 ERA.

Mets fans still shake their heads that the southpaw wasn't brought in to face Mike Scioscia in Game 4 of that year's NLCS, when a 3–1 series lead seemed just a K away.

Many hours of therapy got fans over that, but watching Myers cavort on the mound for the world champion Reds two years later as leader of the "Nasty Boys" caused a few relapses. The Mets had sent him to Cincy in a straight-up challenge blockbuster for John Franco after the '89 season. Myers moved around but continued to get the job done as the Mets went to seed. When he set the then-NL record with 53 saves for the 1993 Cubs, the Mets won 59 times all season.

In 1999 the Mets pulled off a more minor challenge trade: brief visitor **Dan Murray** to Kansas City for **Glendon Rusch** (2000–01). Rusch proudly wore 48 into a starting job in 2000 and turned out to be one of the biggest surprises in baseball. That season, at least. The Mets held onto the man that *Baseball Weekly* proclaimed "the best number five starter in baseball." Then he proceeded to pitch like several previous number 48s. Rusch went to Milwaukee in the Jeromy Burnitz deal and won 10 games in his first year as a Brewer, but he led the league in losses. He bounced around the rest of the decade, calling it quits just under 100 losses for his career and just over the .400 win percentage bar.

Aaron Heilman (2003–07) also experienced the up-and-down ride of the major leagues since being a first-round pick out of Notre Dame in 2001. Heilman looked like a bust when he lost 10 of his first 13 career decisions as a starter. The Mets gave him another chance in 2005, and he tossed a one-hit shutout, opening a lot of eyes and seemingly fixing it in his mind that he *should* be a starter despite his bullpen success and the organization telling him no (repeatedly).

While he had a 5.93 ERA and allowed 22 home runs in 133.2 career innings as a starter, Heilman had a 0.68 ERA out of the pen after the 2005 All-Star break, the best of anyone in baseball. He pitched 74 times in '06 and was generally successful, until Yadier Molina made all the faces at Shea look as sour as Heilman's.

From that nadir at 48, we ascend to the apex. In May of 2014 there was no expectation that this kid with all that hair was going to be any better than **Pat "Swing and a" Misch** (2009–11) or **Frank Francisco** (2012–13) and may not even last as long in Flushing as those two. Starting against the Yankees at Citi Field against their young no name, Chase Whitley, you figured the bullpen would be up early and maybe the Mets might win a slugfest for once.

The Mets didn't hit at all, but **Jacob deGrom** was a smash hit. The soon to be twenty-six-year-old (righty pitcher, lefty batter) even singled his first time up, and if Terry Collins had let the college shortstop hit instead of bunt with two on his next time up, he might have gotten himself the run the Mets never provided. The Mets and deGrom lost, 1–0, but he turned into the biggest find of the season. In an organization filled with blue chip pitchers, the unheralded deGrom got better results than anyone else in 2014. He became the first Met Rookie of the Year since Dwight Gooden, he fanned the first eight Marlins of a September game to approach Tom Seaver's major league record of 10, and the kid just kept getting better.

Dan Carubia

Jacob deGrom was not the most hyped young Mets pitcher, but it did not take long to see that his results were as good as anybody's

Flanked by a staff of talented—and younger—pitchers, he was even more deGrominating his sophomore year. He won 14 times in '15, fanned the side on 10 pitches in his first All-Star Game, struck out 200 for the season, and then—in his first postseason series—won Games 1 and 5 of the NLDS at Dodger Stadium. He beat the Cubs at Wrigley in the NLCS as well.

It's got to be the hair—because it certainly isn't the number.

To wit, predecessors in the lower 48 include **Julio "Iguana-Man" Machado** (1990), baby-faced lefty **Pete Schourek** (1991–93), veteran setter-upper **Roger Mason** (1994), the other **Pedro Martinez** (1996), highly unsuccessful reliever **Ricardo Jordan** (1997), and hard-throwing **Kane Davis**, who made the squad in 2002 and subsequently blew out his arm.

Number 48

Number of times issued: 21 (14 players, 1 DNP, 3 coaches)

Longest tenured: Aaron Heilman (5 seasons, 227 games), Randy Myers (5 seasons, 185 games), Pete Schourek (3 seasons, 98 games), Glendon Rusch (3 seasons, 65 games)

Best single seasons: Jacob deGrom, 2015 (14–8, 2.54 ERA, 205 strikeouts in 191 innings); deGrom, 2014 (9–6, 2.69 ERA, 144 strikeouts in 1401. innings); Myers, 1988 (7–3, 1.72 ERA, 26 saves, 69 strikeouts in 68 innings); Rusch, 2000 (11–11, 4.01 ERA, 157 strikeouts in 190 2/3 innings); Heilman, 2005 (5–3, 3.17 ERA, 106 strikeouts in 108 innings)

Career statistical leaders: RBI (Schourek 8, deGrom 6, Rusch 6), batting average (deGrom .200), wins (deGrom 23, Rusch 19, Heilman 19, Myers 17); saves (Myers 56, Frank Francisco 24); ERA (deGrom 2.61, Myers 2.74),

---

Ghosts in the Machine

Somewhere in the murky mists of Flushing, perhaps in an auto salvage yard over by the Roosevelt Avenue Bridge, is the place where Phantom Mets gather. It's where Mac Suzuki approaches Randy Bobb and, fighting backs tears, asks, "Wanna have a catch?"

Vagaries of the waiver rules, poor planning, bad luck, injuries, trades, or other roster-changing events have resulted in seventeen such men. This group is a bit different than "paper Mets" acquired over an offseason and traded immediately, like Jim Kern, or guys who were traded for but never made it out of the minors. Phantom Mets differ in that they occupied space on the active roster during a season, meaning they were eligible to play and thereby occupied a number. They count, and yet they don't.

Following is a list of Mets uniforms worn by players who never made it into an official game while wearing that uniform in that year. (They are the mysterious players listed as DNP in various chapters.) Some of the players accrued considerable time in other Mets uniforms, while others haunt the Iron Triangle.

No.	Player	Year	Notes
3	**Jason Phillips**	**2001**	Phillips would gather in three additional numbers in subsequent call-ups. He couldn't get No. 3 back because it belonged at the time to Vance Wilson, his rival for the role of Mike Piazza's backup.
5	**Jerry Moses**	**1975**	One of three catchers to start the year with the Mets (Jerry Grote and rookie John Stearns were the others), the veteran Moses was sold to San Diego when they had a sudden catching crisis.
9	**Randy Bobb**	**1970**	Duffy Dyer won the backup catcher job in 1970, although Bobb rode the bench in September.

No.	Player	Year	Notes
16	Mike Jorgensen	1969	Gil Hodges liked small groups. Jorgensen didn't even get a post-clinching inning, although he played in this number subsequently.
21	Ron Gardenhire	1986	Cut shortly after the season began, Gardenhire kept his sense of humor. Fearing he might wind up driving a tractor in Kansas he quipped, "I could go from Dear John to John Deere." Fear not, Ron, a 13-year managerial career awaited in Minnesota.
21	Terrel Hansen	1992	Minor league slugger recalled briefly when Kevin Baez and Vince Coleman were injured; he was sent back down before appearing. Never got a turn at-bat or an inning in the field but hit nearly 200 home runs over thirteen minor league seasons.
22	Billy Cotton	1972	Another minor league catcher who couldn't take innings from Duffy Dyer.
23	Bob G. Miller	1962	Acquired in a trade, then reassigned to the minors before appearing in a game. When Miller returned, Joe Christopher was in 23, so Miller switched to 36.
29	Jason Isringhausen	1995	Asked for—and received—No. 44 before his mound debut.
32	Tyler Yates	2002	When Satoru Komiyama injured his finger in his electric garage door, Yates had three days in the bullpen, but that door never opened. He returned two years and one arm surgery later, wearing No. 33.
34	Mac Suzuki	1999	In what wouldn't be considered Steve Phillips's brightest procedural moment, Suzuki was acquired in a trade for Allen Watson but claimed by Kansas City on waivers when the Mets tried to sneak him down to AAA days later.
35	Jon Matlack	1970	Just getting a September taste; would be up to stay a year later in No. 32.
43	John Gibbons	1985	With the Mets in a pennant race, it was more difficult than usual getting playing time from Gary Carter.
44	Jim Bibby	1970, 1971	Right-hander Bibby had a 12-year career ahead of him, including a no-hitter, but none of it was with the Mets (natch), who in consecutive years promoted Bibby to the club in September only to leave him seated in the bullpen. Traded in '71 to St. Louis in an eight-player deal.
48	Joe Nolan	1973	Catcher was rushed from Tidewater when Jerry Grote suffered a broken arm, Nolan became superfluous when the Mets traded for Jerry May.

No.	Player	Year	Notes
56	**Anderson Garcia**	**2006**	Last of the Armando Benitez trade booty, Garcia filled a space between the entertaining yet ineffective Jose Lima and Alay Soler.
56	**Matt Reynolds**	**2015**	Thanks to Chase Utley knocking Ruben Tejada into Pasadena, the Mets needed a backup shortstop in the 2015 postseason. Reynolds, not called up to New York in September, was the only shortstop available. Not winning (and receiving the bigger World Series share) probably hurt more than not playing.

#49: NIESE KNOWING YOU

Born the day the Mets clinched the 1986 world championship, no Met wore No. 49 close to as long as **Jon Niese** (2008–15) though his timing wasn't great otherwise.

Just when you thought you could trust him in a big game (the Mets played few games that qualified as such in his tenure), he came up short. The lefty from Defiance, Ohio seemed to go with the flow and to that end had an ERA just below 4.00 and a perfectly mediocre 61–61 mark: one winning season, three losing seasons, and five exactly at .500. If only the team he played for had finished .500 that many times in his tenure.

Niese's first and last years were the only years the Mets had winning records, and in each case the Mets did not start him in crucial games. With rookie lefty Steve Matz's hard stuff trumping Niese's looping curveball, the veteran pitched out of the bullpen in the 2015 postseason, perhaps foretelling of a career-lengthening conversion at some point. And it will be in someone else's bullpen. He was traded to Pittsburgh (for Neil Walker) in December 2015, and uncharacteristically took a few shots at the team on his way out. That's not Niese.

Jon Niese was a Mets mainstay from the left side of the mound for eight seasons.

Dan Carubia

You know what else isn't so Niese? Remembering the combination of shut-down stuff punctuated with egregious late-inning meltdowns authored by **Armando Benitez** (1999–2003) over a tumultuous five years in Flushing.

The Mets have a lineage of great relievers, and Benitez famously (or rather, infamously) coughed up the lead in many a crucial spot, but by sheer volume of saves—and, you could look it up, save percentage—the chest-thumping, fastball-firing Armando ranks among the best.

Acquired from the Orioles by GM Steve Phillips in December 1998, Armando had the first 40-save seasons in club history (2000–01), and his 160 saves as a Met ranks ahead of any reliever not named Franco. Considering he didn't take over the closer's role until midway through 1999 and was finally run out of town in July 2003, he averaged close to 40 saves per season. Total blown saves in that time: 25. Seven of those ruined chances came during his one truly awful year as a Met in 2003; ironically, that was the same year he earned his lone All-Star berth as a Met (and never made it back to Shea from the festivities). Getting a save often seemed automatic for Armando. It was when he didn't get the save that the image of Brian Jordan or J.T. Snow or Paul O'Neill repeated in your head again and again as night gave way to dawn.

The relievers following Benitez in 49 have predictably had tough times. **Orber Moreno** (2003–04) got hurt, **Felix Heredia** (2005) got hurt and then suspended for steroids, and **Roberto Hernandez** wore the number for only a few days in 2006 before going back to 39. Still, the mojo must have rubbed off and Bert wasn't nearly the same pitcher he'd been in '05.

Philip Humber (2006–07), the third overall pick in the 2003 draft, never won a game as a Met—including a must-win game where he was handed a 5–0 lead against the fourth-place Nats during the collapse of '07. But the man who would one day pitch a perfect game (for the 2012 White Sox), was part of the haul that landed the pitcher who finally broke the Mets' no-hitter drought: Johan Santana.

Walt Terrell (1982–84) was the first 49 of note in Mets history. Like Benitez, he was pilfered from an AL team (Texas, with Ron Darling in tow). Terrell was 19–23 as a Met with a downright upright 3.53 ERA. His most memorable day came when he homered twice and drove in all four runs in his win at Wrigley in a rare Mets NBC *Game of the Week* appearance in 1983. He left town in a similarly brilliant move; the prize returned from Detroit was Howard Johnson.

Bearded lefty **Kevin Kobel** (1978–80) had experience in losing. He came from a Milwaukee team that finished fifth, fifth, and sixth his first three years in the majors. That proved to be a perfect apprenticeship for a Mets club that would finish sixth, sixth, and fifth in his three years in Flushing.

Kobel fashioned 5 wins and a 2.91 ERA as a swingman with the 1978 Mets. He started 27 games with a 3.51 ERA in '79.

If the Mets' failure to chase down a division title in 1989 can be traced to a single game and a single goat, it might be the August 20 affair at Shea when veteran **Don Aase** (1989) coughed up four 9th-inning runs and a lead to the Dodgers, highlighted by a home run by future Mets manager Willie Randolph.

Ed Hearn (1986) shined playing Gary Carter's understudy when the lights were brightest. That is to say, not quite as incandescently, but bright enough, especially for a reserve backstop whose high number illustrated what a longshot he was. Fondly remembered as a piece of the '86 puzzle, and afterward outbound freight in the David Cone heist.

Others wore 49 while passing through: **John Stephenson** (1964), fourteen years later came **Dyar Miller** (1980–81), **Don Schulze** (1987), **Mike Birkbeck** (1992), **Joe Vitko** (1992), **Pete Walker** (1995), and **Bob MacDonald** (1996). Because 9—the number worn by his dad, Randy, as ironman catcher for the Cubs—was occupied by Gregg Jefferies in Flushing, 49 was the first number for **Todd Hundley** (1990–91).

Joe Crawford was effective (4–3, 3.30) and yo-yoed back to Norfolk during his lone year as a Met in 1997, but he went for the cash and security in Japan. **Brad Clontz** (1998) did nada in his two-game Mets tenure in 1998, but the next year he threw the most important regular-season wild pitch for a New York team since Jack Chesbro's 95 years earlier for the New York Highlanders. Pitching for Pittsburgh in the bottom of the 9th in a tie game on the last day on the schedule, Clontz's first pitch to Mike Piazza with the bases loaded skipped away and brought in Melvin Mora with the run that sent the Mets to a one-game playoff in Cincinnati. What a Clontz!

Number 49

Number of times issued: 20 (all to players)

Longest tenured: Jon Niese (8 seasons, 182 games), Armando Benitez (5 seasons, 333 games), Kevin Kobel (3 seasons, 76 games), Walt Terrell (3 seasons, 57 games)

Best single seasons: Benitez, 1999 (4–3, 1.85 ERA, 22 saves, 128 strikeouts in 78 innings); Benitez, 2000 (4–4, 2.61 ERA, 41 saves, 106 strikeouts in 76 innings); Niese, 2012 (13–9, 3.40 ERA, 155 strikeouts in 190 1/3 innings); Niese, 2014 (9–11, 3.40 ERA, 128 strikeouts in 187 2/3 innings); Terrell, 1984 (11–12, 3.52 ERA, 114 strikeouts in 215 innings); Kobel, 1979 (6–8, 3.51 ERA, 67 strikeouts in 161 2/3 innings)

Career statistical leaders: Home runs (Ed Hearn 4); RBI (Niese 18, Hearn 10); batting average (Hearn .265); wins (Niese 61, Terrell 19, Benitez 18); saves (Benitez 160); ERA (Benitez 2.70, Terrell 3.53)

Games People Play: Appearances by the Numbers

While the Mets have had some excellent pitching talent in their history, they've also had a lot of mound melancholy. And how does one deal with poor pitching? By bringing in more pitchers, of course. As the game has evolved, well-pitched games often require three and four hurlers—if not more—to complete, and two decades have passed since a Mets team reached double figures in complete games in a season.

Below are the numbers that have been called in to pitch the most often in Mets history through 2015. It includes starters, closers, and many classifications of manly men: middle men, setup men, mop-up men, and firemen. Watch out for the odd LOOGY (Left-hand Only One Out Guy) floating around. It can get a little messy.

No.	Games	Notes
45	1,385	When a Mets manager has wanted an arm, he's signaled for 45 more than anyone else. And why not? Tug McGraw (361 games) and John Franco (301) make up more than half of those calls.
39	1,275	Bobby Parnell is your leader with 329 mound appearances—eight of them were starts.
36	1,133	Jerry Koosman started 346 games and relieved 30 times.
27	1,081	Furiously working, and often just plain furious, Dennis Cook made 225 appearances.
38	1,058	Skip Lockwood's 228 games, all in relief, lead the pack.
40	1,048	It was Innis in the Morning (and more often at night): 288 appearances.
47	1,042	It's pretty much a lot of starters, stiffs, and Jesse Orosco (371).
48	1,030	Aaron Heilman appeared 280 times in relief and 25 times as a starter—and would have preferred it the other way around.
35	1,008	Big Dave Weathers crammed 180 appearances into two-and-a-half seasons.
34	995	Balanced attack behind Bob Apodaca (184) and Mike Pelfrey (153). Let's hope Noah Syndergaard (24) climbs this list.

#50: HAWAII 5-0

In an era when educators complain that students are lacking general knowledge in many subjects—geography among them—the Mets have taught plenty of people about our fiftieth state. Hawaii was home for a popular pitcher of the 1980s and a thumping folk hero who rode in on a wave of home runs in 1999 and hit the latest game-ending postseason home run in franchise history (if you ignore the first two words in Robin Ventura's grand-slam single).

Portly portsider **Sid Fernandez** (1984–93) was one of the best pitchers the Mets have ever had. No Met since Tom Seaver went out there with no-hit stuff more frequently. El Sid was lucky to have pitched in the era before pitch counts or he would have been yanked for exceeding 100 pitches often enough to have dwindled his win total to nothing. Maybe his career would have lasted longer if that powerful left arm had been babied, but it's hard to imagine him lasting longer than the ten seasons he spent at Shea, three of which saw El Sid post the best ratio of hits per nine innings in the National League.

Dan Carubia

Sid Fernandez, the original 50, brought great stuff and impressive results from the Aloha State to Shea.

The Mets stole him from the Dodgers and put him in the rotation in July 1984. He only pitched in relief once in his first three seasons, but it was his masterful bullpen work in Game 7 of the 1986 World Series that put the Mets in position to rally to win the world championship.

Fernandez certainly would have reached 100 wins as a Met if his last club hadn't been the brutal '93 edition that he wasted a 2.93 ERA on before getting hurt (5–6 mark in 120 innings). Of his list of impressive numbers, something that can't be overlooked is how he made a uniform number in the 50s fair game for players (thirty-four coaches and managers—and only a handful of call-ups—had worn numbers 50 or higher pre-Sid). Fernandez was proud of his Hawaiian roots and claimed *Hawaii 5-0* to be his favorite program, so 50 it was. No Mets player had worn the number before, and none has lived up to El Sid's legacy. But one guy sure tried hard.

Benny Agbayani (1999–2001) burst onto the scene and became an instant hero and cult figure. Shane Spencer had come up the previous year for the Yankees and crushed homers at an impressive rate. Big whoop. The Yankees were ahead by a hundred games and Shane merely kept the yawning down among the arrogant. The following May, the Mets were in need of an out-fielder and brought up the stocky, hardworking, Honolulu product with the funny name. Whereas Agbayani wore 39 for his unimpressive first tour in '98, this time he snagged 50. He hit 10 homers in his first 19 starts and helped the Mets reach the postseason for the first time in eleven years.

The next year there was no spot for Benny, but the roster flexibility afforded for the season-opening series with the Cubs in Japan got him a seat on the long plane trip to Tokyo. After losing the opener to a poor Cubs club, the second game went into the 11th inning tied, two outs, bases loaded, pitcher's spot up. Why not Benny? Why not indeed. Agbayani's grand slam won the game, and he stayed with the team all year, settling in as a thumper in the eighth spot until Melvin Mora was traded and Benny moved up in the order. He had another solid season and saved his heroics for when they were most needed. Game 3 Division Series, tie game, tie series, 14th inning, wind howling in from left field. Whap! Gone. Shea goes nuts. Everyone loves Benny just a little bit more.

He should have kept his mouth shut when asked for his World Series prediction, but unlike his teammates, he at least brought his bat to the first real Subway Series in forty-four years, driving in the tiebreaking run in the only win for the Mets. But that was it. The spell ended, and those big hits no longer came. Fans started liking the exotic new flavor of Tsuyoshi Shinjo. Agbayani was traded and eventually had a reunion with Bobby Valentine and Matt Franco in Japan; this time toasting the championship with no Yankees rabble to ruin things.

As thrilling as the dual Hawaiian 5-0s were, others suffered by comparison.

Victor Diaz hit an Agbayani-esque home run in the 9th at Shea to start the 2004 Cubs on the road to ruin not unlike the '07 Mets (or '69 Cubs). After he switched to 20, Diaz seemed to find a way of hitting the off switch on his brain at the wrong time. He was quietly dealt during the 2006 season for minor league catcher Mike Nickeas.

Duaner Sanchez went unscored upon in his first 22 innings as a Met in 2006, including seven multiple-inning appearances, as the Mets roared to a big lead in the standings. Even when the National League caught up to him a little, the goggled one was still as good as any reliever the Mets—or the league—had to offer. Then he took a taxi. Not Harry Chapin's taxi, either. If you could go back in time—and you'd already ended poverty, hunger, war, and talked Harry Frazee into keeping Babe Ruth—would you run onto the field before Aaron Heilman's fateful pitch to Yadier Molina or fasten Duaner Sanchez's seat belt? If you chose the latter, there'd have been no Oliver Perez to start that game so magnificently. But if Duaner wasn't hurt, would the Mets have even needed a Game 7? Call it the Duaner Quandary.

Not so thought provoking were the hurlers not named El Sid who came before Sanchez: **Juan Castillo** (1994), **Rick Trlicek** (1997), the miserable **John Thomson** (2002), and **Matt Watson** (2003). Post Duaner relievers were almost as ho hum: **Sean Green** (2009–10), **Michael O'Connor** (2011), **Scott Atchinson** (2013), and **Rafael Montero**, who was the expected rook to rock the rotation when he and Jacob deGrom were called up in May 2014. But deGrom flourished and Montero faltered in '14 and shoulder woes slowed him in '15. You never know what you'll get when you turn 50.

Number 50

Number of times issued: 14 (12 players, 2 coaches)

Longest tenured: Sid Fernandez (10 seasons, 255 games), Benny Agbayani (3 seasons, 311 games)

Best single seasons: Fernandez, 1986 (16–6, 3.52 ERA, 200 strikeouts in 204 1/3 innings, All-Star); Fernandez, 1989 (14–5, 2.83 ERA, 198 strikeouts in 219 1/3 innings); Agbayani, 2000 (.289/.391/.480, 15 HR, 60 RBIs); Duaner Sanchez, 2006 (5–1, 2.60 ERA, 44 strikeouts in 55 1/3 innings)

Career statistical leaders: Home runs (Agbayani 35); RBI (Agbayani 129); batting average (Agbayani .282); wins (Fernandez 98, Sanchez 10); saves (Fernandez 1, Sean Green 1); ERA (Fernandez 3.14, Sanchez 3.48)

"C" You Real Soon: Mets Captains

In the early days of professional baseball, a captain also performed the duties of today's manager. The captain played, made out the lineup, and settled player disputes while the manager operated more like a general manager or business manager of today. Eventually the captain and manager monikers merged, and there didn't seem much purpose for a captain.

And after winning two world championships in their first twenty-five years of existence, the captain-free Mets seemed to do just fine (forgetting, of course, that period from 1962 to 1968 and that eternity between 1977 and 1983). On May 6, 1987, the Mets named their first captain: Keith Hernandez. It seemed an inspired choice. The first baseman was the leader on the field and in the locker room, handing out bon mots as needed to the press that swarmed around his smoky locker.

As if this didn't distinguish him enough, a C was stitched on his uniform. They also sewed one on the upper right corner of Gary Carter's jersey. The Mets doubled—or halved—the honor and made the catcher a captain for '88.

Why co-captains? George Vescey of the New York Times forwarded a theory: "The group-think is that appointing the fiery Hernandez was [Davey] Johnson's natural instinct, and that appointing the sunny Carter six months later was Johnson's way of appeasing Frank Cashen." But two captains couldn't outflank Major Orel Hershiser in battle in the NLCS.

The captains went out together, limping into the sunset—or Cleveland and San Francisco—after their injury-marred 1989. The Kid and Mex were two different personalities, but both were essential to the glory the Mets achieved as a unit in 1986.

The naming of the third captain followed the next World Series appearance. John Franco, a forty-year-old relief pitcher, was named captain on May 4, 2001. This germinated from the mind of none other than Turk Wendell. Wild-eyed Turk got the idea from hockey, where a captain actually has necessary on-ice duties. About the only official function a captain has in baseball is to take the lineup card to home plate (sometimes). Franco did this on his first night wearing the C and explained a Shea Stadium ground rule incorrectly. (He said that a ball hitting off the black backdrop in the picnic area was a live ball. It wasn't. But with meticulous Bobby Valentine in the dugout, players didn't sweat rule idiosyncrasies.) Franco did get the save that night, though.

Ten seasons after Franco threw his last pitch as a Met, former teammate David Wright, having signed a long-term contract and owning or preparing to lease every offensive record in franchise history, was named the fourth Mets captain on March 21, 2013. He was already called "Captain America," and decided he did not need a mask or shield or C.

Mets GM Sandy Alderson explained that Wright "is not a guy who wears it on his sleeve, which probably relates to the C on the uniform and the fact that it won't be there. I don't think David needs it. I don't think that fits his personality. He's not somebody who is a captain in title alone. It's really about the substance underneath the title."

#51–99: THE HIGH NUMBERS

PROGRESSION:

Player	Years
Cookie Lavagetto (coach)	1962–63
Wes Westrum (coach/manager)	1964–65
Roy McMillan (coach/manager)	1973–76
Denny Sommers (coach)	1977–78
Dick Sisler (coach)	1979–80
Deron Johnson (coach)	1981
Jim Frey (coach)	1982–83
Vern Hoscheit (coach)	1984–87
Tom Spencer (coach)	1991
John Stephenson (coach)	1992
Mike Maddux	1993–94
Lance Johnson	1996
Mookie Wilson (coach)	1997 (to Aug. 8)
Mel Rojas	1997–98
Rick White	2000–01
Dave Engle (coach)	2002 (to June 12)
Chris Chambliss (coach)	2002 (from June 12)
Rick Peterson (coach)	2004–08 (to June 16)
Luis Aguayo (coach)	2008 (from June 17)
Luis Alicea (coach)	2009
Chip Hale (coach)	2010–11
Dave Hudgens (coach)	2012–14
Jack Leathersich	2015

Traditionally a netherworld of Metdom, numbers over 50 have become more common since 2010, when Kevin Kierst took over for Charlie Samuels as the club's equipment manager. (Another Kierst numbers innovation was circular labels bearing uni numbers on the knobs of bats for easy ID.)

A series of subtle changes have pushed more numbers higher and higher. Coaches who traditionally occupied the 50s sartorially mingled among the pitchers, catchers, and position players in the lower 50. Uniformed staff has increased overall, meaning numbers for bullpen catchers, batting-practice pitchers, and assistant hitting coaches. Also, relief pitchers have emerged as a kind of separate class from their starting brethren in the 30s and 40s. The result is more freshness in jersey issues over the last five years than in any time since the club's first 40-man roster was assembled in 1962. That's pretty remarkable.

It's early still, however, so our voyage North will encounter more sparsely populated islands than long-settled landmasses. It's also a bit a rough ride, so keep your seatbacks straight and tray tables in their upright and locked positions. Here we go.

Number 51

Can we turn back now?

In this land of the frightening relievers, **Mike Maddux** is the first stop. He went 3–8 with a 3.80 ERA in a thankless role for the 1993 Mets. As the team improved, Maddux imploded in '94. Only the strike could wipe away any recall of the "Bad Maddux," who actually turned into a good pitching coach. (Having Greg Maddux as your little brother can't hurt in an interview.)

Rick White (2000–01) was kind of scary looking, but he did all right on the mound. He was part of that Steve Phillips Friday trading spree in July 2000 that resulted in Bubba Trammell and Mike Bordick both homering in their first Mets at-bats. White, just in from Tampa Bay, picked up a win in his first Mets appearance. He got an even more important win in Game 3 of that year's Division Series. He did some solid work for the Mets in 2001 as well.

There's just no explaining **Mel Rojas** (1997–98). One day he's a superb closer for the Expos. Next, the Cubs sign him to a huge contract and he becomes a batting-practice pitcher. Steve Phillips strolls by with his new allowance and pays full retail for Rojas, who clearly belongs in the 99-cent bin. After trying to hide Rojas and his 6.05 ERA from the Shea boo-birds in '98, the Mets shipped him to Los Angeles for none other than Bobby Bonilla.

Lance Johnson, part of that original deal for Rojas, obligingly changed to 51 for a game in 1996 to let Mookie Wilson have his own day and his own number when he was inducted into the Mets Hall of Fame. "We had to do what we could to make this day perfect," Johnson explained. Almost two decades later it was wild, hard-throwing lefty **Jack Leathersich** (2015) going to the Cubs via waiver claim.

Eighteen coaches have worn 51, including **Rick Peterson** (who couldn't fix Victor Zambrano but patched several other holes and generally sounded smart until the chassis fell off the jalopy in September '07). Two coaches have ridden the number to the manager's chair. **Wes Westrum** finished out the 1965 season in 51 as the hand-picked successor of the incapacitated Casey Stengel, but the following spring he snagged number 9 from Jim Hickman, who took 6. A press corps hooked on Stengelese wished Westrum could have grabbed a fistful of personality while he was at it. Some of those same reporters still on the beat must have had a similar wish when **Roy McMillan** succeeded the colorful, quotable Yogi Berra as manager to finish out the 1975 season. McMillan returned to the quiet coaching lines the following spring.

Number 51

Number of times issued: 23 (5 players, 18 coaches)

Best single season: Rick White, 2001 (4–5, 3.88 ERA, 2 saves, 51 strikeouts in 69 2/3 innings)

PROGRESSION:

Player	Years
Solly Hemus (coach)	1962–63
Don Heffner (coach)	1964–65
Harvey Haddix (coach)	1966–67
Joe Pignatano (coach)	1968–81
Greg Pavlick (coach)	1985–86, 1988–91, 1994–96
Dave Wallace (coach)	1999–2000
Dave Engle (coach)	2001
Randy Niemann (coach)	2002–03
Rick Waits (coach)	2003
Tony Clark	2003 (from June 5)
Don Baylor (coach)	2004
Guy Conti (coach)	2005
Howard Johnson (coach)	2007
Guy Conti (coach)	2008
Razor Shines (coach)	2009–10
Dave Hudgens (coach)	2011
Carlos Torres	2013–15 (to July 31)
Yoenis Cespedes	2015 (from Aug.1)

Number 52

You might have heard something about this **Yoenis Cespedes** guy.

Acquired at the 2015 trade deadline, but only after Plan A fell through, the Cuban slugger arrived from Detroit just in time to reawaken a slumbering Mets lineup and solidify the club for a pennant race in a way only one player had ever done before: Donn Clendenon in 1969.

Cespedes fit the Mets as snugly as the canary-yellow compression sleeve covering his muscular right arm. He smashed 35 extra-base hits including 17 home runs as the club's new center fielder—an OPS of .942—over a resplendent eight-and-a-half weeks during which the Mets not only overtook the Washington Nationals for the NL East title but humiliated them at the same time. Right in the

middle of it was Cespedes, whose signature moments included devastating the Nationals in each game of a fateful series in Washington in September: A seventh-inning, run-scoring double off Matt Thornton to cap a tiebreaking rally Monday; a three-run double off Drew Storen the next night, helping to rescue Matt Harvey as the Mets rallied from a 7–1 deficit to an 8–7 win; and on Wednesday, facing Storen again, crushing one off the back wall of the visiting bullpen to break an 8th-inning tie and lead the Mets to a decisive sweep.

Cespedes cooled, eventually, by the time the club reached the World Series: His awkward pursuit and subsequent kick of Alcides Escobar's

Yoenis Cespedes means "power" in any language.

leadoff drive to center field in Game 1 illustrated his limits as a flycatcher, and resulted in an inside-the-park home run for Kansas City—a bad omen for the games to follow. With reported contract demands seeming beyond the Mets ability to provide them, the club was prepared to go Yo free in 2016 but waited him out and got Cespedes for all of us, at least for another year.

As evidenced by his collection of sports cars, batmobiles, and horses, the man knows how to make an arrival. **Carlos Torres** (2013–15) knew how to get out of the way. He obligingly took 72. Torres approached an unsexy middle-relief role with stoic determination and, often, heroic results: 16 wins, 2 saves and a 3.32 ERA over 149 appearances. Read on for the sad aftermath in Chapter 72.

It was all sad aftermath for the Mets and **Ramon Ramirez**, arriving in a rare dud of a Sandy Alderson trade—the 2012 swap of Angel Pagan to San Francisco, also bringing along center field failure Andres Torres, one of three high-numbered Torres of recent vintage. **Tony Clark** (2003) is known to the outside world as president of the Players Association, but here he is known as the Mets' first player to wear 00 (see "Less Than Zero" for how he and Mr. Met resolved that conflict).

Number 52

Number of times issued: 17 (4 players, 13 coaches)

Best single seasons: Yoenis Cespedes, 2015 (17 HR, 44 RBIs, .604 slugging in 57 games); Tony Clark, 2003 (.232/.300/.472, 16 HR, 43 RBIs); Carlos Torres, 2014 (8–6, 2 saves, 3.06 ERA in 73 games)

Number 53

Mark Guthrie had a 27-inning scoreless streak for the 2002 Mets that stretched over 34 appearances. Did we mention he's left-handed? The streak ended and he got his first loss as a Met when he allowed a three-run blast to Luis Gonzalez that flushed the season down the toilet in early August, culminating with the sorry ending of the Bobby Valentine era. Guthrie, who'd come from the Art Howe Show in Oakland, did not stick around for the East Coast revival.

Chad Bradford of *Moneyball* fame was excellent in his one year as a Met, 2006. He took 53, Marty Noble reported on mlb.com, because he had a thing for 8 and liked to add: 5 + 3. His knuckle-dragging, sidearm slowball drove hitters nuts. It made Peter Angelos a little crazy as well because he threw $10.5 million at Bradford to bring him to Baltimore for three years.

PROGRESSION:

Player	Years
Rogers Hornsby (coach)	1962
Ernie White (coach)	1963
Mel Harder (coach)	1964
Sheriff Robinson (coach)	1966–67
Eddie Yost (coach)	1968–76
Tom Burgess (coach)	1977
Dal Maxvill (coach)	1978
Chuck Cottier (coach)	1979–81
Bud Harrelson (coach)	1982
Bobby Valentine (coach)	1983
Eric Hillman	1992–94
Rafael Landestoy (coach)	1996
Tom Robson (coach)	1997–99, 2000–01
Mickey Brantley (coach)	1999
Dave Engle (coach)	2001
Mark Guthrie	2002
Verne Ruhle (coach)	2003
Jerry Manuel (coach)	2005
Chad Bradford	2006
Jerry Manuel (coach/ manager)	2007–10
Jeremy Hefner	2012–13
Bobby Abreu	2014

Eric Hillman (1992–94) was extremely tall (6-foot-10), **Jeremy Hefner** (2012–13) was extremely unlucky (getting hurt just as Mets started to improve), and **Bobby Abreu** was extremely professional. A Venezuelan On-Base Machine (career OBP .395), Abreu spent the last campaign of an excellent 18-year big-league career with the 2014 Mets, accumulating his 400th steal, 288th home run, and 2,470th hit—a single in his final at-bat (10,081). The same age (and attitude) as Bartolo Colon, Abreu proved still dangerous with a bat—or glove—in his hand.

The Mets didn't score much between 1968 and 1976, so it was crucial that the man sending runners home be daring yet efficient. **Eddie Yost** was both. He was also loyal. He came to the Mets from Washington with Gil Hodges and fellow coaches Rube Walker and Joe Pignatano. Yost watched in disbelief as his trusted friend died in front of him after a round of golf in 1972, and he stayed through Yogi Berra's tenure and lasted a year into Joe Frazier's brief and unhappy reign before hightailing it to Boston. They called him "The Walking Man" because of the staggering 1,614 walks he drew with the old Senators (still in the top ten all-time), but Mets fans knew that keen eye also could see when to try to squeeze a little more offense from a slow-footed Mets runner rounding third on a one-hop single.

Until Willie Mays, the best player in history to serve as a Mets coach was **Rogers Hornsby** for the 1962 club. "Rajah" was a career .358 hitter who won seven batting titles—six in a row—including an unfathomable .424 average for the 1924 Cardinals. Having arguably the greatest-hitting second baseman of all-time coach hitters for the worst team in modern history (no argument there) wasn't a great match. He scared the kids, disturbed the veterans, and at sixty-seven probably could have hit better than any second sacker the '62 Mets could muster. He died that winter, as did coach and first No. 48 Red Kress. Makes one wonder how anyone survived that club.

Lost in the utter hysteria of media outrage that the Mets would dare to fire Willie Randolph following a West Coast night game in 2010 was a remarkable debut for **Jerry Manuel**, who ascended into the manager's office. In a pre-game press conference Manuel in the sleepy-cool style of a jazz disc-jockey calmly and articulately diagnosed every issue that plagued the club, then adroitly diffused a potentially explosive on-field issue after Jose Reyes led off Manuel's first game by promptly having a fit about coming out of the game due to a leg injury. The 2008 Mets under "Gangsta Jerry" were inarguably a better performing club than the same group under Randolph, even if the season ended with a similar thud. In retrospect, however, it was a mistake to offer him a contract extension without interviewing potential successors. Manuel's two successive years were marked by passive offensive strategies and skittish bullpen management—the dearth of talent wasn't his fault—but it resulted in a club that was hard to watch.

Number 53

Number of times issued: 21 (5 players, 15 coaches, 1 manager)

Best single seasons: Mark Guthrie, 2002 (5–5, 2.44, 44 strikeouts in 48 innings), Chad Bradford, 2006 (4–2, 2.90 ERA, 2 saves, 45 strikeouts in 62 innings)

PROGRESSION:

Player	Years
Red Ruffing (coach)	1962
Clyde McCullough (coach)	1963
Whitey Herzog (coach)	1966
Salty Parker (coach/manager)	1967
Rube Walker (coach)	1968–81
Rob Dromerhauser (coach)	1988–91
Mark Clark	1996–97
Al Jackson (coach)	1999–2000
Charlie Hough (coach)	2001–02
Rick Waits (coach)	2004 (see also 52)
Rick Down (coach)	2005–07 (to July 13)
Brian Lawrence	2007 (from Aug. 2)
Alex Torres	2015 (to July 29)
Tim Stauffer	2015 (from Sept. 13)

Number 54

Alex Torres (2015) won't be remembered for his jersey but for his hat. Spooked by an injury to one-time Tampa Bay teammate Alex Cobb, who was struck in the noggin by a batted ball in 2013, Torres took to wearing a conspicuous padded crown on his hat in the event the same ever happened him. Thankfully it didn't, but if only Torres could have taken similar precaution to other calamities awaiting him on the mound with the 2015 Mets: Way too many walks, hits, and runs. Though he had the first save ever for a 54, one Torres was enough for New York and the lefty was banished to the minors in July. His number was reissued to late-arriving bullpen fodder **Tim Stauffer** in September.

GM Joe McIlvaine snagged **Mark Clark** from Cleveland just before the 1996 season started, figuring he needed a veteran to offset Generation K. Good idea. Clark led the Mets in wins, ERA, strikeouts, and innings, while Jason Isringhausen and Paul Wilson combined for 11 wins and a 5.05 ERA (Bill Pulsipher missed the entire year). Clark was solid but not as good in '97, so new GM Steve Phillips sent him home to Illinois in the six-player Turk Wendell deal with the Cubs.

The 2007 Mets tried Mike Pelfrey, Jason Vargas, Dave Williams, and Chan Ho Park for a combined thirteen No. 5 starter appearances before reclamation project **Brian Lawrence** became the first pitcher to win a game (and in his first try). The aforementioned quartet was 0–10 with an 8.28 ERA. After winning in his debut, Lawrence was 0–2 in his five subsequent starts for the collapsible '07 club.

Salty Parker is the least known of any Mets manager. And given that he spent one year as a Mets coach and went 4–7 in his brief tilt at the skipper's wheel in 1967, it should stay that way.

If any coach is ever considered for the Mets Hall of Fame, it should be **Rube Walker**. Taking into account that the process for induction into the exclusive circle has become as hard to interpret as the puffs of smoke from the College of Cardinals (in Rome, not St. Louis), don't hold your breath that Rube will ever get the nod. Consider that Walker served as pitching coach from 1968 to 1981, started the practice of the five-man rotation to protect (but not baby) the franchise's young arms, and served faithfully under Gil Hodges, Yogi Berra, Roy McMillan, Joe Frazier, and Joe Torre without losing his mind (or job). The old Brooklyn catcher was finally shown the door with Torre on the last day of '81, and then accompanied him to Atlanta.

There wasn't much about baseball that Hall of Famer **Whitey Herzog** didn't know, except when it came to kissing up to those who paid the bills. Herzog coached the 1966 team, moved up to director of player development, helped put together the budding farm system, and probably could have moved into the general manager's seat when Johnny Murphy died in 1969 or the manager's office when Gil Hodges passed in 1972. Obviously, neither job came his way. Herzog couldn't keep from continuously telling board chairman and stockbroker M. Donald Grant to stop interfering with personnel matters. How we all wish we could have said that to the Simon Legree of Shea.

Number 54

Number of times issued: 14 (4 players, 10 coaches, 1 manager)

Best single season: Mark Clark, 1996 (14–11, 3.43, 142 strikeouts in 212 1/3 innings)

PROGRESSION:	
Player	Years
Sheriff Robinson (coach)	1972
Joe Fitzgerald (coach)	1973–75
Joe Frazier (manager)	1976–77
Frank Howard (coach/manager)	1982–84, 1994–96
Orel Hershiser	1999
Shawn Estes	2002 (to Aug. 15)
Pedro Feliciano	2002–04
Tom Ñieto (coach)	2005–08 (to June 16)
Ken Oberkfell (coach)	2008 (from June 17)
Randy Niemann (coach)	2009–10
Chris Young	2011–12
Pedro Feliciano	2013
Kelly Johnson	2015

Number 55

Goofy-looking former Mets nemesis **Orel Hershiser** (1999) showed Shea fans, at long last, why his teammates had called him "Bulldog" throughout his career. With nearly nothing left in the tank, Hershiser worked awfully hard to win a miraculous 13 games—including the 200th of his career—as a Met in '99. Who could forget Hershiser casually flinging the ball to second base in an improvised hidden ball trick as he was about to be lifted from a key game with the Braves? Or starting that final game of the season that the Mets had to win against powerful Pirates rookie Kris Benson, who hadn't yet been worn down by his wife, Anna. Or Hershiser's gritty 3 1/3 innings out of the pen in epic Game 5 of the NLCS. It was nice for the Mets to have the Bulldog on their side this time.

Shawn Estes (2002) will be remembered forever as the guy who missed Roger Clemens's butt but who humiliated him with a home run when Clemens finally showed his cowardly face at Shea. Disappointing and disowned, Estes went to Cincinnati in August for a few players, including **Pedro Feliciano** (2002–03, 2013). Feliciano honed his craft by pitching for what seemed like a few minutes every night, wearing 39 and then 25, and after two seasons spent entirely on the disabled list for the Yankees, in 55 again as a 2013 Met. Perpetual Pedro was usually good for an out in any uni number.

Standing tall and throwing softly, former Princeton basketballer **Chris Young** ground out five wins and nine losses as a frequently injured bargain-bin starting pitcher in 2011 and 2012. The Mets encountered him most recently as a healthy enemy combatant in the 2015 World Series. The Mets by then had dressed veteran utilityman **Kelly Johnson** (2015) in 55.

Johnson, who came over in a mid-season trade from Atlanta, played six positions, helping turn the Met bench from a liability to a strength, and contributed two home runs in the September put-away sweep of Washington including an 8th-inning shot off Stephen Strassburg to even the score in the series finale.

Joe Frazier had the name of a fighter. **Frank Howard** looked like one. Frazier was GM Joe McDonald's idea of a good manager when he came up from Tidewater to take over the 1976 Mets. With Tom Seaver coming off his third Cy Young, Jerry Koosman winning 20 and making a push for his own Cy Young, and Jon Matlack winning a career high 17 with 6 shutouts—not to mention Dave Kingman launching balls to Astoria (until he got hurt)—the Mets won 86 times while never even remotely

Joe Frazier vs. New York was not a fair fight. The career minor leaguer suffered a TKO in year two as Mets manager in 1977.

contending in the NL East. Frazier's French Army–like collapse the following spring set the stage for the Joe Torre era. Howard, a 6-foot-7 sweetheart, took over when George Bamberger could no longer hack managing in 1983. Hondo played the kids and let the Mets get the last bit of seven seasons of losing out of their system. He then returned to coach for Davey Johnson as if nothing had happened.

Number 55

Number of times issued: 13 (6 players, 6 coaches, 2 managers)

Best single seasons: Orel Hershiser, 1999 (13–12, 4.58 ERA); Kelly Johnson, 2015 (.258, 5 HR, 13 RBIs in 49 games)

PROGRESSION:

Player	Years
Dyar Miller	1980
Bill Monbouquette (coach)	1982
Gene Dusan (coach)	1983
Jeff Kaiser	1993
Bob Apodaca (coach)	1996
Brian McRae	1997–99
Darren Bragg	2001
Edwin Almonte	2003
Dave Racanelli (coach)	2004
Guy Conti (coach)	2006–07
Juan Lopez (coach)	2008 (to Aug. 18)
Luis Ayala	2008 (from Aug. 19)
Jon Switzer	2009
Dave Jauss (coach)	2010
Jon Debus (coach)	2011
Andres Torres	2012
Scott Rice	2013–14
Matt Reynolds	2015 (did not play)

Number 56

A man came right from work to Shea Stadium one Friday night in August 1997, unaware of Steve Phillips's first trade. The Shea patron stared blankly at the lineup posted on the scoreboard and mumbled in a baffled tone, "Who is number 56, and why is he batting first?" That's how **Brian McRae** came to Shea. B-Mac (1997–99) was the son of Hal McRae, the best designated hitter until Paul Molitor put away his glove. B-Mac possessed power from both sides of the plate, plus speed and fielding skills his father couldn't dream of, yet the numbers he put together in his one full season as a Met didn't resonate like dear old Dad's. Fans got on him, B-Mac got on them back—although not in the same league as Hal's famous Kansas City ashtray-tossing tirade—and the McRae era at Shea lasted just 300 games. It would be the longest and most productive stint of any Met to wear 56. Read on.

Darren Bragg, of Waterbury, Connecticut, chose 56 for Lawrence Taylor, a Giant in a different field. Bragg accrued 57 at-bats somewhat quickly in 2001 and then was set adrift just as fast to ply his hand at evil as a Yankee. Don't like to Bragg, but Darren lasted longer and fared better in Queens than the Bronx.

Dyar Miller was the first Met to break out 56. He did it in his breakout season of 1980. Yes, Mets had occasional breakout seasons in this time period; just nobody knew about them. A 1.93 ERA and 1 home run allowed stabilized a rocky bullpen—even with his penchant for allowing hits on other pitchers' accounts. Miller slipped into No. 49 the next year and his breakout broke.

Guy Conti, coordinator of the spring training schedule for five different Mets managers since 2002, was a confidant of Pedro Martinez. Now 73, he was employed as bullpen coach in New York during Pedro's reign, donning 52 (2005, 2008) between years in 56 (2006–07). David Wright told Tim Rohan of the *New York Times* about once missing curfew—now that's a scoop—and when Conti, the minor league field coordinator, called the teenaged third baseman into his office, Wright said that he felt like he had let down his father.

Scott Rice (2013–14) endured 13 minor-league seasons before finally debuting in the majors with the 2013 Mets, getting all the action the lefty ever wanted—a team-leading 73 appearances. His arm was never the same again. **Luis Ayala** racked up nine late-season saves for a Mets club desperately missing Billy Wagner. But he was no stopper, and there was no stopping the bullpen woes of that 2008 club. **Jeff Kaiser** (1993), **Edwin Almonte** (2003), and **Jon Switzer** (2009) all had forgettable months with really bad teams.

Chase Utley's leg-breaking dirty slide in the 2015 National League Championship Series knocked Ruben Tejada out of action and **Matt Reynolds** into the major leagues for the first time. The infielder, who had spent the entire 2015 season with Class AAA Las Vegas and wasn't even on the 40-man roster, had a rare opportunity to get a first taste of play in the postseason, but fortunately, no more emergencies arose, making him a most unusual phantom Met.

Number 56

Number of times issued: 17 (9 players, 7 coaches, 1 DNP)

Best single seasons: Brian McRae, 1998 (.264/.360/.462, 21 HR, 79 RBIs, 20 stolen bases); Dyar Miller, 1980 (1–2, 1.93 ERA, 1 save, 28 strikeouts in 42 innings); Scott Rice, 2013 (4–5, 3.71 ERA in 73 games)

Number 57

PROGRESSION:	
Player	Years
Bobby Floyd (coach)	1997
Tom Robson (coach)	2002
Jason Roach	2003
Eric Valent	2004–05
John Santana	2008–12
Lamar Johnson (coach)	2014
Kevin Long (coach)	2015

If he wasn't one in a million, **Johan Santana** was one in 8,020. That's how many games the Mets went without a no-hitter before the Venezuelan lefty blanked the St. Louis Cardinals in an exhaustingly tense and hard-fought, five-walk, eight-strikeout, 134-pitch effort on June 1, 2012, that illustrated why Santana was so special: His determination could be even more impressive than his stuff, and his stuff—just ask David Freese—was mighty impressive.

Like Frank Viola eighteen years prior, Santana was a Cy Young award winning lefty acquired from Minnesota in a multiplayer deal and signed to an extravagant multiyear deal. Santana won 16 games and the NL ERA

Dan Carubia

Johan Santana did all he could to try to bring the postseason back to Flushing. He did finally end the no-hit drought.

title in 2008 and never pitched worse than a 3.13 ERA. But shoulder woes cost him all of 2011 and despite the glory of the no-hitter, he appeared in just 10 major league games afterward. While it's tempting to draw a straight line from those 134 max-effort pitches, they're only a drop in a long career of a pitcher who went hard all the time.

Until Santana came along the most historic single-game effort by a Met 57 belonged to **Eric Valent**, a reserve outfielder who hit for the cycle in Montreal's Stade Olympique on July 29, 2004.

Valent, batting seventh—ahead of David Wright!—hit a speaker with his high fly for a ground-rule home run. His 7th-inning triple got him the cycle, one of two three-baggers he had all year. That was enough to tie for the team lead. (Lest ye forget, second baseman Jose Reyes was hurt most of 2004.) The next year Valent couldn't get on track, and 57 was 86ed.

Jason Roach was brought up three times in 2003 and was pummeled twice. **Kevin Long** was imported from the Yankees as hitting coach in 2015 and seemed to steady old pupil Curtis Granderson. Hitting coaches often get too much blame when a team stops hitting, so three long overdue cheers for when a ballclub starts (finally!) knocking the ball around the yard.

Number 57

Number of times issued: 7 (3 players, 4 coaches)

Best single seasons: Johan Santana, 2008 (16-7, 2.53); Eric Valent, 2004 (.267/.337/.481, 13 HR, 34 RBIs)

Number 58

PROGRESSION:

Player	Years
Luis Rosado	1980
Anderson Garcia	2006 (did not play)
Sandy Alomar Sr. (coach)	2008–09
Ken Oberkfell (coach)	2011
Jenrry Mejia	2013–15

Once removed from an aggressive promotion as a twenty-year-old wearing No. 32 in 2010 (and a post-surgical return in those digits in 2012), **Jenrry Mejia** fashioned a tragedy of a career that included intermittent highs as a starter and erstwhile closer wearing 58, only to see it obliterated by three suspensions for steroid use within a year. The last, announced in February of 2016, resulted in a lifetime ban from baseball. The demonstrative, compactly built right-hander rung up 28 saves in 2014. Like Mejia, **Luis Rosado** (1980), a catcher by trade and the only other Met to appear in a game wearing that number, didn't get a hit—leaving 58 in a serious 0-for-32 hole.

Number 58

Number of times issued: 5 (2 players, 2 coaches 1 DNP)

Number 59

PROGRESSION:

Player	Years
Ed Lynch	1980
Alay Soler	2006 (to July 3)
Guillermo Mota	2006 (from Aug. 22)–2007
Dan Warthen (coach)	2008–15

This number brings out the GM, the defector, and the cheater.

Guillermo Mota would have been easier to forgive if he'd struck out Scott Spiezio in Game 2 of the 2006 NLCS, or if Shawn Green had come down with Spiezio's deep drive. That series-changing moment was one of the few failures on Mota's Mets résumé . . . at least until his drug test results were made public a few weeks later. Pre-Mets, Mota was best known for a long-simmering tangle with Mike Piazza during spring-training games in 2002 and again in 2003. The former ended with Piazza throttling Mota at the Vero Beach bullpen after he took a Mota fastball off the hip; in 2003 Mota came inside once then plunked Piazza on the shoulder, sending the usually sedate slugger into a seething rage: Mota threw his glove at a charging Piazza before cowardly retreating to the dugout pursued by a half-dozen bloodthirsty Mets (in citrusy orange spring jerseys). Piazza reportedly stalked Mota through the visiting clubhouse in Port St. Lucie, but never found him.

Alay Soler (2006) started his major league career by walking the first three Phillies he faced, allowing a hit to the next batter, and then being victimized by an error that scored two runs. He persevered and wound up having a marvelous debut. Soler didn't get the win, but the Mets did. He won twice on the ensuing road trip from heaven, including a rare complete game in the Rick Peterson world. Then Soler, who'd risked all to defect from Cuba, couldn't get outs and found himself back in the minors. Despite a million Mets mound questions in spring training 2007, he was one of the first guys cut.

Ed Lynch wound up a general manager with the Cubs, but his first major league win came against Chicago on Senior Citizen's Day before a Saturday throng of 7,259 in 1980. He even picked up his first major league hit that day. Acquired a year earlier as the prospect portion of the Willie Montanez deal with Texas (Mike Jorgensen was the player part), Lynch would slip off 59 for lower numbers and stick around to see other prospects prosper around him.

He lacked the reputation and buttoned-up jacket of predecessor Rick Peterson, but **Dan Warthen** (2008–15) has lasted twice as long as Mets pitching coach and heads into 2016 as the senior member of the on-field staff. Some analysts are crediting his longevity to his ability to teach a signature pitch—the Dan Warthen Slider—that spins less, travels faster, and makes secondary offerings look better, a phenomenon that at least partly explains the success of homegrown hurlers like Jacob deGrom and Hansel Robles. Warthen put aside 59 in order to accommodate new pitching pupil **Antonio Bastardo** in 2016.

Number 59

Number of time issued: 5 (4 players, 1 coach)

Best single season: Guillermo Mota, 2006 (3–0, 1.00 ERA, 19 strikeouts in 18 innings)

PROGRESSION:	
Player	Years
Scott Schoeneweis	2007
Jon Rauch	2012

Number 60

When Chad Bradford escaped New York to Baltimore and the market for veteran brand-name relievers went kerflooey along with him, the Mets abruptly reached into their pockets to be sure they didn't miss **Scott Schoeneweis** (2007–08). That was their second mistake. The lefty with the three-year deal proved remarkably unreliable, although he did wind up with a pair of late-season saves when Billy Wagner collapsed. He actually found ways to end the 2007 and 2008 seasons worse than the Mets. In October 2007 Schoeneweis was outed for receiving shipments of steroids when he was with the White Sox in 2003–04. The next fall he took the loss in the last game at Shea and was subsequently (and mercifully) traded.

By the time the tattooed giant **Jon Rauch** came along in 2012 fans expected such veteran relievers to disappoint them. They mixed it up with him a few times on Twitter but Rauch wasn't as bad as he was tall. Then again, he was really tall.

PROGRESSION:	
Player	Years
Jesse Orosco	1979
Mario Ramirez	1980
Jeff Duncan	2003
Chan Ho Park	2007
Livan Hernandez	2009
Jack Egbert	2012
Dana Eveland	2014

Number 61

By the time **Livan Hernandez** joined the Mets as their fifth starter in 2009, he already played for seven other big-league clubs, been a professional in his native Cuba, and though listed at just thirty-four-years-old, was about as battle-scarred as they came. Relying on signature unpredictability and a wide repertoire of pitches, he won five of his first six decisions before faltering in the dog days of August and drawing his release. Hernandez would play for another three clubs before retiring for good following 2012, wearing No. 61 at every stop.

Jesse Orosco wore 61 for only one day, but he did the undoable. He got the last out in a game for the 1979 Mets. This didn't happen often. On April 5 that year, with two outs in the bottom of the 9th, and Dwight Bernard knocked out of a mop-up situation at packed Wrigley Field on Opening Day, Orosco induced his lone batter, Bill Buckner, to fly out. It was the first of his record 1,252 appearances in the majors. Outfitted in 47 and then sent to the minors, Orosco would return and transform into one of the greatest relievers the franchise has seen.

Journeyman lefty **Dana Eveland** hopped aboard in mid-2014, pitching quite well in a low-pressure role.

While the Mets suffered through Mike Piazza's groin injury in May 2003, the already depleted club reached all the way to Class AA and made **Jeff Duncan**'s life. The twenty-four-year-old outfielder had two hits in his first start, and the team was bad enough and banged-up enough that he played in 56 games despite the fact that he couldn't hit. When Mets continued getting hurt the next year, the smooth-fielding Duncan was back at Shea wearing No. 10, but his .067 average assured there would be no third invitation.

Chan Ho Park was a subplot throughout 2007 spring training, but he dropped out of New York's plans like a stone after getting rocked the second time through the order in his only start. **Mario Ramirez** (1980) spent almost as little time in 61 as Park, but he came back to see further action at No. 3. **Jack Egbert** went quietest of all. His entire Mets career consisted of two-thirds of an inning. It was a perfect two-thirds, though, so he's got that going for him.

Number 61

Number of times issued: 7 (7 players)

Best single season: Livan Hernandez, 2009 (7-9, 4.68)

PROGRESSION:	
Player	Years
Hubie Brooks	1980
Juan Lopez (coach)	2008
Elvin Ramirez	2012
Erik Goeddel	2014–2015

Number 62

For a number closely associated with the Mets, there are few Mets closely associated with 62.

There's **Erik Goeddel** (2014–15), who parlayed some light mop-up duty into becoming probably the least recognized participant in the 2015 postseason (sure looked like Howie Kendrick recognized his fastball, however). **Elvin Ramirez** had stuff intriguing enough to get Rule 5ed out of the Mets system by the Nationals, but they gave him back. The Mets gave him to Anaheim after a rough few outings as a 2014 rookie.

Fresh off the farm, **Hubie Brooks** came to the majors wearing 62. Fittingly, the Mets had been searching for a quality third baseman since '62. Hubie would do quite nicely. Brooks wore the highest number in Mets history until Turk Wendell hopped over the chalk in No. 99. "It was the only uniform they had when I came up, so I had to take it," Brooks told the *New York Times*. "I'm kind of superstitious, so I told [equipment manager Herb Norman] I'd take any number under 62." They gave him 39. He received a respectful 7 the next spring.

Hubie's arrival signaled a shift from the jokes about the multitude of mediocre Mets at the position to a succession of third baseman who could hit, field, and lead, each seemingly better than the last.

Number 63

Chris Schwinden got a few turns in the rotation as the 2011 and 2012 Mets cycled through the remnants of their near-ready Class AAA starters.

Schwinden then pedaled through a tour de France of DFAs: from the Mets to Toronto, Toronto to Cleveland, Cleveland to New York (the Yankees!), then back to the Mets—all within a few weeks in 2012, all without getting another taste of big league play. Cheers to the Lance Armstrong of the waiver wire.

Number 64
Pity **Akeel Morris** (2015). With a wiped bullpen requiring fresh arms, the Mets abruptly yanked the twenty-two-year-old all the way from Class A St. Lucie. He left days later with an ERA (67.50) even higher than his lofty uni number, but with a promotion to Class AA. Like a stray cow wandering the pasture, paunchy journeyman righthander **Elmer Dessens** (2009–10) sauntered onto and off of the Mets over the course of two summers, providing grass-fed relief of R. A. Dickey and USDA Choice setting up of Francisco Rodriguez.

PROGRESSION:	
Player	Years
Elmer Dessens	2009-10
Akeel Morris	2015

Number 66
Bulldoggish lefty **Josh Edgin** (2012–14) is the only member of this exclusive club. He's averaged nearly a strikeout per inning over parts of three seasons, but sat out 2015 to join the more populous Tommy John club.

Number 68
All hail the pioneering **Dario Alvarez** (2014–15)—the first 68, the first Dario, and the first Alvarez in club history.

Number 70
As we learned discussing 56s, the fastest route to the Mets—although the hardly the most desirable—just might be breaking one of Ruben Tejada's bones. When the shortstop broke a fibula in 2013, the Mets reached all the way to Class AA Binghamton for all-glove, light-stick shortstop **Wilfredo Tovar**, issuing him the same number he'd worn as a freshman invitee to spring training that year. Tovar stroked a game-winning RBI single in his debut, but didn't do much else, even in a second September look-see in 2014. When Tejada went down again, thanks to Chase Utley, Tovar missed the chance to be on the 2015 postseason roster due to a concussion. The Mets took him off the 40-man roster after the World Series and he joined the Twins.

Number 71

Reliever **Gonzalez Germen** (2013–14) had strikeout stuff—and some walk stuff, and a little too much home-run stuff, so the Mets eventually let him go. Aside from pioneering the No. 71 jersey, Germen's claim to fame was being the corresponding roster move for the debut of 2014 Rookie of the Year Jacob deGrom.

Number 72

Reliever **Carlos Torres** obligingly surrendered his customary No. 52 upon the 2015 acquisition of Yoenis Cespedes, but being the Mets' first-and-only 72 appeared to do him little good. He was 16–15, 3.32 in the former, and 1–2, 7.31 in the latter. Though 72 is destined to be remembered when our children's children relive the Torres-to-Murphy-to-Torres "hacky-sack" play (Google it).

PROGRESSION:	
Player	Years
Kenny Rogers	1999
Ricardo Rincon	2008
Robert Carson	2012–13

Number 73

Kenny Rogers, "The Gambler," came a-riding in from the west to save the day for the '99 Mets. Save the day? Yes. Take a look at his 12 starts with the Mets that year.

Rogers led the Mets in complete games and won his first five decisions as the team went 10–2 in his starts. A sixth win was denied him when he was injured a few outs shy of qualifying. With everyone assuming the Mets were finished the last weekend of the season, Rogers struck out 10—more than in his three previous starts combined—and the Mets won in extra innings and somehow ended up in the 11th inning of the NLCS with a chance to force a seventh game.

Maybe this is where we should mention he had some control issues and was not at his best pitching for New York teams in the postseason. The Gambler, whose uniform said 73 because the number he wore in every city except New York was retired for Casey Stengel (37), was back in the American League in his accustomed digits the following spring. Know when to fold 'em. That's what happened to the other two 73s—lefty relievers **Ricardo Rincon** (an unanswered Hail Mary in 2008) and **Robert Carson** (who gave out home runs like Johnny Carson gave out jokes: nightly).

Number 75

Smarting from a second straight faltering finish in 2008—a collapse all the more tragic as it presaged the forthcoming rubble of both Shea Stadium and the U.S. economy—the Mets hamfistedly made it a point to place nearly all the blame on their bullpen and set out on a making a show of reckless offseason moves highlighted by an eight-figure contract to free-agent closer **Francisco Rodriguez** of the Angels. Never mind the club had other needs—a lineup, starting pitching, a manager, and a bench among them—and was still paying millions for an unfulfilled multiyear deal to the previous import closer, Billy Wagner.

Becoming the club's first-and-only 75 by reversing his customary 57 (belonging to Johan Santana), K-Rod racked up 83 saves and an All-Star appearance over his first two-and-a-half years. And he actually made you miss Wagner's decorum. Rodriguez had ugly

Dan Carubia

Francisco Rodriguez came to the Mets too late to help them contend.

encounters with coaches, staff, and even his own family, the latter resulting in an arrest and detainment at Citi Field. In the meantime it was clear that Rodriguez was an impossible luxury for a bereft club terrified of vesting option in his contract. He was tossed off to Milwaukee a few weeks before Carlos Beltran was traded in 2011.

Number 77

After Sandy Alderson and his team were summoned to begin a gut renovation of the financially ruined Mets in 2010, his first purchase, announced at the winter meetings in Florida that year, was a new battery: Catcher Ronny Paulino and reliever **D. J. Carrasco**. It was a Triple A battery.

Things would get better for Alderson and the Mets, but not for Carrasco, who pitched to a 6.11 ERA as a Met, including a rare game-losing walk-off balk. In May of 2012, Carrasco was ejected for hitting Milwaukee's Ryan Braun with a pitch following a home run surrendered to the previous hitter. He never came back.

Number 99

Let's skip right to the end, and what an ending! **Turk Wendell** (1997–99) said he chose 99 because 13 was already gone. A lot of big numbers were doled out the day he got to Shea.

The August 8, 1997, trade between the Mets and Cubs sent away advanced-digit wearer Mark Clark (54), one-day 51 Lance Johnson, plus the unadventurous—except when it came to hiding his steroids stash—Manny Alexander (6); in return came Mel Rojas (51), Brian McRae (56), and Wendell in the high-numbers deal of the century for the Mets. Wendell, somewhat dismissed at the time of the trade, turned out to be the most significant player who changed places that day.

Wendell was a man of the people, befriending everyone he came in contact with at Shea and everywhere else. He pumped his fist, slammed the rosin bag, leapt over baselines, and brushed his teeth between innings (though he cut down on in-game brushing after a baseball card appeared with him in the act). Turk got lost hunting mountain lions and wore a necklace of turkey teeth that could have severed his jugular. Behind all that flakiness, though, he worked hard and was willing to do anything within the rules to win, just as it was desire and not sideshows that marked the careers of Tug McGraw and Roger McDowell, the Mets relievers Wendell so vividly brings to mind.

Wendell was the first Met to appear in 80 games in 1999 (the year prior he set a club record by pitching in 9 successive games). His career ERA as a Met was a terrific 3.34 over an astonishing 285 games in four-plus seasons. His rubber arm fell off from a million sliders too many after he was traded to Philadelphia, but he was one Phillie it was hard to root against. And the most memorable 99 this side of Gretzky.

Numbers Not Off Their Backs

Now that we've gone through every uniform (positive) number—and consequently every player—in Mets history, here's ten other Mets numbers to jam into your brain.

1. No-hitter. Thanks, Johan. It sure does beat 0.
2. World championships. (May you be reading this some day in the future and laugh ironically because, of course, the Mets have won titles in multiples of 2. May civilization last this long.)
3. Mets who have finished second in National League MVP voting: Tom Seaver 1969, Keith Hernandez 1984, and Darryl Strawberry 1988.
4. Seasons of 20 wins by Tom Seaver.

5. Strikeouts in a game. The platinum sombrero has been worn by four free-swinging Mets: Ron Swoboda (twice), Frank Taveras, Dave Kingman, and Ryan Thompson.

6. Hits and runs by Edgardo Alfonzo at the Astrodome on August 30, 1999; Alfonzo set one-game Mets records in those categories and for total bases (16).

7. Times Mets pitchers have lost 20 games in a season: Roger Craig and Al Jackson twice, Jack Fisher, Tracy Stallard, and Jerry Koosman.

8. Strikeouts in a row to start a game by Jacob deGrom against the Marlins on September 16, 2014. It set the team mark and tied the major league record from the beginning of a game. It ended two batters short of Tom Seaver's all-time mark of 10 straight Ks in a game, set in 1970.

9. Consecutive hits by Jose Vizcaino in 1996 and John Olerud in 1998.

10. Runs scored in the eighth inning against Atlanta on Fireworks Night 2000, erasing an 8–1 deficit and culminating with a three-run home run by Mike Piazza.

#0–00: LESS THAN ZERO

#0

Some would say the career of Rey Ordoñez was a big, fat zero. That isn't true. Only the first two years of it were. Ordoñez debuted as 0 on April Fools' Day, 1996, in an Opening Day downpour at Shea Stadium. He gunned down a runner at the plate from his knees in left field as the Mets staged a comeback from 6–0 down against the Cardinals. Ordoñez wowed the crowd with his remarkable range, popup slides, and bullet throws. His bat work, however, left a lot to be desired. Ordoñez hit .257—high for him—but he swung at everything, walking just 22 times with a mere 10 unintentional bases on balls in 151 games. He finished fifth in the Rookie of the Year balloting, but a *Newsday* scribe said anyone who voted for Ordoñez, "just isn't paying attention."

Rey-Rey's attention drifted even more in 1997. He lost playing time to Manny Alexander after breaking a bone on his glove hand diving for a ball. After Alexander was traded,

Going with Zero as a rookie summed up Rey Ordonez's offense, but his "D" had people talking.

Luis Lopez saw plenty of time at short. Ordoñez homered on September 2—his only one of the year—and proceeded to go 0-for-37, breaking the thirty-five-year-old franchise mark for position players set by original Met Don Zimmer and tied by Tommie Agee in 1968 (0-for-34). Ordoñez fell just shy of pitcher Randy Tate's 0-for-41 set in his immortal hitless season of '75. The shortstop finished the year at .216, reaching base a quarter of the time while posting an unfathomable .256 slugging percentage.

With Ozzie Smith retired, Ordoñez was the best-fielding shortstop in the league, and he won the first of three consecutive Gold Gloves in 1997. If he'd played in most other eras, when shortstops were expected to field everything and keep the game moving with unproductive at-bats, there'd have been few complaints. But now there was Jeter—a rookie the same year as Ordoñez—and A-Rod, already a batting champ in Seattle; plus this kid in Boston named Nomar, who seemed like quite the hitter. Ordoñez still used a translator, but he had to know that the expectations at the position were getting higher.

So Ordoñez changed numbers. He took 10 in spring training in 1998, stating, "I want to be more than nothing." Oh, he's that. And more.

Outfielder **Terry McDaniel** was the first 0 in franchise history. He debuted on August 30, 1991, and disappeared into nothing just a month later.

Omar Quintanilla, a fringy middle-infield reserve whose disappearances and reappearances had already resulted in two uni-number assignments (6 and then, 3) arrived in Metland a third time in 2014 and took a number that represented the "0" in Omar. Remarkably, Quintanilla's six hits including one double in 29 at-bats as a zero was the exact same line (.207) as McDaniel had in the uniform in 1991. Oh, yeah.

Number 0

Number of times issued: 3

Best single season: Rey Ordoñez, 1996 (.257/.289/.303, 1 HR, 30 RBIs);

Number 00

PROGRESSION:	
Player	Years
Tony Clark	2003 (to June 5)

According to numerologists, zero is the number of nothingness and potentiality. **Tony Clark** asked for a double dose.

Clark arrived in 2003 having worn 17 and 44 as Tony the Tiger before switching to 22 for what became a down year with the Red Sox in 2002. Clark was one of several free agents in camp, but unlike Tom Glavine and Mike Stanton, Clark had to earn his spot. General manager Steve Phillips invited anyone who could walk to spring training, hoping to catch lightning in a bottle. With such a big group in camp, Clark was offered the choice of 00 or 88. He said, "I didn't want to hear any wide-receiver jokes." Instead, he heard a lot of Mr. Met jokes.

When one group too many of school kids asked why he had Mr. Met's number, Clark switched to 52 on June 5. He homered his first time up in the new number. Ten of Clark's 16 homers came following the switch, but none came after Cliff Floyd left the lineup in mid-August. The powerless, punchless Mets stunk up the joint.

Tony Clark vs. Mr. Met: Big Shoes to Fill

Tony Clark, meet Mr. Met. For the chilly opening day festivities on March 31, 2003, the Mets had two 00s: Clark, the backup first baseman, and the team's longtime mascot, Mr. Met. How awkward.

At 6-foot-10, Mr. Met stood just three inches taller than Clark, but he towered over his adversary in so many ways. Mr. Met had first appeared on the cover of the 1963 yearbook in cartoon form, and a year later a man dressed as the mascot, a baseball first, roamed the stands at new Shea Stadium. It was a much more primitive—and smaller—head that Dan Reilly cavorted around in than today's noggin, but the kids loved Mr. Met right off the bat. And since he was popular and beloved, it only made sense that M. Donald Grant put the kibosh on it. Mr. Met was rarely seen through the dwindling days of the deRoulet regime—why bother when there's Mettle the Mule! And disappeared completely when Doubleday and Wilpon took over.

Mr. Met emerged from hiding to make a buck. A venture with Nickelodeon turned Shea into an amusement park beyond right field in 1994. Mr. Met returned for good with a state-of-the-art head and sporting 00 on his pinstripe uniform. It may have been cheesy, but at least someone was having fun as the screeches of kids could be heard above the agony on the field. Kids left the amusement park after the game to run the bases at Shea on certain Sundays.

Mr. Met is all about gallantry, fun, and double zero.

The strike brought a premature end to Nick and the Mets' plans, but Mr. Met stuck around. He got new wardrobes as the Mets broke out new uni after new uni. When it rained he wore a yellow slicker and matching cap not unlike the Gorton's Fisherman of the Islanders' brief logo disaster.

Mr. Met got higher profile, popping up in commercials and TV guest spots, showing his head at civic functions and schools, and appearing at the odd birthday party. In 2013, his other half, Mrs. Met, started showing up again. Once a redhead known as Lady Met, her long disappearance is a mystery best-left unsolved. She too wears 00, by the way.

Back in 2003, Mr. Met—as is his way—didn't say anything when Clark came along and took his number, but Clark knew when he was licked. The night after a long rain delay perhaps gave him time to think, Clark switched to 52. Using the diplomacy necessary as future head of the Players Association, Clark acquiesced. "Mr. Met had 00 long before I got here, and he'll be here long after I leave," Clark told John Rowe of the Bergen Record. "It's his to keep."

5, 7, 15, 17, 18: THE JEFF MCKNIGHTMARE

No player in Mets history has worn as many uniform numbers as Jeff McKnight. Over a sporadic four-year stint with the Mets, the bespectacled utility man suited up in an amazin' five different uniform numbers. His story, naturally, is one of persistence and versatility.

Jefferson Alan "Moon" McKnight had a long journey into Mets history. Born on February 18, 1963 in Conway, Arkansas, McKnight, the switch-hitting son of former Cubs utility man Jim McKnight, was selected by the Mets in the second round of the January 1983 free-agent draft.

One of the five numbers worn by Jeff McKnight as a Met.

He spent the next six and a half years in the Mets farm system, developing into the kind of player who does many things adequately and none particularly well. McKnight could—and did—play all nine positions as a minor leaguer, yet he lacked the power, speed, and fielding skill to project as a big league starter at any of them. Never even invited to major league camp, McKnight by 1987 had settled into a reserve role for AAA Tidewater, and it appeared his chances for success in the big leagues were slim.

Then came 1989. The Mets' bid to repeat as Eastern Division champions ran off the tracks early: Gary Carter and Keith Hernandez hit the disabled list within a week of one another in May. And when starting second baseman Tim Teufel sprained an ankle while jogging outside Wrigley Field on June 5, McKnight, who had logged 1,795 minor league at-bats to that point, finally got the call. The following day, pinch hitting from the left side for Roger McDowell, in the stadium his father played in, McKnight drove a 2–1 delivery from Calvin Schiraldi into left field for a single.

McKnight was wearing No. 15 then. He would see action in another five games, including two starts, before being optioned to Tidewater on June 18 when Teufel returned to active duty.

By all rights the story could have ended then and there. McKnight was not called back up when rosters expanded in September, and like dozens of minor-league vets at similar stages in their careers, he was cut from the 40-man roster following the season.

McKnight signed a minor-league deal with the Orioles that December, and spent the next two years as a part-time Orioles backup and DH, becoming one of thirty-one second basemen to play alongside Cal Ripken during the Iron Man's consecutive-games streak. Non-tendered by Baltimore following the 1991 season, McKnight again caught on with the Mets, who offered him a non-roster invitation to spring training in 1992.

This time, he made the team, wearing No. 5 (Kevin Elster had 15 at that time and 13—McKnight's uni number with the O's—belonged then to Rodney McCray). McKnight spent all of April and most of August and September with the Mets that year. McKnight again had to fight for an Opening-Day job—and won it—in 1993 despite seeing his No. 5 issued to hotshot rookie Jeromy Burnitz, who'd debut later that season. McKnight instead opened 1993 in No. 7 but changed jerseys on May 22 when manager Jeff Torborg and his staff were fired. Dallas Green's new coach, Bobby Wine, wanted No. 7 and got it. McKnight switched to 17; but for the first time as Met, he spent an entire year without a visit to the minors. It may have helped that manager Green was a former teammate of McKnight's father Jim when they were minor leaguers, but McKnight earned his keep, hitting .322 as the club's primary left-handed pinch-hitter.

Once again in 1994, McKnight found himself—and his number—pushed aside for a higher profile teammate. This time it was pitcher Bret Saberhagen, who was unhappy with the No. 18 issued him in 1993 and began '94 in McKnight's 17. Accepting the lot of the twenty-fifth man, McKnight acquiesced and took No. 18. It proved to be a difficult year for McKnight. He learned during spring training that his father had been killed in a car accident in Arkansas. Struggling with a .143 average in June, McKnight went onto the disabled list with a strained rib cage. The *Bergen Record* gave him a midseason grade of F, noting his "only value to the Mets [is that] he's a Bob Dylan fan."

Newspapers speculated that summer that the Mets had "disabled" McKnight merely to create roster space artificially ("You can believe what you want to believe," freewheelin' Jeff told writers). But the Mets hadn't stopped jerking him around. Sent to a Norfolk rehab assignment in July, McKnight was recalled to the majors on August 11 while the team sent its promising young players—Burnitz and Fernando Viña—to AAA so they could continue playing in the event of a strike. That night in Philadelphia, in the top of the 12th inning of a 1–1 game, McKnight entered as a pinch hitter for Eric Gunderson and singled off Tom Edens, only to be thrown out trying to stretch it into a double. The Phillies won the game in the bottom of the

12th, the players struck as threatened at midnight, and Jeff McKnight never played another major league game.

McKnight returned home to Arkansas, and worked at a television station. On March 1, 2015, he lost a ten-year battle with leukemia at age fifty-two. His New York legacy was 4 home runs, 28 RBIs, a .250 average, and a record that might never be broken: five different Mets uniform numbers.

The Three-Number Club

If Jeff McKnight leads the lineup of multiple-number wearing Mets, Ed Lynch is its starting pitcher.

Fans best remember Lynch for wearing No. 36—his digits for 145 of his 167 career games with the Mets. But his 22 other appearances were divided among three numbers on his back during 1980 and 1981.

Lynch owes much of his number collection, indirectly, to Craig Swan, the veteran Mets pitcher whose breakdowns over the tail end of his career provided Lynch with his first three opportunities—and first three uni numbers. Shoulder trouble suffered by Swan in late August of 1980 required the Mets to summon Lynch while on a West Coast trip. Like several Mets call-ups in 1980, Lynch was initially issued a high number (59) for his debut appearance in San Francisco. But Lynch was wearing No. 35 shortly after the Mets returned home to Shea.

In April of 1981, Lynch reappeared in No. 35 after Swan was taken out of action by his own teammate: attempting to catch Tim Raines stealing second in the first inning, catcher Ron Hodges's throw drilled Swan in the back, breaking one of Swan's ribs (needless to say, Raines was safe; he eventually scored to hand Swan an especially hard-luck loss). Lynch was sent back to Tidewater shortly after Swan was reactivated, mere days before a two-month strike interrupted the season. Baseball resumed anew in August, but Swan's shoulder was only older and rustier, and Lynch was back; only this time, he was wearing No. 34. That's because Randy Jones, the former All-Star whose 35 jersey would one day be retired by the Padres, apparently decided during the strike to take back his familiar number (Jones was in 25 previously).

Lynch finally won a roster spot on his own ability in 1982 and remained a good Mets soldier until 1986, in his familiar No. 36.

Utility infielder Kevin Collins, like Lynch, wore four different Mets numbers only to be traded months before the Mets won a world championship. Collins wore one number for each truncated visit with the Mets over four seasons. He debuted in 1965 as No. 10, returned for a September call-up in

1967 as 19, spent four months wearing No. 16 in 1968, and finally inherited Jerry Buchek's former No. 1 in 1969 before becoming outbound freight in the famous Donn Clendenon trade with Montreal.

A hard-nosed, left-handed-hitting infielder out of Springfield, Massachusetts, Collins's path to a full-time job with the Mets was blocked by Bud Harrelson. Collins fashioned himself into a scrappy reserve who by all accounts was a terrific teammate. This was evident in the reaction of his mates when Collins was knocked onto his back at the Astrodome on a jaw-breaking hard slide into third base by Doug Rader in 1968. Coach Joe Pignatano, outfielder Tommie Agee, and pitcher Don Cardwell, who socked Rader above the eye, rushed to his aid and a bench-clearing brawl was on. The scrappy Collins recalled he couldn't participate: He was staring at the Astrodome roof in a daze.

From the Office of McKnight, Lynch, and Collins

Ron Darling switched numbers when he felt like it. Roger Craig changed jerseys to change his luck. But the majority of Mets triple threats were bit players who took what they were given and/or assembled their jersey collection on the way to establishing an identity.

Typical of the below list is Jason Phillips, the backup catcher who suited up in Nos. 7, 26, and 23—and technically, at least, in No. 3. Phillips was called up to Mets from AA Binghamton in May of 2001 due to a player shortage occurring when reliever Tom Martin went down with a sudden injury and outfielder Darryl Hamilton was a day short of returning from the disabled list. Phillips then was issued a jersey, No. 3, but did not appear in a game before being sent back down when Hamilton returned the next day. Later that year, Phillips made his "official" Mets debut in No. 26—No. 3 had in the meantime been issued to reserve backstop Vance Wilson. No. 26 was issued to Marco Scutaro prior to Phillips's September call-up of 2002, so Phillips instead wore No. 7. But in the spring of 2003, the Mets reserved No. 7 for superstar-in-waiting Jose Reyes and told Phillips to take No. 23 instead. That would be his number for the remainder of his Mets career.

Following is a list of membership in the Mets' exclusive three-number club, through 2015:

Name	Numbers Worn
Jeff McKnight	5, 7, 15, 17, 18
Kevin Collins	1, 10, 16, 19
Ed Lynch	34, 35, 36, 59
Darrel Sutherland	43, 45, 47
Cleon Jones	34, 12, 21

Name	Numbers Worn
John Stephenson	12, 19, 49
Jim Hickman	6, 9, 27
Mike Jorgensen	10, 16, 22
Hank Webb	22, 29, 30
Hubie Brooks	62, 39, 7
Clint Hurdle	7, 13, 33
Chuck Carr	1, 7, 21
Kevin Elster	2, 15, 21
Charlie O'Brien	5, 22, 33
Ron Darling	12, 15, 44
Jason Phillips	7, 23, 26
David Cone	16, 17, 44
Jae Seo	40, 38, 26
Roger Craig	13, 36, 38
Lee Mazzilli	12, 16, 13
Pedro Feliciano	55, 39, 25
Mike DiFelice	6, 33, 9
Marlon Anderson	18, 23, 9
Ramon Martinez	22, 26, 6
Robinson Cancel	4, 40, 29
Anderson Hernandez	1, 4, 11
Omar Quintanilla	6, 3, 0

COMPLETE NUMERICAL ROSTER

Following is an alphabetical list of all Mets players and their uniform numbers through 2015. An asterisk (*) indicates that the player was assigned that number but did not appear in a game while wearing it.

A

David Aardsma (2013)	30
Don Aase (1989)	15, 49
Kurt Abbott (2000)	20
Bobby Abreu (2014)	53
Juan Acevedo (1997)	39
Manny Acosta (2010–12)	36, 46
Jon Adkins (2007)	39
Benny Agbayani (1998–2001)	39, 50
Tommie Agee (1968–72)	20
Chris Aguila (2008)	29
Rick Aguilera (1985–89)	38, 15
Jack Aker (1974)	22
Manny Alexander (1997)	6
Edgardo Alfonzo (1995–2002)	13
Neil Allen (1979–83)	46, 16
Jermaine Allensworth (1998–99)	46, 23
Bill Almon (1980, 1987)	25, 2
Edwin Almonte (2003)	57
Roberto Alomar (2002–03)	12
Sandy Alomar Jr. (2007)	19, 28
Sandy Alomar (1967)	5
Jesus Alou (1975)	23
Moises Alou (2007–08)	18
George Altman (1964)	2

Luis Alvarado (1977)	19
Dario Alvarez (2014–15)	68
Chip Ambres (2007)	36
Craig Anderson (1962–64)	20, 29
Jason Anderson (2003)	17
Marlon Anderson (2005, 2007–08)	18, 23
Rick Anderson (1986)	32
Rick Ankiel (2013)	16
Bob Apodaca (1973–77)	34
Kevin Appier (2001)	17
Joaquin Arias (2010)	12
Tony Armas (2008)	44
Jerry Arrigo (1966)	34
Richie Ashburn (1962)	1
Tucker Ashford (1983)	11
Bob Aspromonte (1971)	2
Pedro Astacio (2002–03)	34
Scott Atchison (2013)	50
Benny Ayala (1974, 1976)	18
Luis Ayala (2008)	56
Manny Aybar (2005)	36

B

Wally Backman (1980–88)	28, 6
Mike Bacsik (2002–03)	33
Carlos Baerga (1996–98)	6, 8
Kevin Baez (1990, 1992–93)	36, 1
Bob Bailor (1981–83)	4
Billy Baldwin (1976)	21
James Baldwin (2004)	38
Rick Baldwin (1975–77)	45

Brian Bannister (2006)	40
Rod Barajas (2010)	21
Lute Barnes (1972–73)	1
Jeff Barry (1995)	18
Kevin Bass (1992)	21
Miguel Batista (2011, 2012)	47
Ed Bauta (1963–64)	38
Mike Baxter (2011–13)	23
Jason Bay (2010–12)	44
Billy Beane (1984, 1985)	43, 35
Larry Bearnarth (1963–66)	31
Pedro Beato (2011, 2012)	27
Blaine Beatty (1989, 1991)	38
Jim Beauchamp (1972–1973)	24, 5
Rich Becker (1998)	6
Derek Bell (2000)	16
Gus Bell (1962)	3
Heath Bell (2004–06)	19
Jay Bell (2003)	44
Carlos Beltran (2005–11)	15
Rigo Beltran (1998–99)	43
Armando Benitez (1999–2003)	49
Dennis Bennett (1967)	38
Gary Bennett (2001)	7
Kris Benson (2004–05)	34
Butch Benton (1978, 1980)	15, 19
Juan Berenguer (1978–80)	43
Bruce Berenyi (1984–86)	27, 31
Dwight Bernard (1978–79)	28
Yogi Berra (1965)	8
Angel Berroa (2009)	4

Jim Bethke (1965)	41, 28, 36
Steve Bieser (1997)	29
Mike Birkbeck (1992, 1995)	48, 36
Mike Bishop (1983)	11
Vic Black (2013, 2014)	38
Willie Blair (1998)	46
Henry Blanco (2010)	4
Jerry Blevins (2015)	13
Terry Blocker (1985)	21
Bruce Bochy (1982)	9
Tim Bogar (1993–96)	23, 11
Brian Bohanon (1997–198)	46
Bruce Boisclair (1974, 1976–79)	26, 4
Danny Boitano (1981)	36
Mark Bomback (1980)	36
Bobby Bonilla (1992–95, 1999)	25
Mike Bordick (2000)	17
Toby Borland (1997)	43
Don Bosch (1967–68)	17
Daryl Boston (1990–92)	7, 6
Ken Boswell (1967–74)	24, 12
Ricky Bottalico (2004)	34, 20
Ed Bouchee (1962)	11, 3
Larry Bowa (1985)	2
Blaine Boyer (2011)	23
Ken Boyer (1966–67)	14
Chad Bradford (2006)	53
Mark Bradley (1983)	9
Darren Bragg (2001)	56
Craig Brazell (2004)	9
Ed Bressoud (1966)	1

Lance Broadway (2009)	35
Rico Brogna (1994–96)	26
Hubie Brooks (1980–84, 1991)	62, 39, 7
Terry Bross (1991)	46
Andrew Brown (2103–14)	47, 30
Emil Brown (2009)	29
Kevin Brown (1990)	43
Leon Brown (1976)	23
Mike Bruhert (1978)	26
Brian Buchanan (2004)	10
Jerry Buchek (1967–68)	1
Taylor Buchholz (2011)	33
John Buck (2013)	33
Damon Buford (1995)	2
Ambiorix Burgos (2007)	40
Greg Burke (2012–13)	46
Tim Burke (1991–1992)	4
Jeromy Burnitz (1993–94, 2002–03)	5, 20
Larry Burright (1963–1964)	6
Ray Burris (1979–80)	26, 34
Brett Butler (1995)	22
Marlon Byrd (2013)	6
Paul Byrd (1995–96)	43
Tim Byrdak (2011–13)	40

C

Miguel Cairo (2005)	3
Mike Cameron (2004–05)	44
Eric Cammack (2000)	29
Eric Campbell (2014–15)	29
Robinson Cancel (2008–09)	40, 4, 29

John Candelaria (1987)	45
John Cangelosi (1994)	44
Chris Cannizzaro (1962–65)	8, 5
Buzz Capra (1971–73)	38
Chris Capuano (2011)	
José Cardenal (1979–80)	6
Don Cardwell (1967–70)	27
Buddy Carlyle (2014–15)	44, 43
Duke Carmel (1963)	1
Chuck Carr (1990–91)	7, 1, 27
D. J. Carrasco (2011–12)	77
Mark Carreon (1987–91)	32, 45
Robert Carson (2012–13)	73
Chris Carter (2009–10)	23
Gary Carter (1985–89)	8
Raul Casanova (2008)	30
Alberto Castillo (1995–98)	30
Juan Castillo (1994)	50
Luis Castillo (2007–10)	1
Tony Castillo (1991)	36
Ramon Castro (2005–10)	11
Frank Catalanotto (2010)	27
Darrel Ceciliani (2015)	1
Roger Cedeño (1999, 2002–03)	19
Ronny Cedeño (2012)	13
Juan Centeno (2013–14)	36
Jaime Cerda (2002–03)	43
Rick Cerone (1991)	13
Yoenic Cespedes (2015)	52
Elio Chacon (1962)	7
Dean Chance (1970)	27

Kelvin Chapman (1979, 1984–85)	10, 11
Ed Charles (1967–69)	24, 5
Endy Chavez (2006–08)	10
Bruce Chen (2001–02)	32
Rich Chiles (1973)	29
Harry Chiti (1962)	44
John Christensen (1984–85)	35, 7
McKay Christensen (2002)	23
Joe Christopher (1962–65)	23
Ryan Church (2008–09)	19
Galen Cisco (1962–65)	26
Brady Clark (2002, 2008)	15, 44
Mark Clark (1996–97)	54
Tony Clark (2003)	00, 52
Donn Clendenon (1969–71)	22
Gene Clines (1975)	1
Tyler Clippard (2015)	46
Brad Clontz (1998)	49
Choo Choo Coleman (1962–63, 1966)	17, 20
Vince Coleman (1991–93)	1, 11
Willie Collazo (2007)	36
Kevin Collins (1965, 1967–69)	10, 19, 16, 1
Bartolo Colon (2014–15)	40
David Cone (1987–92, 2003)	44, 17, 16
Michael Conforto (2015)	30
Jeff Conine (2007)	28, 19
Bill Connors (1967–68)	38, 33, 45
Cliff Cook (1962–63)	6, 1
Alex Cora (2009–10)	3, 13
Dennis Cook (1998–2001)	27
Tim Corcoran (1986)	29

Mark Corey (2001–02)	27
Mardie Cornejo (1978)	47
Reid Cornelius (1995)	47
Billy Cowan (1965)	3
Collin Cowgill (2013)	4
Roger Craig (1962–63)	38, 36, 13
Jerry Cram (1974–75)	38
Joe Crawford (1997)	49
Mike Cubbage (1981)	3
Michael Cuddyer (2015)	23

D

Jeff D'Amico (2002)	13
Travis d'Arnaud (2013–15)	15, 7
Vic Darensbourg (2004)	39
Ron Darling (1983–91)	44, 12, 15
Brian Daubach (2005)	13
Ray Daviault (1962)	35
Ike Davis (2010–14)	29
Kane Davis (2002)	48
Tommy Davis (1967)	12
Jacob deGrom (2014–15)	48
Mike DeJean (2004–05)	35
Carlos Delgado (2006–09)	21
Wilson Delgado (2004)	17
John DeMerit (1962)	29
Matt den Dekker (2013–14)	6
Bill Denehy (1967)	44
Joe DePastino (2003)	10
Elmer Dessens (2009–10)	64
Mark Dewey (1992)	43

Carlos Diaz (1982–83)	32
Mario Diaz (1990)	34
Victor Diaz (2004–06)	50, 20
R. A. Dickey (2010–12)	43
Mike DiFelice (2005–07)	33, 6, 9
Jack DiLauro (1969)	31
Steve Dillon (1963–64)	39
Jerry Dipoto (1995–96)	45
Chris Donnels (1991–92)	23
Octavio Dotel (1999)	29
D. J. Dozier (1992)	7
Sammy Drake (1962)	12
Mike Draper (1993)	47
Lucas Duda (2010–15)	21
Jeff Duncan (2003–04)	61, 10
Shawon Dunston (1999)	12
Jim Dwyer (1976)	25
Duffy Dyer (1968–74)	18, 10
Lenny Dykstra (1985–89)	4

E

Damion Easley (2007–08)	3
Tom Edens (1987)	32
Josh Edgin (2012–14)	64
Jack Egbert (2012)	61
Dave Eilers (1965–66)	38
Larry Elliot (1964, 1966)	42, 17
Dock Ellis (1979)	35
Kevin Elster (1986–92)	2, 21, 15
Brad Emaus (2011)	4
Scott Erickson (2004)	19

Alex Escobar (2001)	25
Nino Espinosa (1974–78)	48, 39
Alvaro Espinoza (1996)	12
Shawn Estes (2002)	55
Chuck Estrada (1967)	33
Francisco Estrada (1971)	5
Nick Evans (2008–11)	6
Dana Eveland (2014)	61
Carl Everett (1995–97)	3

F

Jorge Fabregas (1998)	12
Pete Falcone (1979–82)	33
Jeurys Familia (2012–15)	27
Kyle Farnsworth (2014)	44
Jesus Feliciano (2010)	
Pedro Feliciano (2002–04, 2006–10, 2013)	55, 39, 25
Chico Fernandez (1963)	7
Sid Fernandez (1984–93)	50
Tony Fernandez (1993)	1
Sergio Ferrer (1978–79)	3, 1
Nelson Figueroa (2008–09)	27
Tom Filer (1992)	44
Jack Fisher (1964–67)	22
Mike Fitzgerald (1983–84)	20
Shaun Fitzmaurice (1966)	5
Don Florence (1995)	36
Gil Flores (1978–79)	17
Wilmer Flores (2013–15)	4
Cliff Floyd (2003–06)	30
Doug Flynn (1977–81)	23

Tim Foli (1970–71, 1978–79)	19
Rich Folkers (1970)	38
Brook Fordyce (1995)	5
Bartolome Fortunato (2004, 2006)	43
Larry Foss (1962)	27
Casey Fossum (2009)	47
George Foster (1982–86)	15
Leo Foster (1976–77)	1, 19
Joe Foy (1970)	5
Frank Francisco (2012–13)	48
John Franco (1990–01, 2003–04)	31, 45
Julio Franco (2006–07)	23
Matt Franco (1996–2000)	15
Jeff Francoeur (2009–10)	12
Jim Fregosi (1972–73)	11
Bob Friend (1966)	20
Danny Frisella (1967–72)	29, 34
Mike Fyhrie (1996)	40

G

Brent Gaff (1982–84)	45
Bob Gallagher (1975)	22
Dave Gallagher (1992–93)	8
Danny Garcia (2003–04)	12
Karim Garcia (2004)	20
Ron Gardenhire (1981–85)	19, 21*
Jeff Gardner (1991)	19
Rob Gardner (1965–66)	29
Wes Gardner (1984–85)	27
Wayne Garrett (1969–76)	11
Rod Gaspar (1969–70)	17

Dillon Gee (2010–15)	35
Gary Gentry (1969–72)	39
Germen Gonzalez (2013–14)	71
John Gibbons (1984, 1986)	8, 35, 43*
Bob Gibson (1987)	38
Paul Gibson (1992–93)	45
Shawn Gilbert (1997–98)	12
Brian Giles (1981–83)	23, 15
Bernard Gilkey (1996–98)	23
Sean Gilmartin (2015)	36
Joe Ginsberg (1962)	12
Matt Ginter (2004)	13
Mike Glavine (2003)	27
Tom Glavine (2003–07)	47
Ed Glynn (1979–80)	48
Erik Goeddel (2015)	62
Carlos Gomez (2007)	27
Jesse Gonder (1963–65)	16, 12
Dicky Gonzalez (2001)	39
Geremi Gonzalez (2006)	32
Raul Gonzalez (2002–03)	21
Dwight Gooden (1984–94)	16
Greg Goossen (1965–68)	20, 10
Tom Gorman (1982–85)	29
Jim Gosger (1969, 1973–74)	18, 19, 5
Ruben Gotay (2007)	6
Mauro Gozzo (1993–94)	45
Bill Graham (1967)	26
Wayne Graham (1964)	4
Curtis Granderson (2014–15)	3
Danny Graves (2005)	32

Andy Green (2009)   29

Dallas Green (1966)   27

Pumpsie Green (1963)   18

Sean Green (2009–10)   50

Shawn Green (2006–07)   20

Charlie Greene (1996)   7

Kenny Greer (1993)   35

Tom Grieve (1978)   2

Jeremy Griffiths (2003)   46

Jerry Grote (1966–77)   15

Joe Grzenda (1967)   43

Lee Guetterman (1992)   35

Eric Gunderson (1994–95)   40

Mark Guthrie (2002)   53

Ricky Gutierrez (2004)   6

H

Don Hahn (1971–74)   25

Scott Hairston (2011–12)   12

Tom Hall (1975–76)   42, 19

Shane Halter (1999)   11

Darryl Hamilton (1999–2001)   18

Jack Hamilton (1966–67)   32

Justin Hampson (2012)   45

Ike Hampton (1974)   20

Mike Hampton (2000)   32

Tim Hamulack (2005)   46

Todd Haney (1998)   18

Aaron Harang (2013)   44

Jason Hardtke (1996–97)   19

Shawn Hare (1994)   19

Tim Harkness (1963–64)	3
Pete Harnisch (1995–97)	27
Bud Harrelson (1965–77)	3
Greg Harris (1981)	20
Lenny Harris (1998, 2000–01)	19
Willie Harris (2011)	22
Greg Harts (1973)	6
Matt Harvey (2012–15)	33
Andy Hassler (1979)	44
Tom Hausman (1978–82)	32
LaTroy Hawkins (2013)	32
Ed Hearn (1986)	49
Richie Hebner (1979)	3
Danny Heep (1983–86)	25
Jeremy Hefner (2012–13)	53
Jack Heidemann (1975–76)	12
Aaron Heilman (2003–08)	48
Bob Heise (1967–69)	23, 28
Ken Henderson (1978)	10
Rickey Henderson (1999–2000)	24
Steve Henderson (1977–80)	5
Bob Hendley (1967)	33
Sean Henn (2013)	43
Phil Hennigan (1973)	34
Doug Henry (1995–96)	35
Bill Hepler (1966)	28
Ron Herbel (1970)	31
Felix Heredia (2005)	49
Anderson Hernandez (2005–07, 2009)	1, 4, 11
Keith Hernandez (1983–89)	17
Livan Hernandez (2010)	61

Luis Hernandez (2010)	3
Manny Hernandez (1989)	36
Orlando Hernandez (2006–07)	26
Roberto Hernandez (2005–06)	39, 49
Tom Herr (1990–91)	28
Daniel Herrera (2011)	19
Dilson Herrera (2014–15)	2, 16
Rick Herrscher (1962)	6
Orel Hershiser (1999)	55
Mike Hessman (2010)	19
Jim Hickman (1962–66)	9, 27, 6
Joe Hicks (1963)	22
Richard Hidalgo (2004)	15
Joe Hietpas (2004)	10
Chuck Hiller (1965–67)	2
Dave Hillman (1962)	34
Eric Hillman (1992–94)	53
Brett Hinchliffe (2001)	32
Jerry Hinsley (1964, 1967)	24, 40
Gil Hodges (1962–63)	14
Ron Hodges (1973–84)	42
Scott Holman (1980, 1982–83)	26, 28
Jay Hook (1962–64)	47
Wayne Housie (1993)	2
Mike Howard (1981–83)	5
Pat Howell (1992)	38
Chin-lung Hu (2011)	25
John Hudek (1998)	43
Jessie Hudson (1969)	38
Keith Hughes (1990)	12
Philip Humber (2006–07)	49

Todd Hundley (1990–98)	49, 9
Ron Hunt (1963–66)	33
Willard Hunter (1962, 1964)	29, 38
Clint Hurdle (1983, 1985, 1987)	33, 13, 7
Jonathan Hurst (1994)	13
Butch Huskey (1993, 1995–98)	10, 42

I

Ryota Igarashi (2010–11)	18
Jeff Innis (1987–93)	40
Kaz Ishii (2005)	23
Jason Isringhausen (1995–97, 1999, 2011)	29,* 44, 45

J

Al Jackson (1962–65, 1968–69)	15, 38
Darrin Jackson (1993)	3
Roy Lee Jackson (1977–80)	31
Mike Jacobs (2005, 2010)	27, 35
Jason Jacome (1994–95)	47
Gregg Jefferies (1987–91)	9
Stan Jefferson (1986)	27
Chris Jelic (1990)	46
Ben Johnson (2007)	4
Bob D. Johnson (1969)	29
Bob W. Johnson (1967)	25, 6
Howard Johnson (1985–93)	20, 44
Kelly Johnson (2015)	55
Lance Johnson (1996–97)	1, 51
Mark Johnson (2000–02)	5, 20
Rob Johnson (2012)	16
Barry Jones (1992)	46

Bobby J. Jones (1993–2000)	28
Bobby M. Jones (2000, 2002)	21
Chris Jones (1995–96)	5
Cleon Jones (1963, 1965–75)	34, 12, 21
Randy Jones (1981–82)	25, 35
Ross Jones (1984)	21
Sherman Jones (1962)	36, 28
Ricardo Jordan (1997)	48
Mike Jorgensen (1968, 1970–71, 1980–83)	10, 16, 22
Jorge Julio (2006)	34

K

Jeff Kaiser (1993)	56
Rod Kanehl (1962–64)	10
Takashi Kashiwada (1997)	18
Jeff Kent (1992–96)	39, 12
Jeff Keppinger (2004)	6
Dave Kingman (1975–77, 1981–83)	26
Mike Kinkade (1998–2000)	33
Wayne Kirby (1998)	11
Bobby Klaus (1964–65)	6
Jay Kleven (1976)	22
Lou Klimchock (1966)	6
Brandon Knight (2008)	28, 44
Ray Knight (1984–86)	22
Kevin Kobel (1978–80)	49
Gary Kolb (1965)	18
Satoru Komiyama (2002)	7
Dae-Sung Koo (2005)	17
Cal Koonce (1967–70)	34
Jerry Koosman (1967–78)	36

Ed Kranepool (1962–79)   21, 7

Gary Kroll (1964–65)   25

Eddie Kunz (2008)   44

L

Clem Labine (1962)   41

Aaron Laffey (2013)   47

Juan Lagares (2013–15)   12

Jack Lamabe (1967)   34

David Lamb (2000)   26

Hobie Landrith (1962)   5

Ced Landrum (1993)   26

John Lannan (2014)   32

Frank Lary (1964–65)   17

Bill Latham (1985)   44, 33

Brian Lawrence (2007)   54

Matt Lawton (2001)   23

Terry Leach (1981–82, 1985–89)   43, 26

Tim Leary (1981, 1983–84)   38

Jack Leathersich (2015)   51

Ricky Ledee (2006–07)   9

Aaron Ledesma (1995)   11

Al Leiter (1998–2004)   22

Fred Lewis (2012)   15

Johnny Lewis (1965–67)   24

Dave Liddell (1990)   36

Cory Lidle (1997)   11

Jose Lima (2006)   17

Jim Lindeman (1994)   29

Doug Linton (1994)   30

Phil Linz (1967–68)   2

Mark Little (2002)   21

Graeme Lloyd (2003)	17
Paul Lo Duca (2006–07)	16
Ron Locke (1964)	45
Skip Lockwood (1975–79)	38
Mickey Lolich (1976)	29
Phil Lombardi (1989)	39
Kevin Lomon (1995)	44
Terrence Long (1999)	26
Braden Looper (2004–05)	40
Luis Lopez (1997–99)	17
Al Luplow (1966–67)	18
Zach Lutz (2012–13)	19
Ed Lynch (1980–86)	59, 35, 34, 36
Brandon Lyon (2013)	34
Barry Lyons (1986–90)	33

M

Rob MacDonald (1996)	49
Julio Machado (1989–90)	31, 48
Ken MacKenzie (1962–63)	19
Elliott Maddox (1978–80)	21
Mike Maddux (1993–94)	51
Dave Magadan (1986–92)	29, 10
Pat Mahomes (1999–2000)	23
John Maine (2006–10)	33
Pepe Mangual (1976–77)	11, 21
Phil Mankowski (1980, 1982)	2, 8
Jim Mann (2000)	39
Felix Mantilla (1962)	18
Barry Manuel (1997)	26
Josias Manzanillo (1993–95, 1999)	39
Shaun Marcum (2013)	38

Eli Marrero (2006)	32
Dave Marshall (1970–72)	18
Jim Marshall (1962)	6
Mike A. Marshall (1990)	6
Mike G. Marshall (1981)	28
J. C. Martin (1968–69)	9
Jerry Martin (1984)	9
Tom Martin (2001)	34
Fernando Martinez (2009–11)	26
Pedro A. Martinez (1996)	48
Pedro Martinez (2005–08)	45
Ramon Martinez (2008–09)	22, 6
Ted Martinez (1970–74)	17, 23
Roger Mason (1994)	48
Jon Matlack (1971–77)	35,* 32
Kaz Matsui (2004–06)	25
Daisuke Matsuzaka (2013–14)	16
Gary Matthews (2002, 2010)	25, 19
Mike Matthews (2005)	27
Steven Matz (2015)	32
Jerry May (1973)	20
John Mayberry Jr. (2015)	44
Brent Mayne (1996)	17
Willie Mays (1972–73)	24
Lee Mazzilli (1976–81, 1986–89)	12, 16, 13
Jim McAndrew (1968–73)	43
Bob McClure (1988)	27
Terry McDaniel (1991)	0
Roger McDowell (1985–89)	42
Chuck McElroy (1999)	34
Joe McEwing (2000–04)	47, 11

Tug McGraw (1965–67, 1969–74)	45
Ryan McGuire (2000)	40
Collin McHugh (2012–13)	36
Jeff McKnight (1989, 1992–94)	15, 5, 7, 18, 17
Greg McMichael (1997–99)	36
Roy McMillan (1964–66)	11
Brian McRae (1997–99)	56
Kevin McReynolds (1987–91, 1994)	22
Doc Medich (1977)	22
Jenrry Mejia (2010–15)	32, 58
Carlos Mendoza (1997)	6
Orlando Mercado (1990)	35
Butch Metzger (1978)	45
Jason Middlebrook (2002–03)	27
Doug Mientkiewicz (2005)	16
Felix Millan (1973–77)	16, 17
Lastings Milledge (2006–07)	44
Bob G. Miller (1962)	23,* 36
Bob L. Miller (1962, 1973–74)	24, 30
Dyar Miller (1980–81)	56, 49
Keith Miller (1987–91)	25
Larry Miller (1965–66)	35
Ralph Milliard (1998)	26
Randy Milligan (1987)	27
John Milner (1971–77)	28
Blas Minor (1995–96)	34
Pat Misch (2009–11)	48
John Mitchell (1986–89)	43
Kevin Mitchell (1984, 1986)	32, 35, 7
Vinegar Bend Mizell (1962)	26
Dave Mlicki (1995–98)	38

Herb Moford (1962)	26
Gustavo Molina (2008)	6, 29
Johnny Monell (2015)	19
Willie Montanez (1978–79)	25
Rafael Montero (2014–15)	50
Joe Moock (1967)	18
Tommy Moore (1972–73)	19, 39
Bob Moorhead (1962, 1965)	22, 21
Melvin Mora (1999–2000)	6
Jerry Morales (1980)	25
Al Moran (1963–64)	40
Jose Moreno (1980)	4
Orber Moreno (2003–04)	49
Kevin Morgan (1997)	10
Akeel Morris (2015)	64
Guillermo Mota (2006–07)	59
Carlos Muniz (2007–08)	38, 32
Danny Muno (2015)	16
Billy Murphy (1966)	23
Daniel Murphy (2008–15)	28
Dale Murray (1978–79)	22
Dan Murray (1999)	48
Eddie Murray (1992–93)	33
Dennis Musgraves (1965)	34
Jeff Musselman (1989–90)	13
Randy Myers (1985–89)	48
Bob Myrick (1976–78)	44

N

Xavier Nady (2006)	22
Danny Napoleon (1965–66)	16
Tito Navarro (1993)	36

Charlie Neal (1962–63)	4
David Newhan (2007)	17
Mike Nickeas (2010–12)	13, 4
Randy Niemann (1985–86)	46, 40
Jon Niese (2008–2015)	49
Kirk Nieuwenhuis (2012–15)	9
Fernando Nieve (2009–10)	38
C. J. Nitkowski (2001)	40
Trot Nixon (2008)	6
Junior Noboa (1992)	3
Joe Nolan (1972)	35
Hideo Nomo (1998)	16
Dan Norman (1977–80)	33, 8
Abraham Nunez (2008)	6
Edwin Nunez (1988)	45
Jon Nunnally (2000)	26

O

Charlie O'Brien (1990–93)	22, 33
Michael O'Connor (2011)	50
Darren O'Day (2009)	36
Eric O'Flaherty (2015)	44
Tom O'Malley (1989–90)	27
Alex Ochoa (1995–97)	22
Jose Offerman (2005)	35
Bob Ojeda (1986–90)	19
John Olerud (1997–99)	5
Darren Oliver (2006)	26
Garrett Olson (2012)	38
Jose Oquendo (1983–84)	2
Rey Ordoñez (1996–2002)	0, 10
Jesse Orosco (1979, 1981–87)	61, 47

Joe Orsulak (1993–95)	6
Junior Ortiz (1983–84)	34
Brian Ostrosser (1973)	19
Ricky Otero (1995)	1
Amos Otis (1967, 1969)	28, 25
Henry Owens (2006)	36
Rick Ownbey (1982–83)	20

P

John Pacella (1977, 1979–80)	20
Tom Paciorek (1985)	44
Juan Padilla (2005)	28
Angel Pagan (2008–11)	16
Craig Paquette (1998)	18
Chan Ho Park (2007)	61
Harry Parker (1973–75)	31
Rick Parker (1994)	11
Bobby Parnell (2008–15)	39
Jose Parra (2004)	46
Tom Parsons (1964–65)	27
Val Pascucci (2011)	15
Ronny Paulino (2011)	4
Jay Payton (1998–02)	25, 44
Bill Pecota (1992)	32
Al Pedrique (1987)	25
Mike Pelfrey (2006–12)	34
Brock Pemberton (1974–75)	2
Alejandro Pena (1990–91)	26
Oliver Perez (2006–10)	46
Timo Perez (2000–03)	6
Yorkis Perez (1997)	25
Robert Person (1995–96)	29

Roberto Petagine (1996–97)   20, 10

Bobby Pfeil (1969)   1

Andy Phillips (2008)   29

Jason Phillips (2001–04)   3*, 26, 7, 23

Mike Phillips (1975–77)   5

Tony Phillips (1998)   6

Mike Piazza (1998–2005)   31

Jimmy Piersall (1963)   34, 2

Joe Pignatano (1962)   5

Kevin Plawecki (2015)   22

Grover Powell (1963)   41

Todd Pratt (1997–2001)   43, 7

Jason Pridie (2011)   20

Rich Puig (1974)   6

Charlie Puleo (1981–82)   25

Bill Pulsipher (1995, 1998, 2000)   21, 25

J. J. Putz (2009)   22

Q

Omar Quintanilla (2012–14)   6, 3, 0

R

Gary Rajsich (1982–83)   21

Elvin Ramirez (2012)   62

Mario Ramirez (1980)   61, 3

Ramon Ramirez (2012)   52

Lenny Randle (1977–78)   11

Willie Randolph (1992)   12

Bob Rauch (1972)   44

Jon Rauch (2012)   60

Jeff Reardon (1979–81)   45, 44

Anthony Recker (2013–15)   20

Tim Redding (2009)	44
Prentice Redman (2003)	20
Addison Reed (2015)	43
Darren Reed (1990)	28, 6
Jeremy Reed (2009)	18
Rick Reed (1997–2001)	35
Steve Reed (2002)	39
Desi Relaford (2001)	8
Mike Remlinger (1994–95)	43
Hal Reniff (1967)	32
Argenis Reyes (2008–09)	4, 11
Jose Reyes (2003–11)	7
Matt Reynolds	56*
Ronn Reynolds (1982–83, 1985)	8, 9
Tommie Reynolds (1967)	16
Armando Reynoso (1997–98)	40
Dennis Ribant (1964–66)	17, 18, 30
Scott Rice (2013–14)	56
Gordie Richardson (1965–66)	41
Jerrod Riggan (2000–01)	34, 38
Ricardo Rincon (2008)	73
Royce Ring (2005–06)	22, 43
Luis Rivera (1994)	3
Jason Roach (2003)	57
Kevin Roberson (1996)	18
Dave Roberts (1981)	15
Grant Roberts (2000–04)	36
Hansel Robles (2015)	47
Francisco Rodriguez (2009–11)	75
Rich Rodriguez (2000)	46
Kenny Rogers (1999)	73

Les Rohr (1967–69)	31, 33
Mel Rojas (1997–98)	51
Luis Rosado (1977, 1980)	58, 35
Brian Rose (2001)	23
Don Rose (1971)	31
Vinny Rottino (2012)	33
Don Rowe (1963)	29
Glendon Rusch (1999–2001)	48
Dick Rusteck (1966)	43, 40
Nolan Ryan (1966, 1968–71)	34, 30

S

Bret Saberhagen (1992–95)	18, 17
Ray Sadecki (1970–74, 1977)	33
Joe Sambito (1985)	35
Amado Samuel (1964)	7
Juan Samuel (1989)	7
Duaner Sanchez (2006, 2008)	50
Rey Sanchez (2003)	10
Ken Sanders (1975–76)	33
Johan Santana (2008–2012)	57
Rafael Santana (1984–87)	3
Jose Santiago (2005)	33
Omir Santos (2009)	9
Mackey Sasser (1988–92)	2
Josh Satin (2011–14)	3, 13
Doug Saunders (1993)	2
Rich Sauveur (1991)	39
Mac Scarce (1975)	44
Jimmie Schaffer (1965)	17
Dan Schatzeder (1990)	43

Calvin Schiraldi (1984–85)	40
Al Schmelz (1967)	44
Dave Schneck (1972–74)	23, 16
Brian Schneider (2008–09)	23
Scott Schoeneweis (2007–08)	60
Dick Schofield (1992)	11
Pete Schourek (1991–93)	48
Ted Schreiber (1963)	43
Don Schulze (1987)	49
Chris Schwinden (2011–12)	63
Mike Scott (1979–82)	30
Marco Scutaro (2002–03)	26
Ray Searage (1981)	44
Tom Seaver (1967–77, 1983)	41
David Segui (1994–95)	10, 21
Aaron Sele (2007)	30
Dick Selma (1965–68)	39
Frank Seminara (1994)	34
Jae Seo (2002–05)	38, 40, 26
Art Shamsky (1968–71)	24
Bob Shaw (1966–67)	26
Don Shaw (1967–68)	35
Gary Sheffield (2009)	10
Norm Sherry (1963)	5
Tsuyoshi Shinjo (2001, 2003)	5
Craig Shipley (1989)	35
Bart Shirley (1967)	6
Kelly Shoppach (2012)	6
Bill Short (1968)	40
Paul Siebert (1977–78)	43, 48
Doug Simons (1991)	43

Ken Singleton (1970–71)	29
Doug Sisk (1982–87)	39
Bobby Gene Smith (1962)	16
Charley Smith (1964–65)	1
Dick Smith (1963–64)	16
Joe Smith (2007–08)	35
Pete Smith (1994)	32
Esix Snead (2002, 2004)	23, 1
Duke Snider (1963)	11, 4
Alay Soler (2006)	59
Jorge Sosa (2007–08)	29
Warren Spahn (1965)	21
Tim Spehr (1998)	33
Shane Spencer (2004)	43
Bill Spiers (1995)	19
Dennis Springer (2000)	34
Steve Springer (1992)	13
Larry Stahl (1967–68)	25
Roy Staiger (1975–77)	35, 2
Tracy Stallard (1963–64)	36
Leroy Stanton (1970–71)	23, 44
Mike Stanton (2003–04)	32
Rusty Staub (1972–75, 1981–85)	4, 10
Tim Stauffer (2015)	54
John Stearns (1975–84)	16, 12
John Stephenson (1964–66)	49, 19, 12
Randy Sterling (1974)	35
Kelly Stinnett (1994–95, 2006)	33, 36
Josh Stinson (2011)	64
Brian Stokes (2008–09)	43
George Stone (1973–75)	40

Tobi Stoner (2009-10)	29
Pat Strange (2002–03)	38
Darryl Strawberry (1983–90)	18
Scott Strickland (2002–03)	25, 28
John Strohmayer (1973–74)	39
Brent Strom (1972)	40
Dick Stuart (1966)	17
Tom Sturdivant (1964)	47
Bill Sudakis (1972)	9
Cory Sullivan (2009)	19
John Sullivan (1967)	20
Darrell Sutherland (1964–66)	47, 43, 45
Craig Swan (1973–84)	27
Rick Sweet (1982)	8
Jon Switzer (2009)	56
Ron Swoboda (1965–70)	14, 4
Noah Syndergaard (2015)	34

T

Pat Tabler (1990)	35
Hisanori Takahashi (2010)	47
Ken Takahashi (2009)	36
Shingo Takatsu (2005)	10
Jeff Tam (1998, 1999)	36, 38
Frank Tanana (1993)	29
Kevin Tapani (1989)	26
Tony Tarasco (2002)	40
Randy Tate (1975)	48
Fernando Tatis (2008–10)	17
Jim Tatum (1998)	19
Frank Taveras (1979–81)	11

Billy Taylor (1999)	26
Chuck Taylor (1972)	42
Hawk Taylor (1964–67)	19
Ron Taylor (1967–71)	42
Sammy Taylor (1962–63)	16
Taylor Teagarden (2014)	23
Ruben Tejada (2010–15)	11
Dave Telgheder (1993–95)	38, 40
Garry Templeton (1991)	11
Walt Terrell (1982–84)	49
Ralph Terry (1966–67)	38
Tim Teufel (1986–91)	11
Dale Thayer (2011)	46, 36
George Theodore (1973–74)	18, 9
Josh Thole (2009–12)	30
Frank Thomas (1962–64)	25
Ryan Thompson (1992–95)	44, 20
John Thomson (2002)	50
Lou Thornton (1989–90)	4, 1
Marv Throneberry (1962–63)	2
Gary Thurman (1997)	10
Dick Tidrow (1984)	32
Rusty Tillman (1982)	34
Jorge Toca (1999–2001)	30
Jackson Todd (1977)	30
Andy Tomberlin (1996–97)	33
Joe Torre (1975–77)	9
Alex Torres (2015)	54
Andres Torres (2012)	56
Carlos Torres (2013–15)	52, 72
Mike Torrez (1983–84)	30

Kelvin Torve (1990–91)	24, 39
Wilfredo Tovar (2013–14)	70
Steve Trachsel (2001–06)	29
Bubba Trammell (2000)	33
Alex Treviño (1978–81, 1990)	29, 6
Rick Trlicek (1996–97)	34, 50
Michael Tucker (2006)	22
Justin Turner (2010–13)	2
Wayne Twitchell (1979)	36
Jason Tyner (2000)	11

U

Del Unser (1975–76)	25
Lino Urdaneta (2007)	19
Juan Uribe (2015)	2

V

Mike Vail (1975–77)	31, 6
Raul Valdes (2010)	22
Jordany Valdespin (2012–13)	1
Wilson Valdes (2009)	4
Eric Valent (2004–05)	57
John Valentin (2002)	4
Jose Valentin (2006–07)	18, 2
Bobby Valentine (1977–78)	1
Ellis Valentine (1981–82)	17
Julio Valera (1990–91)	34
Jose Valverde (2014)	47
Claudio Vargas (2008)	39
Jason Vargas (2007)	43
Mo Vaughn (2002–03)	42
Jorge Velandia (2000–01, 2003)	11, 13

Robin Ventura (1999–2001)	4
Logan Verrett (2015)	35
Tom Veryzer (1982)	11
Fernando Viña (1994)	1
Frank Viola (1989–91)	29, 26
Joe Vitko (1992)	49
Jose Vizcaino (1994–96)	15

W

Billy Wagner (2006–09)	13
Bill Wakefield (1964)	43
Chico Walker (1992–93)	34
Pete Walker (1995, 2001–02)	49, 43
Tyler Walker (2002)	46
Donne Wall (2001)	33
Derek Wallace (1996)	47
Gene Walter (1987–88)	31
Claudell Washington (1980)	15
Allen Watson (1999)	30
Matt Watson (2003)	50
Dave Weathers (2002–04)	35
Hank Webb (1972–76)	42, 29, 30
Al Weis (1968–71)	6
Turk Wendell (1997–01)	99
David West (1988–89)	46
Mickey Weston (1993)	43
Dan Wheeler (2003–04)	39
Zack Wheeler (2013–14)	45
Rick White (2000, 2001)	51
Wally Whitehurst (1989–92)	47
Ty Wigginton (2002–04)	9
Rick Wilkins (1998)	39

Carl Willey (1963–65)	28
Nick Willhite (1967)	29
Charlie Williams (1971)	35
Dave Williams (2006–07)	32
Gerald Williams (2004, 2005)	6, 21
Mookie Wilson (1980–89)	1
Paul Wilson (1996)	32
Preston Wilson (1998)	11
Tom Wilson (2004)	6
Vance Wilson (1999–2004)	3
Herm Winningham (1984)	21
Matt Wise (2008)	38
Gene Woodling (1962)	11
Chris Woodward (2005–06)	4
David Wright (2004–15)	5
Billy Wynne (1967)	35

Y

Tyler Yates (2004)	32,* 33
Masato Yoshii (1998–99)	29, 21
Anthony Young (1991–93)	33, 19
Chris B. Young (2014)	1
Chris R. Young (2011–12)	55
Eric Young (2013–2015)	22, 1
Joel Youngblood (1977–82)	18

Z

Pat Zachry (1977–82)	40
Victor Zambrano (2004–06)	38
Todd Zeile (2000–01, 2004)	9, 27
Don Zimmer (1962)	17

ACKNOWLEDGMENTS

This book has been a long time coming. Since 1962, yes, but the Mets by the Numbers website (mbtn.net) has been up and running since 1999.

Neither the book nor the site would be possible without those who could run, hit, throw, and instruct well enough to be worthy of major league uniform. We may sometimes be flip in our assessments, but anyone good enough to wear a Mets uniform and number without having to pay for the privilege automatically has our respect.

Our deepest gratitude is reserved for Mark Weinstein at Skyhorse Publishing, who erased three years of angst in three minutes by starting negotiations for this book the day after the Mets clinched the 2006 division title. Mark has moved on since the first edition but to this day remains one of the project's biggest champions. We're just as grateful for a second go-round under the guidance of Jason Katzman and Skyhorse's sister, Sports Publishing LLC.

We sincerely thank Howie Rose for writing the foreword to this book. Also thanks to Lou Schwartz, president of the American Sportscasters Association, for putting us in touch with Eric Spitz at WFAN, who generously made entreaties on our behalf. Special thanks also to the players who have addressed unsolicited questions over the years about their uniform numbers, especially the all-good-guy team of George Theodore, Lenny Randle, Joe McEwing, Ed Hearn, Kevin Collins, Kevin Plawecki, and Kelvin Torve.

And we couldn't have done it alone. Sources that were especially helpful beyond all the scorecards and media guides include the following reference works: *The Cultural Encyclopedia of Baseball*, 1st edition, Jonathon Fraser Light (Jefferson, NC: McFarland & Co., 1997); *The Baseball Encyclopedia*, 4th edition, Gary Gillette and Pete Palmer (New York: Sterling Publishing, 2007); *Total Baseball*, 7th edition, John Thorn, Pete Palmer, and Mike Gershman (Kingston, NY: Total Sports Publishing, 2001); and *The New Bill James Historical Baseball Abstract* (New York: The Free Press, 2001). And while our research was independent of the two definitive books on uniform numbers, the fact that these had been published didn't hurt: *Baseball by the Numbers*, Mark Stang and Linda Harkness (Lanham, MD: The Scarecrow Press, 1997), and *Now Batting, Number . . .*, by Jack Looney (New York: Black Dog and Leventhal Publishers, 2006).

Books on the Mets are many in number, but the ones that we referred to faithfully for this project were the following: *This Date in N.Y. Mets History*, Dennis D'Agostino, (Briarcliff Manor, NY: Scarborough, 1981); The *Complete Year-by-Year N.Y. Mets Fan's Almanac*, Duncan Bock and John Jordan (New York: Crown, 1992); *The New York Mets: Twenty-Five Years of Baseball Magic*, Jack Lang and Pete Simon (New York: Henry Holt, 1986); and *The New York Mets*, Leonard Koppett (New York: Macmillan, 1974).

We bounced in and out of countless Web sites to track down information or just jog the memory. The most important of these hold the cryptic details of every game played, plus the stats of every player, and in some cases, uniform number info. The Ultimate Mets Database (ultimatemets.com) deserves special recognition for integrating the very research behind this book into its awesome repository of Mets statistics.

Fans since the Mets' inception have been spoiled by terrific, informative, and engaging daily newspaper reporters and columnists, whose work yesterday and today we admire and rely on. Marty Noble, whose work at *Newsday* and later mlb.com showed an interest in the uniform number, was a particular inspiration. Thanks also to Jared Diamond, Anthony DiComo, Adam Rubin, Marc Carig, Joel Sherman, Ken Davidoff, Andy Martino, and their colleagues. Historical info and insight on the team we're here for was offered by friends and comrades on the Internet especially those at the Crane Pool Forum, Amazin' Avenue, Mets Police, MetsBlog, and basically all of #MetsTwitter, to name only a few.

Uniforms are a visual sensation and not just a statistical listing, so photography is crucial to a book on the subject. Most of the images from the first book were no longer available, so we went digging to find photos to match the number.

Photo credits can be found under most photos, but that does not convey the appreciation for the dozens of images loaned to us, gratis, from people who either had the right camera or the photo rights. Dan Carubia, was—and still is—poised near (or on) the field to get photos of Mets players dating all the way back to the Second Kingdom of Kong, circa 1981. For images before that period, we were aided by Jacob Kanarek, author of *From First to Worst: The New York Mets 1973–1977* (Jeffersonville, NC: McFarland, 2008), the all too true story of the 1970s slide from surprise pennant winners to baseball Sibera. He also helped in the acquisition of the rights to an undeveloped roll of film from Wrigley Field taken on July 14, 1969. But there were still a few holes in our collection, and into the breech came the photographic talents of Lou Longobardi, Dave Murray, Jim Singer, Dan Twohig, David G. Whitman, and Sharon Chapman. Uncredited photos provided by metsilverman.com.

Matt: Help with yearbooks and other materials came from Robert Pizzella, Brad Smith, and Syd Silverman, who bought and brought home plenty of materials in the Dark Ages of Mets baseball. It all would have been tossed away if not for my mother, Jan McNally Silverman, who went against the old stereotype and carefully stashed this Mets gold away against fire and time. And she didn't even like baseball. Also thanks to friends Bruce Markusen, Bill Nowlin, Todd Radom, Linc Wonham, Al Yellon, and Alec Dawson. An endeavor requiring much time scouring the archives for arcane—yet vital—information couldn't be possible without the moral assistance of family: Debbie, Jan, and Tyler Silverman. I'll pick the yearbooks, scorecards, and books off the floor now. Or tomorrow.

Jon:
After seventeen years online, the friends of, and contributors to, the Mets by the Numbers project are far too many to mention individually. Many in the early days helped to complete the historical picture, in particular Ed Armstrong and Jason Ellersick: kind, knowledgeable and patient enough to share their own research whenever I asked.

Many more regular contributors to the site keep me informed, on my toes and laughing, even if I don't know many of them beyond their screen handles. They include: Matt Buscemi, Gordon Handler, Pete Mahoney, Doug Hoffman, Dennis D'Agostino, Chris Sullivan, Michael Grimaldi, Michael Weil, Kasey Ignarski, Gene Fry, Scott Pirrung, Steve Bulota, Joe Hickey, Bob Finkel, Mark Simon, Glenn Larsen, Kenny Bumbaco, Ken Mattucci, Aaron Weiss, Rich Kroebel, Ernie Alston, Mitchell Pak, Shari Forst, Richard Hochroth, Jonathan S. "52" Weissman, Edward Hoyt, Kevin Carter, Dave Murray, Steve J. Rogers, Rob Safuto, Kevin Brotzman, Bill McEvoy, Alex Giobbi, "Jetropolitans" "Shorty," "Mookie," "Keiran," "Howie R," "Paul C.," "Lazylou," "Irv," "Keith," "Ellis," "Glen," "Mike J.," "Mark in Japan," "Jack" "Alf Tanner" and of course, "9th-string catcher." I'm leaving out way too many others.

Paul Lukas (Uniwatch) and Greg W. Prince (Faith & Fear in Flushing) were early discoverers and supporters of the project and both are perceptive, funny and influential writers who inspire me every day. Josh Wilker

(Cardboard Gods) writes so beautifully about baseball it makes me want to stop doing it. Thank you Phil Hartman of Two Boots for the support and the forum for Mets talk, and all the pizza. Behind the scenes David Moore, Scott Turner, Dirk Lammers, and especially, Richard DiStefano, make it sing.

Thanks to all my friends in Greenpoint including Word Books and Propeller Coffee. To my resilient and supportive family. And especially to Heidi and Ivan.